PERGAMON RUSSIAN CHESS SERIES

The Application
of Chess Theory

The Application of Chess Theory

By

Y. P. GELLER

International Grandmaster

Translated by

KENNETH P. NEAT

PERGAMON PRESS

OXFORD · NEW YORK · BEIJING · FRANKFURT
SÃO PAULO · SYDNEY · TOKYO · TORONTO

U.K.	Pergamon Press plc, Headington Hill Hall, Oxford OX3 0BW, England
U.S.A.	Pergamon Press, Inc., Maxwell House, Fairview Park, Elmsford, New York 10523, U.S.A.
PEOPLE'S REPUBLIC OF CHINA	Pergamon Press, Room 4037, Qianmen Hotel, Bejing, People's Republic of China
FEDERAL REPUBLIC OF GERMANY	Pergamon Press GmbH, Hammerweg 6, D-6242 Kronberg, Federal Republic of Germany
BRAZIL	Pergamon Editora Ltda, Rua Eça de Queiros, 346, CEP 04011, Paraiso, São Paulo, Brazil
AUSTRALIA	Pergamon Press Australia Pty Ltd., P.O. Box 544, Potts Point, N.S.W. 2011, Australia
JAPAN	Pergamon Press, 5th Floor, Matsuoka Central Building, 1-7-1 Nishishinjuku, Shinjuku-ku, Tokyo 160, Japan
CANADA	Pergamon Press Canada Ltd., Suite No. 271, 253 College Street, Toronto, Ontario, Canada M5T 1R5

English translation copyright © 1984 K. P. Neat

First edition 1984
Reprinted 1987, 1989

Library of Congress Cataloging in Publication Data

Geller, Efim Petrovich, 1925–
The Application of Chess Theory
(Pergamon Russian chess series)
Includes index.
1. Chess—Collections of games. 2. Chess—Openings.
I. Title. II. Title: The Application of Chess Theory
III. Series.
GV1452.G44   1983   794.1'5   83-2406

British Library Cataloguing in Publication Data

Geller, Efim
The Application of Chess Theory—(Pergamon Russian chess series)
1. Geller, Efiim   2. Chess—Collections of games
I. Title
794.1'59   GV1439 G/

ISBN 0-08-026914-1 (Hardcover)
ISBN 0-08-029738-2 (Flexicover)

Printed in Great Britain by BPCC Wheatons Ltd, Exeter

Contents

The Trademark of Yefim Geller

The name of grandmaster Yefim Geller does not require any special introduction, as it is well enough known in the chess world. He was one of the most striking representatives of that "new wave", which soon after the Second World War confidently set about storming the most important chess heights. In the Soviet Union his contemporaries were Tigran Petrosian, Mark Taimanov and Yuri Averbakh; in Yugoslavia—Svetozar Gligoric and, a little later, Borislav Ivkov; in the USA—the brothers Donald and Robert Byrne, and in Hungary—László Szabó. To a greater or lesser degree they all competed successfully with the chess stars of the older generation, and although only one of them became World Champion (over a period of almost 100 years there have only been 12 of them!), the contribution of this "wave" to the treasury of chess is very considerable.

One can, of course, compare the purely competitive results of Yefim Geller with the achievements of the world's leading grandmasters, and come to the conclusion that he is one of them. But I should like to draw the attention of the reader to something else. The point is that in the creative sense Geller has always been distinguished, and he has always occupied a special place. There are few players who "in their lifetime" have earned a characterization such as that given to Geller by one of the most authoritative World Champions, Professor Mikhail Botvinnik: "Before Geller we did not understand the King's Indian Defence". Of course, the point relates not just to one opening, even though it be important and topical, but to the fact that one of the strongest aspects of his talent was and is his ability to research, to seek the new, and to discover the secret essence of chess.

Of course, it is not only by this that Geller has drawn attention. From his very first steps in the Soviet and world arenas he shone with his rich and brilliant play. Chess players will never forget how in 1949, making his debut in the USSR Championship as a candidate master, he literally smashed a whole rank of grandmasters and almost became champion of the strongest chess power in the world. But nevertheless, one-move mistakes occur more often with him than with other players of his class, perhaps because he was late in learning to play. It was this that prevented him from making the final few steps up the staircase leading to the chess throne. On the other hand, for his wealth of ideas in the most varied chess directions, Geller is one of the most prominent grandmasters of all time. And in this book he readily invites all readers into his creative laboratory: so that they can see how ideas are conceived, and, perhaps, themselves learn how to do this.

Especially since, like the majority of active grandmasters, Geller used to prepare his ideas for practical play, whereas now he has become one of the most interesting authors with a wide range of chess views.

However, all this by no means rules out the fact that even today Geller remains one of the strongest grandmasters in the world. At the respectable age of 55 he became USSR Champion, and if he is continuing to play it means that he feels within him the strength to do so. This means that he will test his ideas in practice, and they will emerge supplied with the trade-mark "Yefim Geller", a mark with the highest of reputations.

Mikhail Tal
Ex-World Champion

From the Author

The games collected in this book were played during the 35 years of my career in big-time chess. Do I number them among my best? In the main, yes, because victory in them brought me that which attracts me more than anything in chess. Defeats are also instructive, of course, but that is a quite different topic...

The games are grouped in a rather unusual way—according to opening. This is not by acci-dent. All my life I have been working on the problems of chess theory, and to a certain extent such a grouping enables the book to be regarded as a "report on the work carried out". But the main thing is that, by playing through a whole group of games played, for example, with the Sicilian Defence, I think that simultaneously the reader will be able to master a whole series of stratagems, typical of the given opening.

In a separate section are games played by the author against grandmasters with the highest title—that of World Champion. Not every game here is a contender for the epithet of "best", but all, without exception are memorable. But then, there is no way that battles with the chess kings could be otherwise....

PART 1 (grouped according to opening)

Ruy Lopez

Geller–Mecking

Interzonal Tournament
Palma de Mallorca, 1970

The hobbling knight

There are openings in which Black's successful defence depends upon whether or not he can solve satisfactorily the problem of developing a particular minor piece. Lovers of the French Defence know just how much trouble the "French" bishop at c8 can cause, and King's Indian players are often concerned about the knight at a5. In the Ruy Lopez Black has often suffered because of his "Spanish" knight being stuck over on the Q-side, and this is what happened here to the young Brazilian grandmaster Henrique Mecking. White built his entire game around shutting the knight at b7 out of play. The result was a strategically complete game, one of those where victory is achieved without any obvious mistake by the opponent. Such encounters afford no less satisfaction than the most complicated combinations and the most dashing attacks.

1 e4	e5
2 Nf3	Nc6
3 Bb5	a6
4 Ba4	Nf6
5 0–0	Be7
6 Re1	b5
7 Bb3	d6

8 c3	0–0
9 h3	Na5
10 Bc2	c5
11 d4	Qc7
12 Nbd2	Nc6
13 d5	

The classical way of handling this position. White blocks the centre, and undertakes to play actively against the black king.

13 ...	Na5

More common is 13 ... Nd8, with Rubinstein's idea of ... Ne8, ... g6, ... Ng7, ... f6 and ... Nf7. The text move has always been regarded with suspicion, although Keres, on the basis of his game with Alexander (White) at Hastings 1937–1938, considers that after 13.....Na5 14 b3 Bd7 15 Nf1 Nb7 16 c4 Black obtains sufficient counter-play. The present game, as well as certain others, do not confirm this opinion. The point is that White himself has no need to initiate play on the Q-side by 16 c4. He aims to block it, and as regards activity he is interested in the opposite side of the board. The knight at a5 must remain a perpetual reproach to Black.

14 b3	Bd7
15 Nf1	Nb7
16 Ng3	c4
17 b4	

Both sides have made all the usual "Spanish" moves, and preparations for battle are complete.

| 17 ... | Rfc8 |

Vacating a square for the retreat of his bishop. The construction of barricades on the K-side à la Rubinstein would clearly have been too late now. Possibly Black should have played 17 ... a5 immediately, but what is he to do next? Even on the Q-side he has no particular prospects.

18 Nf5	Bf8
19 Nh2	a5
20 Re3	

This simultaneously pursues several aims. Firstly, control is taken of the c3 square, which after the coming exchange will be vacated by the white pawn. Secondly, the rook intends to take up a temporary post at g3, to force Black to exchange on f5. An attack by pieces alone will be unable to breach the black king's position, but after the exchange on f5 the scope of the bishop at c2 is increased, White obtains an excellent spring-board for his pieces at e4, and the pawn at f5 comes into direct contact with the black king's shelter.

| 20 ... | a×b4 |
| 21 c×b4 | B×f5 |

This move could have been delayed, but the doubling of rooks on the a-file does not promise Black anything—White simply plays a2–a3, and sooner or later the exchange on f5 is forced.

| 22 e×f5 | c3 |

Not wishing to await his downfall on the K-side, Black attempts to gain some counter-play, by using the c4 square to attack the pawns at d5 and b4. Thus the routine 23 g4, for example, would have been answered by 23 ... Qc4. Therefore White immediately regains control of e4, so as to place his rook there and deprive the opposing pieces of the slightest activity.

23 Ng4!	Be7
24 N×f6+	B×f6
25 Re4	

White has carried out the basic part of his strategic plan. He is ready to begin a pawn storm against the black king position, and at the same time he does not object to exchanges, since if now all the pieces were to be removed from the board, except the bishop at c2 and knight at b7, Black could immediately resign.

25 ...	Qd7
26 Qf3	Rc7
27 h4	Qe7

The threat was g2–g4–g5.

| 28 g3 | Nd8 |

Alas, from here, too, the knight has only one way: back to b7.

| 29 a3 | Rcc8 |

2

Mecking openly waits. There is nothing else for him to do, and before continuing his attack White decides to surround and eliminate the breakaway black pawn at c3.

30 Rb1	Rc7
31 Qe2	Rb8
32 Rb3	Qd7
33 Qf3	

Creating two threats. One is 34 g4, and if Black parries it by 34 ... Qe7, then White carries out the second, by attacking the pawn at c3 three times.

33 ...	Be7
34 Re3	Bf6

The correct defence (*35 Rb×c3 R×c3 36 R×c3 e4*). Having "tested" his opponent, White varies his threat.

35 Re4	Be7
36 g4	

Forcing Black's reply, after which the pawn at c3 is doomed, and White maintains his attack.

36 ...	f6
37 Re3	Nf7

The knight has acquired a certain freedom, but it is too late.

38 Rb×c3	Rbc8
39 Be4	

Black must be denied the "satisfaction" of giving up a second pawn by ... e4, but of establishing his knight at e5.

39 ...	Bd8
40 Bd2	Rc4
41 R×c4	R×c4

If 41 ... b×c4 42 Rc3, and White now "surrounds" a pawn at c4 (*Bb1–a2* and *Qe4*).

42 Rc3	Bb6
43 R×c4	b×c4
44 g5	

It turns out that, even without the rooks, the pawn storm is highly formidable, since the queens are still on the board.

44 ...	f×g5
45 h×g5	Bd8
46 Qh5	c3
47 Be3	

With the terrible threat of 48 g6.

47 ...	h6
48 f6	Resigns

Few variations had to be calculated during the course of the game, but all the links in the plan were subordinate to one aim. To a certain extent this makes the game a text-book example.

No. 2 Ruy Lopez

Geller–Antoshin

Moscow, 1970

A rook in the enemy rear

White carried out a typical method of attack: he first tied down the opposing forces on the Q-side, and then made a timely transference of the weight of the struggle to the opposite side of the board. To do this he had to sacrifice the exchange, but on the other hand he gained an advantage in force on the decisive sector of the battlefield.

The game was awarded a special prize "For the most fighting and interesting game of the tournament".

1 e4	e5
2 Nf3	Nc6
3 Bb5	a6
4 Ba4	Nf6
5 0–0	Be7
6 Re1	b5
7 Bb3	d6
8 c3	0–0
9 h3	Na5

10 Bc2	c5
11 d4	c×d4
12 c×d4	Bb7

The drawback to this move is that White can advance d4–d5, restricting the activity of the black bishop.

13 Nbd2	Nc6
14 d5	Nb4
15 Bb1	a5
16 Nf1	Qc7

Uniting the rooks and preparing 17 ... Rfc8 with the threat of ... Nc2. The "voluntary" retreat of the knight, 16 ... Na6, is more usual, but in the game Fischer–Unzicker, Leipzig, 1960, for example, after 17 Ng3 Bc8 18 Bd3 Bd7 19 Be3 White gained a clear initiative on the Q-side.

17 Ng3	g6

So as not to allow Nf5, Black agrees to a weakening of his K-side. However, for the moment White is contemplating an attack on the other side of the board.

18 a3	Na6
19 Bd3	b4
20 Be3	Nc5
21 Rc1	

Disclosing the drawbacks to Black's 16th move: he cannot maintain his hold on c5.

21 ...	Nfd7

22 Bb5!

This confirms White's advantage. The threat of B×d7 is highly unpleasant, and Black's reply is essentially forced.

22 ...	Qb8
23 Nd2	Rd8
24 Qe2	Kg7
25 Rc2	

Preparing to double rooks. Black has no active counter-play, and he tries to weaken the pressure on the Q-side by exchanging the white-squared bishops. But very often the side with the initiative acquires one type of positional advantage in return for another: here the c6 square becomes open for invasion.

25 ...	Ba6
26 B×a6	N×a6

Forced, since 26 ... R×a6? 27 B×c5 N×c5 28 R×c5 leads to loss of material.

27 Rc6	Ndc5

Black's pieces have been diverted to the Q-side, and the preconditions for an attack on the black king have appeared.

28 Qg4	Kh8
29 Bh6	

Renewing the threat of Nf5.

29 ...	Rg8
30 Nc4	Qd8
31 Re3	

The last preparations. White prevents ... Nd3.

31 ...	f6

The immediate 31 ... Nb8 fails to 32 R×c5 d×c5 33 N×e5, with a very strong attack.

32 f4   Nb8

33 R×c5!   d×c5

White was intending to sacrifice the exchange when he made his 28th move. During the game I first expected here 33 ... e×f4, but then I found the variation 34 Q×f4 d×c5 35 e5! Bf8 (after *35 ... f×e5 36 N×e5* Black is lost) 36 B×f8 R×f8 37 e6 Q×d5 38 e7 Re8 39 Q×f6+ Kg8 40 Nh5! (*40 Nd6 Nd7 41 N×e8 R×e8*) 40 ... Q×h5 41 Nd6, and Black is forced to give up his queen, which can merely delay his defeat.

The continuation in the game does not require any special commentary.

34 f×e5	f5
35 e×f5	g×f5
36 Q×f5	Q×d5
37 Nd6	Rg6
38 Rd3	Qe6
39 Qf3	Ra7
40 Nf7+	Kg8
41 Nd8	

Here the game was adjourned. After sealing

41 ...   Qa2

Black resigned without resuming. White has several ways of continuing his attack. The simplest, evidently, is 42 b3, when against the numerous threats (in particular *43 Qf7 mate*) there is no defence.

No. 3 Ruy Lopez

Stein–Geller

Kislovodsk, 1966

Profiting from a loss

The piece sacrifice made by Leonid Stein could have proved successful, if the game had gone into an ending. But an endgame was not reached, since Black created an attack on the white king. It was obvious that he had to aim for complications, but for this Black had to "sell" his extra piece four times more cheaply than he had acquired it. After which the mass of white pawns were witnesses to the downfall of their king.

I cannot avoid mentioning that White's 8th move is less favourable than the main variation with c2–c3, h2–h3, etc. Either Stein had a liking for 8 d4, or else he was frightened by the spectre of the Marshall Attack. The second supposition is perhaps more probable.

1 e4	e5
2 Nf3	Nc6
3 Bb5	a6
4 Ba4	Nf6
5 0–0	Be7
6 Re1	b5
7 Bb3	0–0

Lurking on the horizon is the Marshall Attack. At that time Black's successes in it were so serious, that even such genuine "Spaniards" as Tal and Stein sought ways of avoiding 8 ... d5.

8 d4	d6
9 c3	Bg4
10 d5	

Immediately releasing the tension in the centre. Stein did not like the variations after the double-edged 10 Be3, and I knew this.

10 ...	Na5
11 Bc2	c6
12 h3	

Five years later, in the 34th USSR Championship, Leningrad, 1971, Stein chose here the more usual 12 d×c6 Qc7 13 Nbd2 (the chances were also equal after *13 h3 Be6 14 Bg5 Nc4 15 Qc1 h6* in Bronstein–Pachman, Amsterdam, 1964) 13 ... Q×c6 14 h3 (preferable is *14 Nf1 Nc4 15 Qe2 Rae8 16 a4 Bd8 17 a×b5 a×b5 18 h3* with a slight plus for White, Trifunovic–Barcza, Zagreb, 1955; however, this variation is by no means obligatory) 14 ... Be6 15 Ng5 Bd7 16 Qe2 h6 17 Ngf3 Rfc8, but again failed to achieve anything. Black later advanced ... d5 and gained a slight advantage.

The present game could have done much to decide the winner of the tournament. Only a win would suit White, and it was probably for this reason that Stein invited his opponent to follow a comparatively unexplored path. But "there is nothing new under the sun": Stein's continuation occurred back in 1922 at Hastings in the game Yates–Rubinstein.

12 ...	B×f3
13 Q×f3	c×d5
14 e×d5	Rc8

In the aforementioned game Rubinstein played 14 ... Nc4 15 Nd2 Rc8, which during the game, to be frank, I did not know. The text move to some extent provokes White into an immediate attack on Black's weakened pawns on the Q-side. I played it reluctantly, and mainly because the more "normal" 14 ... Qc7 is unpleasantly met by 15 Bg5, with the threat of 16 B×f6 and 17 Qf5.

| 15 Nd2 | g6 |

15 ... b4 fails to 16 Bf5 b×c3 17 B×c8 c×d2 18 B×d2 Nc4 19 Bg5 Q×c8 20 Rac1, when the knight cannot be saved. Therefore Black sets about creating a pawn centre, although it was not yet too late to follow the path of Rubinstein — 15 ... Nc4, with the threat in some cases of ... Nb6.

16 Bd3

White is consistent in his actions, but he has no choice. The attempt to create a weak black pawn at b5 by 16 b4 Nc4 17 N×c4 R×c4 18 a4 is not so attractive, in view of the mutual weakness at c3.

| 16 ... | Nh5 |
| 17 a4 | f5 |

18 a×b5

This move, offering a piece sacrifice, was played instantly by Stein. It can be assumed that he considered 19 Bf1 inadequate, and decided to employ drastic measures. It seems to me that such a decision does not follow from the needs of the position.

| 18 ... | e4 |
| 19 N×e4 | |

Played after 50 minutes' thought. In analysis after the game Stein expressed the opinion that he should have retained his knight and played 19 B×e4, with the possible sequel 19 ... f×e4 20 Q×e4 Bg5 21 b×a6 Qb6 22 Nf3 B×c1 23 Ra×c1, but here too 23 ... Nb3 24 Rcd1 Nc5 25 Qe2 Nf4 leads to a clear advantage for Black. Stein realized that 19 B×e4 would reduce his chances on the Q-side, and hence also his only hope of a successful outcome to the game.

It must also be mentioned that it is impossible to make a definitive analysis of such a position, the variations calculated in it are merely approximate ones, and all that can be relied upon is the accuracy of one's general assessment.

19 ...	f×e4
20 Q×e4	Nb3
21 R×a6	

The rook sacrifice 21 Q×e7 Q×e7 22 R×e7 N×a1 is obviously incorrect.

| 21 ... | N×c1 |
| 22 R×c1 | |

Here we can sum up the results of the manoeuvre begun on White's 18th move. It is clear that he has not suffered from a material point of view, and if he could take play into an ending he would have excellent winning chances. But the king is always present! He cannot be exchanged, and his downfall leads to defeat. Therefore Black, exploiting his advantage in pieces, strikes on the K-side, the opposite-coloured bishops merely intensifying his attack.

| 22 ... | Bh4 |
| 23 Rc2 | |

Similar play would have resulted after 23 g3 Qg5 24 Rf1 (*24 Rd1 Nf4*) 24 ... B×g3.

| 23 ... | Rc7! |

The last black piece not participating in the storm is transferred to an attacking position.

24 g3

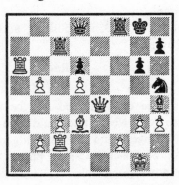

| 24 ... | B×g3 |

White in his time gave up a piece for four pawns, whereas Black returns it for only one!

| 25 f×g3 | Qg5 |

The weakness of the king's pawn screen and the remoteness of the rook at a6 make White's position indefensible. In the main variation 26 Rg2 Re7 27 Qd4 Re1+ 28 Kh2 Qc1 he comes under a mating attack.

26 g4	Re7
27 Qd4	Qh4
28 Ra1	

If only the rook hadn't moved from this square!...

28 ...	Re1+
29 R×e1	Q×e1+
30 Kh2	Qg3+
31 Kh1	Q×h3+
32 Kg1	

Or mate in three moves: 32 Rh2 Ng3+ 33 Kg1 Rf1+.

| 32 ... | Ng3 |

White resigns

No. 4 Ruy Lopez

Zhukhovitsky–Geller

*Central Chess Club Tournament
Moscow, 1970*

Weakness of a strong point

According to the rules of military strategy, the defences should be breached at their weakest place, and that is usually what happens. But how much more striking is a blow at the most invulnerable point, especially if it is situated in the centre of the board. Of course, its invulnerability must be imaginary, otherwise the blow will simply not succeed. To seek out such a weakness behind its apparent strength—this is where the difficulty lies.

1 e4	e5
2 Nf3	Nc6
3 Bb5	a6
4 Ba4	Nf6
5 0-0	Be7
6 Re1	b5
7 Bb3	0-0
8 h3?	

Black was "threatening" the Marshall Attack, and White decided to forestall it, by employing a move of more than 20-year antiquity (Taimanov–Lilienthal, Moscow, 1948). I was not familiar with this game, but Tal had played the move against me in 1966 at Kislovodsk. After this I found a plan, enabling Black to transpose into the Smyslov Variation with an extra tempo, since he advances ... d5 not in two moves, but in one.

8 ...	Bb7
9 d3	

In the aforementioned game Taimanov played 9 Nc3, which led to equality after 9 ... d6 10 Nd5 Na5. After 9 d4 Black can choose either 9 ... d6 10 c3 with normal play, or else the sharper 9 ... N×d4 10 B×f7+ R×f7 11 N×e5 Rf8 (*11 ... Nc6 12 N×f7 K×f7 13 e5*, with a very strong attack) 12 Q×d4 c5, with good counter-play for the pawn.

9 ...	h6

This move had not occurred before in practice. It is necessary, so as to be able to defend the e5 pawn with the rook, at the same time avoiding the pin on the knight at f6.

10 Nbd2	Re8
11 c3	Bf8

12 Nf1	Na5
13 Bc2	d5

Black's plan could not have been more successful. He could first have played 13 ... c5, with the likely sequel 14 Ng3 d5 15 e×d5 Q×d5 16 Ne4, but this would most probably have transposed into a possible continuation from the game.

14 e×d5	Q×d5
15 b4!?	

A good move which, however, is the first step of a dubious plan. The unpleasant 16 ... c5, completely restraining the white centre, is now forestalled, but ...

15 ...	Nc6
16 a4	

White should have refrained from this. He is unable to exploit the weakness at b5, and consequently his activity on the flank is merely a loss of time. Black, on the other hand, is centralizing all his forces to the maximum extent.

Better is 16 Ng3, establishing additional control over e4.

16 ...	Rad8
17 Ng3	Qd7

The square d5 is needed for the knight, otherwise by 18 Ne4 White could have forced some exchanges, and in the endgame the weakness of Black's Q-side pawns would become more appreciable.

18 Bd2	Nd5
19 Qb1	

White should have held the position by 19 a×b5 a×b5 20 Bb3, and if 20 ... Nf4, then 21 B×f4 e×f4 22 R×e8 and 23 Ne5, while on 20 ... Nf6 he can make a tacit offer of a draw by 21 Bc2. All the battle would then still have been to come.

19 ...	Nf4
20 a×b5	a×b5
21 d4	

White misses the one possibility, as given above, of maintaining comparative equality (21 B×f4, etc.). He had obviously not anticipated that his position would be blown up at the apparently invulnerable d4 point.

21 ...	N×d4!
22 N×d4	

If 22 c×d4, then 22 ... B×f3 23 g×f3 Q×h3 24 B×f4 e×f4 25 Bf5 Qh4 26 Ne2 (or 26 Ne4 g6) 26 ... Rd5 with a decisive attack. Or 23 B×f4 e×f4 24 Bf5 Q×d4, winning. Defeat would only have been delayed by 23 Bf5 Q×d4 24 Be3 Q×b4 25 g×f3 g6, when the h3 pawn falls, after which Black has more than sufficient pawns for the piece.

22 ...	N×g2
23 Bf5	Qd6
24 Be4	

24 Ne4 is inadequate — 24 ... Qd5! 25 Nf3 N×e1 26 B×e1 Kh8, and 27 ... g6 is threatened, while if 27 Ned2, then 27 ... e4.

24 ...	N×e1
25 B×b7	e×d4
26 c×d4	c6!

The forcing variation begun on Black's 21st move has concluded. The material situation is roughly level, but White's position is in shreds. His white-squared bishop is not destined to take any further part in the game.

27 B×e1	Qc7
28 Ba6	R×d4
29 Bc3	Rc4
30 Qb2	Qd7
31 Kh2	

Or 31 Kg2 Rh4 32 Rh1 Qd5+ 33 Kg1 Qf3.

31 ...	Rh4
32 Qd2	Q×h3+
33 Kg1	Rg4
34 Re1	R×e1+
35 Q×e1	h5

White resigns

No. 5 Ruy Lopez

Parma–Geller

*Capablanca Memorial Tournament
Havana, 1965*

Tactics against strategy

Plans which appear favourable from the viewpoint of the general laws of strategy sometimes encounter unexpected refutations, based on the tactical peculiarities of the position. This by no means contradicts the unshakeable law regarding the priority of strategy. It simply means that the formulation of correct plans demands a precisely chosen time, and that account must be taken of combinational counter-possibilities. Bruno Parma overlooked that after penetrating into the enemy position his queen might be trapped, and that by attacking it Black would obtain the preconditions for launching a counter-attack.

1 e4	e5
2 Nf3	Nc6
3 Bb5	a6
4 Ba4	Nf6
5 0–0	Be7
6 Re1	b5
7 Bb3	0–0
8 c3	d6

I quite often threaten the Marshall Attack (*8 ... d5*), but it is by no means always that I wish to play it. But the opponent, of course, does not know what I have decided before the start of the game, and sometimes avoids the possible attack, which affords Black additional chances in playing the opening.

9 h3	h6

"Informing" the opponent that he will have to battle against the Smyslov System, one of the most modern and soundest defences. Preventing the pin of his knight at f6, Black securely defends e5 and prepares in some cases to counter in the centre with ... d5. Here an alternative move order is also possible — 9 ... Re8 10 d4 h6.

10 d4	Re8
11 Nbd2	Bf8
12 Nf1	

White follows the main line of the system. In the Keres–Spassky Candidates Match (1965) the attempt 12 a3 Bd7 13 Ba2 a5 14 Qb3 Qe7 15 Nf1 a4 16 Qc2 g6 17 Ne3 Bg7 did not really achieve anything for White. After the immediate 12 d5 White again cannot count on an opening advantage.

12 ...	Bd7

This is what the system's inventor himself usually plays. The alternative, 12 ... Bb7,

is constantly chosen by Gligoric. It is sufficient to recall his match from the 1968 Candidates cycle with Tal.

The reader will see that in games with Portisch (No. 6) and Gligoric (No. 7), I too had to face this move.

13 Ng3	Na5
14 Bc2	Nc4

14 ... c5 can be answered by 15 b3, with the idea of restricting the knight at a5 (Geller–Gufeld, Armed Forces Team Championship, Odessa, 1965, Fischer–Spassky, Havana Olympiad, 1966, and other games). After 15 ... Nc6 White must immediately close the centre by 16 d5, since after 16 Be3 c×d4 17 c×d4 e×d4 18 N×d4 d5 Black can equalize. Nevertheless, 14 ... c5 is perfectly playable, as is 14 ... g6 with the possible sequel 15 Bd2 Bg7 16 Qc1 Kh7 17 b3 c5 18 Be3 (*18 d5!* is better) 18 ... c×d4 19 c×d4 Nc6 20 Qd2 e×d4 21 N×d4 d5 (Tal–Geller, 37th USSR Championship, Moscow, 1969— by transposition), or 15 b3 c5 16 d5 Bg7 17 Nh2 Nh7 18 Be3 Qh4 19 Nf3 Qe7 (Stein–Geller, ditto).

15 a4	

This was also played against me later by Stein in the Moscow International Grandmaster Tournament of 1967. I consider that the plan associated with this move is not the best. In principle, White has to prepare play on the K-side, and the opening of the a-file is more likely to favour Black. In recent times a stronger manoeuvre has been found— 15 Nh2 followed by f2–f4, which reduced the number of adherents to this system of defence for Black.

15 ...	c5
16 a×b5	

Stein played more cunningly in the aforementioned 1967 game: 16 b3! Na5 (unpleasant is *16 ... Nb6 17 a5 Nc8 18 b4*, etc.

—Tal–Minic, Budva, 1967) 17 a×b5 a×b5 18 d5 Qb6 19 Be3, and although White's position is preferable, Black has some counter-play thanks to the open a-file. White also stands slightly better after 16 d×c5 d×c5 17 Nh2 Nd6.

16 ...	a×b5
17 R×a8	Q×a8
18 d×c5	d×c5
19 Nh5	

This is the point of White's forcing manoeuvre begun on the 16th move. Since Black cannot contemplate 19 ... Bc6 20 N×f6+, White gains the advantage of the two bishops. On general grounds this idea should favour White, but he underestimated the fact that his queen's retreat would be cut off.

19 ...	N×h5
20 Q×d7	Nd6!

It turns out that White is threatened with the loss of his queen: 21 ... Nf6 22 Qc7 Rc8 23 Qb6 Rc6. He has to retreat it to the K-side, where it is out of play.

21 Qg4	Nf6
22 Qh4	Re6!

A very strong move in such positions, and one to which Spassky frequently resorts. Black's defences are securely strengthened along the 6th rank, and he can begin play on the other side of the board.

23 Nd2

White plans Nf1–e3–f5, since he has no other active possibility.

23 ...	c4
24 Nf1	b4

Immediately undermining White's Q-side. In view of the threat of 25 ... b3 26 Bb1 Qa1, his reply is forced.

25 c×b4	Nb5

Black's queen and bishop, lying in ambush, begin to make their presence felt. The outcome of the game is decided.

26 Bd2	Qa2
27 Qg3	

27 Rb1 can be met by 27 ... c3, or 27 ... Na3, or 27 ... Nd4.

27 ...	Q×b2
28 Ba4	Nd4
29 Qc3	Qa2
30 Qa1	

No better is 30 Bd1 Nb5 31 Qc1 c3 32 B×c3 Rc6.

30 ...	Q×a1
White resigns	

After 31 R×a1 c3 32 Be3 B×b4 further loss of material is inevitable.

No. 6 Ruy Lopez

Geller–Portisch

International Grandmaster Tournament
Moscow, 1967

A life lasting one evening

On encountering a theoretical innovation, I think not so much about how to avoid danger, as how to find a refutation or an optimal reply to it. In the given instance I was helped by associations with another game, played about a year and a half earlier. As a result the innovation died, without managing to bloom.

1 e4	e5
2 Nf3	Nc6
3 Bb5	a6
4 Ba4	Nf6
5 0–0	Be7
6 Re1	b5
7 Bb3	d6
8 c3	0–0
9 h3	h6

In deciding on the Smyslov System, which also features in my repertoire, Lajos Portisch was intending to infuse some "fresh blood" into the normal line, in which he had prepared an innovation. Besides, in the opening I would in effect have to battle against myself. ...

10 d4	Re8
11 Nbd2	Bf8
12 Nf1	Bb7

The most active move, and, strictly speaking, the most thematic. Black immediately begins a battle for the d5 and e4 squares. The alternative 12 ... Bd7 is more passive, but safer, since it maintains control of f5. Smyslov and I usually play 12 ... Bd7, while Spassky and especially Gligoric prefer 12 ... Bb7. This, however, does not mean that we never "change places". ...

13 Ng3   Qd7

The innovation was not long in coming (the usual continuation is *13 ... Na5 14 Bc2 Nc4*, and if *15 a4*, then *15 ... d5*—Stein–Spassky, Amsterdam Interzonal, 1964). Black unites his rooks, and wishes after ... Rad8 to complete his development. This plan appears quite attractive, but the momentarily insecure position of the black queen suggested to me (in analogy with game No. 5, Parma–Geller, where it was a black

bishop that was left undefended at d7) the following forcing continuation. What's more, in contrast to the aforementioned game with Parma, White's plan here does not have a tactical flaw.

14 d×e5!

The alternative 14 a4 Na5 15 Bc2 e×d4 16 c×d4 c5 would have led to a complicated position with slightly the better chances for White.

14 ...   d×e5

14 ... N×e5, a typical recapture in such positions, is unpleasantly met by 15 N×e5 d×e5 16 Qf3, when White firmly seizes the initiative (he threatens both *17 B×h6*, and *17 Nf5*).

15 Nh5!

"Offering" the opponent the choice between going into an inferior ending after 15 ... Q×d1 16 N×f6+ g×f6 17 B×d1, and continuing with the queens on. Portisch chooses the latter, although if he had foreseen White's 18th move he would have reconciled himself to a difficult ending.

15 ...	Qe7
16 Nh4	N×h5
17 Q×h5	Na5

This attempt to drive away the active bishop from b3 leads to an immediate debacle.

More tenacious was 17 ... Nd8, when

White would have continued the attack by 18 Re3, with the rather unpleasant threat of transferring the rook to g3. For example:

(a) 18 ... Kh7 19 Rg3, when 19 ... B×e4 is bad because of 20 B×h6!, and if 20 ... g×h6 then 21 Qg4.

(b) 18 ... Kh8 19 Rg3 B×e4, and White has a very strong attack after 20 Bg5 (here *20 B×h6 is wrong because of 20 ... g×h6 21 Qg4 Bh7*) 20 ... g6 (there is nothing else) 21 B×e7 g×h5 22 Bf6+ Kh7 23 Re1.

(c) 18 ... Qg5 (this immediate pawn sacrifice seems Black's best chance) 19 Q×g5 h×g5 20 Nf3 c5 21 N×g5 c4 22 Bc2, although even here White can hope gradually to realize his advantage.

18 Bg5!

18 ... h×g5 allows mate after 19 Ng6, while if 18 ... Q×g5 19 Q×f7+, and Black is defenceless.

18 ...	Qd7
19 Rad1	Bd6
20 B×h6	g×h6

Black also fails to save the game after 20 ... N×b3 21 B×g7 K×g7 22 Nf5+.

21 Qg6+	Kf8
22 Qf6	

Forcing mate in a few moves. Now 22 Ng6+ is threatened.

22 ...	Kg8
23 Re3	**Resigns**

No. 7 Ruy Lopez

Geller–Gligoric

"Match of the Century"
Belgrade, 1970

A continuing duel

Quite often the chess world witnesses some curious creative duels, which sometimes last for several years. They proceed according to the following typical scheme. Two players have played a game. On meeting each other again, they choose the same variation, without any prior agreement, of course, thus adding a psychological struggle to the purely chess struggle. Over each of them, like the sword of Damocles, hangs the anxious thought: why is the opponent repeating the previous game? On what move has he prepared a surprise, and has he in fact prepared one? Should I wait for the unpleasant surprise, or should I be the first to deviate from the familiar path? And if I deviate, then when and how?

Such a complex of questions concerned Svetozar Gligoric and myself during the following game, since up to a certain point it repeated our meeting from the USSR–Yugoslavia match at Sochi in 1968. Then I had attempted unsuccessfully to pierce my opponent's defences. On this occasion I was successful, because Gligoric himself deviated from the correct move order.

This game was played in the first round, and in the third our duel was continued. The Yugoslav grandmaster reverted to the set-up which had occurred in Sochi, improved it, and rehabilitated this variation for Black. But chess is too diverse to give a definitive assessment to the resulting position. So that in principle the duel has not yet concluded: the ball is now in White's court.

On the conclusion of the match this game was judged the best of those won by the Soviet grandmasters, and received a special prize.

1 e4	e5
2 Nf3	Nc6
3 Bb5	a6
4 Ba4	Nf6
5 0–0	Be7
6 Re1	b5
7 Bb3	d6
8 c3	0–0
9 h3	h6

The Smyslov System begun with this move was Gligoric's main weapon against the Ruy Lopez, which was once picturesquely called the "Spanish torture" for Black. The Yugoslav grandmaster is one of the world's greatest experts on this system.

10 d4	Re8
11 Nbd2	Bf8
12 Nf1	Bb7
13 Ng3	Na5
14 Bc2	Nc4

Other moves to be tried here are:

(a) 14 ... c5, which can be answered by 15 d5 Nc4 16 Nh2 g6 (Tal–Smyslov, Baku, 1961), or by the immediate 15 b3.

(b) 14 ... g6 15 Nh2 Bg7 16 f4 e×f4 17 B×f4 c5 18 b3 Nc6 (Gheorghiu–Panno, Mar del Plata, 1965).

(c) 14 ... d5!?, sacrificing a pawn and obtaining an open game.

For the moment my opponent follows our Sochi game.

15 b3

For the time being for me too there is no reason to deviate. Especially since Tal, in his 1968 match with Gligoric, twice failed to achieve anything after 15 a4 d5!? He then resorted to 15 Bd3, employed a week earlier by Korchnoi in his match with Reshevsky, but to me this continuation seems rather artificial.

15 ...	Nb6
16 Bb2	Nbd7

Only Gligoric could give a completely authentic explanation of his train of thoughts at this point. From the side it looks like a vote of no confidence in himself. Fearing some surprise, Black varies from the approved continuation of the Sochi game, where after 16 ... c5 17 d×e5 d×e5 18 c4 Qc7 (in the 3rd round of the "Match of the Century" Gligoric played the more exact *18 ... Nbd7*,

immediately starting the knight on the route d7–b8–c6–d4, and not determining for the moment the position of the queen) 19 Qe2 b4! (*19 ... b×c4 20 b×c4* gives White the square a4, and the advantage) 20 Rad1 Nbd7 21 Nd2 Nb8 22 Nf5 Nc6 23 f4 g6 24 f×e5 N×e5 25 Ng3 Bg7 Black maintained the balance, and on the 28th move a draw was agreed.

17 Qd2

Gligoric regards this move as not the strongest, recommending that the withdrawal of the knight from b6 should be exploited by 17 a4. Nevertheless the white queen is comfortably placed at d2 (not *17 Qe2? e×d4 18 c×d4 N×e4!*), and White is aiming for active play in the centre, after bringing up his queen's rook.

17 ...	c5
18 Rad1	Qa5

Too active. Less committing is 18 ... Qc7, and after 19 d×e5 d×e5 20 c4 Nb8! Black's position is sufficiently sound.

19 d×c5	d×c5

On 19 ... Q×a2 White would have had a pleasant choice between 20 c6, and 20 Ra1 Q×b2 21 Reb1 with the advantage after 21 ... Q×b1+ 22 R×b1 N×c5 23 Re1.

20 c4	b4

The lesser evil was to go into a slightly inferior ending by 20 ... Q×d2. But Gligoric was hoping to equalize by the usual manoeuvre in such positions, ... Nb8–c6–d4, and overlooked or underestimated a combinational blow by the opponent. Note, incidentally, that after 20 ... Q×a2 White would have had not only the straightforward 21 Ra1 Q×b2 22 Reb1 Q×b1+ with a fairly sound position for Black, but also the less obvious 21 Bc3 b4 22 Ra1 b×c3 23 Q×c3 Q×a1 24 R×a1 with the advantage.

21 a4

The weakness at a2 is eliminated, and the pressure in the centre maintained. White stands better.

21 ...   Qc7

Freeing the knight at d7 from the defence of the e5 pawn, and continuing to dream of transferring it via b8 and c6 to d4. But, to this end, better was 21 ... Re6 followed by ... Rae8, as suggested by Bondarevsky.

22 Nf5   Nb8

The decisive moment of the game. Only one move, ... Nc6, separates Black from complete happiness, and White has no right to delay. The alternative suggestion of 22 ... Rad8 would have left White with the advantage both after 23 Qe2, and after 23 Nd6 B×d6 24 Q×d6 Q×d6 25 R×d6.

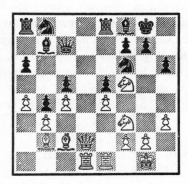

23 N×e5!

At just the right time! In giving up two minor pieces for rook and pawn, White sees that the swift advance of his e- and f-pawns will drive the black forces back into unfavourable positions.

23 ...   R×e5
24 B×e5   Q×e5
25 f4   Qe6

After 25 ... Qc3 26 Qf2 the black queen would have been trapped, for example: 26 ... Nc6 27 e5 Ne8 28 Re3 Qb2 29 N×h6+ g×h6 30 Bh7+.

26 e5   Ne8

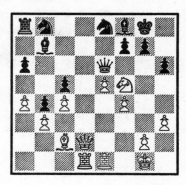

Offering White the tempting possibility of losing his way after 27 Nd6 N×d6 28 e×d6 Qf6 29 d7 Nc6 30 Re8 Nd4!

It is unlikely that Black would have saved the game after 26 ... Ne4 27 R×e4! Q×f5 28 Ree1 Qe6 (28 ... *Qh5* is unpleasantly met by *29 Qd3*) 29 f5, with a highly dangerous attack. His misfortune is that his Q-side pieces can merely stand and watch the destruction of his king's position.

27 Nh4!

The most energetic continuation. Black's h7 now becomes a fatal weakness.

27 ...   Nc6
28 Qd3   g6
29 f5   g×f5
30 N×f5

Threatening mate in three moves by 31 Ne7+, etc. Black's reply is forced, since after 30 ... Bg7 31 N×g7 K×g7 (*31 ... N×g7 32 Qh7+ Kf8 33 Qh8+*) 32 Qh7+ Kf8 33 Bf5! his queen has no good retreat — 33 ... Qe7 34 Qh8 mate.

30 ...   Qg6
31 Qe2!

31 Qd7 would also have won, but White wishes to deny his opponent the slightest chance.

31 ...   Qg5

This leads to the loss of the queen, but Black's position was no longer tenable. Thus after 31 ... Qe6 32 Qe4 Qg6 during the game I considered two winning continuations:

(a) 33 Re3 Nd8 34 Rd5 B×d5 35 c×d5 etc.

(b) 33 Rd7! Bc8 34 e6! B×d7 (34 ... Q×e6 35 Ne7+) 35 e×d7 Ng7 (35 ... Nc7 36 Nh4!) 36 N×g7 K×g7 37 Q×g6+ f×g6 38 Be4.

| 32 h4 | Qf4 |
| 33 g3 | |

It is not often that the queen is trapped in the centre of the board. The remainder is simple.

33 ...	Q×e5
34 Qg4+	Qg7
35 N×g7	Nf6
36 Qf4	B×g7
37 Qc7	Rb8

Three minor pieces are adequate compensation for a queen, but here White also has an extra rook.

38 Rd6	Ng4
39 R×c6	Bd4+
40 Kf1	Resigns

No. 8 Ruy Lopez

Kupreichik–Geller

37th USSR Championship
Moscow, 1969

One plan is better than two

In this USSR Championship I did not set myself any creative goals. In my opinion, any discoveries, even "intuitive" ones, are founded on knowledge, on the basis of what has been assimilated. But knowledge requires

study, study requires time, and before the Championship I had absolutely no time. As I was seconding Boris Spassky in his match for the World Championship, I was unable even to play in the Semi-Final, and was included in the Final, which had the status of a Zonal Tournament, at virtually the last minute. Therefore I had only one goal—to reach the Interzonal Tournament.

Even so, I managed to play some games comparatively cleanly and consistently from the creative point of view. The present game is one of them.

1 e4	e5
2 Nf3	Nc6
3 Bb5	a6
4 Ba4	Nf6
5 Qe2	

This queen move—before castling—is now frequently employed by grandmaster Gurgenidze, and in the 1920s it was played by Alekhine, Bogoljubov and Spielmann. In the 1968 Kislovodsk tournament I had to defend as Black against Gurgenidze, and so I was familiar with certain features of the position.

| 5 ... | Be7 |

Here the usual continuation is 5 ... b5 6 Bb3 Be7, and now:

(a) 7 d4 d6, and if 8 c3, then according to Grünfeld 8 ... Bg4 gives Black a reasonable game, for example: 9 Bd5 N×d5 10 e×d5 Na5 11 d×e5 d×e5 12 Q×e5 B×f3 13 g×f3 Nc4.

(b) 7 a4 Rb8 8 a×b5 9 d4 d5! 10 c3 N×e4 11 N×e5 N×e5 12 d×e5 0–0, with approximate equality.

The text move took my opponent unawares, since 6 d4 (it later transpired that this is what Kupreichik had been intending to play) simply loses a pawn. In the aforementioned game Gurgenidze continued 6 B×c6 d×c6 7 b3, taking play along the lines of the Exchange Variation. Kupreichik decides to carry out a mixture of two other plans, but his idea proves unsuccessful.

6 c3	b5
7 Bb3	

Of course, on 7 Bc2 Black replies 7 . . . d5.

7 . . .	0–0
8 d4	d6
9 d×e5	

This exchange, removing the tension in the centre, is taken by White from the move order 5 Qe2 b5 6 Bb3 Be7 7 d4 d6 8 d×e5, which gives him a minimal advantage.

9 . . .	N×e5
10 N×e5	d×e5
11 a4	

The advance of the rook's pawn is borrowed from the plan given in the note to Black's 5th move. Each of White's two moves (his 9th and 11th) is all right on its own, but taken together they have led to the important c5 square being seized by the black pieces, to a loss of time, and hence to the loss of the initiative. White should have played 11 0–0.

11 . . .	Bb7
12 f3	Nd7

Heading for c5, and not fearing the loss of the b5 pawn: 13 a×b5 a×b5 14 R×a8 Q×a8 15 Q×b5 B×e4! 16 Q×d7 Bh4+ gives Black a very strong attack.

13 Be3	Nc5
14 Bc2	Bc6
15 a5	

Within a move or two (*0–0* and *b2–b4*) White will have everything in order, but it is at this point that Black begins his offensive.

15 . . .	b4!
16 0–0	

White has no time to take the pawn: 16 c×b4 Ne6, and 17 0–0 fails to 17 . . . Bb5.

16 . . .	Rb8
17 Rd1	Qc8
18 Nd2	

To concede the d4 square is equivalent to suicide for White. However, in any case his position is not easy.

18 . . .	b×c3
19 b×c3	Rb2!

This invasion by Black's rook consolidates his advantage, since White is unable to evict it.

20 Qf2	R×c2
21 B×c5	Qe6
22 B×e7	Q×e7
23 Qe3	

The attempt to get rid of the annoying black rook—23 Rdc1—would have led to loss of material: 23 . . . R×c1 24 R×c1 Qa3.

23 . . .	Rd8
24 Nc4	

A pseudo-active move. 24 Nf1 was more circumspect, although even then White cannot hold onto to both of his weak pawns at a5 and c3.

24 . . .	R×d1+
25 R×d1	h6

In spite of the simplification Black has retained a big positional advantage. Each of his pieces is more active than its white opponent.

26 Qd3

Conceding the g1–a7 diagonal is equivalent to capitulation, although the better 26 h3 Bb5 27 Nd2 Qa3 would only have prolonged the struggle.

| 26 ... | Qc5+ |
| 27 Kh1 | Ba4! |

This wins, since against the threat of 28 ... Bb3 there is no satisfactory defence.

| 28 Qd8+ | Kh7 |
| 29 Qc8 | |

In the hope of perpetual check, but...

| 29 ... | Q×c4 |

White resigns, since f7 is defended by the queen.

No. 9 Ruy Lopez

Hübner–Geller

Interzonal Tournament
Palma de Mallorca, 1970

Adjourning for revenge

This game took place in the fifteenth round, when with 9 points I was sharing 3rd and 4th places, while Robert Hübner was in 5th–7th place on 8½. However, the leading group was so tightly packed that even with Black my trainer, grandmaster Eduard Gufeld, and I were thinking only of victory. The question was: what to play? Not long before our game Hübner had played 6 Qe2 in the Ruy Lopez against Portisch. This would have suited me, since in my time I had done a great deal of work on a sharp system involving the sacrifice of a pawn. But Gufeld expressed his fears: what if Hübner, as in an earlier game with Gligoric, should exchange on c6, set up a solid position, and gain a draw? The argument seemed convincing, but somewhat abstract. Firstly, Hübner had played Gligoric at the start, when he had the "status" of a debutant in an Interzonal Tournament, whereas by the 15th round he was one of the leaders, and a possible Candidate for a match with the World Champion. Competitive logic demanded that he should not avoid a fight. And secondly, there is no reason for avoiding an equal and quiet game, provided only that there is plenty of play in prospect. This was confirmed in a game from the last round by Smyslov, who outplayed Hübner from such a situation.

1 e4	e5
2 Nf3	Nc6
3 Bb5	a6
4 Ba4	Nf6
5 0–0	Be7
6 Qe2	b5
7 Bb3	0–0
8 c3	d5

Here Portisch played 8... d6 against Hübner, and White retained an advantage: 9 a4 b4 10 d4 e×d4 11 N×d4 Bd7 12 Rd1 Qb8 13 Nd2 Qb7 14 Bc2 Rfe8 15 Nc4. The move in the game, which was first employed by Schlechter, allows Black sharply to complicate the game after the most crucial line 9 e×d5 Bg4! 10 d×c6 e4 11 d4 e×f3 12 g×f3 Bh5, with a strong attack in return for the two pawns.

After the game some commentators expressed the opinion that Hübner was unprepared for this variation. That may be so, but to be fair it has to be said the natural continuation 9 e×d5 has also been avoided in games with me by theoretically better prepared players (to say nothing of their playing strength), such as Paul Keres (Budapest, 1952) and Boris Spassky (Leningrad, 1960). Obviously the point is that there are few players with White who are prepared to go immediately onto the defensive!

9 d3	Bb7
10 Rd1	

Hübner himself, annotating this game in *Informator*, considers this move dubious. In the aforementioned Keres–Geller game White played more solidly: 10 Re1 Re8 11 Nbd2 Qd7 12 Nf1 Rad8 13 Bg5 Na5 14 Bc2 d×e4 15 d×e4. But up to a certain point Hübner repeats (with a transposition of moves) the game Bisguier–Geller (Stockholm, 1962), where Black avoided an early … Bb7 but also gained an excellent position.

10 …	Re8
11 Nbd2	Bf8
12 Nf1	Na5
13 Bc2	c5

This position is quite in the spirit of the Smyslov System, which is considered one of the most "pleasant" for Black in the Ruy Lopez. White has lost the advantage of the first move: he is a long way from an attack on the K-side, and on the Q-side and in the centre his opponent has the initiative.

14 Bg5

To be considered was 14 Ng3, completing the knight manoeuvre and aiming for f5.

14 …	h6
15 Bd2	Qc7
16 Ng3	Rad8

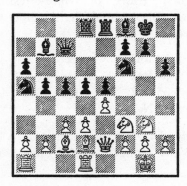

17 h4?

The idea of this move was evidently to place the pawn at h5 and then invade with the knight at f5, whereas after the immediate 17 Nf5 Kh7 the knight cannot be maintained at f5, since Black has prepared … g6. However, Hübner should have been thinking not about activity, but about defence. This aim was best met by 17 Rac1, placing the rook opposite the black queen and preparing in case of necessity to retreat the bishop to b1.

After losing time and weakening his K-side, White finds himself in a difficult position.

17 …	c4!
18 b3!	

Black is intending to destroy White's defensive lines at e4. The exclamation mark is attached to White's move because, in an inferior position, when many a player would have lost heart, Hübner begins playing very tenaciously, and by the threat of c3–c4 hinders Black to the maximum extent in realizing his advantage.

18 …	c×d3
19 B×d3	Qc8!

The soundest way of increasing the advantage, although the more direct 19 … d×e4 20 B×e4 (*20 N×e4 Nd5 21 c4 Nf4*) 20 … N×e4 was also perfectly possible.

Black exploits the fact that 20 e×d5 loses a piece to 20 … e4, and puts the square g4 under fire. Now on 20 c4 there follows 20 … d×e4, and if 21 B×a5, then 21 … R×d3 22 R×d3 e×d3 23 Q×d3 e4.

20 Bc2

As soon as c3–c4 is no longer on the agenda, Black begins transferring to the centre of events his one passively placed piece—his knight at a5. Exchanges do not worry him: there are already organic weaknesses in White's position.

20 …	d×e4
21 N×e4	B×e4

In my younger days, when my aim in practically every game was to mate the opposing king, I would have preferred 21 ... Nd5. I think that both continuations are feasible; a position has been reached where various solutions are possible.

| 22 B×e4 | N×e4 |
| 23 Q×e4 | Nb7 |

This is the point. The stereotyped 23 ... Nc6 would have limited the knight's scope, whereas now it is aiming for d3.

| 24 Ne1 | Nd6 |

White only has to defend the invasion square, and the knight unexpectedly changes course.

| 25 Qe2 | Nf5 |
| 26 h5 | |

26 g3 would not have saved White from the mounting threats—26 ... Bc5.

| 26 ... | e4 |
| 27 Nc2 | |

A reflex reaction to the cramped position of the white knight. 27 a4 should have been considered, although it is possible that White was afraid of being immediately crushed in the variation 27 ... Bc5 28 a×b5 Ng3 29 Qc4 R×d2 30 R×d2 e3.

| 27 ... | Rd3 |
| 28 Qg4 | |

In his notes Hübner suggests instead 28 Nb4, but what can White do after the simple 28 ... B×b4 29 c×b4 Nd4 30 Qf1 Qg4?

| 28 ... | Bc5 |
| 29 Nb4 | |

Now Black has two "romantic" ways of concluding the game. After 29 Ne3 he would have had the prosaic task of realizing

an extra pawn in a rook ending: 29 ... N×e3 30 Q×c8 R×c8 31 B×e3 B×e3 32 R×d3 e×d3 33 f×e3 R×c3. This should not have caused any particular difficulty.

| 29 ... | Rg3 |

When the game was adjourned, I very much regretted that I had not played 29 ... B×f2+. After 30 K×f2 Qc5+ White's king has nowhere to go, and he will also not last long if he declines the sacrifice. I will reveal the "secret": I preferred the text move because I expected that White, who was losing his queen, would resign immediately. But Hübner forced me to analyse, and then to resume the game ...

30 Qf4	Bd6
31 f×g3	B×f4
32 B×f4	e3

The first "fruits" of White's resistance. Of course, Black should have simply taken the c3 pawn.

33 Rd3	e2
34 Re1	Qc5+
35 Kh2	Qf2
36 Nc2	

Merely delaying the inevitable. All the same White cannot save the game: 36 Bd2 Re3!

| 36 ... | Nh4 |

A blow is struck from the other side.

37 g×h4	Q×f4+
38 Kg1	Q×h4
39 Rh3	Qg5
40 Nd4	Qd2
41 Kf2	

With the faint hope that Black will take on a2, when 42 b4 followed by 43 R×e2 will allow White to put up a lengthy resistance.

41 ...	Qf4+
42 Kg1	Qd2
43 Kf2	Qf4+
44 Kg1	

Having repeated the position to gain time on the clock, after analysis Black starts a decisive regrouping of his forces. For this he has to give up his e-pawn.

44 ...	a5
45 a3	

White can allow ... b4 only if both of the black Q-side pawns are exchanged. He dare not capture the pawn: 45 N×b5 Re3.

45 ...	Re4
46 N×e2	

Forced, in view of the threat of 46 ... R×d4 47 c×d4 Q×d4+ and 48 ... Qf2. But the resulting pin is highly unpleasant for White.

46 ...	Qe5
47 Kf1	Qf5+
48 Rf3	

Or 48 Kg1 Qe6 49 Kf1 Q×b3, and Black creates a passed pawn on the Q-side.

48 ...	Q×h5
49 Rd1	Qe5
50 Rf2	f6
51 Rd2	Re3
52 Rd4	Kh7

Of course, not 52 ... R×c3?? 53 Rd8+.

53 Rd1	Qe4

There is simply nothing for White to move: 54 Rc1 R×e2.

54 Re1	Qc2
55 b4	a4
56 g4	Qe4
57 Rg2	Rf3+
White resigns	

No. 10 Ruy Lopez

Geller–Keres

41st USSR Championship
Moscow, 1973

A quarter of a century of "torture"

It would seem that Paul Keres had forgotten about our meeting nearly 25 years earlier on that same stage of the Railway Workers' Central House of Culture. Again Black did not manage to equalize. A quarter of a century later the "Spanish torture" enabled White to take to its logical conclusion an advantage, which at the time had remained unrealized.

1 e4	e5
2 Nf3	Nc6
3 Bb5	a6
4 Ba4	Nf6

Keres, an expert on the Ruy Lopez, varies his systems: a few rounds earlier he had played 4 ... d6 against Spassky, and after 5 B×c6+ b×c6 6 d4 e×d4 7 N×d4 c5 he gradually equalized. But in the given game he failed to cope with his opening problems.

5 0–0	Be7
6 Re1	d6
7 c3	0–0
8 d4	

If here White plays 8 h3, after 8 ... Bd7 9 d4 Re8 10 Nbd2 Bf8 the normal move of his knight from d2 to f1 is hindered by the threat of ... e×d4. I encountered this in a game with Kholmov (Match–Tournament of Three USSR Teams, Moscow, 1973), and was forced to continue 11 d5, after which White had essentially no advantage.

It is curious that, when analysing my game with Keres in 1949, I established that in this position White answers 8 ... b5 with the unexpected 9 Bc2 (*9 Bb3* leads to normal variations), when after 9 ... Bg4 10 d5 Na5 11 Nbd2 Black is unable to undermine the centre by 11 ... c6? because of 12 b4.

In the game Black tries to hold the centre, at the cost of a temporary immobilization of his Q-side.

| 8 ... | Nd7 |
| **9 Be3** | |

The most accurate. The stereotyped 9 Nbd2 would have given Black the chance to "regain" the tempo on which White has economized (he has managed without *h2–h3*) by 9 ... Bf6 with the threat of 10 ... e×d4, and if 10 Nf1, then 10 ... Nb6 and ... Bg4.

| 9 ... | Bf6 |
| **10 Nbd2** | |

Already White could have advantageously advanced his pawn to d5, but the natural continuation in the game also places Black in a difficult dilemma. He has to choose between conceding the centre — 10 ... e×d4 11 c×d4 Nb6 12 Bc2, spoiling his pawn formation without any compensation — 10 ... Nb6 11 B×c6 b×c6 12 d×e5, and the move in the game. Only later did it become clear that the least evil would have been to concede the centre, although even in this case White would have won the opening battle.

| 10 ... | Re8 |
| **11 d5** | |

With even greater force than before. It transpires that all Black's pieces are badly placed. The pinned knight at d7 prevents the development of his Q-side, and the bishop at f6 prevents him from creating counter-play with ... f5. Less noticeable for the moment, but no less significant, is the weakening of the f7 square. All this is the consequence of the passive plan chosen by Black in the opening (*8 ... Nd7*).

| 11 ... | Ne7 |
| **12 b4** | |

More exact than 12 c4, when Black might yet have replied 12 ... c5. Now this is impossible due to the loss of a pawn: 13 B×d7 and 14 b×c5 (or in the reverse order).

| 12 ... | g6 |

12 ... Ng6 is parried by the simple 13 g3, when it is not clear what Black can do next.

13 c4

This advance could have been prepared by 13 Rc1, but I wanted to provoke ... c6, which is now obligatory (otherwise White has time to play *c4–c5*).

| 13 ... | c6 |

14 Rc1

Black was hoping for a piece sacrifice —14 c5 d×c5 14 d6 b5 followed by ... c×b4, which would have given him three pawns and counter-play. Besides, in the variation similar to that which occurred in the game, I did not see how after 14 c5 d×c5 15 b×c5 c×d5 16 e×d5 N×d5 17 Ne4 N×e3 18 R×e3 (*18 N×f6+ N×f6*) 18 ... Bg7 19 Rd3 Re7 I could exploit the pin on the d-file. Thus on 20 Nd6 Black simply replies 20 ... N×c5 21 N×c8 Q×c8, and the threat of 22 ... e4 is highly unpleasant.

Now White prepares the breakthrough c4–c5, and simultaneously removes his rook from the X-ray action of the black bishop.

14 ...	Bg7

14 ... c×d5 looks the lesser evil, when White has a choice between the quiet 15 c×d5 and the sharper 15 e×d5. Now on 15 ... Nf5 he continues 16 c5, threatening to advance the c-pawn further and win the exchange, while 15 ... b5 16 Bb3 leads to a familiar "Sicilian" formation with a weak square for Black at c6. In general, from the strategic point of view Black's position must be considered lost.

15 c5!	d×c5

Black is still hoping to "buy off" his opponent with a piece in the variation given earlier, but by a pawn sacrifice White opens the centre and begins a decisive offensive. The withdrawal of the black bishop to g7 gives him an important tempo for the attack.

16 b×c5	c×d5
17 e×d5	N×d5
18 Bg5	Ne7

Black retreats his "hanging" knight from d5, since the alternatives are bad:

(*a*) 18 ... Bf6 19 Ne4! B×g5 20 Nf×g5 Ne7 21 B×d7 B×d7 22 Q×d7 winning a piece.

(*b*) 18 ... Qa5 19 Nc4 Q×c5 20 Nc×e5, winning material.

19 Ne4	h6

20 Nd6!	h×g5

Black has nothing else — 20 ... Rf8 21 B×e7 and 22 N×c8.

21 N×f7!!

This second piece sacrifice completely destroys Black's K-side. The capture of the knight leads to the loss of the queen or to mate: 21 ... K×f7 22 N×g5+ Kf6 (*22 ... Kg8 23 Bb3+, or 22 ... Kf8 23 Ne6+*) 23 Nh7+ Kf7 24 Bb3+.

21 ...	Qa5

No better is 21 ... Qc7 22 N7×g5, when the threat of 23 Bb3+ cannot be parried, while in certain variations there is also the possibility of Ne6.

22 N7×g5	Rf8
23 B×d7	

The simplest way. White restores material equality and retains a winning attack.

23 ...	Q×a2
24 Re2	

Black tries to keep control of the vitally important a2–g8 diagonal, but White begins driving away the black queen.

24 ...	Qa3

It turns out that after 24 ... Qd5 25 Rd2 the black queen is caught!

25 Re3	Qb4

25 ... Qa2 again leads to the loss of the queen: 26 Rc2, and if 26 ... Qd5, then 27 Rd3. But now White achieves his aim: the e6 square is in his power.

26 B×c8	Ra×c8

27 Qd7	Nf5

After 27 ... Rce8 Black suffers heavy losses, while 27 ... Rfe8 leads to a variety of smothered mate: 28 Qe6+ Kh8 29 Nf7+ Kh7 30 N3g5+ Kg8 31 Nh6++ Kh8 32 Qg8+ N(R)×g8 33 Nhf7 mate.

28 Qe6+	Kh8
29 Q×g6	Resigns

Sicilian Defence

No. 11 Sicilian Defence

Geller–Kogan

Odessa Team Championship, 1946

In search of adventure

My chess childhood was considerably extended because of the war, and this interesting though far from faultless game was played when I had first category rating. At that time the romance of chess held an irresistible attraction for me, and I did not yet understand the strict logicality of the laws of chess strategy, which I frequently broke for the sake of cavalier attacks on the enemy king, for which I was often punished. But I did not complain, since the emotional satisfaction from a successful brilliant attack, accompanied by a cascade of sacrifices, more than compensated for any isolated misfortunes.

It is from this viewpoint that the reader should consider this game from the distant romantic past. To a certain extent it played the role of a catalyst, giving me confidence in my powers, without which the development of a chess player is impossible.

1 e4	c5
2 Nf3	d6

3 d4	c×d4
4 Q×d4	

The attitude to this move of the Leningrad Master M. Noakh has varied with the times. At first it provoked interest, then it was almost completely supplanted by the main continuation 4 N×d4, and now it has again acquired a certain recognition by the efforts in particular of Karpov and Vasyukov. It leads to less well studied, but interesting and sharp positions.

4 ...	Nc6
5 Bb5	Bd7
6 B×c6	B×c6

6 ... b×c6 is also satisfactory.

7 Nc3	Nf6
8 Bg5	e6
9 0–0	

At the present time 9 0–0–0 is more often played. In my opinion, Q-side castling in this position is a double-edged weapon, since the white king is less securely placed and can become the target for a dangerous counter-attack. Those readers who find such an assessment too abstract are referred, among others, to the game Hecht–Geller, Belgrade, 1969: in it White achieved nothing from the opening.

9 ...	Be7
10 Rad1	0–0
11 Rfe1	Qc7

Black has played the opening accurately. White gains nothing from the win of a pawn —12 B×f6 B×f6 13 Q×d6 Q×d6 14 R×d6 B×c3 15 b×c3 Rfc8, and the resulting ending is completely without danger for Black.

12 h3

This simple, at first sight waiting move is the start of an original, but alas, fanciful plan of direct attack on the opposing king.

12 ...   Rfd8

Black has completed his final preparations, and his offensive in the centre and on the Q-side promises to be highly formidable. But I was lured by the mirage of my intended attack, and I calmly continued manoeuvring, with a view to creating future threats against the black king. Today in this position I would probably play 13 a3, so as to answer 13 ... b5 with 14 e5 d×e5 15 Q×e5.

13 Nh2	b5
14 Rd3	

Typical romanticism! In bringing out the rook in front of my pawns, I was hoping to smash open the black king's position by an onslaught of my pieces alone. Meanwhile, Black has no weaknesses, and it is clear that White's attack should simply not succeed.

14 ...   a5

An imperceptible mistake, after which the struggle intensifies. Although tempting, the immediate 14 ... b4 did not work because of 15 B×f6 B×f6 16 Q×b4 Rab8 17 Qc4!, and if 17 ... R×b2, then 18 Ng4, obtaining an attacking position and retaining the threat of Nd5. But had Black played 14 ... Rab8, he would have nipped in the bud White's aggression, as later becomes clear.

15 Rf3	b4

16 R×f6

It begins! Incidentally, it should be said that White had already burned his boats, since on 16 Nd1 there would have followed 16 ... e5 and 17 ... d5, when his position collapses like a house of cards.

16 ...   b×c3

At the very first clash Black misses the strongest continuation. It is true that the text move looks highly tempting, since the white rook is stuck at f6 and cannot painlessly retreat.

Correct is 16 ... g×f6, when although White can continue his attack for a certain time, he does not have compensation for the sacrificed material. For example: 17 Ng4 e5 18 Qc4, and now not 18 ... f×g5, which after 19 Nh6+ Kg7 (*19 ... Kh8 20 Nd5 Qd7 21 N×e7 Q×e7 22 N×f7+ Kg7 23 N×d8*) 20 Nd5 Qd7 21 Nf5+ gives White a very strong attack, but 18 ... b×c3! 19 Nh6+ Kh8 20 N×f7+ Kg7 21 Bh6+ Kg6, and if 22 Re3, then 22 ... d5, when White's attack reaches an impasse.

But now it takes on a real form: the white pieces steal up on the g7 square, although for the moment it does not appear to be threatened.

17 Ng4	h5

Black is crushed after 17 ... g×f6 18 N×f6+ Kh8 19 Q×c3!, when there is no defence to the threat of Nd5.

18 Bh6 **e5**

18 ... h×g4 would have lost to 19 Rg6!, for example: 19 ... e5 20 R×g7+ Kh8 21 Qc4! Rf8 22 R×f7 d5! 23 R×e7 Q×e7 24 B×f8 d×c4 25 B×e7 c×b2 26 Bf6+ Kh7 27 B×e5. After the move in the game an extraordinary position is reached! Under attack are White's queen, rook, bishop and knight, and in addition the black pawn at c3 is not so far away from the queening square!

19 Qe3 **h×g4**

Inevitable mate follows after 19 ... g×f6 20 Qf3!

20 B×g7 **K×g7?**

This allows White triumphantly to conclude his attack. Black could have extricated himself by 20 ... B×f6 21 B×f6 Kf8! 22 Qg5 c×b2, when White has nothing better than to give perpetual check: 23 Qg7+ Ke8 24 Qg8+ Kd7 25 Q×g4+, etc. But after the game my opponent said that at this point, being two pieces up, he was hoping to win and was not thinking in terms of a draw.

21 Qh6+ **Kg8**
22 Rf5 **Be8**

23 Rh5 **f6**
24 Rh4!

Threatening 25 Qh7+ Kf8 26 R×g4, when mate is inevitable.

24 ... **Qc8**

Black hopes to give up his queen for the white rook, but in doing so he leaves his bishop at e7 without defence.

25 Qh8+ **Kf7**
26 Rh7+ **Ke6**
27 Qg7 **Kd7**

In view of the threats of 28 Q×g4 mate and 28 Q×e7 mate this is the only move. Black intends to evacuate his king via c6, after which he could have hoped to realize his extra piece: 28 Q×e7+ Kc6 29 Re3 Qd7.

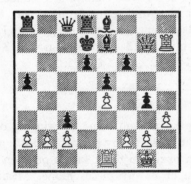

28 Re3!

The winning intermediate move. Black is not saved even by the appearance of a new queen with check!

28 ... **c×b2**
29 Q×e7+ **Kc6**
30 Rc3+ **Kb6**
31 R×c8 **b1=Q+**
32 Kh2 **Rd7**
33 Q×e8 **R×h7**
34 Qc6+ **Resigns**

No. 12 Sicilian Defence

Geller–Vatnikov

*USSR Championship Semi-Final
Kiev, 1950*

A miniature–cum–monograph

To play a miniature game without a serious mistake by one of the sides is impossible. But there are mistakes and mistakes. In the given case the efforts of many players over a number of years were needed to give an exact diagnosis of the manoeuvre ... Na5 and ... b6.

As for the specific course of the game, White had long ago noticed that the weakening of Black's control over the centre (when the knight goes to the edge of the board) normally allows him to make the favourable advance e4–e5. Moreover, this relates not only to the given variation, but also to many other Sicilian set-ups. Therefore White's swift attack, although found at the board, rests on the foundation of accumulated knowledge about the methods of play in typical positions.

1 e4	c5
2 Nf3	Nc6
3 d4	c×d4
4 N×d4	Nf6
5 Nc3	d6
6 Bc4	

This move has an interesting history. It was played as long ago as 1923 in a game Spielmann–Euwe (Scheveningen), but was not then associated with a pawn offensive on the K-side. Then it was employed against Rokhlin in the 6th USSR Championship in 1929 by the Soviet master Sozin, and the system developed by him received the name of the Sozin Attack. But it did not find any fervent followers, and attention was drawn to it only after an excellent victory by Boleslavsky over Aronin in the 17th USSR

Championship. Fashion exists also in chess: in tournaments during the 1950s, along with the Rauzer Attack, the Sozin Attack occurred quite often. In the 1960s one of its adherents became Fischer, and it served him faithfully up to the 4th game of his match with Spassky. Moreover, at first White used to castle K-side in the Sozin Attack, then it was modernized and he began playing Qe2 and 0-0-0.

The Sozin Attack was not part of my basic opening repertoire. I chose it for the reason stated in the introduction to the game.

6 ...	e6
7 0-0	Be7
8 Be3	

In the given position this is stronger than the more flexible 8 Kh1. This will become especially clear after White's 13th move.

8 ...	0-0
9 Bb3	

Prophylaxis before the commencement of positive action. Against Taimanov in the tournament at Szczawno–Zdroj, 1950, Grynfeld played the weaker 9 f4?, and Black immediately seized the initiative: 9 ... d5 10 e×d5 e×d5 11 Be2 Re8.

There is little justification for recommendations such as 9 a3. White preserves his bishop at c4 from exchange, but gives Black a highly important tempo for creating counter-play. For example, 10 Ba2 Qc7 11 Qe2 a6 or 11 ... b6.

9 ...	Na5

Recommended in the theoretical review of the 17th USSR Championship by Bondarevsky and Kéres. In the aforementioned game against Boleslavsky, Aronin played this a move later — 9 ... a6 10 f4 Na5 11 Qf3 Qc7 (*11 ... b5 should have been played*) 12 g4 b5 13 g5 Nd7 14 N×e6 f×e6 15 B×e6+ Kh8 16 Nd5, and White gained a very strong attack.

It is interesting to see how Botvinnik

assesses this crucial moment in his notes to the games Padevsky–Botvinnik (Alekhine Memorial Tournament, Moscow, 1956) and Neikirkh–Botvinnik (Leipzig Olympiad, 1960):

"The manoeuvre ... Na5 and ... b6 is not without its advantages, since: 1. Black exchanges off the bishop at b3; 2. The bishop at c8 reaches b7 a move earlier in comparison with ... Na5, ... a6 and ... b5, and 3. In some cases the bishop at b7 can be defended by the knight at a5. ..."

"Even so, the diversion of the knight to the edge of the board causes serious doubts".

Once again Botvinnik was not let down by his positional feeling. The latest word of theory for Black in the Sozin Attack must for the moment be considered 9 ... a6 10 f4 N×d4 11 B×d4 b5 12 a3 Bb7 13 Qd3 a5!, when for the planned f4–f5 White does not have time, since he has to reckon with 14 ... b4. After the forced 14 e5 d×e5 15 f×e5 Nd7 16 N×b5 Nc5 17 B×c5 B×c5+ 18 Kh1 Qg5 Black gained more than sufficient compensation for the pawn in Fischer–Spassky (4th match game, 1972).

Thus, after a creative discussion lasting many years, Black's plan beginning with 9 ... Na5 has been shown to be dubious.

10 f4　　　　b6
11 e5!

At that time another USSR Championship Semi-Final was taking place in Gorky, where almost simultaneously a game Estrin–

Aronin was played. There was no exchange of information between the towns, and I made the acquaintance of it only after the tournament. By choosing here 11 g4 N×b3 (*11 ... Bb7* is even better) 12 Nc6 Qc7 13 N×e7+ Q×e7 14 a×b3 Bb7 15 e5 d×e5 16 f×e5 Nd5 White achieved nothing from the opening.

Against Botvinnik, Padevsky tried 11 Qf3 Bb7 12 g4 Rc8 13 g5, when by sacrificing the exchange — 13 ... R×c3! — Black would have seized the initiative even after the strongest reply 14 g×f6 R×e3! In general, it should be said that if Black succeeds in posting his bishop at b7, and then exchanges on b3 at the appropriate moment, he stands well. But here the unpleasantness begins earlier than he normally expects it.

11 ...　　　　Ne8

Of course, Black was not attracted by 11 ... d×e5 12 f×e5 Nd5 13 N×d5 e×d5 14 Qf3, but nevertheless this was the lesser evil. Totally bad (after *11 ... d×e5 12 f×e5*) is 12 ... Nd7, which allows the immediately decisive 13 R×f7! R×f7 (or *13 ... K×f7*) 14 N×e6.

12 f5　　　　d×e5

12 ... e×f5 fails to 13 e6 N×b3 14 Nc6 Qc7 15 Nd5, or 13 ... f6 14 Bd5 Bb7 15 B×b7 N×b7 16 Nc6 Qc7 17 Nd5. White has a very strong attack in the variation 12 ... N×b3 13 Nc6! Qc7 14 N×e7+ Q×e7 15 f6.

13 f×e6!

This position was the starting point for a series of later games. Incidentally, had White played 8 Kh1 instead of 8 Be3, Black could have confidently replied 13 ... e×d4 14 e×f7+ Kh8 15 f×e8=Q Q×e8, when White is restricted by the weakness of his back rank. But now he simply plays 16 B×d4 when he is a pawn up with an attack.

On the basis of analyses by Ratner and Lipnitsky, the exchange 13 ... N×b3 was deemed totally bad in view of 14 Nc6! Qd6 (14 ... Q×d1? 15 N×e7+ Kh8 16 Ra×d1 Nd4 17 B×d4 e×d4 18 R×f7) 15 Nd5 N×a1 16 Nc×e7+ Kh8 17 R×f7! Rg8 and now 18 Ng6+ h×g6 19 Qg4 or even 18 Qh5! Q×e6 19 N×g8! Q×d5 20 Rf8 g6 21 Nf6+ Kg7 22 Bh6 mate.

But in the 1961 European Team Championship a sensational game Bilek–Petrosian occurred: 13 ... N×b3 14 Nc6 Qd6 15 Nd5 Bh4! 16 e×f7+ R×f7 17 R×f7 N×a1! 18 Qf1 Bf6 19 N×f6+ N×f6, and White resigned.

But even earlier, in the 1957 Polish Championship, in a game Kostro–Doda White found a very simple and convincing refutation of 13 ... N×b3 14 Nc6 Qd6 — 15 Q×d6! B×d6 16 a×b3 B×e6 17 N×a7, when he obtained a superior, evidently even won ending. This evaluation was not shaken by the game Fischer–Korchnoi (Curacao, 1962) although White contrived to lose the ending.

13 ...	f6

In making such a plausible move, Black was hoping that the worst was over, since after the withdrawal of the knight from d4 he exchanges on b3 and wins the pawn at e6.

14 Nf5	N×b3

The dangerous bishop is eliminated, but too late.

15 Nd5

The white knights are deployed most picturesquely.

15 ...	Nd4

Or 15 ... N×a1 16 Nd×e7+, winning the queen.

16 Nd×e7+	Kh8
17 Ng6+!	Resigns

No. 13 Sicilian Defence

Gereben–Geller

Budapest, 1952

On the altar of attack

It is obvious that White did not play as well as possible. Otherwise Black in this game, which was judged the most brilliant in the tournament, would simply not have been able to lay on the altar of attack first a bishop, and then two exchanges. Such generous sacrifices cannot be considered excessive when the king is being pursued: in the event of success it is all repaid!

1 e4	c5
2 Nf3	d6
3 d4	c×d4
4 N×d4	Nf6
5 Nc3	a6
6 h3	Nc6
7 g4?	

While White's previous passive move cannot be considered a mistake, this "energetic" advance is a serious loss of time.

7 ...	N×d4
8 Q×d4	e5
9 Qd3	Be7
10 Bg2	Be6
11 b3?	

A further neglect of the law of rapid development. Black has a marked lead in the mobilization of his forces, and the position is of an open nature. . . .

11 ...	0–0
12 Bb2	b5
13 0–0–0?	

Courageous and... foolhardy. White "hides" his king in the very epicentre of the battle. However, outwardly he appears to have even an attacking position, and if he had two or three moves of quiet life he could hope for counter-play in the centre. But after his mistakes on the 7th, 11th and 13th moves he gains no such respite to the very end of the game.

13 ...	b4
14 Ne2	

Black's attack also develops freely after 14 Nd5 B×d5 15 e×d5 Nd7.

14 ...	a5
15 f4	Nd7
16 f5	Nc5
17 Qf3	

17 ...   a4!

17 ... Bd7 is also perfectly possible, but the move played is much more vigorous. It is bad now to accept the sacrifice, since 18 f×e6 f×e6 19 Qg3 Bh4 20 Qh2 Rf2 21 Rhe1 Bg5+ wins quickly for Black.

18 h4	a×b3
19 a×b3	

Now the rook's file becomes the invasion route for Black's heavy pieces.

19 ...	Ra2!

The decisive move. The threat of ... Qa5 and ... R×b2 followed by ... Qa3+ and ... Ra8 cannot be averted.

20 f×e6	f×e6
21 Qe3	Qa5
22 c4!	R×b2!
23 K×b2	Qa3+
24 Kb1	Ra8
25 Nc1	Qa1+
26 Kc2	

One more move, and the white king will slip out of the firing line, but...

26 ...	Ra2+

The final sacrifice, after which Black begins regaining with interest his missing material.

27 N×a2	Q×a2+
28 Kc1	N×b3+
29 Q×b3	Q×b3

The outcome of the game is decided. Black has a queen and two pawns for two rooks, and in addition the white king is "bare". As soon as Black includes in the attack his black-squared bishop, which has no opponent, it will all be over.

30 Rd2	Qc3+
31 Rc2	Qe3+

32 Kb2	Qa3+
33 Kb1	b3
34 Rb2	Qb4
35 g5	Bd8
36 Rc1	Bb6
37 Bh3	Kf7
38 h5	Bd4
39 g6+	h×g6
40 h×g6+	Ke7

White resigns

No. 14 Sicilian Defence

Geller–Najdorf

Candidates Tournament
Zurich, 1953

Strength in movement

From time to time, like many other players, I glance through my own games of earlier years, and return to positions and variations which have gone out of practice. I attempt to restore them, to find new ideas and plans. In this search much has to be deemed exhausted, but much remains and is worked out more precisely and in more detail. In a well-known scheme nuances are found, and past intuition is reinforced by knowledge.

Something of this nature can be said about a position which arose in this game. To this day it occurs in my games, including the most important encounters from the competitive point of view, such as, for example, one with Fischer at Curacao. It is true that in the handling of it certain subtleties have appeared, as will be related in the note to White's 10th move.

1 e4	c5
2 Nf3	d6
3 d4	cxd4
4 Nxd4	Nf6
5 Nc3	a6

6 Be2	e5
7 Nb3	Be6
8 0–0	Nbd7
9 f4	Qc7
10 f5	

Today, instead of 10 f5 I would possibly choose 10 Kh1, not revealing my cards and maintaining the tension in the centre (as occurred in my game with Donner in the 1970 IBM Tournament), and would also wonder whether or not to advance the pawn to f4 a move earlier, before castling. After all, in the game Black could have answered 9 f4 not only with 9 ... Qc7, but also more flexibly — 9 ... Rc8, avoiding determining immediately the position of the queen.

Is all this of any significance? I think it is, since by no means always does it reduce to a simple transposition of moves. As for the time when this game was played, then, nearly thirty years ago, opening positions were studied much less, and at times neither I, nor the majority of my colleagues, would pay any attention to such subtleties.

10 ...	Bc4
11 a4	

This move is part of a plan to occupy the centre and blockade Black's Q-side. Later the reader will be able to see that I quite often carry out such a plan against the Sicilian. Moreover, formerly I did this purely intuitively, whereas now intuition is based on conviction. Why? It is wrong to suppose that White's overall idea in the Sicilian Defence is an attack on the K-side. After all, in systems where his knight retreats from d4 to b3, all White's minor pieces, plus his queen's rook and queen are normally directed towards the Q-side, where Black is weakened due to the advance of his a- and b-pawns, and sometimes also the e-pawn (the d5 square). Therefore it makes sense first to tie down Black's forces by activity on the Q-side, and only then, if the opportunity arises, to set one's sights on the black king.

In the present game I managed to embody this idea in pure form.

| 11 ... | Rc8 |
| 12 Be3 | Be7 |

Black obviously underestimates the entire danger of the threatened squeeze in the centre and on the Q-side, otherwise he would have played here 12 ... d5 13 N×d5 (*13 e×d5 Bb4*) 13 ... N×d5 14 e×d5 B×b3 15 c×b3 Bc5. For this reason it is more accurate for White to withdraw his king — 12 Kh1, as occurred in later games. But, I repeat, then such nuances would at times remain beyond the bounds of analysis.

| 13 a5 | h5? |

Not so much a weakening of the K-side, which White in fact did not manage to exploit, so much as a loss of precious time: the pawn will have to be advanced further. In this connection 11 ... Rc8 must be considered inaccurate, provided only that Black did not associate it with 12 ... d5. It was better, as later played by Fischer, to castle on the 11th move followed by ... Rfc8 and ... b5, which is not now possible due to the weakness of the a-pawn. However, it soon transpires that Najdorf disregards this factor.

| 14 B×c4 | Q×c4 |
| 15 Ra4 | Qc7 |

15 ... Qc6 would not have made any essential difference.

16 h3	h4
17 Rf2	b5
18 a×b6	N×b6

Najdorf was pinning considerable hopes on his 17th move. Indeed, his position would appear highly promising in the event of White accepting the temporary pawn sacrifice. For example: 19 R×a6 Nc4, when on 20 Bc1 there follows 20 ... Qb7, and on 20 Qc1 — 20 ... N×b2 21 Nb5 Qb7 22 N×d6+ B×d6 23 R×d6 Nc4 followed by the capture on e4. But the point is that White does not engage in pawn-grabbing, but carries out a plan which Black with his last move was unable to prevent. Here are the steps of this plan:

(*a*) Place the queen at e2 and transfer the rook from f2 to a1, tying down all Black's heavy pieces to the defence of the a6 pawn.

(*b*) Transfer the knight from b3 to e3, taking firm control of the d5 square.

(*c*) Invade d5 with a knight, obtaining the typical formation of good knight against bad bishop.

As will be seen, it takes White twelve moves to implement his plan. He begins by eliminating one of the black pieces which is capable of defending d5.

19 B×b6!	Q×b6
20 Qe2	Ra8
21 Kh2	0–0

22 Rf1	Ra7
23 Rfa1	Rfa8
24 R1a2	

It is not a question of exaggerated orthodoxy, as stated in his book on the tournament by Bronstein, who suggests 24 Qd3 followed by 25 Nd2, when 25 ... Q×b2 fails to 26 Rb1, but simply one of technique. The f2 square has to be covered against possible invasion by the black queen, which could have led to unnecessary complications in a position where White's advantage is undisputed.

24 ...	Bd8
25 Na5	Rc8
26 Nc4	

In a similar position against Fischer at Curacao, I played Nd5, and answered ... N×d5 with e×d5, obtaining the square c6 for my knight. But here White's plan is close to fruition, and without necessity, as the saying goes, you should not change horses in midstream.

26 ...	Qc6
27 Ne3	a5
28 Rc4	Qa6
29 b3	

Forestalling the further advance of the a-pawn.

29 ...	Bb6
30 R×c8+	Q×c8
31 Ned5	N×d5
32 N×d5	

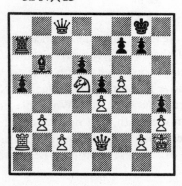

The character of the position has stabilized, and strategically Black's position can be considered lost.

32 ...	Qc5
33 Ra1	Qf2

Black appears to have an excellent opportunity here to play 33 ... a4, and if 34 b×a4 then 34 ... R×a4. But it was here that White would have gained the chance to strike at the king: 34 Qg4 a×b3 35 f6 g6 36 Q×h4, when he mates a move earlier. Black would have had to play 34 ... Qf2 35 f6 Qg3+ 36 Q×g3 h×g3+ 37 K×g3 a×b3 38 R×a7 B×a7 39 c×b3, with an easily won ending for White.

34 Q×f2

Unnecessary, although favourable complications would have resulted after 34 Qg4 Bd8 35 b4 a4.

34 ...	B×f2
35 Rf1	

An important move, ensuring freedom for the white king. If now Black checks at g3, it is his bishop that will be shut in.

35 ...	Bd4
36 c3	Bc5
37 g4	h×g3+
38 K×g3	Rb7
39 Rb1	

It is clear that Black is unable to prevent the creation of a passed pawn on the b-file and its support by the king from c4. Therefore he must remove his king from the back rank, to have the possibility of switching his rook to h8 with counter-play against the h-pawn. This, and also his desire to undermine the pawn at f5, explains Black's next move, after which a purely text-book ending is reached. Black's pawns are on squares of the same colour as his bishop, the white knight has an eternal post in the centre, and the white king is free to move along the white squares. The win in such a position is merely a matter of time.

39 ...	f6
40 Kf3	Kf7
41 Ke2	Rb8
42 b4	g6
43 Kd3	

The game would have concluded more quickly after 43 f×g6+ K×g6 44 b×c5 R×b1 45 c6 Rb8 46 c7 Rh8 47 c8=Q R×c8 48 Ne7+. Occupied with the implementation of my plan, I overlooked this tactical possibility.

43 ...	g×f5
44 e×f5	a×b4
45 c×b4	Bd4

Here we can sum up: White has two isolated passed pawns, whereas Black's two are connected. But the white pawns are mobile, and the black pawns are not!

46 Rc1	Kg7
47 Rc7+	Kh6
48 Ke4	Kg5
49 Rh7	Bf2
50 Rg7+	Kh4
51 Kf3	Be1
52 Kg2	

Threatening mate in 3 moves: 53 Rg4+, 54 N×f6+ and 55 Rg6 mate.

52 ...	Rf8
53 b5	Ba5
54 b6	B×b6

Otherwise b6–b7–b8 will lead to mate.

55 N×b6	Rb8
56 Rg4+	Kh5
57 Nd5	Resigns

No. 15 Sicilian Defence

Geller–Ivkov

*AVRO-Tournament
Hilversum, 1973*

The all-powerful pawn

If on the 23rd move White had exploited his advantage more precisely, we would not have seen the exotic concluding position, where a queen and rook were powerless against a pawn. So that an old saying is perfectly applicable to the outcome of this game—"it's an ill wind...".

1 e4	c5
2 Nf3	d6
3 d4	c×d4
4 N×d4	Nf6
5 Nc3	a6
6 Be2	e5
7 Nb3	Be7
8 0–0	Be6
9 f4	Qc7
10 a4	Nbd7
11 Kh1	

The reader has the chance to satisfy himself that White follows his own recommendations, as given in the note to White's 10th move in Game No. 14 against Najdorf. It is true that here, too, White played f2-f4 only on the ninth, and not the eighth move, but the reason for this was Black's transposition of moves: first ... Be7 and then ... Be6.

11 ...   **Rc8**

Perhaps Black avoided 11 ... 0–0 because he feared a swift but double-edged offensive on the K-side — 12 f5 Bc4 13 g4. After the frequently-played move in the game the lack of defence for his a6 pawn makes it difficult for him to advance ... b5.

12 f5	Bc4
13 a5	0–0
14 B×c4	Q×c4
15 Ra4	Qc6

The exchange on c4 shows either that White is keeping the pawn storm (*g2–g4*) in reserve, or ... that he does not intend to carry it out in the present game. Black's last move is provoked by a desire to keep the white rook at a4 for some time, by tying it to the defence of the e4 pawn. On 15 ... Qc7 White would have continued, as in the game, with 16 Be3.

16 Be3	Rfd8
17 Qf3	

Unequivocally letting it be known that the pawn storm is still on the cards. Ivkov thought for a long time and...

17 ...   **h6**

A clever move. If White responds with the direct 18 g4, Black successfully regroups by exploiting the position of the rook at a4: 18 ... Nh7, when 19 Nd5 is inadequate in

view of 19 ... Q×a4, while 19 Raal is answered at just the right time by 19 ... Ndf6, and without h2–h4 the g4–g5 break-through becomes impossible.

The alternative 17 ... Nc5 did not appeal to Black because of 18 Rc4! (*18 N×c5 d×c5 19 g4 Rd4!*) 18 ... b5 (there is nothing else) 19 a×b6 Q×b6 20 b3, with a clear advantage to White.

18 Raal!   **Nc5**

Here too Black answers 19 N×c5 d×c5 20 g4 with the stereotyped but strong 20 ... Rd4! Therefore White goes a different way, and tries to exploit the weakening of the king's position caused by ... h6.

19 Nd5	N×d5
20 e×d5	Qb5
21 N×c5	d×c5
22 Qg4	

With a multitude of threats: 23 f6, 23 B×h6 and 23 c4. Black's reply is practical-ly forced, after which 23 f6 is not possible due to the rook at al being undefended.

22 ...	Q×b2
23 B×h6	

Natural and ... inaccurate. After 23 c4 Black is helpless against the threats of 24 B×h6 and 24 Rabl followed by R×b7. But now he gains the opportunity to confuse matters, and White is required to play very precisely.

23 ...	e4
24 Rabl	

Here, too, the immediate 24 c4 was better.

24 ...	Qe5
25 c4	e3

This is the point. The black pawn succeeds in crossing the blockading square e3 and causes White considerable trouble. White could have obtained this same position, but with his bishop at e3 and the black pawn at e4, which is undoubtedly in his favour.

26 Rbe1

In view of the threat of 26 ... Bd6 followed by the advance of the e-pawn, White has no time to make the capture 26 R×b7. Now his chief enemy is Black's passed pawn.

| 26 ... | Qd4 |
| 27 Rf4 | Qf6 |

27 ... Qc3 encounters the strong reply 28 Ref1, when the threat of 29 f6 is very unpleasant (28 ... Bf6 29 B×g7).

28 Re4!

Forcibly transposing into a won ending.

28 ...	Q×h6
29 R×e7	Re8
30 Qe4	R×e7
31 Q×e7	Qf4
32 h3	

Opening an escape square for the king, and with a curious rook ending in view. The pawn at e3 will not run away.

| 32 ... | Q×f5 |
| 33 d6 | Qe6 |

Losing control of the queening square d8. The only way to continue resisting was by 33 ... Qf6, but then an interesting rook

ending arises: 34 Q×f6 g×f6 35 R×e3 Rd8 36 Rd3. White wins since, even if Black picks up the d6 pawn, he finishes a pawn up but with a lost pawn ending — a rather unusual occurrence. It is here that the role of the a5 pawn is important, blocking Black's Q-side!

| 34 d7 | Resigns |

No. 16 Sicilian Defence

Pilnik–Geller

Interzonal Tournament
Göteborg, 1955

Clarity is not always necessary

Herman Pilnik stabilized the position too early, after which White's possible initiative on the Q-side was easily neutralized. A more flexible implementation of his plan would have given White good play.

The game received a prize as one of the best in the tournament.

1 e4	c5
2 Nf3	Nc6
3 d4	c×d4
4 N×d4	Nf6
5 Nc3	d6
6 Be2	

Allowing Black to play the Boleslavsky System in its pure form. Therefore much more usual now are the active Rauzer Attack—6 Bg5, and the Sozin Attack—6 Bc4.

6 ...	e5
7 Nb3	Be7
8 0–0	0–0
9 Be3	

White chooses a plan involving an attack on the Q-side. He intends to reinforce his e4 pawn, place his knight on d5 and after its exchange recapture on d5 with the pawn, and then try to break through with c2–c4–c5. The alternative plan of pressure in the centre and on the K-side is less dangerous for Black. For example, after 9 f4 a5 10 a4 Nb4 11 Be3 Qc7 White's actions are restricted, and Black prepares the counter ... d5.

| 9 ... | Be6 |
| 10 Bf3 | |

According to Tarrasch "the bishop at f3 always stands badly", but otherwise the knight cannot be advanced to d5. For this reason I once played 9 f3, and met 9 ... Be6 with an immediate 10 Nd5.

| 10 ... | a5 |
| 11 Nd5 | B×d5 |

The tempting 11 ... a4 12 Nc1 a3 after 13 b3 would merely strengthen the c2–c4–c5 breakthrough.

| 12 e×d5 | Nb8 |

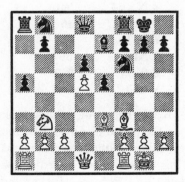

13 c4?

Too straightforward. Now Black easily sets up a blockade on the Q-side, and on the K-side he will have the initiative. White should have continued 13 Qd2 or 13 a4, and then endeavoured to transfer his bishop to the important square b5, from where it could have severely restricted Black's actions.

13 ...	Na6
14 Bd2	b6
15 Bc3	Nc5
16 N×c5	

In this way White deprives the black knights of their excellent post at c5. At this point I realized that Pilnik was no longer thinking of playing actively on the Q-side, and had gone totally onto the defensive.

16 ...	b×c5
17 Qe1	Nd7
18 Bd1	a4

Not allowing the bishop to go to a4, and preserving his "promising" knight from exchange.

| 19 Bc2 | f5 |
| 20 Rd1 | |

Passive defence is bound sooner or later to lead to White's defeat. Here he misses the last chance of complicating the game. After 20 f4 e4 21 g4 Bf6 22 g×f5 Re8! a sharp position favouring Black is reached, but nevertheless White would have had certain counter-chances. Black's next move excludes this possibility.

| 20 ... | g6 |

Black reveals his simple but logical plan: to place his bishop at f6 and advance his pawn to e4, after which e5 will become an excellent outpost for his knight. Then he will begin a pawn offensive on the K-side, also putting pressure on the b-file if necessary.

| 21 Qe2 | Bf6 |
| 22 f3 | e4 |

Of course, at the given moment this pawn sacrifice is not essential, but all the same the advance ... e4 is part of Black's plan.

23 B×f6	Q×f6
24 f×e4	f4

In spite of his extra pawn, White's position can be considered lost. Against the pawn storm he has no satisfactory defence.

25 Rf2	Ne5
26 Rdf1	Qh4

The most exact. The queen stands at the head of the attacking pawn chain.

27 Bd1	Rf7
28 Qc2	g5
29 Qc3	Raf8
30 h3	h5
31 Be2	g4

The concluding blow.

32 R×f4	R×f4
33 R×f4	R×f4
34 g3	Nf3+

Of course, simpler was 34 ... Q×h3 35 g×f4 g3 with a quick mate, but Black was in time trouble and so chose a variation which he had calculated beforehand.

35 Kf2

Or 35 B×f3 Q×g3+.

35 ...	Q×h3
36 g×f4	g3+
37 K×f3	g2+
38 Kf2	Qh2

White resigns

No. 17 Sicilian Defence

Geller–Polugayevsky

28th USSR Championship
Moscow, 1961

The king's Achilles' heel

White could have employed the plan of blockading the Q-side, which had brought him a number of points in the most important events. But, firstly, just as it is wrong to work on chess by studying only the first 10–15 moves, so it is wrong to play one and the same opening system, even though it be rich in variations and nuances. Such a bias threatens to narrow a player's outlook. Secondly, each of us is familiar with the purely human desire sometimes to seek something new, even though it may be not altogether prudent.

1 e4	c5
2 Nf3	d6
3 d4	c×d4
4 N×d4	Nf6
5 Nc3	a6
6 Be2	e5
7 Nb3	Be7
8 0–0	0–0
9 Be3	Qc7

Since Black has avoided developing his bishop on the h1–a8 diagonal, he should not have determined without necessity the position of his queen. More expedient was the immediate 9 ... Be6, as, for example, in Game No. 16 Pilnik–Geller.

10 Qd2

In my opinion, 10 a4 is objectively stronger. In this book the reader will find numerous examples of the blockade of Black's Q-side, but this completely correct plan nevertheless does not exhaust all the possibilities of the position. For the moment White masks his intentions, cherishing in his heart hopes of an attack on the K-side.

| 10 ... | Be6 |
| 11 f4 | e×f4 |

The surrender of the centre is to all appearances forced, since 11 ... Nbd7 12 f5 Bc4 13 g4! is unpleasant for Black. The assessment of this position depends upon whether or not Black's counter-blow in the centre — 13 ... d5, which involves a pawn sacrifice — succeeds. Analysis shows that possible is either 14 N×d5 N×d5 15 e×d5 B×e2 16 Q×e2 Nb6 17 B×b6 Q×b6+ 18 Kh1, with a very sharp position in which White's chances are nevertheless preferable, and the simple 14 e×d5, when 14 ... Bb4 is strongly answered by 15 d6!

12 R×f4

White begins to reveal his intention of a direct attack on the king. A highly-important step in the plan is to transfer his knight from b3 to f5, and to post his bishop at d4. Had Black sensed this, he would now have played 12 ... Nc6, controlling White's key "transit" square d4, and then directed his other knight to e5 via d7.

| 12 ... | Nbd7? |

This fails to prevent White's planned piece arrangement, and his attack now develops without hindrance.

| 13 Nd4 | Ne5 |
| 14 Nf5 | Rac8 |

Both here and later it is unfavourable for Black to play 14 ... B×f5 15 R×f5 Nc4 16 B×c4 Q×c4 17 Bd4!, but to be considered was 14 ... Rfd8 with the possible idea of freeing his position by ... d5.

| 15 Raf1 | Rfe8 |
| 16 Bd4 | Bf8 |

Black's position is difficult. He is deprived of active counter-play, and so he tries as far as possible to strengthen the position of his king. He succeeds in this only partly...

| 17 Bd3 | Nfd7 |
| 18 Rh4! | |

The squares f7 and g7 are more or less securely reinforced, but next to the king there is also the square h7, and White's heavy pieces begin to set their sights on it.

| 18 ... | Ng6 |
| 19 Rh3 | Nde5 |

Black has done everything possible for the defence, but even this is insufficient. White's centralized group of pieces is just too strong, and the only defender of h7 is the black king....

| 20 Qd1 | b5 |
| 21 Qh5 | h6 |

The rank of black pawns on the K-side has been broken. A sacrifice on h6 is clearly in the offing, after which the black king will be exposed. Possible now was 22 g4 with the threat of 23 g5, and on 22 ... f6 — 23 Nd5. But it is better if possible to attack without weakening the position of one's own king. The move played also prepares the knight advance to d5, after which the force of the storm will become too great.

| 22 Rg3 | Kh7 |

This move is essential. If 22 ... b4, then 23 Nd5 B×d5 24 e×d5, and on 24 ... N×d3 White replies 25 R×g6! f×g6 26 Q×g6, with an irresistible attack.

23 Nd5

Even stronger was 23 Kh1 and 24 h4, since in the meantime Black could not have improved his position.

23 ...	B×d5
24 e×d5	N×d3

Already in the air were threats such as 24 N×h6 g×h6 25 B×e5 R×e5 26 R×f7+, etc., and White could have carried them out at the most favourable opportunity.

25 c×d3	Qb7

Black runs into a curious mate after 25 ... Ne5 26 N×h6 g6 (*26 ... g×h6 27 B×e5 and 28 R×f7+*) 27 Ng4+! g×h5 28 Nf6+ Kh6 29 Be3 mate.

26 Kh1

The most exact. In the variation 26 ... Q×d5 27 N×g7 Black will take on d4 without check — 27 ... Q×d4 28 N×e8 R×e8 29 R×f7+ Kh8 30 R×f8+!

26 ...	Rc2
27 Ne3!	

By no means the signal to retreat. The knight switches with gain of tempo to the important square g4, from where it attacks

not only h6, but also f6. At the same time the file is opened for the rook at f1.

27 ...	Rd2
28 Ng4	

More forceful than the alternative possibility of 28 Qf5, with the threats of 29 h4 and 29 Q×f7.

28 ...	Qd7

Instead 28 ... Rde2 was recommended, so as to exchange White's attacking rook by 29 ... Re1. But it too fails to save the game, since White replies 29 Be3, threatening to win the exchange by 30 Nf6+, and on 29 ... Rc2 he plays the thematic 30 B×h6.

29 h4!

The tempting 29 Q×h6+ will not run away. Now this threat is even stronger: after 30 Q×h6+ g×h6 31 Nf6+ Kh8 32 N×d7+ Bg7 33 B×g7+ K×g7 34 h5 Black loses a piece.

29 ...	Qe7
30 Re3	Qd7
31 Q×h6+	Kg8

The queen cannot be taken: 31 ... g×h6 32 Nf6+ Kh8 33 N×d7+ Ne5 34 Bc3 Rc2 35 d4.

32 R×e8	Resigns

Mate at g7 is threatened, and the rook at d2 is attacked.

No. 18 Sicilian Defence

Geller–Panno

*Interzonal Tournament
Göteborg, 1955*

Three in one

Several times in my career situations have occurred which are known by the name of "twin games". This was the case when in the

19th USSR Championship two games were played, between Geller–Flohr and Petrosian–Smyslov, which up to a certain point were identical. In one of the rounds of the 1956 USSR–Yugoslavia match the games Geller–Karaklajic and Averbakh–Ivkov coincided, and at the international tournament in Budapest in 1973 the same happened in Geller–Karpov and Hort–Hecht. Finally, the present game had simultaneously two "twin brothers": Keres–Najdorf and Spassky–Pilnik — a unique instance in the history of chess! Subsequently it received the name of the "Argentinian tragedy".

In twin games it is in principle more advantageous to occupy the second position, since it is possible to introduce corrections using the experience of one's neighbour. Unfortunately, it has never worked out that way: it has always been me who has had to commit himself first. Sometimes this was provoked by an urge to solve the problems of the position myself, sometimes because I learned of the existence of the "twins" later than my colleagues.

At times I had to pay for my "haste" (against Flohr and Karaklajic), whereas my neighbours, Petrosian and Averbakh, achieved more. In the present game, on the other hand, priority was rewarded by a quicker win than in the other games.

1 e4	c5
2 Nf3	d6
3 d4	c×d4
4 N×d4	Nf6
5 Nc3	a6
6 Bg5	e6
7 f4	Be7

In several games of the previous rounds Black had been unable to solve satisfactorily his defensive problems in this variation, and it was obvious that for this unusual USSR–Argentina match on three boards the Argentinians had prepared something new. Even so, for the moment White has no real justification for deviating.

| 8 Qf3 | h6 |
| 9 Bh4 | g5 |

This advance is the idea of the defence worked out by the Argentinian players. They wanted, by exchanging the f4 pawn, to obtain the eternal square e5 for a knight, which, in their opinion, should compensate for White's superior development. Even so this whole manoeuvre is too slow, and at the cost of two pieces White gains the opportunity to begin a direct attack on the king.

| 10 f×g5 | Nfd7 |

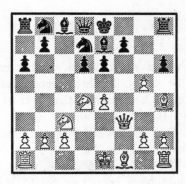

| 11 N×e6(!) | f×e6 |
| 12 Qh5+ | Kf8 |

And here something unexpected occurred. The point was that at this moment Spassky and Keres were still deliberating over whether to sacrifice the knight on e6, and their opponents Pilnik and Najdorf were observing our game and animatedly discussing something. Then Najdorf came up to me and very brusquely, interrupting my thoughts, declared: "Your game is lost; all this has been analyzed by us!"

By this time I had managed to find a continuation of the attack, and I replied by playing:

13 Bb5!

Aimed indirectly against the future black knight at e5, on which Black's entire system of defence is based. The quiet 12 Be2 or 12 Bd3 would have allowed him after 13 ... Ne5 14 0–0+ Kg7 15 Bg3 to support the knight at e5 with his other knight—15 ... Nbc6. But now White will take on c6, then on e5, and will give mate!

However, later it transpired that in their preparations the Argentinians had made a cursory examination of this move, but had "found" a defence and relaxed. Even so, when I played this Najdorf and Pilnik grew rather nervous and returned to their boards. Later they glanced at our game only once more, and saw that their prepared variation contained a flaw.

13 ...   Ne5
14 Bg3!

The whole point! Black's game can no longer be saved. In their preparations the Argentinians had assumed that after 14 0–0+ Kg8! 15 Bg3 h×g5 White's attack would misfire. They overlooked that, after the move order employed in the game, 14 ... Kg8 fails to 15 B×e5 and 16 Qg6+, while 14 ... Kg7 could have been met by 15 B×e5+ d×e5 16 0–0 Qg8 17 Be8, etc.

Incidentally, Najdorf and Pilnik awaited the development of events in our game, saw that things were bad for Black, and diverged from their prepared analysis by playing 13 ... Kg7. This merely enabled them to prolong their resistance.

The strongest defence for Black was found much later, after a vast amount of research had appeared in virtually all the world's chess magazines. It is 13 ... Rh7!, and has in mind the following main continuation: 14 0–0+ Kg8 15 g6 Rg7 16 Rf7 B×h4 17 Q×h6 R×f7 18 g×f7+ K×f7 19 Qh7+

Ke8, when White can either give perpetual check (*20 Qh5+ Kf8 21 Qh8+*), or continue the attack by 20 e5 or after 20 Qh5+ Kf8 by 21 Rf1+ Bf6 22 e5. Without setting myself the aim of giving an exhaustive analysis of this position, I can say that Black would nevertheless appear to have a draw, and therefore in the diagram position White more often plays now 11 Bg3 or 11 Qh5, avoiding such forcing variations.

It is equally clear that, having been transformed from the hunter into the hunted, at the board the Argentinians were unable to find this one very complex saving continuation, which enables Black to balance on the edge of the abyss.

14 ...   B×g5
15 0–0+

First 15 B×e5 d×e5 and then 16 0–0+ would have won even more simply.

15 ...   Ke7
16 B×e5   Qb6+

No better is 16 ... Be3+ 17 Kh1 d×e5 18 Q×e5 Bd4 19 Nd5+ Q×d5 20 Qc7+.

17 Kh1   d×e5
18 Qf7+   Kd6
19 Rad1+   Qd4

Or 19 ... Kc5 20 Rd5+ e×d5 21 Q×d5+ Kb4 22 Qc4+ Ka5 23 b4 (Qa4) mate.

20 R×d4+   e×d4
21 e5+   Kc5

21 ... K×e5 allows a pure mate by 22 Qc7.

22 Qc7+   Nc6
23 B×c6   Resigns

23 ... b×c6 is met by 24 Qa5+ Kc4 25 b3 mate.

No. 19 Sicilian Defence

Geller–Nikolayevsky

Ukrainian Team Championship, 1962

It is easier to be a pawn down

Black was let down by two factors. Firstly, he did not go on to the defensive for a time: in general, Nikolayevsky is a player who prefers to attack. Secondly, he failed to take into account that, with both pairs of rooks on the board, opposite-coloured bishops do not yet presage a draw, but, on the contrary, strengthen the attack of the more active side. What evidently told here was the purely subconscious desire to restore material equality at the very first opportunity. It so often happens that, after sacrificing a pawn, a player aims not to obtain the initiative for it, but to regain sacrificed material.

This is a typical mistake, but it is instinctively committed even by strong and experienced masters.

1 e4	c5
2 Nf3	Nc6
3 d4	c×d4
4 N×d4	Nf6
5 Nc3	d6
6 Bg5	Qb6

One of the ways of countering the Rauzer Attack: Black decides to avoid the heavily-analysed variations.

7 Nb3	e6
8 Be2	

White is contemplating the exchange on f6, and is ready to battle against the bristling "hedgehog" of black pawns in the centre. In the alternative plan White avoids the capture on f6, and the game can continue roughly as follows: 8 Bd3 Be7 9 0–0 0–0

10 Kh1 followed by f2–f4 and activity on the K-side.

8 ...	Be7
9 0–0	0–0
10 B×f6	g×f6

10 ... B×f6, which is possible after Q-side castling by White, does not promise Black anything here: he has no compensation for the pawn.

11 Bh5

Today I would play the more mature move 11 Kh1, without which White in any case cannot get by. The battle against Black's pawn centre demands that its mobility be restricted, which is best achieved by f2–f4–f5. Only in the event of 11 ... Kh8 should White play 12 Bh5, preventing the manoeuvre ... Rg8–g7, after which Black has everything in order.

In the present game, it is true, things merely reduce to a transposition of moves.

11 ...	Kh8
12 Kh1	Bd7
13 f4	a5

An interesting attempt, by means of a flank attack, to carry out a breakthrough... in the centre. Since White is forced to halt the further advance of the rook's pawn, Black obtains for his knight the square b4 from where it supports the freeing ... d5. Even so, it would seem sounder not to move the knight away from the king and from the square e5, but first to make defensive preparations such as ... Be8 and ... Rg8–g7, then relieve the bishop of its surveillance of the f7 pawn and think of active measures.

14 a4	Nb4
15 Qd2	Rad8
16 Rf3	

Both sides consistently carry out their plans, but White's threats are growing more quickly: 17 Rh3, 18 f5, 19 Qh6 and mate. For his last preparatory move 16 ....Bc6 Black no longer has time, but he finds an excellent chance.

16 ...   d5!

Now the thematic 17 Rh3 d×e4 18 f5 is parried by 18 ... e3!

17 e×d5	Bc6
18 Qf2	N×d5
19 N×d5	

With the centre opened a flank attack is doomed to failure, and White changes course, heading for a slightly more favourable ending.

| 19 ... | Q×f2 |
| 20 R×f2 | B×d5 |

The attempt to defend the a-pawn (20 ... R×d5) is unsuccessful, since the black rook is restricted on the 5th rank: 21 Bf3 Rf5 22 B×c6 b×c6 23 g4 Rd5 24 c4.

| 21 N×a5 | Bc5 |

For the pawn Black has two excellent bishops, and all the battle is still to come.

| 22 Re2 | b6 |
| 23 Nb3 | B×b3 |

The correct decision. The opposite-coloured bishops and doubled white pawns make the position a virtual draw.

| 24 c×b3 | Rd3 |
| 25 Rc2! | |

White's main chance, despite the apparent unreality of it, is to set in motion his Q-side pawns. Thus on 25 ... R×b3 there follows 26 a5, when the a-pawn causes Black a mass of trouble.

| 25 ... | Bb4 |
| 26 g3 | R×b3? |

A mistake, after which White is the first to begin an attack, which is merely strengthened by the opposite-coloured bishops. Black should not have conceded the second open file, and so the best for him was 26 ... Kg7 27 Rc6 Rd6 (*27 ... Bc5* or *27 ... Ba5–28 b4*).

| 27 Rd1 | e5 |

Black cannot hold the f7 square by passive defence, and he tries for a counter-attack.

28 Rd7	e×f4
29 B×f7	Re3
30 Rcc7	f3
31 h4	

White has parried the threat of mate, but how is Black to do the same?...

| 31 ... | Re1+ |
| 32 Kh2 | Re2+ |

The appearance of a new black queen would coincide with mate: 32 ... f2 33 Bc4 f1=Q 34 R×h7 mate.

| 33 Kh3 | Re5 |

44

The only way of defending h7.

34 Bd5	Rh5
35 B×f3	Rh6
36 Rc6	

Arresting his opposite number at h6. Another solution to the same problem was also possible: 36 g4 Be1 37 h5 followed by Be4.

36 ...	Ba5
37 Be4	Be1
38 Rd1	Bf2
39 Rf1	Bd4
40 Bf5	Re8
41 Rfc1	Bf2

Also after 41 ... B×b2 42 Rc8 White is essentially playing with an extra rook.

42 Rc8	R×c8
43 R×c8+	Kg7
44 Kg4	Resigns

No. 20 Sicilian Defence

Geller–Larsen

*Candidates Match for 3rd Place
Copenhagen, 1966*

Pursuit of the king

The attack by Bent Larsen on the knight at c3 unexpectedly strengthened the concentration of white pieces preparing for an assault on the king. However, this was perhaps not so unexpected, since the saying "the threat is stronger than its execution" has a very real basis. To threaten some attack means to tie down the opponent's forces, and so force him to take extensive prophylactic measures to parry the possible danger. To carry out the attack sometimes means untying the opponent's hands, enabling him to take concrete defensive measures or even to disregard the attacked object.

It should also be mentioned that general positional considerations would not have allowed White to find the strongest continuation on the 22nd move. It was prompted only by a specific calculation of variations.

1 e4	c5
2 Nf3	Nc6
3 d4	c×d4
4 N×d4	Nf6
5 Nc3	d6
6 Bg5	

Play in the Rauzer Attack is difficult for both sides, which is what makes it attractive. Although White, as the active side, has the advantage, Black is prepared to be subjected to pressure since he has possibilities of counter-play.

6 ...	e6
7 Qd2	a6
8 0–0–0	Bd7
9 f4	Be7
10 Nf3	b5
11 B×f6	g×f6

The strength of Black's resulting pawn "hedgehog" lies in its solidity and in its control over the central squares. Its weakness lies in the chronic weakening of the K-side, and in that it provides a target for attack. This position is well known to theory, which "demands" from White 12 f5, after which 12 ... Qb6, 12 ... Qa5 and 12 ... b4 have all been tried, but with best play by White have not given Black equality.

It is possible that the healthy developing move in the game is no worse. It does not determine White's plan, but, firstly, leaves him a choice between f4–f5 and e4–e5, and, secondly, retains the possibility of the standard attack Nd5 (after ... *b4*).

12 Bd3	Qa5

Directed, in the first instance, against the possibility after 12 ... Qb6 13 Rhe1 b4 of 15 Nd5.

13 Kb1   b4

The first and last inaccuracy in this game, after which Black's position is difficult. The immediate 13 ... Rg8 was better, not fearing 14 e5 (*14 ... d5!*), hindering the harmonious deployment of the white pieces, and keeping the advance ... b4 in reserve. But now the white knight switches from c3 to g3, where it is ready to take part in the attack on the K-side.

14 Ne2   Rg8
15 Ng3   Qc5
16 Rhe1   Ra7

Black senses that the e4–e5 breakthrough is about to follow, and takes measures to defend his bishop at d7. He would have liked to castle, but, alas, the weakening ... b4 has already been played.

17 e5!   d×e5
18 f×e5   N×e5

Forced, since 18 ... f5 19 Qh6 leads at least to the loss of a pawn.

19 N×e5   f×e5
20 Qh6   f5

The correct defence, but nevertheless inadequate. If White's knight were to reach e4 his attack would become irresistible.

21 Q×h7   Rf8
22 b3!

A concrete approach to the position. The immediate evacuation of the king after 22 Qh5+ Kd8 was part of Black's plans. Therefore White sets his sights on the e6 pawn, for which he has to provide a post for his bishop at c4. The weakening of the a1–h8 diagonal, which seems not without its dangers in view of the existence of Black's king's bishop, is not able to be exploited by the opponent. For example: 22 ... Qc3 23 Nh5 e4 24 B×e4 (*24 Bc4 Bf6 25 N×f6+ Q×f6, and Black consolidates*) 24 ... f×e4 25 Ng7+ Kd8 26 N×e6+ Ke8 27 Qg6+ Rf7 28 Qg8+.

22 ...   e4
23 Bc4   Qe5

Defending against 24 Qg6+ and 25 B×e6. On 23 ... Bf6 White, of course, would not have continued 24 Nh5 Qe5, but as in the game.

24 Qh5+   Kd8
25 R×e4   Qc3
26 Ne2

26 Rd3 f×e4 would have been the lesser evil for Black. White now forcibly transposes into a complicated ending, in which middle-game motifs of attack on the king continue to play the leading role.

26 ...   Qh8
27 Q×h8   R×h8
28 R×e6   R×h2
29 Rg6

This wins more quickly than 29 R×a6 R×a6 30 B×a6 Kc7 31 Nf4 Bc6. The threat of 30 Rg8+ Kc7 31 Rg7 is extremely unpleasant.

29 ...	Rh4
30 Nd4	Kc7
31 Rg7	Bf6

31 ... Re4 fails to 32 Ne6+.

| 32 Ne6+ | Kb6 |
| 33 Rg6 | |

The pursuit of the king continues. Especially since the capture of the bishop at d7 would have led to mate ... by Black.

| 33 ... | Bc3 |

More tenacious was 33 ... Bh8, on which White had prepared 34 g3 Rh2 35 Nc5 and 36 N×a6.

| 34 Nc5+ | Bc6 |

As before the position of the bishop at c4 is important: 34 ... K×c5 35 Rd5 mate.

35 Na4+	Kc7
36 N×c3	b×c3
37 Rg3	

The attack now proceeds along the files. Therefore the c3 pawn is more important than the one at g2.

37 ...	Kb6
38 R×c3	B×g2
39 Rd6+	Kc5
40 Rd2	

Instead of obtaining three passed pawns in the endgame (40 R×a6), White gains a tempo for the creation of a mating net.

40 ...	Kb4
41 Kb2	Be4
42 a3+	Ka5
43 Rd6	

Under the threat of inevitable mate in a few moves, **Black resigned.**

No. 21 Sicilian Defence

Geller–Kholmov

Match Ukraine–Lithuania
Vilnius, 1957

Repeating the past

The history of this game is as follows. Not long before the match with Lithuania, the Ukrainian team had played a friendly match with a team from the Russian Federation, led by the Leningrad grandmaster Mark Taimanov. Taimanov and I played a very sharp game, full of combinational blows by both sides, which ended (after a time trouble oversight by me) in a draw. Obviously before our meeting Kholmov had been able to see this game: with his very first move he offered me the chance of going into the Sicilian, and later followed a recommendation by Taimanov, attempting to improve Black's defence. For me it was interesting to repeat the past. Especially since at that time the opening variation in question had not lost its topicality.

1 Nf3	c5
2 e4	a6
3 d4	

Nowadays Black's 2nd move is hardly ever played. A plan for White beginning with 3 c3 has been found, and with the creation of a pawn centre by d2–d4 the advance ... a6 proves to be a loss of time.

At that time opening guides considered the best reply to 2 ... a6 to be 3 c4, playing for pressure in the centre, a recommendation which is rather subjective. More to my taste was the livelier play resulting in the open Sicilian formations.

3 ...	c×d4
4 N×d4	Nf6
5 Nc3	e5

Having said "a" (*2 . . . a6*), Black says "b", and begins double-edged counter-play in the centre. It was in connection with this plan that the old and rather unusual move 2 . . . a6 was employed in the 1940s and 1950s. Less consistent, although perfectly possible, was 5 . . . d6, transposing into normal variations, such as the "Göteborg".

| 6 Nf3 | Bb4 |
| 7 Bc4 | |

The most crucial reply to Black's set-up. Not fearing possible loss of material, White gives the game an open nature and counts on his lead in development. If instead he had played 7 Bd2 (as examined in the most fundamental opening guide at that time, Pachman's *Modern Chess Theory*), Black's tactics would have been justified. For example: 7 . . . d6 8 Bd3 Nbd7 9 0–0 Nc5 10 Qe2 0–0 (Snaevarr–Euwe, Reykjavik, 1949), or 9 a3 B×c3 10 B×c3 Nc5 11 Bb4 Qc7 12 Nd2 Be6 13 0–0 0–0 (Schmidt–O'Kelly, Beverwijk, 1949).

| 7 ... | Qc7 |
| 8 Bb3 | d6 |

Taimanov's recommendation. He himself played 8 . . . 0–0 9 0–0 and ended up in a difficult position, after making a mistake: 9 . . . B×c3 (better is *9 . . . d6*, and if *10 Nd5 N×d5 11 B×d5*, then *11 . . . Nd7*) 10 b×c3 N×e4 11 Re1! Bad, of course, is the immediate 8 . . . B×c3+ 9 b×c3 Q×c3+ 10 Bd2 Qc7 11 Ng5 0–0 12 Bb4, or 8 . . . N×e4 9 B×f7+ K×f7 10 Qd5+ Ke8 11 Q×e4 B×c3+ 12 b×c3 Q×c3+ 13 Ke2!

| 9 0–0 | B×c3 |

Otherwise 10 Nd5 gives White a marked positional advantage.

| 10 b×c3 | N×e4 |
| 11 Ba3 | Bg4? |

Black should not have clung to his extra material, but given preference to 11 . . . 0–0 12 Qd5 N×c3 (*12 . . . Nc5 13 Rad1*) 13 Q×d6, or 11 . . . Nc5, not fearing 12 B×c5 d×c5 (*12 . . . Q×c5 13 Ng5 0–0 14 Qh5*) 13 N×e5 0–0. It is true that White would probably not have played 12 B×c5, but either 12 Qd2, intensifying the pressure on d6, or 12 Ng5, and if 12 . . . 0–0 then 13 f4, with an attack. But in these variations Black could have hoped, by returning the pawn at a convenient moment, to parry the assault.

But now Black's pieces are hanging without defence, and they come under attack.

| 12 Re1 | Nc5 |
| 13 B×c5 | Q×c5 |

13 . . . d×c5 is decisively met by 14 B×f7+ Q×f7 (*14 . . . K×f7 15 Ng5+*) 15 R×e5+. However, this same idea is carried out in the game.

14 B×f7+

From this point and right to the end, White's entire game is based on exploiting the "centralized" position of the black king.

| 14 ... | Ke7 |
| 15 Rb1 | Ra7 |

This apparently absurd move is in fact the strongest. After 15 . . . b5 16 Bd5 Black all the same has to play 16 . . . Ra7 (*16 . . . Nc6 17 B×c6 Q×c6 18 N×e5*). In addition, from a7 the rook is soon able to defend the g7 pawn!

16 Bd5	Rf8
17 Qd2!	

This simultaneously pursues both defensive and attacking aims. The first of these is to take care of the c3 pawn, and the second, more important, is the check at g5. The b7 pawn is also attacked. All these threats can be parried only by Black parting with his white-squared bishop, but then the opponent begins play on the weakened white squares in his position. It should be mentioned in passing that on 17 ... h6 White would not have needed to hurry over the capture on b7, but could first have played 18 Nh4.

17 ...	B×f3
18 Qg5+	Ke8
19 B×f3	b6
20 Rbd1	

Black's position is not eased even by exchanges—his king is in the centre!

20 ...	Rf6
21 Re3	Re7
22 Qh4	

Having reinforced his weak pawns, White sets about creating threats against the black king, although to do so is not so easy. The king is hidden behind the central pawns, and Ratmir Kholmov defends with exceptional tenacity.

22 ...	h6
23 Qe4	Qc7
24 Bh5+	Kd8
25 Qd5	

Having carried out a part of his plan—that of weakening the white squares, White nitends to combine attacks on the d6 and e5 pawns with threats to invade on the Q-side with his heavy pieces. Black's misfortune is

that he is condemned to defend passively, since he has no counter-play.

25 ...	Qc6

Black is ready to give up a pawn after 26 R×e5 Q×d5 27 Re×d5 Kc7, but White quite justifiably hopes for more.

26 Qg8+	Kc7
27 Bf3	Qb5

28 a4!

A useful inclusion, since the capture of the pawn allows the white rook to transfer with gain of tempo to the key square c4 via e4.

28 ...	Qc5
29 Qb3	Kd8

Stubborn defence: the threat of 30 Rd5 is parried (*30 ... Qc7*), so White "calls in" from the other side.

30 Qg8+	Kc7
31 h3	

Prophylaxis prior to the decisive events. White's plans include 32 Re4 b5 33 a×b5 a×b5 34 Ra1.

31 ...	Nd7

With the hope after 32 ... Rf8 of evacuating the king via b8 to a7.

32 Qa8	a5
33 Rd5	Qa3
34 c4	

34 Re4 would have allowed Black to hold on by 34 ... Rf4.

34 ...	Qc1+

Defensive functions are no longer within the black queen's powers: 34 ... Q×a4 35 Rb5, and the threat of 36 Qc6+ is decisive (35 ... Q×c4 26 Rbb3).

35 Rd1	Q×c2

At the cost of a pawn White has neverthe-less gained "access" to the opposing king. The following repetition of the position is to gain time on the clock in time trouble.

36 Qb7+	Kd8
37 Qa8+	Kc7
38 Qc6+	Kd8
39 Red3	Ree6

Otherwise the key d6 pawn cannot be defen-ded. But now the black rook comes within the "field of view" of the white bishop.

40 R3d2	Qb3
41 Bg4	Ke7
42 B×e6	R×e6
43 Kh2	

To be honest, here this move was not necessary, although it could have come in useful later.

43 ...	Qb4
44 Rd5	

Depriving the black queen of the important c5 square.

44 ...	g5
45 Qc7	

Here the time scramble ended, and **Black resigned.** The threat of 46 Rb5 followed by R×b6 or c4–c5 is irresistible.

No. 22 Sicilian Defence

Geller–Reshevsky

Interzonal Tournament
Palma de Mallorca, 1970

The queen in ambush

When sending his rook forward at such an early stage of the game, Black should have thought in advance about its safety. As a result the outcome of the game was mainly decided in the opening. But also of consi-derable importance was the transition stage from opening to middlegame, carried out by White in accordance with a well-known scheme of Maróczy.

1 e4	c5
2 Nf3	e6
3 d4	c×d4
4 N×d4	Nc6

Immediately excluding for White the possibility of employing the 6 g4 variation, which is possible after 4 ... Nf6 5 Nc3 d6. But to be honest, I had no intention of devia-ting from the system of the splendid Hungari-an grandmaster Géza Maróczy, which I had taken up and studied in some detail, and which first occurred in a game of his with Euwe in 1923. The reader could satisfy himself that it had brought me numerous successes, and, as the saying goes, "let well alone".

5 Nc3	d6
6 Be2	Nf6
7 0–0	Be7
8 Be3	0–0
9 f4	Bd7
10 Nb3	

The basis of this retreat is that Black is deprived of the possibility of the "relieving" manoeuvre ... N×d4 and ... Bc6. It is

50

known that 10 Qe1 leads to equality: 10 ...
N×d4 11 B×d4 Bc6 12 Qg3 g6.

10 ...   a5?!

A theoretical innovation. The usual continuation is 10 ... a6 11 a4 Na5.

11 a4   e5

This came as a surprise to me. The logical move was 11 ... Nb4. And although in the end it reduces to a simple transposition of moves, it was hardly right for Black to determine the central pawn formation earlier than necessary. Reshevsky thinks that with a knight at b4 the weakness of d5 is immaterial, but sooner or later it is bound to tell.

12 Kh1   Nb4
13 Bf3   Rc8
14 Rf2!

White carries out a kind of symbiosis of two plans. One of them is obvious, and is to defend the c2 pawn and to set up pressure on the d-file. The other, more masked, came as an unpleasant surprise to Reshevsky.

14 ...   Rc4

This square should have been kept for the bishop, since the pressure on the e4 pawn is illusory, and the black bishop stands badly at c6. It is better developed at e6, and so Black's entire plan begun with his 14th move can be considered incorrect.

15 f×e5   d×e5
16 Rd2

In this way White prevents the immediate 16 ... Bc6, and gains time for carrying out his plan.

16 ...   Qc7
17 Qg1!

It turns out that, in addition to the weakness of the b6 square which is usual for the Scheveningen Variation, the a5 pawn is also weak. Also important is the fact the advanced black rook is trapped, and the whole question now is of how and when to eliminate it. White's position must be considered won.

17 ...   Bd8

There is no other way of parrying 18 Bb6.

18 Rad1   Bc6

The combination 18 ... N×c2 does not achieve its aim: 19 R×c2 B×a4 20 Na1, and White's minor pieces will soon dominate the board.

19 Bc5

The immediate 19 Qf1 would have allowed Black some compensation in parting with the exchange: 19 ... R×e4 20 N×e4 N×e4. The move in the game is aimed at weakening the f7 square.

19 ...   Re8
20 Qf1

Now the variation given above would look like this: 20 ... R×e4 21 N×e4 N×e4 22 B×e4 23 Rd7. It is not surprising that Black finds a different way to give up the exchange.

20 ...	R×c5
21 N×c5	Qe7
22 Nb3	

Exchanges favour White, but 22 Nd3 would not have achieved anything: 22 ... Bb6 23 N×b4 Q×b4, and the a- and e-pawns are both attacked.

22 ...	Bb6
23 Qe2	g6

With White's black-squared bishop on the board such a move would have been suicidal, but now it is perfectly possible.

24 Nb5	Ra8

Planless, but Black has no counter-play. All he can do is to parry the concrete threats and to wait. In addition, Reshevsky was running short of time.

25 Nc1

With his previous move White defended his a4 pawn, and at the same time vacated his c3 square. It is needed for the second knight, which is aiming for d5 via c1–a2–c3.

25 ...	Na6

Black cannot prevent the knight ma-noeuvre: if not via a2, then via e2 it will all the same reach c3.

26 Na2	Nc5
27 Nac3	h5

Temporarily halting the invasion: 28 Nd5 B×d5 29 e×d5 e4, with complications unnecessary for White. But he has other possibilities.

28 Re1	Qf8
29 Rd6	

The threat of 30 Nd5 becomes a reality: 30 ... B×d5 31 R×b6. Reshevsky finds the best defence.

29 ...	Ncd7
30 Rdd1	

Time trouble had also caught up with White. Even so the move has a certain point: the d2 square is predestined for the queen.

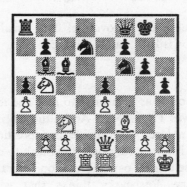

30 ...	Qh6

Typical of the American grandmaster. In a mutual time scramble he tries to play sharply: the opponent may make a mistake. Especially since in the given position he himself has nothing to lose.

The move played has the intention of creating play on the K-side if possible.

31 Qd2

The possibility must not be allowed!

31 ...	Qf8
32 Qd6	Qh6
33 Qd2	Qf8
34 h3	Re8
35 Nd6	Rd8
36 Nc4	Bc7
37 Nd5	

This decides the game.

37 ...	N×d5
38 e×d5	Nf6
39 Qg5	N×d5
40 N×e5	Qg7
41 c4	

An unnecessary move in time trouble. Simpler, of course, was 41 N×c6 b×c6 and only then 42 c4, although this does not affect the outcome of the game. After thinking for eight minutes, **Black** played

> **41 ...**   **f6**

and ... **stopped the clocks.** There is no sense in playing on after 42 Q×g6.

No. 23 Sicilian Defence

Geller–Polugayevsky

Match-Tournament of Three Grandmasters
Portoroz, 1973

The bishop was cramped at c6...

This was the initial cause of all Black's difficulties. True, later analysis showed that, at the point when Black mentally conceded the game, he could still have put up a stiff resistance. This once again demonstrates that it is never too late to resign, even at heart.

1 e4	c5
2 Nf3	d6
3 d4	c×d4
4 N×d4	Nc6
5 Nc3	e6
6 Be2	Nf6
7 Be3	Be7
8 f4	0–0
9 0–0	Bd7
10 Nb3	a5
11 a4	

This position will already be familiar to the reader from Game No. 22 with the American grandmaster Reshevsky, and so there is no need to repeat the notes to Black's 4th move and to the 10th moves of both players. I should merely like to add that the reproaches addressed at 11 a4, and based on the variation 11 ... Nb4 12 Bf3 Bc6 followed by ... d5, are groundless: White

plays 13 Nd4 followed by Ncb5 (after ... *d5* and *e4–e5*) and c2–c3.

11 ...	Nb4
12 Bf3	e5
13 Kh1	

The alternative was 13 Qe2, immediately starting a battle for the b6 square, and vacating d1 for a rook.

13 ...	Bc6?

It has already been said that in the Maróczy system the bishop is extremely badly placed at c6. Of course, if White were to play, as against Reshevsky, 14 Rf2, Black would obtain good counter-play after 14 ... d5. The exchange of pawns, eliminating the tension in the centre, immediately deprives Black of this possibility, and White firmly seizes the initiative. Black should have considered, for example, 13 ... Be6, and if 14 Rf2 e×f4 15 B×f4 Qb6 with a double-edged game. Thus on 16 Nd4 Black succeeds in transferring his knight to e5 — 16 ... Nd7. Therefore 13 Qe2 looks more accurate than 13 Kh1: the above variation is ruled out because of 14 f5 (in reply to *13 ... Be6*).

14 f×e5	d×e5
15 Qe2	Qc7
16 Qf2	Nd7

Forced, since Black's Q-side weaknesses are already beginning to tell.

17 Rad1   Kh8

Black is bound to aim for ... f5, since he has no other counterplay, but the immediate 17 ... f5 loses material after 18 e×f5 R×f5 19 Nd5 B×d5 20 B×d5+ N×d5 21 Q×f5 N×e3 22 Qe6+ and 23 R×d7.

18 Bg4

So as to win either a pawn after 19 B×d7 B×d7 20 Bb6, or ... time for thought after the continuation in the game.

18 ...	Nf6
19 Bf3	**Nd7**
20 Bg4	**Nf6**
21 Bf5	**g6**

There is nothing else, so Black accepts the temporary sacrifice of the e4 pawn, subjecting himself to an attack over the entire front.

22 Bb6	**Qb8**
23 Bh3	**N×e4**
24 N×e4	**B×e4**
25 Rd7	

Black's position appears to be on the verge of collapse, and it is not surprising that he commits a fatal inaccuracy. The main thing for him is control over f6, and the only move which meets this is 25 ... Bg5! Since on 26 Bc5 Black replies 26 ... f5, White would have had to make a difficult choice between 26 Nc5, 26 Be3, 26 Qc5, 26 R×f7, 26 N×a5, 26 B×a5, or ... some other continuation. In the majority of the lines White retains an advantage in the middlegame or the endgame, but Black could still have put up a stiff resistance.

The move played leads to him conceding the f6 square and to a quick defeat.

25 ...   Qe8

26 Bc5	**B×c5**
27 Qf6+	**Kg8**
28 N×c5	

The threat of 29 Ne6 cannot be parried without loss of material.

28 ...	**Nd5**
29 Qd6	

The alternative was 29 Qh4, when e6 could have been invaded by the white bishop.

29 ...	**Ra6**
30 N×a6	**b×a6**
31 Rf×f7	**R×f7**
32 Be6	**B×g2+**

With the last hope of 33 K×g2 Nf4+.

33 Kg1   Resigns

No. 24 Sicilian Defence

Geller–Filip

*Candidates Tournament
Curacao, 1962*

An instinctive reaction

The note to White's 12th move indicates a different, quieter plan, which would have retained for White all the advantages of his position. Why I chose the path of outright aggression is difficult to say. Even after a game it is not always possible to give a precise explanation for one's conduct and actions at the board.

A priori I can suppose that it was my opponent's good-nature, serenity and rather slow manner of play which prompted me into taking such a sharp decision. Although not for one moment did I forget that Filip defends, and likes to defend, more than he does to attack.

1 e4	c5
2 Nf3	d6
3 d4	c×d4
4 N×d4	Nf6
5 Nc3	a6
6 Be2	

As "justification" for this apparently modest old move, I can only say that it appeals to me.

6 ...	e6
7 0–0	Qc7
8 f4	Be7
9 Be3	

From my notes to other Sicilian games, the reader will find that nowadays in this position I play 9 Kh1. Indeed, why should White over-protect his knight at d4, before Black has attacked it even once? And if it is only a question of completing his development, it is not yet clear where the black-squared bishop will best be placed.

After the move played White has to reckon with the immediate 9 ... b5 followed by 10 Bf3 Bb7 11 e5 d×e5, etc., as well as with the positionally more justified 9 ... 0–0, and if 10 Qe1, then 10 ... b5 followed by ... Bb7 and ... Nbd7.

Filip chooses a different move order, after which White has the opportunity to upset his opponent's plans.

| 9 ... | Nbd7 |
| 10 Bf3 | |

The ... b5 advance is temporarily halted, and it can now be carried out only by the preparatory 10 ... Rb8. This is probably what Black should have played, since the idea of exploiting at an early stage the weak c4 square frequently suffered a fiasco in games from even before the war: Lasker–Pirc, Moscow, 1935 (true, in a rather different set-up), Kan–Ragozin, Moscow, 1936, and others.

| 10 ... | Nb6 |
| 11 Qe2 | 0–0 |

The plausible 11 ... Nc4 encounters an immediate combinational refutation: 12 e5 d×e5 13 Ndb5 a×b5 14 N×b5, and after 15 Q×c4, in view of the threat of 16 Nc7+, White also picks up the e5 pawn.

12 g4

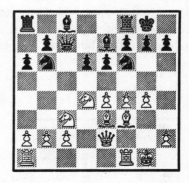

It very often happens that a position can be resolved in two or even several ways, the choice normally being between a quiet and a sharper continuation. This is also the case here: apart from the aggressive move played, White also had the solid 12 Rad1, when 12 ... Nc4 can be answered by 13 Bc1 followed by driving away the black knight.

| 12 ... | Nc4 |

The thematic invasion. The standard counter-blow in the centre in reply to a flank attack would have led after 12 ... d5 13 e5

Nd7 14 Rad1 Nc4 15 Bc1 to a "French" set-up, in which the white pieces are excellently placed to support the K-side pawn storm.

13 g5   Nd7

After 13 ... N×e3 Black loses material: 14 g×f6 N×f1 15 f×e7 Q×e7 16 R×f1. One has to agree with the recommendation by Kan, who annotated this game in the tournament bulletin, of 13 ... Ne8, when the following knight move by White would be impossible. But at e8 the knight no longer controls e5, and White could if he wished have continued his swift offensive with 14 f5, not wasting time on Bc1.

14 Nf5!

Black obviously overlooked this blow. It is bad to take the knight, since after 14 ... e×f5 15 Nd5 White immediately regains his piece with an overwhelming advantage. By 14 ... Re8 Filip could have retarded the development of White's initiative, but he decided to retain both his bishops.

14 ...   Bd8
15 Bd4!

This move could also have followed, along with 15 N×e7+, on 14 ... Re8. White's threats have now become very real. Black can defend his g7 pawn in four ways, of which three are unsuccessful: 15 ... e5 16 Nd5 and 15 ... e×f5 16 Nd5 Qc6

17 e×f5 give White a very strong attack, while 15 ... g6 allows an immediate mate by 16 Nh6. There only remains the move played.

15 ...   f6
16 Kh1

In order to use the g-file for attack. Black cannot unite his knot of pieces on the Q-side, since on 16 ... b5 there follows 17 g×f6 g×f6 (17 ... B×f6 18 e6) 18 Qg2+ Kf7 19 Bh5 mate.

16 ...   Ndb6
17 g×f6!   B×f6

Doctor Miroslav Filip is a cautious player, who attempts to avoid even those positions where there only may be some danger. In positions where there is indeed some danger, he feels very much at home. At the board it is unlikely that he would have calculated a variation such as 17 ... e×f5 18 f×g7 Re8 19 Bh5 Bd7 20 Bf7+ K×f7 21 g8=Q+ R×g8 22 Qh5+ Kf8 23 Qh6+ Ke8 24 Rg1, when the position reached is worthy of a diagram.

Black's big material advantage cannot save his king from White's concluding mating attack. Therefore, evidently purely intuitively, Filip declined the piece sacrifice, and attempted to defend by exchanging.

18 B×f6   R×f6
19 N×d6!

The strongest continuation of the attack. Bad now is 19 ... N×d6 20 e5 R×f4 21 e×d6 Q×d6 22 Rad1 Qc7 23 Be4 with dangerous threats.

| 19 ... | R×f4 |
| 20 N×c4 | N×c4 |

20 ... Q×c4 leaves Black in difficulties after 21 Qd2 Rf8 22 Be2! But now it appears at first sight that the game is level, and that after the inevitable 21 ... Ne5 Black will stand well, but this is not so.

21 e5!!

By including his bishop in the attack, White makes it irresistible. 22 Nd5 winning the exchange is threatened, and it is not apparent how Black can simultaneously defend his king, save his "hanging" pieces on the 4th rank, and complete his development. From the following variations one gains the impression that he already has no satisfactory defence:

(a) 21 ... Q×e5 22 Be4.

(b) 21 ... N×e5 22 Nd5 e×d5 23 B×d5+ Rf7 24 R×f7 N×f7 25 Qe8 mate.

(c) 21 ... Rf7 22 Nd5 Qc5 23 b4!

(d) 21 ... Qf7 22 Bh5 R×f1+ 23 R×f1 Qc7 24 Bf7+ Kh8 25 Be8! g6 26 Rf7 Qc5 27 Ne4.

| 21 ... | Bd7 |
| 22 Nd5 | |

This immediately concludes the game. After 22 ... e×d5 23 B×d5+ Kh8 24 R×f4 N×e5 25 Re1 White is the exchange up with an attack, while on 25 ... Ng6 there follows 26 Rf7 Nf4 27 Qe8+! with inevitable mate. Therefore **Black resigned.**

No. 25 Sicilian Defence

Geller–Mikhalchishin

46th USSR Championship Tbilisi, 1978

Another trapped knight

As was mentioned in my notes to Game No. 1 with Mecking, often the fate of a variation and of an entire game is decided by the position of one piece. There Black suffered on account of his "Spanish" knight at a5, whereas here it was his "Sicilian" knight at g7 that was crippled!

1 e4	c5
2 Nf3	d6
3 d4	c×d4
4 N×d4	Nf6
5 Nc3	a6
6 Be2	e6
7 0–0	Be7
8 f4	0–0
9 Kh1	

I consider this move useful in many lines of the Scheveningen Variation. It is played here because White hopes to provide work for his black-squared bishop not only at e3.

| 9 ... | Qc7 |

Black aims in the first instance to develop his bishop at b7. In recent years 9 ... Nc6 has been more popular.

| 10 a4 | b6 |

And here 10 ... Nc6 was essential, since

Black must watch very carefully for the thematic e4–e5 break.

11 Bf3	Bb7

12 e5!	Ne8

The attempt to attack the e5 pawn after 12 ... d×e5 13 f×e5 Nfd7 14 B×b7! Q×b7 15 Bf4 Nc6 16 Qf3 Rac8 17 Ne4 gives White every chance of an attack, with a highly-important role being assigned to his knight at e4. By the move in the game Black prevents the knight from playing to this central square, and he hopes in the future to activate his knight from e8.

13 Be3	Nc6
14 Qe2	

Exploiting a tactical chance, White reinforces his outpost at e5 and efficiently completes his development. 14 Qe1, with the same aim, would not have worked, as will be seen a litt.: later.

14 ...	g6

Black attempts to connect his rooks, although it transpires that this plan has its drawback. But it is already difficult to offer him any good advice, since 14 ... d×e5 14 f×e5 N×e5 fails to 16 Bf4. With the white queen at e1 this variation would not have been possible due to 16 ... N×f3.

15 Rad1	d×e5?

Also bad is 15 ... Ng7 because of 16 e×d6 B×d6 17 Ndb5, or 15 ... Rd8, since the a6 pawn is hanging. But Black should have continued the struggle with 15 ... d5, although in this case White's positional advantage is very great. He controls d4, and with the centre closed there is nothing to hinder his preparations for a K-side pawn storm.

16 f×e5	Ng7

Here too capturing on e5 with the knight is not possible due to 17 Bf4. Now it would appear that Black's main difficulties are behind him, but...

17 N×c6!	

The most efficient way to win is via the exchange of queens!

17 ...	B×c6
18 Qc4	Rfc8
19 Q×c6	Q×c6
20 B×c6	R×c6
21 Rd7	Re8
22 g4!	

In this way White succeeds in exploiting the shortcoming of the manoeuvre begun by Black on his 14th move. The knight at g7 is shut out of play, and, strangely enough, will soon be caught.

22 ...	h5
23 h3	h×g4

24 h×g4	b5
25 a×b5	a×b5
26 Ne4	

White's pieces are actively enough placed to conclude the game with an attack on the king, although the quieter 26 Rf2 was also possible.

26 ...	R×c2
27 Nf6+	B×f6
28 e×f6	R×b2
29 f×g7	f5

The g7 pawn is taboo, since White has a choice between winning the rook by 30 Bd4+ and mating by 30 Rf×f7+, etc.

| 30 Rf3 | f×g4 |

The threat was 31 Rh3 and mate at h8.

| 31 Rf4 | Rc8 |
| 32 Bc5 | Resigns |

No. 26 Sicilian Defence

Geller–Anikayev

*47th USSR Championship
Minsk, 1979*

I want to attack!

It was Emanuel Lasker who rightly remarked that the battle on the chess board is not conducted by white and black pieces, but by people. People who have different states of health, different tournament positions, and also different moods. And at times this can be decisively reflected in the pattern of a chess game. The choice of opening, whether to aim for quiet or risky play, depends not only on the style of a player, but also on the disposition with which he sits down at the board.

Who knows how my game with Yuri Anikayev would have gone, had I not been in an especially aggressive mood that evening. I did not just want to win—this is almost always the case. I wanted to sacrifice, I wanted to attack. And the attack succeeded! I will not hide the fact that the finish gave me considerable pleasure and... a special prize.

1 e4	c5
2 Nf3	e6
3 d4	c×d4
4 N×d4	Nf6
5 Nc3	d6
6 Be2	Be7
7 0-0	0-0
8 f4	Nc6
9 Be3	a6

It soon transpires that Black is planning the relieving operation ... N×d4 and ... Bd7–c6. But he should have begun carrying it out without ... a6, as was played against me, for example, by Polugayevsky a year earlier in the 46th USSR Championship at Tbilisi. In this case, if White wants to try for an opening advantage, in reply to 9 ... Bd7 he has to lose a tempo and remove his knight from the centre by 10 Nb3.

| 10 a4 | Bd7 |

After the inclusion of the moves 9 ... a6 10 a4, it very shortly transpires that the retreat of the knight is no longer necessary. Therefore 10 ... Qc7 looks more logical, intending the possible 11 ... N×d4 and 12 ... e5, or transposing into normal set-ups after 11 Nb3 b6.

11 Bf3

I do not think that this is a new move, although in opening books of recent years it is not mentioned in this particular situation. Normally 11 Nb3 is recommended here.

The text move is designed to emphasize the drawbacks to Black's chosen move order.

11 ...   Na5

It turns out that here the relieving operation 11 ... N×d4 12 B×d4 Bc6 allows White to seize control of the weakened b6 square (*13 a5*), with a secure blockade of Black's Q-side pawns. Therefore my opponent decided to try and refute White's plan, by exploiting the lack of control of c4 by transferring his knight there. This manoeuvre may be justified, but again 11 ... Qc7, with the aforementioned possibilities, was sounder.

12 Qe2

White's alternative plan was to advance 12 e5, driving the knight back to e8.

12 ...   Qc7
13 g4

More solid, and possibly stronger, was the plan with 13 Rad1 Nc4 14 Bc1. But, as I have already said, on that evening I was in an "attacking mood". ...

13 ...   Rfc8?

Black wishes to bring his rook into play, hoping without its help to parry the attack on the K-side. But in doing so he not only loses time, but—more important— irreparably weakens his f7 square. Also slow in the given situation is 13 ... Rac8, which seems no better after 14 g5 Ne8 15 f5 Nc4 16 f×e6 f×e6 17 Bg4 N×e3 18 Q×e3, with a very strong initiative.

The sharpness of the position demanded immediate positive action of Black, along the lines of 13 ... Nc4. During the game I considered in reply to this 14 g5 Ne8 15 Nf5!? Bd8 (*15 ... e×f5 16 Nd5 Qd8 17 Q×c4*) 16 Bd4 e×f5 17 Rae1 or even 17 Kh1 with a strong attacking position for the sacrificed piece.

14 g5   Ne8
15 f5   Nc4
16 Bh5

Perfectly sufficient was 16 f×e6 f×e6 (*16 ... B×e6 — 17 N×e6 f×e6 18 Bg4*) 17 Bg4, when Black cannot successfully defend his e6, since after 17 ... N×e3 18 Q×e3 Qc4 the simple 19 Qf2 is decisive. But the move in the game is also highly effective, since it forces Black to weaken completely his king's position. Besides, White had calculated everything practically to the end.

16 ...   g6
17 f×g6   f×g6
18 Qf2   Ne5
19 Nf3

With the exchange of his only defender —the knight at e5— Black's position will collapse. Therefore he resourcefully brings up reserves.

19 ...   Ng7
20 N×e5   Rf8
21 Nf7   N×h5?

This allows a spectacular and forcing conclusion. More tenacious was 21 ... g×h5, although again after 22 Bd4 White's attack can hardly be parried (*22 ... B×g5 23 Qg3*).

22 Nd5!

Black must be prevented from blocking the long black diagonal by ... e5.

| 22 ... | e×d5 |
| 23 Nh6+ | Kg7 |

Or 23 ... Kh8 24 Bd4+ Ng7 25 B×g7+ K×g7 26 Qd4+ Bf6 27 R×f6 Qc5 28 Rf7 mate.

24 Qf7+!

This is much quicker and more rational than 24 Bd4+ Bf6 25 g×f6+ K×h6 26 Qh4 g5 27 Be3 Rg8 28 f7 etc.

24 ...	R×f7
25 R×f7+	Kh8
26 Bd4+	Bf6
27 R×f6	Resigns

27 ... N×f6 allows 28 B×f6 mate.

No. 27 Sicilian Defence

Geller–Andersson

*Interzonal Tournament
Moscow, 1982*

In search of the truth

1 e4	c5
2 Nf3	d6
3 d4	c×d4
4 N×d4	Nf6
5 Nc3	e6
6 Be2	Be7
7 0–0	Nc6
8 Be3	0–0
9 f4	e5

This paradoxical move—after all, a few moves earlier Black advanced his e-pawn only one square— was first played by Spassky against Karpov in their 1974 Candidates Match. The position now reached is typical of the Boleslavsky Variation. Black attempts to show that the tempo lost is of no great importance. And it has to be said that the first attempt in the aforementioned game concluded successfully, since with the help of his new idea Spassky gained his only win in the match.

10 f×e5

For a long time 10 Nb3 was considered strongest here, when Black would hold the centre and play 10 ... a5 as in the Boleslavsky Variation. But I was very soon able to demonstrate in practice that the lost tempo gives White the chance of gaining a clear advantage, and my game against Spassky given later in the book (No. 93) for a long time discouraged players with Black from repeating such a plan.

But a few years ago several players, among them Kasparov and Andersson, began answering 10 Nb3 with 10 ... e×f4. This is a more justified continuation, since after

11 B×f4 White, too, has lost a tempo, while after 11 R×f4 the white rook is awkwardly placed. Among those to suffer was myself. Neither against Kasparov, Moscow 1981, after 11 B×f4 Be6 12 Kh1 d5! 13 e5 Nd7 14 N×d5 Nd×e5 15 c4 Bg5!, nor against Andersson, London 1982, after 11 R×f4 Ne8! 12 Qd2 Bf6, did I gain any advantage as White.

It was my turn to seek an improvement in White's play, and it has to be said that in such cases this is a difficult task. At which point of the variation should one deviate from the accepted paths? It was only a stroke of fortune that helped me to guess the right direction, whereas normally one would have to sift through a mass of different variations. It was necessary for me to do this work, since in the Moscow Interzonal both Kasparov and Andersson were playing, and the pairings might give me the white pieces against them.

It would seem that I managed to "strike gold", and fate rewarded my efforts not only in the present game. I also had White against Kasparov, and part of that game is given below.

10 ...	d×e5
11 Nf5	B×f5
12 R×f5	Rc8

Andersson was not satisfied by the course of the Geller-Kasparov game, played at the start of the tournament. There, after 12 ... Qa5 13 Kh1 Rad8, instead of the theoretical line 14 Qg1 g6 15 Rff1 Nd4 with advantage to Black (Stean-Tal, Nice Olympiad, 1974) there followed the innovation 14 Qf1! White wishes to transfer his bishop to c4 and set up pressure on the f-file, and also to seize control of d5. Kasparov replied 14 ... Qb4? (*14 ... Nd4* was rather better), and after 15 Rb1 Qd6 16 Bc4 White held the initiative.

| 13 Kh1 | g6 |
| 14 Rf1 | Q×d1 |

Andersson hopes to equalize in the endgame, but White's two bishops make this a difficult task.

| 15 Ra×d1 | Kg7 |

An imperceptible mistake, allowing White to develop a serious initiative. 15 ... Rfd8 was essential, to prevent a possible invasion of the seventh rank by the white rook. By 16 R×d8 R×d8 17 g4 White would have kept the initiative, but there would not have been any immediate unpleasantness in store.

16 g4!

The virtues of this move are not only that White threatens g4–g5 and that he creates an escape square for his king. In addition the f5 square is attacked by the pawn.

| 16 ... | h6 |
| 17 Nd5! | N×e4? |

After this move Black's game is lost. Better drawing chances were offered by 17 ... N×d5, although after 18 R×d5 White's advantage is obvious.

| 18 N×e7 | N×e7 |
| 19 Rd7 | Ng8 |

Black cannot play ... Nf5, a move which would have been possible had not the white pawn been at g4.

20 R×b7	Ngf6
21 c4	Nd6

21 ... Rb8 22 Rb5 would have lost Black a tempo, since his e-pawn, blocking the a1–h8 diagonal, is attacked, as well as his a-pawn.

22 Rb4	Rb8
23 R×b8	R×b8
24 b3	Nde4
25 Bf3	

Black has not yet lost any material, but at any moment the white bishops will break out and support the advance of their Q-side pawns.

25 ...	a5
26 Re1	Nc3

The threat of 27 B×e4 N×e4 28 Ba7 forces Andersson to open up, allowing a quick knock-out.

| 27 Ba7 | Rd8 |

Equally bad is 27 ... Re8 28 Bb6 a4 29 Re3 N×a2 30 b×a4.

28 R×e5	N×a2
29 Re3	Rd6
30 c5	Rd2
31 c6	Resigns

No. 28 Sicilian Defence

Geller–Taimanov

*27th USSR Championship
Leningrad, 1960*

At the origin of a new system

This was one of the first games in which White encountered a system which was later to become fashionable—the "hedgehog" of pawns along the 6th rank. Of course, I did not know then that subsequently this set-up would cause White so much trouble, and perhaps for this reason I was not at all afraid of it?!? My general understanding of position enabled me in this game to hit upon a method of play, which, in my opinion, is not without interest...

1 e4	c5
2 Nf3	e6
3 d4	c×d4
4 N×d4	Nc6
5 Nb5	d6

Black's delay in developing his king's knight allows White to include his c-pawn in the struggle for the centre, since its path has not been blocked by a knight at c3. However, apart from the immediate 6 c4 which is nowadays considered strongest, also possible is the continuation in the game, aimed at weakening the d5 square.

| 6 Bf4 | Ne5 |

Of course, 6 ... e5 was essential, although 7 Be3 would have led to a position which White wanted to play, and Black did not. It stands to reason that now Mark Taimanov would have chosen this move without thinking. However, at that time the so-called "Chelyabinsk Variation" (or "Pelikan Variation") was not in fashion and was considered incorrect.

| 7 c4 | |

Later it was shown that, by employing an exact move order, White can immediately refute the opponent's manoeuvre. This is achieved by 7 N1a3! (first 7 B×e5 d×e5 8 Q×d8+ K×d8 and then 9 N1a3 allows Black equal chances after 9 ... Bc5 10 Nc4 f6 11 Nbd6 Ke7 12 Rd1 Nh6 13 Be2 Rd8, Karaklajic–Langeweg, Beverwijk, 1968) 7 ... Nf6 (7 ... a6 is very unpleasantly met by 8 B×e5 d×e5 9 Q×d8+ K×d8 10 0-0-0+, and if 10 ... Bd7, then 11 Nc4!, and Black cannot avoid loss of material) 8 B×e5 d×e5 9

Q×d8+ K×d8 10 Rd1+ (f2 must remain defended by the king, so that Q-side castling is not needed here) 10 ... Ke7 11 Nd6, and White has an enormous positional advantage.

However, theory is created with the years, and draws its conclusions on the basis of chess practice. In addition, White's 7th move in the game fits in with his basic strategic plan—that of creating pressure in the centre.

7 ...	a6
8 N5c3	Nf6
9 Be2	Be7
10 0–0	0–0
11 Nd2	

White is close to completing his development, and his spatial advantage is fairly stable.

11 ...	b6

Characteristic of the set-up which has now become very popular.

12 Be3

Also possible is 12 Bg3, but I decided to attack the b6 pawn straight away: an interesting, and, it would seem, correct reaction to the set-up chosen by Black.

12 ...	Bb7

13 f4

White is aiming to open up the game, so as to weaken the opponent's line of pawns on the 6th rank. But Black is confident that behind its cover he can calmly complete his development. A joint analysis after the game established the interesting fact that each of us considered such an opening of the position to favour himself.... The alternative plan was to intensify the pressure on the centre and on b6 by the regrouping f2–f3, Qe1–f2, Rfd1 and Rac1.

13 ...	Ng6
14 Qb3	Nd7
15 f5	

White consistently carries out his plan, although he could have first mobilized his queen's rook, retaining his advantage in space. Forcing play now begins.

15 ...	Bg5

Bad is 15 ... Nge5 16 f×e6 f×e6 17 c5 N×c5 18 B×c5 b×c5 19 Q×e6+, when there are too many vulnerable points in Black's position.

16 B×g5	Q×g5
17 f×g6	Q×d2
18 g×f7+	R×f7
19 R×f7	K×f7
20 Rd1	Qe3+
21 Kh1	Qc5?

A far from obvious but significant mistake, after which by energetic play White creates an attack on both wings. Meanwhile, Black should not have been concerned about the defence of his d6 pawn, but should have tried for counter-play by 21 ... Nf6, and if 22 R×d6 then 22 ... N×e4.

22 Na4	Qa5

The d6 pawn is again invulnerable due to mate by the queen on the back rank, but...

23 c5!!

Into a four-fold attack! Three of the captures are obviously bad, while the fourth — 23 ... N×c5 — diverts the knight from the defence of the K-side, and White continues 24 Rf1+ Kg8 25 Qf3, with an irresistible attack which wins at least a piece after 26 Qf7+, 27 N×c5 and 28 Q×b7.

Therefore Black "buys" his opponent off with a pawn, but he can no longer save the game.

| 23 ... | Re8 |
| 24 N×b6 | N×b6 |

Black loses immediately after 24 ... N×c5 25 Qf3+ Ke7 (*25 ... Kg8 26 Rf1*) 26 Nc4.

25 c×b6	B×e4
26 Bf3	B×f3
27 Q×f3+	Qf5
28 R×d6	Rc8
29 Q×f5+	e×f5
30 h3	Rb8

The invasion 30 ... Rc2 is pointless in view of 31 b4, when Black does not have time to take the a2 pawn.

31 a4	Ke7
32 Rc6	a5
33 b4!	

The simplest. By temporarily sacrificing a pawn, White creates two connected passed pawns, and this decides the game.

33 ...	a×b4
34 a5	b3
35 Rc3	Kd6
36 R×b3	Kc6
37 Re3	f4

Or 37 ... Ra8 38 Re5 g6 39 Kh2 Kd6 40 b7 Rb8 41 a6.

| 38 Re7 | Kb5 |
| 39 Ra7 | |

Quicker than 39 R×g7 K×a5 40 b7 h5 41 Kg1, etc.

39 ...	g5
40 b7	h5
41 a6	**Resigns**

No. 29 Sicilian Defence

Geller–Vasyukov

*6th USSR Spartakiad
Riga, 1975*

Don't betray yourself

This complicated and very tense game contained a number of mistakes. The reason for this was a mutual time scramble, which is practically inevitable when the players are seeking new and untrodden paths. And although in principle I prefer games which are more complete, nevertheless the interesting strategic and tactical struggle (how many variations remained behind the scenes!) forced me to include this game in the book.

It should also be added that, if at the decisive moment White had gone along with his opponent, Black's plan would have been implemented in full. But White did not betray his principle: even at the board to seek the vulnerable aspects of a new set-up constructed by the opponent. The result — a piece sacrifice, and a persistent and highly-complicated combinational attack.

1 e4	c5
2 Nf3	Nc6
3 d4	c×d4
4 N×d4	Qc7
5 Nc3	

I avoided the possible and fairly popular 5 Nb5 Qb8 6 c4, because in the present game I was aiming for lively piece play, rather than to squeeze Black in the centre. The immediate 5 c4, on the other hand, forces White to offer a highly problematic pawn sacrifice after 5 ... Qe5 or 5 ... Nf6 6 Nc3 N×e4 7 N×e4 Qe5.

5 ...	e6
6 Be2	Nf6
7 0–0	N×d4

An interesting idea, and very much in the spirit of the Paulsen System — to develop the black-squared bishop with gain of time. However, as soon transpires, it also has its drawbacks.

8 Q×d4	Bc5
9 Qd3	a6
10 Bg5	

Here are the first unattractive consequences of Black's plan. Since castling is now dangerous in view of the simple exchange on f6, and to lose a tempo by retreating the bishop to e7 is inconsistent, for the moment the black king remains in the centre. This evidently led Black to the idea of starting counterplay on the K-side, at the same time shutting in White's black-squared bishop.

10 ...	h6
11 Bh4	d6
12 Rad1	Bd7
13 a3	

Directed against the possibility of Q-side castling. In addition, the d6 pawn is indirectly attacked (*14 b4* is threatened).

13 ...	Rc8

Against 13 ... 0–0–0 White has two unpleasant replies:

a) 14 Qf3!, unexpectedly winning a pawn.

b) 14 Kh1 with the idea of f2–f4, when 14 ... g5 15 Bg3 e5 fails to 16 b4 Ba7 17 Q×d6.

14 Kh1	g5

14 ... B×a3 was too dangerous in view of 15 B×f6! g×f6 16 Nd5! e×d5 17 Q×a3, when one variation is sufficient to illustrate the strength of White's position: 17 ... Q×c2 (perhaps the most crucial and interesting reply) 18 Q×d6 Q×e2 19 e×d5 Q×b2 (White wins brilliantly after *19 ... Qb5 20 Rfe1+ Kd8 21 Rc1!! R×c1 22 Q×f6+ Kc7 23 R×c1+ and 24 Q×h8*) 19 Rfe1+ Kd8 20 Re7, with a very strong attack. Besides, Black consistently carries out an interesting plan.

15 Bg3	e5

The barricades have been erected, and now the attempt to free the black-squared bishop by 16 f3 would allow Black to carry out the manoeuvre ... Nh5–f4. But the black king is in the centre, and so...

16 f4!!

The f-file is opened, and that means that there will be no quiet life for the black king for some time, if, of course, at all. It stands to reason that I was unable to calculate all the variations in the coming attack, and relied, firstly, on a general assessment of the position, and, secondly, on ... intuition.

16 ...   e×f4

After 16 ... g×f4 the bishop sacrifice is by no means obligatory: also good is 17 Bh4 Nh7 18 Nd5 or 18 g3.

17 B×f4

Also to be considered was 17 R×f4 g×f4 18 Bh4.

17 ...   g×f4
18 R×f4   Nh7
19 Nd5

White also has a very strong attack after 19 e5! Be6 (*19 ... d×e5 can be met by 20 R×f7! K×f7 21 Bh5+ Ke7 22 Nd5+ Kd8 23 N×c7 R×c7 24 Qg6 Be7*—otherwise the invasion at g7 is decisive—*25 Qg7 Bf6 26 Qf7*, and Black loses, since against the threat of *27 Bg4* even *26 ... Kc8* does not save him in view of *27 R×d7 R×d7 28 Bg4*) 20 e×d6 Qd7 21 Ne4.

19 ...   Qd8

Necessary, both to defend f6, and to avoid after 19 ... Qc6 the piquant variation 20 R×f7! K×f7 21 Bh5+ Ke6 (*21 ... Kg7 22 c3+*, or *21 ... Kg8 22 Ne7+*) 22 Qh3+ Ke5 23 Qg3+ Ke6 24 Qg6+ Ke5 25 Qg7+ Ke6 26 Bg4 mate.

20 b4   Ba7
21 e5!   Be6

After 21 ... d×e5 White's idea—the rapid inclusion of his queen in the attack—would have been realized in full: 22 R×f7! K×f7 23 Bh5+ Ke6 24 Qg6+ Nf6 25 N×f6 Q×f6 26 Bg4+ with mate in 3 moves.

22 e×d6   Rc6

22 ... Bb8, controlling c7, would have appeared to fit in with Black's basic defensive idea. But it seems to me that Yevgeny

Vasyukov avoided it purely intuitively, since in this case the availability to White of his d4 square would have acquired decisive significance. By continuing 23 Bg4, White could have set his opponent virtually insoluble problems. Thus the d6 pawn is immune — 23 ... Q×d6 (*23 ... B×d6 24 B×e6 B×f4 25 B×c8*, and White now has a material advantage plus a very strong attack) 24 B×e6 Q×e6 25 Re4 Be5 26 Nf4, while on 23 ... B×g4 White gains a favourable ending after 24 Qd4! Rf8 (*24 ... Rg8 25 Qe4+ Be6 26 Q×h7*, and there is no satisfactory defence against the knight check at f6) 25 R×g4 Q×d6 26 Re4+ Kd8 27 Nb6!

Therefore by switching his rook to the 6th rank Black tries both to weaken the pressure on the d-file, and to hold the key point e6.

23 Bg4?

A purely mechanical mistake in approaching time trouble. Having prepared this move against 22 ... Bb8, White also plays it now, immediately turning a won game into a lost one. The logical continuation of the attack on e6 was 23 Nc7+ R×c7 (or *23 ... Kd7 24 R×f7+ B×f7 25 Bg4+*) 24 d×c7 Q×c7 (*24 ... Q×d3 25 B×d3 0–0 loses to 26 B×h7+ K×h7 27 Rd8 Kg7 28 Re4*) 25 Bg4 0–0 26 Qg3!!, immediately deciding the game.

23 ...   R×d6

Up to a certain point—or, more precisely, until time trouble interferes—Black defends excellently.

24 B×e6   R×e6

White wins by force after 24 ... f×e6 25 Qg6+ Kd7 26 Qg7+ Kc8 27 Ne7+ (more spectacular is *27 Rc4+ Kb8 28 Rc7!*) 27 ... Q×e7 28 Rc4+! Kd8 29 Q×h8+ Nf8 30 Rf1.

25 Nf6+

White seems to win immediately by 25 Qc3, with the threats of 26 Q×h8+, 26 Nc7+, and even 26 Nf6+, but the "ultra-late" 25 ... 0-0! parries all his aggressive intensions. Therefore in the meantime the opponent must be denied the right to castle.

25 ...   Ke7
26 Nd5+   Kf8

This move was wrongly condemned by certain commentators, since 26 ... Ke8 would now have been answered by 27 Qc3.

27 Rdf1   Ng5
28 h4

If the black knight abandons its position, White's attack will become decisive. In addition g2–g3 and Kg2 is threatened, after which the knight cannot be maintained at g5. But Black's defensive resources are not yet exhausted, and Vasyukov makes excellent use of his chances.

28 ...   Bb8!
29 Rc4

Or 29 Rf5 Ne4! 30 R×f7+ Ke8 and Black has numerous threats (*31 ... Q×h4+, 31 ... Ng3+*, etc.), while 29 Rd4 is very strongly met by 29 ... Be5.

29 ...   Re5
30 Rd4   Ne6?

A time trouble mistake, allowing White to develop a strong and this time decisive attack. After 30 ... Ba7! White's initiative would have been slightly weakened, and Black's material advantage would have acquired decisive significance.

31 Qg6!   Qe8
32 Rd3

A quiet reply, after which it is very difficult for Black to find a reasonable continuation. Even his extra piece does not help. Thus, for example, he loses after:

(*a*) 32 ... Re2 33 Qg4 R×c2 34 Nf6 Qc8 35 Nd7+ Ke8 (or *35 ... Ke7 36 R×f7+!!*) 36 Qf5 Nd8 37 Re3+.

(*b*) 32 ... Rg8 33 Q×h6+ Ng7 34 Nf6 Re1 35 Nh7+.

(*c*) 32 ... Bd6 33 Rdf3.

Comparatively best was 32 ... Nd8, planning counter-play with ... Re1. Then 33 Qf6 Rh7 34 Nf4 does not work in view of 34 ... Re1! 35 R×d8 R×f1+ 36 Kh2 R×f4!!, but 34 Nb6! Re1 35 Nd7+ Kg8 36 N×b8 R×f1+ 37 Q×f1 leaves White a pawn up with the better position.

In time trouble Black attempts to clarify the situation, but he runs into a masked counter-blow.

32 ...   R×d5
33 R×d5   Nf4
34 Qf6!

This quiet move decides the game. Black cannot defend simultaneously against the threats of 35 Q×h8+ and 35 Rd8.

34 ...	**Rg8**

No better is 34 ... N×d5 35 Q×h8+ Ke7 36 Re1+.

35 Rd8	**Rg6**
36 R×e8+	**K×e8**
37 Qh8+	

and within a few moves **Black resigned**.

No. 30 Sicilian Defence

Geller–Kuzmin

46th USSR Championship
Tbilisi, 1978

The dragon must be attacked!

It is well known that the "Dragon" Variation received its name from the snake-like formation of Black's K-side pawns. I have devoted a considerable amount of time to the study of this line, which always leads to a very sharp struggle. I have played a number of games both with White, and with Black; some of these games have been in highly-important events, including Candidates Matches for the World Championship. And I have come to the conclusion that in chess, as in fairy-tales, White must attack the "dragon" with the utmost energy. Only on this condition can he hope to "cut off its head"!

1 e4	**c5**
2 Nf3	**d6**
3 d4	**c×d4**
4 N×d4	**Nf6**
5 Nc3	**g6**

It is this move that is the dragon's "trade-mark". The next few moves of both sides are well known to theory. White prepares a K-side pawn storm, while Black relies on his long-range bishop at g7 for counter-play in the centre and along the half-open c-file.

6 Be3	**Bg7**
7 f3	**Nc6**
8 Qd2	**0–0**
9 Bc4	**Bd7**
10 h4	**Rc8**
11 Bb3	**h5**

Sharp play results from 11 ... Ne5 12 h5 N×h5 (if Black declines the sacrifice, White gains an attack "for free") 13 g4 Nf6 14 0–0–0 Nc4 15 B×c4 R×c4, when White has the initiative for the pawn, although it is not yet completely clear whom this variation favours. Nevertheless, in recent times Black has switched to the blockading continuation employed in the present game, with the aim of hindering his opponent's attack.

12 0–0–0	**Ne5**
13 Bg5	

The alternative plan is to transfer the bishop to the long black-squared diagonal by 13 Kb1 Nc4 14 B×c4 R×c4 15 Nb3 Be6 16 Bd4. It should also be mentioned that after 13 Bh6 B×h6 14 Q×h6 R×c3 15 b×c3 Qa5 Black gains counter-play for the exchange, and White's activity on the K-side is hindered in particular by the well-placed knight at f6.

13 ...	**Nh7?**

A dubious idea: the knight abandons its ideal post. Incidentally, after this game this move was no longer played, preference being given to 13 ... Rc5.

14 Bh6!	**B×h6**
15 Q×h6	**R×c3**
16 b×c3	**Qa5**

17 Kb1

Of course, the immediate 17 f4 does not work because of 17 ... Q×c3 18 f×e5 Qa1+. It can be assumed that Gennady Kuzmin was following the game Tal–Mista, Dubna, 1973, where White defended his c3 by 17 Ne2. To me this seems to lose time for the attack, allowing Black to create dangerous counter-play by 17 ... Bb5. Here, on the other hand, White makes a useful move, after which the threat of f3–f4 becomes especially strong.

17 ...	Q×c3

Black plays this not so much to win a pawn, as to parry that same threat of 18 f4, on which there would now follow 18 ... Nc4 19 B×c4 Q×c4, when it is unlikely that the exposed white king can be saved. But ...

18 Ne2!

This gives White an important tempo for the attack, in which, however, he has to be prepared to sacrifice.

18 ...	Qc5

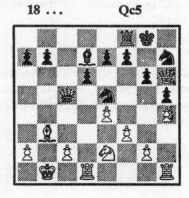

19 g4!

Here too 19 f4 does not achieve its aim, since unnecessary complications result after 19 ... Ng4 20 Q×g6+ Kh8 21 B×f7 Qb5+ 22 Ka1 (or *22 Bb3*) 22 ... Q×e2.

19 ...	N×f3

After 19 ... h×g4 20 f4! Nf3 (even worse is *20 ... Qe3 21 h5*) 21 Q×g6+ Kh8 22 Qh6 White has numerous threats. The move played looks very strong, but it meets with a precise refutation.

20 Rd5!	Qf2
21 g×h5	g5

There is no other defence against the mating attack.

22 h×g5	

It is not often that one sees the g- and h-pawns changing places, and, moreover, in the vicinity of the enemy king!

22 ...	Qe3

Halting the advance of the g-pawn, but...

23 Rhd1!

Up to here my opponent had played, as they say, *a tempo*, spending a total of not more than fifteen minutes. Here he sank into thought for an hour and a half, but there is already no way to save the game. The threat of evicting the black queen from the c1–h6 diagonal is decisive.

23 ...	Bg4

No better is 23 ... Nh×g5 24 R×g5! Q×g5 25 Rg1!

24 R1d3	Q×e2
25 g6	Nfg5

Or 25 ... Nf6 26 g7.

26 R×g5	Qf1+
27 Kb2	N×g5

28 Q×g5	Qf6
29 Q×f6	e×f6
30 h6	Bh5

And without waiting for 31 B×f7+, **Black resigned.**

No. 31 Sicilian Defence

Geller–Suetin

Moscow, 1981

The shortest game

This highly-interesting event was a match-tournament of four USSR teams: first and second teams, and veteran and youth teams. I was appearing for the first team, and my opponent for the veterans. Since I was faced with a game against a well-known theorist, and since it was definitely a friendly event, on the 6th move I chose a little-studied continuation.

The game turned out to be the shortest of the 96 played in the match-tournament.

1 e4	c5
2 Nf3	e6
3 d4	c×d4
4 N×d4	a6
5 Bd3	Bc5

This move was introduced into modern practice by Polugayevsky, and has the aim of immediately removing the white knight from the centre, whereas after 6 Nb3 the bishop finds a fairly convenient post at a7.

6 c3

In previous games too (for example, with Filip in the Candidates Tournament, Curacao, 1962, where *6 Be3* was played) I had often tried to maintain the knight in its active position.

| 6 ... | Ne7 |

Of course, the knight would have been more active at f6, but the immediate 6 ... Nf6 fails to 7 e5, and therefore the preparatory 6 ... d6 would have been very useful.

6 ... d5!? is interesting, but after 7 Nd2 Black has to part with his bishop and play 7 ... B×d4 8 c×d4 d×e4 9 N×e4 Nc6 with a very sharp position, since in the event of 7 ... Nf6 8 e5 Nfd7 9 N2f3 he simply has nowhere to put his king: after K-side castling it will come under a fatal attack, Haag–Kapelan, Budapest, 1972.

Therefore the most popular is 6 ... Nc6, with the possible sequel 7 Be3 Qb6 8 Qb3 Qa7 9 Nd2 N×d4 10 c×d4 B×d4 11 B×d4 Q×d4 12 Nf3 Qa7 13 0–0, when White's lead in development compensates for the sacrificed pawn.

| 7 0–0 | Nbc6 |

In the game Geller–Taimanov, 39th USSR Championship, Moscow, 1969, after 7 ... 0–0 White immediately went onto the offensive by 8 Qh5, and gained a slight advantage — 8 ... d6 9 Nd2 Nd7 10 N2b3.

| 8 Be3 | Qb6 |

An erroneous plan. With his development incomplete, Black himself aims for tactical complications. Moreover, his main piece—his queen—comes under attack. Preferable was 8 ... d6.

| 9 Nd2! | d5 |

In order not to allow the knight to c4, Black is forced to open up the game with his king uncastled, since he cannot settle for either 9 ... Q×b2 10 Nc4 Q×c3 11 Rc1 Qb4 12 a3 trapping the queen (*12 ... Qb5 13 Nd6+*), or 9 ... N×d4 10 c×d4 B×d4 11 Nc4 Qc5 12 b4 Qa7 13 Nd6+ with a very strong attack on the king.

10 N2b3	B×d4
11 c×d4	d×e4
12 B×e4	Qd8

White's isolated pawn is a small price to pay for his two bishops, his lead in development, and the chance to begin a direct attack. It is interesting to see how, with the most simple, natural moves, he simultaneously prevents the opponent from castling and brings his own forces into play.

13 Qh5	Nd5
14 Bg5	Nce7
15 Rfe1	h6
16 Rad1	Qd6

Black still cannot castle, if only because of 17 B×h6. But now his seemingly solid central defences collapse.

17 B×e7!	N×e7
18 d5!	e×d5

After 18 ... e5 19 Bb1 there is no way of defending the e5 pawn.

19 B×d5	Qf6

No better is 19 ... Qg6 20 B×f7+! K×f7 21 R×e7+.

20 B×f7+

In view of the loss of his queen — 20 ... Q×f7 21 Rd8+ — **Black resigned.**

No. 32 Sicilian Defence

Geller–Hübner

Las Palmas, 1976

Whose plan is superior?

The chairman of the jury, grandmaster Bent Larsen, awarded this game a special prize as the best played in the tournament. There were no obvious mistakes in it, and both sides consistently carried out their plans. But Black's plan proved to be impracticable, and the subsequent tactical complications ended in favour of White.

1 e4	c5
2 Nf3	e6
3 d4	c×d4
4 N×d4	a6
5 Bd3	

At the present time this is the most popular continuation in reply to the Paulsen System. White wishes in the first instance to castle, without allowing Black after 5 c4 Nf6 6 Nc3 to develop his bishop at b4. It is curious that this was the very opening of a game Porges–W. Paulsen in... 1892!

5 ...	g6

A comparatively fresh idea in this old variation. The plan with the development of the bishop at g7 was introduced into modern practice after a series of games by Gipslis in the 1967 Interzonal Tournament in Sousse. True, on the basis of his acquaintance with one of the Paulsen brothers' manuscripts,

Bent Larsen asserts that in the system suggested by them they tried literally everything, including perhaps ... the move 5 ... g6.

| 6 0–0 | Bg7 |
| 7 c3 | |

Since this was the third time that Robert Hübner had employed this set-up against me, I decided to restrict myself to this modest move. It has its virtues—in particular it restricts the scope of Black's fianchettoed bishop. But since White declines to take control of the central squares (his knight does not go to c3, nor his pawn to c4), he cannot expect too much from the opening.

Therefore objectively stronger is 7 Be3 (the loss of a tempo—*7 Be2*—does not create any difficulties for Black, as was confirmed by the game Ivkov–Gipslis, Sousse, 1967, which continued *7 ... Ne7 8 Nc3 0–0 9 Bg5 d6 10 Qd2 Nbc6 11 Nb3 Qc7 12 Bh6 b5 13 B×g7 K×g7 14 a3 Bb7*, with roughly equal chances), and after 7 ... Ne7 8 c4 d5 9 c×d5 e×d5 10 Nc3 0–0 11 e×d5 N×d5 12 N×d5 Q×d5, Miagmarsuren–Gipslis, Sousse, 1967, instead of 13 Bc2 White could have played 13 Be2 and transferred his bishop to f3, with pressure on Black's Q-side.

| 7 ... | Nf6 |
| 8 Nd2 | Qc7 |

It was to secure the post for the queen at c7 that the Paulsen brothers played ... a6.

9 a4

This move follows logically from White's intended plan. Normally ... b5 is prevented by the white pawn at c4, so here the a-pawn takes on this role.

| 9 ... | 0–0 |
| 10 Re1 | |

Threatening 11 e5 Nd5 12 Nc4, and simultaneously vacating a square for the retreat of the white-squared bishop.

| 10 ... | d6 |
| 11 a5 | Nbd7 |

Black does not wish to lose control of b6, which would be the case after 11 ... Nc6 12 Nc4.

| 12 Nc4 | d5 |
| 13 e×d5 | N×d5 |

A debatable decision. Things would perhaps have been easier for Black with an isolated pawn at d5, since then his problems over the development of his Q-side would have disappeared.

14 Bf1   Nc5

And this is a serious inaccuracy. Black aims for the freeing advance ... e5 (which does not work immediately in view of *15 Nf5*), but, as we will see, in the immediate future this proves impossible. Therefore Black should have tried to exchange off the strong white knight at c4 by 14 ... Ne5, and retreated the knight to c6 in the event of White avoiding the exchange.

It can also be added that Black is unable to carry out his plan because of certain tactical nuances.

15 Bg5

Not only preventing 15 ... e5, which would lead to the loss of a pawn after 16 Nf3, but also intending the transfer of the bishop via h4 to g3, with strong and unpleasant pressure on the weakened black squares.

| 15 ... | f6 |
| 16 Bh4 | e5 |

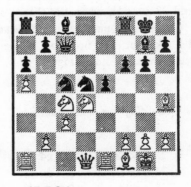

17 Qf3!

Had the white knight retreated, Black would have had everything in order. But this *zwischenzug* changes the picture, since the b6 square ends up in White's hands. And as a consequence of this, the weakening of the a2–g8 diagonal also tells.

17 ...   **Nf4**

Forced, since after 17 ... Rd8 Black cannot avoid loss of material—18 N×e5 f×e5 19 B×d8 Q×d8 20 Bc4, and if 20 ... e×d4, then 21 B×d5+ Kh8 22 Qf7 Bd7 23 c×d4 B×d4 24 Re7 Qg8 25 Q×g8+ R×g8 26 B×g8 K×g8 27 Rd1 Bf6 28 Rd×d7, and White emerges the exchange ahead.

18 Nb6   **Rb8**
19 Bg3

Weaker is the immediate 19 Bc4+ Kh8 20 b4 Nd7, when the bishop at c4 is "hanging". Therefore the bishop check is better kept in reserve.

19 ...   **g5**
20 B×f4   **g×f4**
21 b4   **Ne6**

Or 21 ... e×d4 22 b×c5, and Black's position is in tatters (*22 ... Q×c5? 23 Q×f4 Bf5 24 c×d4*).

22 Bc4   **Re8**

On 22 ... e×d4 White would have answered 23 c×d4!, when the threat of d4–d5–d6 would not have allowed Black to defend his knight. But now too White gains by force a material advantage.

(see diagram next column)

23 N×c8   **Q×c4**
24 Nd6   **N×d4**
25 c×d4   **Qe6**

Both 25 ... Q×b4, and 25 ... Q×d4 would have allowed a smothered mate—26 Qd5 (b3)+ Kh8 27 Nf7+ Kg8 28 Nh6++ Kh8 29 Qg8+ R×g8 30 Nf7 mate.

26 N×e8   **Q×e8**

White is the exchange up, and its realization does not present any particular difficulty.

27 d×e5   **f×e5**
28 Rac1   **Qf7**
29 Red1   **Re8**
30 Qe4   **Bf8**
31 Rd5   **Qg6**
32 Re1   **Q×e4**
33 R×e4   **Rc8**

Or 33 ... Bg7 34 Rd7.

34 Rd×e5   **B×b4**
35 Re8+

Blundering into the mate by 35 R×b4?? is not obligatory.

35 ...   **R×e8**
36 R×e8+   **Kf7**
37 Rb8   **B×a5**
38 R×b7+   **Kg6**
39 Ra7   **Bc3**
40 R×a6+   **Kg5**
41 Kf1

With the time control reached, **Black resigned.**

French Defence

No. 33 French Defence

Geller–Sokolsky

*18th USSR Championship
Moscow, 1950*

Five swift steps

Black was faced with a considerable temptation in the form of an undefended white pawn at e5, and in the end it proved too strong for him.

In general the game has the character and certain features of a miniature, which cannot be played without the "assistance" of the opponent. It received a prize as one of the best games of the Championship.

1 e4	e6
2 d4	d5
3 Nc3	Bb4
4 e5	c5
5 a3	B×c3+
6 b×c3	Ne7
7 Qg4	

Intending after 7 ... c×d4, which was introduced by Botvinnik (Ragozin–Botvinnik, Moscow, 1935), to offer a pawn sacrifice instead of the standard 8 Q×g7 Rg8 9 Q×h7, etc. At that time, and in fact nowadays, the variation in the game was played rather rarely, and it does not yet have a definitive assessment.

7 ...	c×d4
8 Bd3	Qc7

The alternative is 8 ... Qa5 9 Ne2 0-0.

9 Ne2	d×c3

The strongest move. In a later game Bonch-Osmolovsky–Rovner, Lvov, 1951, Black tried 9 ... Q×e5, but after 10 Bf4! (*10 c×d4*

h5! 11 Qh4 Qc7) 10 ... h5 11 Qh4 Nf5 12 Qg5 Qf6 13 Q×f6 g×f6 14 B×f5 e×f5 15 B×b8 R×b8 16 c×d4 White gained an advantage in the ending. He also has the better ending after 10 ... Qf6 11 c×d4 h5 12 Qg3 Nbc6 13 Bg5 Nf5 14 B×f6 N×g3 15 B×g7 Rg8 16 h×g3 R×g7 17 R×h5.

10 Q×g7	Rg8
11 Q×h7	Q×e5

Here, too, it was better to avoid the temptation to eliminate White's central pawn. Bonch–Osmolovsky, the inventor of the move 8 Bd3, suggested 11 ... Nbc6, aiming for development. Continuations which have occurred in practice are 12 f4 Bd7, and 12 Bf4? Bd7 13 0-0 0-0-0 14 Qh5 d4 15 Bg3 Be8! (Unzicker–Uhlmann, Varna, 1962). Now, however, White gains the opportunity to play his main trump—his passed h-pawn, supported by his pieces (in particular the black-squared bishop).

12 Bf4	Qf6

Or 12 ... Qh8 13 Q×h8 R×h8 14 Be5 Rf8 15 B×c3 Nbc6 16 f4, and the h-pawn cannot be stopped.

13 h4	Nbc6

If 13 ... e5, then 14 Bg5 Qg7 (*14 ... Qb6 15 B×e7 R×g2 16 Bg5 Q×f2+ 17 Kd1*) 15 Q×g7 R×g7 16 Bf6 and then h4–h5, etc.

14 Bg5	Qe5
15 Qh6	

White consistently carries out his plan. His queen is to be transferred to f6, clearing the way for his h-pawn.

15 ...	Bd7
16 Qf6	Rc8

Nothing is achieved by the attempt to

75

complicate matters by 16 ... Q×f6 17 B×f6 e5 18 Bh7 d4 19 h5 (or *19 Ng3*) 19 ... Bf5 20 B×f5! N×f5 21 h6, when after 21 ... N×h6 22 R×h6 Black does not even have time to take the g2 pawn.

17 f4!	Qe3
18 h5	e5
19 h6	e4
20 Bb5	R×g5

With the last hope of 21 Q×g5? Nd4.

21 h7!

The threat of 22 Qh8+ is very strong.

21 ...	Bg4
22 Q×g5	Qd2+
23 Kf1	B×e2+
24 B×e2	Nd4
25 h8 = Q+	Resigns

No. 34 French Defence

Geller–Stahlberg

*Interzonal Tournament
Stockholm, 1952*

Gratuitous suffering

One method of defence is for the defending side to "stock up" (if possible) with extra material, and then attempt, by returning it, to alleviate the mounting pressure. The ex-perienced Swedish grandmaster Gideon Stahl-berg neglected this possibility, and pinned his hopes on the method of "defence with counter-attack". The result was a quick defeat, although Black did not make any obvious mistake.

An explanation may be sought in the fact that, a few rounds earlier, in his favourite variation 3 ... c5 4 e×d5 Q×d5 5 Nf3 c×d4 6 Bc4 Qd8, etc. Stahlberg incurred a difficult position against Averbakh, and, evidently fearing some further improvement for White, avoided his normal continuation and ended up in an insufficiently familiar position.

1 e4	e6
2 d4	d5
3 Nd2	Nf6

Theory regards this variation as difficult for Black, but from the way that Stahlberg made his third move it seemed to me that Black had prepared something. The question immediately arose — at what point could a surprise be expected?

| 4 e5 | Nfd7 |
| 5 Bd3 | c5 |

From the tree of variations at Black's disposal, one branch stands out: Botvinnik's favourite but little-studied (especially at that time) continuation 5 ... b6, with the idea of exchanging the white-squared bishops by ...Ba6 and thus reducing White's chances of a K-side attack.

| 6 c3 | Nc6 |
| 7 Ne2 | Qb6 |

An interesting struggle results from 7...f6, which occurred not long before the tourna-ment at the Helsinki Olympiad in the game Keres–Czerniak. Black leaves his queen in its initial position, since it is needed both for 8 ... Qe7 (after *8 Nf4*) and for 9...Q×f6 (after *9 e×f6*). Having passed by this varia-tion, Black is practically "obliged" to spring his surprise (assuming, of course, that he has prepared one!) in one of the two remaining main variations.

8 Nf3	c×d4
9 c×d4	f6
10 e×f6	

This move is aimed at gaining control of e5. At that time theory was more in favour of 10 Nf4. But, firstly, even then it seemed to me that this leads to highly unclear play, and, secondly, it was here that Stahlberg could have found some improvement. Since no surprise came in the game itself, it is highly probable that this was the case.

10 ...	N×f6
11 0–0	Bd6
12 Nf4	

At that time both White and Black were merely feeling their way in this complicated position. The line which is now regarded as strongest, 12 Nc3 0–0 13 Re1 or 13 Be3 Bd7, and now not 14 a3 Rae8 with chances for both sides (Pachman–Uhlmann, Prague, 1954, and Boleslavsky–Pietzsch, Berlin, 1967), but 14 Ne5!, was not then known.

Black's counter-play is along the f-file, and therefore White's immediate aim is to attempt to force the black rook to move from f8 to e8. In the event of 12 Bf4 B×f4 13 N×f4 0–0 14 Re1 Black has the reply 14 ... Ne4, and if 15 B×e4 then 15 ... R×f4.

12 ...	0–0

It would have been rash to play 12 ... B×f4 13 B×f4 Q×b2 14 Bd6.

13 Re1	B×f4?

After the immediate 13 ... Re8 White could have provoked favourable complications, for example: 14 Ne5 N×d4 14 Nh5!, and it is not easy to parry White's attack. Even after the best defence 15 ... Rf8 16 N×f6+ R×f6 17 Ng4 Rf7(f8) 18 Be3 it is

not clear what Black is to play. 18 ... e5 fails to 19 N×e5! B×e5 20 Qh5, with an inevitable debacle.

The pawn sacrifice 13 ... Nd7, which was later suggested, can also hardly be correct.

Black should have played 13...Ne4. *E.C.O.* then gives 14 g3, leading to an advantage for White (Keres), but this move has gone out of practice. The reason for this can be sought in the fact that White weakens the white squares in the vicinity of his king, and although he wins a pawn, in doing so he has to give up his white-squared bishop. Of course, these are general considerations, but it seems to me that the *E.C.O.* evaluation is too categorical. Besides, it would be interesting to try 14 ... g5!?, when 15 Nh5 is met by 15 ... N×f2!, so that White is obliged to enter the complications of 15 N×g5.

14 B×f4	Bd7

The critical point of the game. Black does not sense the danger. Meanwhile, the advantages of White's position are so great that Black should have been thinking not about development, but about how to complicate the game. This could have been achieved either by 14 ... Ne4, or 14 ... Q×b2 (if he has to suffer, let it at least be for a pawn). In the second variation, the most critical, the battle would still have been to come. But now White gains a strong initiative with material level, for free.

15 Bd6	Rfe8
16 Bc5	Qc7

Black can no longer win the pawn: 16 ... Q×b2 17 Rb1 Qc3 (*17...Q×a2 18 Ra1 Qb2 19 Re2 Qc3 20 Ra3*) 18 R×b7.

17 Rc1	Qf4
18 Ne5	Rac8

After 18...N×e5 19 d×e5 Ng4 20 g3 Qg5 21 h4 Qh5 22 Be2 White wins a piece.

19 Rc3

White's threats mount, both concretely— 20 B×h7+ K×h7 21 Rh3+ Kg8 22 Rh8+, and more abstractly—he intends to retreat his bishop to b1 and to transfer very strongly his rook to the K-side. Therefore Black decides to try to exploit the position of the bishop at c5. The direct 19 ... b6 does not succeed: 20 Bd6 N×d4 21 N×d7 Q×d6 22 N×f6+ g×f6 23 Qg4+, so Stahlberg contemplates a counter-attack.

19 ...	N×e5
20 d×e5	R×c5

After 20 R×c5 Ng4 Black's hopes would have been justified, but White has no intention of going on to the defensive.

21 g3!	Qb4

The queen is forced to abandon the decisive part of the battlefield, otherwise Black simply loses the exchange.

22 a3	Qb6
23 e×f6	

Black's K-side is in ruins. He loses after 23 ... R×c3 24 Qg4, or 23 ... g6 24 Qc1, or 23...g×f6 24 B×h7+ Kf8 (if *24...K×h7* or *24...Kg7*, then *25 Qc2*) 25 Qd4.

23 ...	Kf7
24 f×g7	R×c3
25 Qh5+	K×g7
26 Q×h7+	Kf6
27 b×c3	

It is obvious that the black king cannot survive.

27 ...	Qd8
28 Bg6	Rf8
29 Bh5	d4
30 c×d4	Qa5
31 Qg6+	**Resigns**

No. 35 French Defence

Geller–Vaganian

*43rd USSR Championship
Yerevan, 1975*

Against the spirit of the variation

In this variation Black voluntarily concedes to his opponent both a lead in development, and an advantage in space, but holds on thanks to the closed nature of the position. Here White succeeded—not without the opponent's help—in opening up the position, and the superior mobilization of his forces immediately proved decisive.

1 e4	e6
2 d4	d5
3 Nd2	Nc6

This move appears completely antipositional, since Black himself impedes the thematic French attack on the white centre by

... c5. In fact he immediately prepares a quite different idea: the central counter ... e5, which is possible, for example, after 4 c3. But in the main variation, which occurs in this game, Black has to work hard to undermine White's centre.

4 Ngf3	Nf6
5 e5	Nd7
6 Bd3	Nb4

The evaluations of theory are constantly changing. At any rate, they cannot be called permanent, and this is one of the attractions of chess. Thus, for example, here 6 ... f6!? is considered promising for Black, although on the basis of the game Luckis–Stahlberg, Mar del Plata, 1942, which continued 7 Ng5 Nd×e5 8 d×e5 f×g5 9 Qh5+ Kd7 10 Nf3 it used to be thought to favour White. But in fact, interposing 9 ... g6! 10 B×g6+ Kd7 gives Black at least a complicated, double-edged game after 11 f4 (*11 Nf3 allows Black an advantage — 11...h×g6 12 Q×g6 Be7 13 B×g5 Qg8 14 Q×g8 R×g8 15 h4 b6*, Chekhov–Yurtayev, USSR, 1978) 11 ... g×f4 12 Nd3 Nb4, Faibisovich–Monin, USSR, 1979.

7 Be2	c5
8 c3	Nc6
9 0–0	Qb6

This is not yet a mistake, but a kind of overture to one. The immediate 9 ... f6 10 e×f6 Q×f6 11 c4! allows the undermining of Black's centre, but better is 9 ... c×d4, as was played against me a few rounds later in the same USSR Championship by Doroshkevich. The game continued 10 c×d4 f6 11 e×f6 (*11 Re1!? deserves consideration*) 11 ... N×f6, when the pawn sacrifice 12 Ne5 N×d4 13 Qa4+ did not achieve anything real.

| 10 Nb3 | a5? |

But this is a mistake. Although Black attempts to intensify the pressure on the centre by driving the knight from b3, in doing so he concedes the square d4, which is especially important in the French Defence. In combination with the weakening of the b5 square, this becomes extremely dangerous. Correct was 10 ... c×d4 11 c×d4 Be7.

11 d×c5!

According to the rules of strategy, a lead in development demands positive action, otherwise it may gradually disappear.

| 11 ... | Qc7 |

It stands to reason that the variation 11 ... N×c5 12 Be3 a4 13 Nbd4, in which White improves to the maximum the placing of all his pieces, does not appeal to Black. But his position is already very difficult.

12 Bf4	N×c5
13 Nbd4	Bd7
14 Nb5	Qb6
15 Be3	Qd8

15 ... N×e5 16 N×e5 B×b5 17 b4! B×e2 18 Q×e2 a×b4 19 c×b4 Q×b4 20 Rab1 Qa4 21 Rfc1 leads to a decisive attack on the black king stranded in the centre. But now, too, the wanderings of the black queen up and down the a5–d8 diagonal cannot go unpunished.

| 16 c4! | d×c4 |
| 17 B×c4 | Qb8 |

79

Black vainly attempts somehow to cover the weak points in his position. No better, however, is 17 ... Be7, as suggested by certain commentators, if only because of 18 Nd6+ B×d6 19 Q×d6 Ne4 20 Qd3.

18 Qe2	a4

On 18 ... Be7 White would have continued as in the game.

19 Rfd1	Na5
20 b4!	N×c4

After 20 ... a×b3 21 a×b3 the threat of 22 b4 is especially terrible.

21 Q×c4	Na6

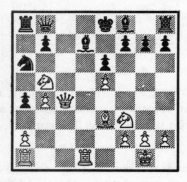

22 R×d7!

Now the black king is totally exposed.

22 ...	K×d7
23 Rd1+	Ke8
24 Nd6+	B×d6

Or 24 ... Ke7 25 Bg5+ f6 26 e×f6+ g×f6 27 B×f6+! K×f6 28 Qh4+ Kg7 29 Qg5 mate.

25 e×d6	

Threatening both 26 d7+, and, as a minimum, 26 b5 winning the knight.

25 ...	Qd8
26 Bg5	

In view of the variations 26 ... f6 27 Q×e6+ Kf8 28 Ne5, and 26 ... Rc8 27 Qb5+ Qd7 28 Q×d7+ K×d7 29 Ne5+, **Black resigned.**

No. 36 French Defence

Geller–Vaganian

*44th USSR Championship
Moscow, 1976*

Yet another idea ...

Calmly following a familiar variation, Black clearly did not anticipate any particular danger in the opening, but he nevertheless encountered a surprise. This game once again testifies to the inexhaustibility of fresh chess ideas, and shows how carefully one has to play even in the most simple and well-known positions.

1 e4	e6
2 d4	d5
3 Nd2	c5
4 Ngf3	c×d4
5 e×d5	

In the event of 5 N×d4 Black has no reason to attempt to gain a tempo by 5 ... Bc5?!; after 6 N2b3 Nb6 7 Bb5+ Bd7 8 e×d5 White gives his opponent an isolated pawn. But 5...Nc6 gives Black a comfortable game.

5 ...	Q×d5

This leads to a variation in which, by a temporary pawn sacrifice, White gains a lead in development, and hence possibilities of active play.

6 Bc4	Qd6

Theory considers this strongest. 6 ... Qa5 allows White after suitable preparation to gain a tempo by Nb3. At d8 the queen occupies a more passive position, while 6...Qh5 allows White to gain an endgame advantage by 7 0-0 Nc6 8 Nb3 Nf6 (*8...e5* loses to *9 N×e5!*) 9 Nb×d4 10 N×d4 Q×d1 11 R×d1 a6 12 Bf4.

7 0-0	Nf6
8 Nb3	Nc6
9 Nb×d4	N×d4
10 N×d4	Be7

The other common continuation is 10...a6, with the idea of attacking the bishop with gain of tempo by ...Qc7 and of playing ...Bd6, when possible is 11 Bb3 Qc7 12 Qf3 Bd6 13 h3, or 11 Re1, or, as I played against Stahlberg at Göteborg, 1955, 11 b3 Qc7 12 Qe2 Nd6 (better is *12...b5 13 Bd3 Bb7*) 13 Nf5! B×h2+ 14 Kh1 0-0 15 N×g7!, with advantage to White.

But Black copies the game Tal–Petrosian, Varese, 1976, where from the opening White did not achieve anything.

11 b3

For the moment 11 Nb5 does not achieve its aim: 11...Qc6! 12 Qe2 0-0 13 Bf4 a6 14 Nd4 Qc5 15 Nb3 Qc6, and in Tal–Petrosian, USSR, 1976, Black equalized.

11...	0-0
12 Bb2	Qf4

Black has an inferior ending after 12...e5 13 Nb5 Q×d1 14 Rf×d1 Bf5 15 Rac1, Tal–Uhlmann, Moscow, 1967.

13 Qe2!

A new idea. In the aforementioned Tal–Petrosian game in Varese, White tried to exploit the advanced position of the black queen by 13 Nf3 b6 14 Be5 Qg4 15 Nd4 Q×d1 16 Ra×d1 Bb7 17 Nb5, but after 17...Bc5 Black had equal chances. But here White first of all brings up his reserves.

13...	Qe4

Sensing the danger, Black offers the exchange of queens, but subsequently this allows White to gain a further tempo for the attack.

14 Qd2!	Rd8

The pin on the knight is illusory, whereas the weakening of the f7 square, especially in view of the bishop at c4, is very marked. This motif immediately attracted my attention, and in fact it was to save Black from an even more rapid defeat.

15 Rfe1	Qh4
16 Rad1	Bc5

Otherwise Black's previous moves, beginning with his 13th, would be illogical. But now White has the possibility of a new and brilliant idea.

17 Re5

He overlooks it! Although he retains all the advantages of his position, much stronger was 17 Qa5!, when Black has nothing better than to block completely his Q-side by the awkward move 17...Nd7. The point is that 17...b6 and 17...Bb6 are decisively met by 18 Q×c5!! and 18 Q×b6!! respectively followed by 19 Nf3, after which the weakness of Black's back rank tells.

17...	Ng4

Since he loses after 17...Bf8 18 g3 Qh3 (*18...Qg4 19 Be2 Qg6 20 Bd3 Qg4 21 Rg5*) 19 Bf1 Qg4 20 Rg5 Qe4 21 Bg2, Black tries to complicate the situation as much as possible by sacrificing a piece.

| 18 R×c5 | Q×h2+ |
| 19 Kf1 | e5 |

19...Qh1+ 20 Ke2 Q×g2 21 Qf4 is inadequate. Black's misfortune is that he is pursuing the king with too few forces. Therefore he attempts to include his bishop in the attack.

| 20 Qg5 | Nf6 |

After 20...Bd7 21 Nf3 Qh1+ 22 Ke2 Q×g2 23 Qh4 e4 24 Ng5 it is White who has a decisive attack.

21 B×f7+!

Black's plan would to a certain extent have been justified after 21 R×e5 Bg4! with great complications. Besides, for a long time White has had his sights on the f7 square. ...

| 21 ... | Kh8 |

Or 21...K×f7 22 Rc7+, and bad is 22...Bd7 23 Nf3 Qh6 24 Q×h6 g×h6 25 B×e5, or 22...Rd7 23 R×d7+ B×d7 24 Nf3 Qh6 26 N×e5+.

| 22 R×e5 | |

Now that the black rooks have been deprived of the e8 square, and after a possible transition into an endgame he will not even have two pawns for his piece (this will become clear a little later), this capture is perfectly justified.

| 22 ... | Bg4 |
| 23 f3 | Rac8 |

After 23...Qh1+ 24 Ke2 Q×g2+ 25 Ke3 neither 25...Re8 nor 25...B×f3 is possible. But now the threat of 24...R×c2 is easily parried.

24 Rd2	Rf8
25 Be6	Rce8
26 Rde2	Qh1+
27 Kf2	h5
28 Nf5	Resigns

Caro-Kann Defence

No. 37 Caro-Kann Defence

Geller–Hort

"Solidarity Tournament"
Skopje, 1968

Quickly into the endgame

An example of how it is sometimes possible to go from opening to middlegame in the hope of achieving a favourable endgame.

It is not always possible to carry this out consistently: the opponent endeavours, before it is too late, to change things. But Vlastimil Hort was lulled somewhat by the apparent simplicity of the position, and was late in sensing the danger. His reaction proved unfortunate, although it was already very difficult to do anything about it.

It is remarkable that, right up to the point when he capitulated, Black did not suffer even the slightest loss of material.

1 e4	c6
2 d4	d5
3 Nd2	

A little finesse. Against the usual 3 Nc3 certain players, Botvinnik for example, like to play 3 ... g6. But now this continuation loses its point, since White can always defend his d4 pawn by c2–c3. Thus Black's choice in the opening is restricted.

3 ...	d×e4
4 N×e4	Bf5
5 Ng3	Bg6
6 Nf3	Nd7
7 h4	h6
8 h5	Bh7
9 Bd3	B×d3
10 Q×d3	Qc7
11 Bd2	e6
12 0-0-0	

Up to this point both sides have followed the main line of the old classical variation of the Caro–Kann Defence. Here theory considers the strongest to be 12 Qe2, when White, retaining the option of castling on either side, masks his plans. In reply to 12 ... 0-0-0, according to Boleslavsky's recommendations, he can continue immediately with 13 Ne5, or else can make this move after 12 ... Ngf6 13 0-0-0 0-0-0. This was the course taken, for example, by the game Spassky–Botvinnik, Moscow, 1966, and by the 13th game of the Spassky–Petrosian World Championship Match of 1966.

In the present game, however, I did not especially conceal my intentions. White deliberately goes in for exchanges, with the intention of exploiting the restriction of Black's K-side (by the pawns at h5 and—subsequently—at e5!) in the endgame. Moreover, it is rather difficult for Black to avoid exchanges which favour his opponent.

12 ...	Ngf6
13 Ne4	N×e4

Black should not have fallen in so readily with White's plans: the exchange on e4 should have been delayed.

14 Q×e4	0-0-0
15 g3	Be7

After 15 ... Bd6 16 Rhe1 Nf6 17 Qh4, followed if necessary by Qh1, all the same Black would have been unable to prevent the invasion of the knight at e5. Even so, this was the lesser evil.

16 Kb1

A useful move. Otherwise Black can meet Bf4 with ... Qa5. The intended Ne5 would have been premature here, since Black has control of d5, and by 16 ... N×e5 17 d×e5 Rd5 he could have forced White to play either 18 Bc3, depriving him of c2–c4, or 18 f4, depriving his queen of the important f4 square.

16 ...	Rhe8
17 c4	c5
18 Bf4	

It is obvious that 18 Ne5 would again have been inopportune: 18 ... N×e5 19 d×e5 Rd4.

18 ...	Bd6
19 Ne5	

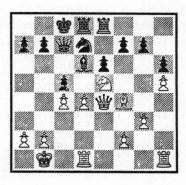

19 ...	N×e5

It would seem that at this point Hort did not yet sense the danger threatening him, for simultaneously with this move he offered a draw. But all the same it is difficult for Black to devise anything. The capture with the bishop on e5 is not worth considering: it leaves a yawning hole at d6, and the knight has no convenient post (it is a long way to d4, and even there it cannot be maintained). 19 ... f5 fails to the unexpected 20 Nf7! Nf6 (Black cannot accept the sacrifice: *20 ... f×e4 21 N×d6+ Kb8 22 Nf7 e5 23 d×e5 Ka8 24 e6 Qc6 25 N×d8 R×d8 26 Rd6,* or *24 ... Qc8 25 Nd6 Qc6 26 N×e8, 27 e×d7* and *28 Rd6*) *21 N×d6+ Q×d6 22 Qe2,* and White has a marked positional advantage. But also after the move played White probably has a won ending.

20 d×e5 Bf8

After the game Hort stated that 20 ... Be7 would have been better, so as to free his K-side by ... f6, and if e×f6 B×f6. But in this case too the weakness at e6, plus the pawns fixed on black squares at g7 and h6, would have ensured White a persistent advantage.

21 Be3

In the words of Hort, here he felt he was in trouble, and decided, after exchanging both pairs of rooks, to take his king across to the defence of his K-side. I, too, had no reason to avoid the exchanges. On the contrary: after the disappearance of the rooks White can attack more boldly.

21 ...	R×d1+
22 R×d1	Rd8
23 R×d8+	Q×d8
24 Kc2	Qa5
25 a3	Qa4+
26 Kc1	Kc7?

This loses. Black should have played 26 ... Be7, retaining his queen in its active position, and agreeing if necessary to the sacrifice of one of his K-side pawns for the sake of counter-play. Then the direct 27 Qg4

achieves nothing for White after 27 ... Bg5, a move which can also follow on 27 Qf4. Therefore I was intending to play 27 f4, threatening 28 f5, and on 27 ... Kc7—28 g4.

Black played the king move to prepare 27 ... b5.

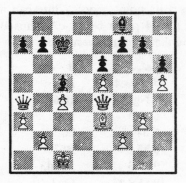

27 Qf4! Qd7

The search for perpetual check after 27 ... Be7 28 Q×f7 Q×c4+ 29 Kd2 Qd5+ 30 Ke1 Qh1+ 31 Ke2 is in vain, and Black is forced totally onto the defensive.

28 b3

An important move. The coordination of the Q-side pawns is restored, and the white king finds a safe shelter from the checks at c2.

28 ...	Kd8
29 Kc2	Ke8
30 Qe4	

All Black's pawns are protected, but the fate awaiting his pieces is to be passive witnesses to the opponent's mounting activity.

30 ...	Qc7
31 f4	Be7
32 g4	Bh4
33 f5	Bg3

The counter-play against the e5 pawn is of little consequence, since White continues his attack along the white squares.

34 f×e6 f×e6

35 Qg6+	Kf8
36 Q×e6	B×e5
37 Kd3!	

A white-square path has been opened for the king into the opponent's position. Black has no defence against its advance.

37 ...	Bg3
38 Ke4	Bh2
39 Kf5	Bg3
40 Bd2	

This is more exact that 40 Kg6 Qd6 41 Q×d6 B×d6 42 Bc1 Be5, when White still has to work to achieve the win. He now threatens an attack on g7.

40 ...	Bh2
41 Bc3	Qf7+

Here the game was adjourned, but **Black resigned** without resuming, in view of the obvious variation 42 Q×f7+ K×f7 43 Ke4 and 44 Kd5.

Pirc Defence

No. 38 Pirc Defence

Geller–Ciocaltea

Malta Olympiad, 1980

Those brief decisive minutes

No, on this occasion we are not talking about time trouble, which so often decides the fate of a game. It was the minutes which were available to prepare for this game that were brief. After all, with the Swiss system, on which the Olympiad was held, the name of one's opponent is discovered not long before the gong announcing the start of play. But during these minutes I looked through a number of games by the Rumanian player, and noticed his way of handling the Pirc Defence with ... c6 and a subsequent interesting knight manoeuvre. Literally on the way to the tournament hall I managed to outline a general plan of campaign. ...

I should also mention that the game was played in the last round of the Olympiad, and my task was simultaneously complicated and simplified by the fact that the position of our team demanded a win at all costs!

1 e4	d6
2 d4	Nf6
3 Nc3	g6
4 Nf3	Bg7
5 Be2	0–0
6 0–0	c6
7 h3	Na6

With the idea of transferring the knight to c7 (instead of the usual 7 ... Nbd7), and then if possible of advancing ... d5. In some previous games Victor Ciocaltea had played the preliminary 7 ... a5, but had then avoided this inclusion, since after a subsequent ... d5 and e×d5 Black could not take on d5 with the pawn in view of the weakening of his b5 square.

8 Re1	Nc7

Black has carried out his plan, and prevents the bishop at c1 from taking up a convenient post (9 Bg5—9 ... Ne6). On the other hand, his queen's knight cannot be called active, and this must be considered an achievement for White. Also, Black cannot hope to advance ... e5.

9 Bf1

It would have been inexcusably careless to hope that my opponent would not be familiar with the game Geller–Panno, Bogota, 1978, and that after 9 a4 he would repeat the mistake made there by Black, 9 ... b6?!, after which White mounted strong pressure, and then an attack: 10 Bf4 Bb7 11 Qd2 Re8 12 Rad1 Qd7 13 Bh6 a6 14 e5! Nfd5 15 B×g7 K×g7 16 Ng5.

9 ...	d5
10 e5	Nfe8
11 Ne2	

While Black is unable to play ... c5, White transfers his "unemployed" knight to an active post at f4.

11 ...	Ne6
12 Nf4	

Again the undermining of the centre by the c-pawn is impossible, while White does not fear the exchange on f4 ...

12 ...	N8c7

After 12 ... N×f4 13 B×f4 Nc7 14 Qd2 Ne6 15 Bh6 White retains his opening advantage: Black cannot get by without ... f6, but on this White exchanges bishops, doubles rooks on the e-file, and later advances c2–c4. But after the move played Black is obviously cramped.

13 Nd3!

Avoiding the now unnecessary exchange, and again stopping the black c-pawn.

13 ...	f5
14 e×f6	

The aims of the two sides are diametrically opposed. Black is trying, in spite of the limited mobility of his pieces, to block the position, while for White it is essential to open it up — only then will the more harmonious development of his forces tell.

14 ...	e×f6

15 a4!

At first sight a pointless move. But the weakening of the enemy K-side can be exploited only by starting a battle in the centre. Hence White's plan: b2–b3 and c2–c4. But first it is useful to cramp Black on the Q-side, especially since this is achieved without loss of time: the white bishop is provided with a good post at a3.

15 ...	a5
16 b3	Re8
17 Ba3	Bf8?

It is natural that Black should want to exchange off the opponent's strong bishop, and at the same time obtain the d6 square for his queen. But in doing so he markedly weakens the position of his king. Interesting therefore was 17 ... Bh6!?, halting for the moment the advance c2–c4. But it would seem that Black had not yet guessed his opponent's intention.

18 B×f8	R×f8

To be considered was 18 ... N×f8, although even then White retains the initiative after 19 Qd2 and c2–c4. And in any case the exchange of bishops has made the weakness at f6 more acute.

19 Qd2	Qd6
20 Rad1	b6
21 Qc1	

Completing the preparations for c2–c4.

21 ...	Ba6
22 c4	Qd7

Parrying the unpleasant threat of 23 c5. Unsatisfactory was 22 ... d×c4 23 b×c4 N×d4 in view of 24 N×d4 Q×d4 25 Ne5 Qh4 (or *25 ... Qc5 26 Nd7*) 26 N×c6, with complete domination by the white pieces.

23 Nf4

The black knights are defending each other, and after the exchange of one of them the other is deprived of its "strong point". In addition, the opposition of the bishops favours White: in certain variations the bishop at a6 can be "hanging".

23 ...	N×f4
24 Q×f4	Rad8

The validity of the previous comment would have been confirmed after 24 ... Rae8 — 25 R×e8 N×e8 26 c×d5, and after 26 ... B×f1 27 d×c6 Black loses a pawn.

The point of the move played is to defend the queen and to prepare to switch the knight via e6 to g7, and, if possible, to f5. On the immediate 24 ... Ne6?! White would have replied 25 Qg4, pinning the knight.

25 Re3	Ne6

Black should have gone totally onto the defensive — 25 ... Bb7 26 Rde1 Rf7.

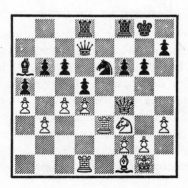

26 R×e6!	Q×e6
27 c×d5	Qc8
28 B×a6	Q×a6
29 d×c6	

Two strong passed pawns are more than sufficient compensation for the exchange. The rest can be regarded as a matter of technique, although the game continues to remain interesting and sharp, especially in view of the mutual shortage of time.

29 ...	g5
30 Qc1	

With the threat of 31 Qc4+, exchanging queens.

30 ...	Rd6
31 d5	Rfd8
32 Nd4	

The threats of 33 Nf5 and Nb5 force Black to swim with the current.

32 ...	R×d5
33 c7	Re8
34 Qc6	Qa8

White wins immediately after 34 ... Rde5 35 Nf3.

35 Q×b6

In time trouble White overlooks a quicker win: 35 c8=Q! R×c8 36 Qe6+ Kh8 (or *36 ... Kg7 37 Nf5+ and 38 R×d5*) 37 Q×f6+ Kg8 38 Nf5!, and if Black takes the rook, after 39 Kh2 one of the three mates is guaranteed.

35 ...	Qc8
36 Rc1	Qd7
37 Nb5	g4
38 Qa6	g×h3
39 c8=Q	Rd1+
40 R×d1	Q×d1+
41 Kh2	Resigns

Alekhine's Defence

No. 39 Alekhine's Defence

Geller–Bronstein

Interzonal Tournament
Petropolis, 1973

A reserve variation

During this game I suddenly sensed that my opponent was aiming to obtain the same position as had occurred in my game with Hecht at the tournament in Budapest six months earlier. What did David Bronstein have in mind: to follow an improvement suggested by me, or to try some other possibility? Only he can give the answer to this. Even so, I think that I guessed my opponent's intention, and so on the 15th move I switched to a reserve variation. It was fortunate that after my game with Hecht I had also studied this line. . . .

Black, being denied his secret weapon, proved to be unprepared, and he promptly committed a serious mistake.

1 e4	Nf6
2 e5	Nd5
3 d4	d6
4 Nf3	Bg4
5 Be2	e6
6 0–0	Be7
7 h3	

An important move, the main point of which is revealed in the normal variation 7 c4 Nb6 8 e×d6 c×d6 9 Nc3 0–0 10 Be3 Nc6 11 d5 e×d5 12 N×d5 13 Q×d5. Here, if he is seeking equality, Black plays 13 ... Bf6 (for example, Lein–Smyslov, 34th USSR Championship, 1967), or he can go in for complications — 13 ... Be6 14 Qd2 d5?! After the inclusion of the moves 7 h3 Bh5,

in this variation Black's bishop comes under attack, and he has to waste a tempo, which gives White a clear advantage: 14 ... Bg6 Rad1.

7 ...	Bh5
8 c4	Nb6
9 Nc3	0–0
10 Be3	d5

Black begins an immediate battle for the c4 square.

11 c5	B×f3

After 11 ... Nc4 12 B×c4 d×c4 Black, not without reason, fears for the safety of his c4 pawn.

12 B×f3

The recommendation of 12 g×f3 followed by f3–f4 seems highly dubious to me.

12 ...	Nc4

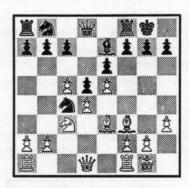

The key position of this variation. In the first instance White must decide what to do with his black-squared bishop. 13 Bc1 delays the development of his Q-side, and by undermining the centre with ... b6 and ... f6 Black obtains satisfactory play. In the 19th game of his match with Fischer (Reykjavik, 1972), Spassky tried 13 b3, giving up his bishop, which also appears dubious.

In my game with Hecht (Budapest, 1973) I had preserved my bishop by 13 Bf4. Now 13 ... N×b2 14 Qb3 gives White a marked advantage, while after 13 ... Bg5 14 B×g5 Q×g5 15 b3 Black cannot play 15 ... Nd2 because of 16 B×d5! and 17 f4 (*16 ... N×f1 17 B×b7 Ne3 18 Qd2*). Therefore 15 ... Na5 is forced, when 16 Be2 and 17 f4 allows White to reinforce his centre and gain the initiative.

In the present game, too, I decided to retain my bishop.

13 Bf4	Nc6
14 b3	N4a5
15 Rc1	

Against Hecht I played 15 Qd2 (preventing ... *Bg5*) 15 ... b6 16 Racl b×c5 17 d×c5. Here Black made a mistake — 17 ... B×c5, and after 18 N×d5 he quickly lost. Digressing slightly, it should be mentioned that in this system attacks on the apparently strong d5 point occur fairly often, and Black must constantly keep this in mind in his calculations.

Annotating this game later in *Informator*, I suggested for Black 17 ... Rb8, which in view of the threat of ... Rb4 virtually forces White into the double-edged 18 B×d5 e×d5 19 N×d5 followed by b3-b4. I would not have objected to such a position with White, but at the board I suddenly thought: what if Bronstein should play not 17 ... Rb8, but 17 ... Qb8? White then has to forget about

the d5 square, and in reserve Black may find some improvement.

Having weighed all this up, I switched to another variation. The decision proved correct, since Bronstein stubbornly continued trying to draw me into repeating the game with Hecht. Thus, instead of the move in the game, Black could have continued 15 ... f6 or 15 ... Bg5, to which in the latter case White would have replied 16 B×g5 Q×g5 17 Bg4, preparing 18 f4, and on 17 ... Qf4 — 18 Ne2.

15 ...	b6
16 Na4	

16 Qd2 would have led by transposition of moves to the position that my opponent was wanting.

| 16 ... | b5? |

A strategic mistake. By closing the game on the Q-side, Black relieves White of any worries over his c5 square, and allows him to concentrate his forces on maintaining control of e5. Here, too, he should have considered 16 ... f6 or 16 ... Bg5.

17 Nc3	b4
18 Ne2	f6

Now 18 ... Bg5 no longer achieves its aim: the d4 square is securely defended, and White is able to carry out the plan indicated in the note to his 15th move.

19 e×f6	B×f6
20 Bg4	Qd7
21 Qd3	a6

White was threatening by 22 Qa6 to tie down both the enemy knights.

22 Rce1	Qf7
23 Bh2	Rfe8
24 Rd1	

By the threat of 24 Nf4 White diverted the black rook from the f-file, and now he sets about implementing the plan of a direct attack on the K-side. For a certain time I hesitated over whether to play 24 f4 followed by Kh1 and Ng1–f3, but then I decided that such a regrouping was too slow.

By the move in the game White securely defends his d4, and at the same time prevents a possible ... e5.

24 ...	Nb7
25 Kh1	Nbd8
26 f4	

Forcing Black, in passing, to parry the unpleasant f4–f5, which weakens still further position of his king.

26 ...	g6
27 Bf3	

Finally choosing in favour of the pawn storm: it was not yet too late to transfer the knight to e5.

27 ...	Ne7
28 g4	Ndc6
29 f5	e×f5

Perhaps Black should have sacrificed a pawn, and sought salvation in the ending after 29 ... e5 30 d×e5 N×e5 31 B×e5 B×e5 32 f×g6 Q×g6 33 Q×g6+ h×g6 34 B×d5+ N×d5 35 R×d5.

30 B×c7	Kh8
31 Bh2	Red8
32 Qe3	

White intends by 33 g5 to cramp his opponent completely, then place his knight at f4 and begin advancing his h-pawn (*h3–h4–h5*), after first seizing the e-file.

32 ...	g5

An act of desperation, but it is difficult to offer Black any good advice.

33 g×f5	N×f5
34 Qf2	

The impression is that Black's position will disintegrate at any moment, but by heroic efforts Bronstein somehow manages to hold on.

34 ...	Ng7
35 Bg4	Rf8
36 Be5	Ne8
37 Ng3	Ra7
38 Bh5	Qg8
39 Qb2	

After the direct 39 B×e8 N×e5 40 d×e5 Bg7 Black can hold on.

39 ...	B×e5

Now 39 ... N×e5 is unpleasant in view of 40 d×e5 Bg7 41 Nf5, and after the exchange on g7 the opposition of the white queen and black king on the a1–h8 diagonal is not in favour of the latter. ...

40 d×e5	d4

Blocking the long black diagonal, and preparing ... Qd5.

41 R×f8	Q×f8

42 Rf1	

The sealed move. Black finds the best reply.

42 ...	Qg8

On 42 ... Qe7 White had prepared 43 Qf2 Nc7 44 Nf5, with a very strong attack.

43 Qf2	Ng7
44 Bf7	Qd8
45 Bc4	Ra8
46 Ne4	Nh5

Up to here everything had strictly followed my adjournment analysis. I did not consider Black's last move, but in this position a virtually universal winning continuation was found to be 47 Nd6. It would also have worked here: On 47 ... Qe7 there would have followed 48 Qf3, on 47 ... Qd7 — 48 e6, and on 47 ... N×e5 — 48 Re1.

Changing plan (after lengthy reflection!), I was tempted by some mating threats, and thus allowed Black to prolong the struggle.

47 Qf7	Nf4

All very simple. It turns out that on 48 Nf6 Black has the reply 48 ... Ra7!

48 Qb7	Na5
49 Qf7	Ng6

Black does not even attempt to repeat the position, since on 49 ... Nc6 White replies 50 Qf5 h6 51 h4. In addition, he hopes to get rid of the strong bishop at c4.

50 Bd5	Rc8
51 Nd6	

At last!

51 ...	Rc7

The c5 pawn is taboo: 51 ... R×c5 52 Qa7 Qc7 53 Qa8+.

52 Qf5	Qe7
53 Nf7+	Kg7
54 N×g5	Rd7
55 e6	Rc7
56 N×h7	

Black overstepped the time limit, but all the same his game is lost. After 56 ... K×h7 White wins by 57 Qh5+ Kg7 58 Rf7+ or 58 Rg1.

Queen's Gambit

No. 40 Queen's Gambit

Geller–Fuderer

*Interzonal Tournament
Göteborg, 1955*

Check equals mate

How often is it impossible to evaluate correctly the nature of the struggle in a game, without referring to the tournament positions of the players and to the purely competitive aims facing them at the given moment! This game with Andrija Fuderer is a striking confirmation of this. It took place in the 17th round, and was preceded by the following circumstances.

After starting the tournament with a win,

in the next nine games I did not manage to gain a single victory, whereas I lost three games, and after eleven rounds I was sharing places 15–19 out of the 21 competitors. It was stipulated that the first nine players would go through to the Candidates Tournament, and all I could do was to pin my hopes on the second half of the event. Experience told me that to my 4 points I would have to add a further 7–8 out of 10, in order to be one of the nine. This would not have been easy, even if I had been in good form. And if my form was letting me down, without drastic chess measures such a result was simply impossible.

It is true that by the game with Fuderer I was already sharing 7th place. But, firstly, he was a rival, and was only half a point behind me. Secondly, a win would practically ensure me a place in the Candidates Tournament. And thirdly—and this is perhaps the most important factor—from inertia I was unable to switch suddenly to quiet play "with the draw in hand". Finally, there was the obligation of having the white pieces. . . .

1 d4	d5
2 c4	e6
3 Nc3	c6
4 Nf3	Nf6
5 e3	a6
6 Bd3	Ndb7
7 0–0	

7 e4 is more energetic. Now a position from the Queen's Gambit Accepted is reached, where White has lost a tempo on Bd3×c4, and Black on . . . c6–c5.

7 . . .	d×c4
8 B×c4	b5
9 Bb3	

If it returns to d3, the bishop weakens the subsequent pressure of the white rook on the d-file, and the advances e3–e4 and (should the possibility arise) d4–d5 will not be so dangerous for Black.

9 . . .	c5
10 Qe2	Bb7
11 Rd1	Qc7

Black avoids the most commonly occurring continuations in this problem position (*11 . . . Be7*, *11 . . . b4*, *11 . . . Qb8* and *11 . . . Bd6*, the latter, however, only being suggested in 1959), and White has to make a crucial choice regarding his subsequent plan. He has the following possibilities:

(*a*) 12 d5 N×d5 (after *12 . . . e×d5* Black has to reckon with *13 e4*, and if *13 . . . d×e4*, then *14 Ng5 c4 15 Nc×e4*, while on *13 . . . d4* there can follow *14 Nd5*) 13 N×d5 B×d5 14 B×d5 e×d5 15 R×d5, or first 15 a4.

(*b*) 12 e4 c×d4 13 N×d4 Bc5 14 B×e6, with great complications.

The attempt by White to maintain the tension in the centre, without disclosing his plans, relieves Black of his opening difficulties. Thus in the game Furman–Uusi (Semi-Final of the 22nd USSR Championship, Gorky, 1954) after 12 a3 Bd6 Black easily equalized.

White chooses a new but highly-risky path, involving the sacrifice of a piece. The reasons for such a decision are described in some detail in the introduction to the game. It can also be added that the 24-year-old Fuderer, a talented international master, himself liked—and was highly capable of!—attacking, and I naturally wanted to force him to solve defensive problems.

12 e4	c×d4

13 Nd5!?	e×d5
14 e×d5+	Be7

How should White continue the attack? On 15 R×d4 there follows 15 . . . Kf8! 16 Bf4 Bd6 17 Rc1 Qb8, and there is nothing obvious. However, the move played should not, against best defence, have proved successful.

15 Bg5	Nc5?

Black wants to retain the right to castle, but he should have sacrificed it by 15 . . . Kf8! The position is so sharp that one mistake by the opponent suffices for White to gain a decisive advantage.

16 d6!	Q×d6
14 N×d4	Nce4

After 17 ... Nfe4 18 B×e7 Q×e7 19 Nf5 the knight check at d6 wins outright.

18 Ne6!

A stroke which Black had failed to take into account. He had reckoned only with 18 Nf5. Now on 18 ... Qe5 White plays 19 Bf4, trapping the queen in the centre of the board, while 18 ... f×e6 or 18 ... Q×e6 leaves him with a very strong attack.

18 ...	Qc6
19 N×g7+	Kf8
20 Bh6	Kg8
21 Qf3	

White would also appear to win by 21 Bd5, and if 21 ... N×d5, then 22 Nf5 with numerous threats: 23 R×d5 followed by 24 N×e7, 23 Qg4+. ... In general, the position of the black king is so unfortunate that the first check may essentially be equivalent to mate.

The move in the game pursues two aims. One of them is to forestall a possible counter-attack by Black along the a8–h1 diagonal. The other, which follows from the first, is to prepare 22 Rac1 (which did not work a move earlier because of *21 ... Nc3*), and in event of 22 ... Qb6—to invade with the rook at d7.

21 ...	Bc5
22 Rac1	B×f2+

A problem-like mate could have resulted after 22 ... Qb6 23 Rd7 Rf8 24 R×b7 Q×b7 (or *24 ... B×f2+ 25 Kh1 Q×b7 26 Nf5 Rd8 27 Bd5! R×d5 28 Rc8+*) 25 R×c5 N×c5 26 Qg3 Nce4 27 Nh5+ N×g3 28 N×f6 mate.

23 Q×f2	N×f2

On 23 ... Q×c1 White wins elegantly by the same motifs: 24 R×c1 N×f2 25 Nf5 Re8 26 Rc7 Bd5 27 Rc8, etc.

24 R×c6	N6g4

Both white rooks are immune: 24 ... B×c6 25 Nf5 Re8 26 Rd8!, or 24 ... N×d1 25 R×f6 Rf8 26 Nh5 with an inevitable and pretty mate after 27 Rg6+ h×g6 28 Nf6. Black also loses after 24 ... N2g4 25 Nf5 N×h6 26 R×f6 N×f5 27 R×f7.

25 B×f7+	K×f7
26 Rc7+	

It is not surprising that the calculation of the rather complex variations had demanded of White a mass of time, and he was in serious time trouble. Hence the check with the wrong rook. He could have won immediately by 26 Rd7+ Kg8 27 Ne6, and mate next move.

26 ...	Kg8

It is easy to check that moving into the centre — 26 ... Kf6 27 Rd6+ Ke5 28 Re6+ etc. — would not have saved Black.

27 Rdd7

Again 27 Ne6 would have led to mate.

27 ...	Bd5
28 R×d5	N×h6
29 Ne6	

At last!

29 ...	Nf7
30 Rg5+	Resigns

No. 41 Queen's Gambit

Geller–Unzicker

Interzonal Tournament
Stockholm, 1952

A step towards the truth

In top class events it comparatively rarely happens that the competitors play the opening part of the game (and, hence, the entire game, since in my opinion the study of the opening is fruitful only when it develops into the study of the middlegame and even the endgame) "at sight". Whether or not it is apparent to the chess world, behind each victory or defeat is invariably concealed a history of searchings, findings, and disappointments.

The game with Wolfgang Unzicker is an example of this. The Slav Gambit offered by White was introduced anew into the practice of Soviet players by Tolush in a game against Smyslov (15th USSR Championship, 1947). Then for many years the gambit served as a testing ground, on which were constantly improved the strength of White's blows and the soundness of Black's defences. I tried to vindicate the critical position of the gambit for White. I consider it not altogether right that nowadays the gambit should have disappeared from the scene, since it leads to interesting play, rich in chances for both sides.

I had twice played the Slav Gambit against Smyslov, and prior to the present game the "incident" in the 13th round of the 19th USSR Championship was still fresh in everyone's memory. There in the twin games Geller–Flohr and Petrosian–Smyslov White rather quickly lost the opening battle. For this reason, obviously, Unzicker quite calmly accepted the challenge.

1 d4	d5
2 c4	c6

Already here Black declares that he is ready to undergo the testing by gambit, since he can hardly be happy to transpose on the 4th move into the old Orthodox or Cambridge-Springs Defences (by *4 . . . e6*).

3 Nf3	Nf6
4 Nc3	d×c4
5 e4	b5
6 e5	

More flexible play results from 6 Qc2, as Spassky later used to continue.

6 . . .	Nd5
7 a4	e6

In the aforementioned game with Tolush, Smyslov played 7 . . . Be6, but practice showed this move to be poor, and supporters of the gambit for Black (in particular, Smyslov himself) switched to 7 . . . e6.

8 a×b5	

Also perfectly possible is 8 Be2, which has been successfully tried (the game Borisenko–Flohr, Semi-Final of the 19th USSR Championship, Lvov, 1951, where from the opening Black gained the advantage, should be ignored). In the games Geller–Smyslov (18th USSR Championship, 1950, and Budapest, 1952) White from the opening gained excellent play, which in addition is of a less forcing nature that in the present game. But I was intending to improve White's play in comparison with the aforementioned twin games.

8 . . .	N×c3
9 b×c3	c×b5
10 Ng5	Bb7
11 Qh5	

White tries to provoke a pawn weakening on the K-side, and otherwise in certain variations there is the threat of N×h7–f6+.

11 . . .	g6

The natural reaction. Later 11 . . . Qd7 was tried, after which White's uncertain play in the game Bagirov–Demirkhanian, USSR, 1963 — 12 N×h7 Qd5 13 Nf6+ g×f6 14 Q×h8 b4 15 Be2 Q×g2 16 Rf1 Qe4 17 Bh6 Nd7 18 B×f8 N×f8 19 c×b4 Q×d4 20 Rc1 Rd8 led even to an advantage for Black. But 12 Be2 (with the threat of *Bf3*) gives White the better game after 12 ... Na6 13 N×h7 0–0–0 14 N×f8. Besides, an interesting position also arises in this variation after the untried 13 d5!?

| 12 Qg4 | Be7 |
| 13 Be2 | |

Also to be considered is 13 h4 h5, and now not 14 Qg3, which is mentioned by Flohr in his comments to a game with me (*Shakhmaty v SSSR*, 1952, No.3), but 14 Qf4, forcing 14 ... B×g5 15 h×g5 and fixing Black's pawn weaknesses on the K-side.

| 13 ... | Nd7 |
| 14 Bf3 | |

In the aforementioned twin games, both I and Petrosian played 14 h4?, when Black gained good defensive possibilities: 14...h5 15 Qg3 (with the black pawn at h5, *15 Qf4 B×g5 17 h×g5* no longer has any point) 15...Nb6 16 0–0 a5!, when he seized the initiative. I continued 17 Rb1 b4 18 f4 Qd7 19 Ra1 b3, and lost. Petrosian, who had delayed his decision, saw that White stood badly, and so he tried for complications by 17 d5!? Smyslov promptly went wrong with

17 ... N×d5? (*17 ... B×d5* was essential, not allowing the white knight to reach *e4*), and went on to lose.

14 Bf3 was recommended after the twin games by Lilienthal and Petrosian, and in the present game was being tried for the first time. True, the authors of the move thought that Black could continue simply 14 ... B×f3 15 Q×f3 0–0, but then 16 h4 maintains good attacking chances against the black king.

| 14 ... | Qc7 |

Unzicker follows a recommendation by Flohr. Probably better is 14 ... Qc8, defending e6 in readiness for a possible ... f5. For example, if White plays 15 Ne4, as in the game, then after 15 ... 0–0 16 Bh6 f5! 17 e×f6 18 N×f6+ R×f6 Black gains the advantage. Therefore White would have continued 15 h4, provoking a further weakening of Black's K-side.

| 15 Ne4 | Nb6 |
| 16 Bh6 | |

16 Bg5 is also good. But White wishes to place his bishop on g5 only after the black knight has gone to d5, when Black cannot take with his bishop on e4. In addition, 17 Bg7 Rg8 18 Nf6+ is now threatened.

| 16 ... | Rg8? |

A mistake, of course, but how is Black to continue? If 16...B×e4, then 17 B×e4 Nd5 18 B×d5 e×d5, when possible is either the explosive 19 e6 f5 20 Qf3, or the quieter 19 0–0. He would have probably have had to reconcile himself to 16...Nd5 17 Bg5 0–0 18 B×e7 Q×e7 19 Nf6+, when White's initiative appears pretty formidable.

17 Bg5	B×e4
18 B×e4	Nd5
19 B×d5	e×d5
20 B×e7	Q×e7

21 0–0

The exchange of all the minor pieces has not eased Black's position. His rooks are disconnected, and his king is in the centre. The position continues to be very much a middlegame one.

It hardly has to be said that the pawn sacrificed by White is a small price to pay for all these advantages.

21 ...   Kf8

Unzicker contemplates artificial castling, in order to avoid a direct attack.

22 Rfb1   a6
23 Qf3!

Much stronger than 23 R×b5 a×b5 24 R×a8+ Kg7, when the weakness of White's c-pawn prevents him from winning. In general, Black would be glad to return the pawn to go into an ending.

23 ...   Qe6?

Now Black is quickly crushed. Correct was 23...Kg7, although his position would remain very difficult, for example, 24 Q×d5 Rgd8 25 Qe4 Qe6 26 f4 (but not *26 R×b5 a×b5 27 R×a8 R×a8 28 Q×a8 Qf5 29 Qa1 Qc2*) 26...f5 27 Qf3, and if 27...Rd5, then 28 R×b5.

24 Qf6!

Even without the queens White maintains a mating attack on the king: 24...Q×f6 25 e×f6 g5 26 R×b5 Rg6 27 R×a6!, etc. Objectively speaking, Black could have resigned at this point.

24 ...   Qc8
25 f4   Qb7
26 Ra5   Ke8
27 Rba1   b4

Desperation.

28 c×b4   Q×b4
29 R×d5   Qb7
30 e6   Resigns

No. 42 Queen's Gambit

Geller–Keres

*Interzonal Tournament
Petropolis, 1973*

Victory through simplification

Early exchanges do not necessarily signify that the players, or at least one of them, are in a peaceable mood. Thus in the present game an endgame was reached practically straight after the opening. But in agreeing to, and sometimes provoking exchanges, White constantly maintained the slight advantage gained back in the opening. And when there were few forces remaining on the board, the black pieces were unable to cope with their increased work load. ...

1 c4	c6
2 d4	d5
3 Nf3	Nf6
4 Nc3	e6
5 Bg5	h6
6 B×f6	

From time to time in my games I resort to this exchange, exploiting the fact that the black queen is not altogether well placed at f6. This is of no small significance, as was confirmed, for example, by the games Geller–Botvinnik, Moscow, 1959, and Geller–Tal, Moscow, 1966.

6 ...	Q×f6
7 e3	Nd7
8 Bd3	Bb4

In the aforementioned game Tal continued 8 ... Bd6, and after 9 0–0 Qe7 10 c5 Bc7! 11 b4 e5 12 e4! White gained the better chances. Keres plays against me the same move that almost twenty years earlier I myself played against Petrosian.

| 9 0–0 | Qe7 |
| 10 a3 | B×c3 |

In the game Petrosian–Geller, Moscow, 1954, I attempted to retain the two bishops— 10 ... Ba5, but the loss of time proved highly significant.

| 11 b×c3 | 0–0 |

An apparently imperceptible, but serious inaccuracy. It was essential to exchange first by 11 ... d×c4, and only then play 12 ... 0–0 or immediately 12 ... e5. Now White himself exchanges on d5, depriving the opponent of a possible pawn counter in the centre, and Black has serious difficulties over the development of his Q-side.

| 12 c×d5 | e×d5 |
| 13 a4 | |

Intending by the advance of the a-pawn to block Black's Q-side pawn majority.

| 13 ... | Rd8 |

Black vacates a square for his knight, since he has to develop his queen's wing, and 13 ... Nf6 concedes e5 to White: 14 Ne5 and then, in case of necessity, f2–f4.

| 14 a5 | Nf8 |
| 15 Qa4 | |

Now the road for White's king's rook to the Q-side is open!

| 15 ... | Bd7 |

Black's rooks are at last connected, but, alas, not for long.

| 16 Rfb1 | Rb8 |
| 17 Qa3 | |

The simplest. With the exchange of queens a number of vulnerable points are created in the black position, and the attempt to avoid the exchange leads after 18 Qc5 a6 to the total blockade of Black's Q-side. In this case White's hands would be completely freed for action on the other parts of the board.

| 17 ... | Q×a3 |
| 18 R×a3 | c5 |

Black cannot "stand still": the threat was Rab3, Ba6 and Ne5.

19 Ra2	Rdc8
20 Rab2	Rc7
21 h3	

The point of this move is not only to create an escape square for the king, as becomes clear slightly later.

| 21 ... | Ne6 |
| 22 Ne5 | Bc8 |

The bishop has returned home, and Black's Q-side is again undeveloped.

23 Bf5	Kf8
24 Bg4	

The outline of White's plan takes shape: the bishop is securely defended by the h3 pawn, and the knight can head via d3 to c5.

24 ...	c×d4
25 c×d4	Rc3

Black seeks counter-play, by attacking the white a-pawn from the rear. Possible now was 26 B×e6 f×e6, when the knight dominates over the bishop, but White also has no objection to exchanges: he retains all the advantages of his position.

26 Rb3	R×b3
27 R×b3	b5

This leads to loss of material, but Black is no longer able to parry the threat of 28 Bf3.

28 Bf3	b4
29 Nc6	Rb7
30 B×d5	

White is a pawn up, and — more important —each of his pieces is more active than its black opponent. There are several ways to win, and the remainder does not require any commentary.

30 ...	Bd7
31 Ne5	Ba4
32 B×b7	B×b3
33 Nd3	Ke7

34 N×b4	Kd6
35 f3	f5
36 Bc8	g5
37 B×e6	B×e6
38 f4	g×f4
39 e×f4	Bc4
40 Kf2	Be6
41 Kf3	Bb3
42 g4	

42 ... Ke6 was sealed, but **Black resigned** without resuming.

No. 43 Queen's Gambit

Geller–Ivkov

Beverwijk, 1965

The dominant queen

On finding himself in a difficult position, Black parted with his queen, for which he gained a sufficient material equivalent. The different "calibres" of the forces remaining on the board demanded of White especially energetic play, and at times there was only one correct continuation. As a rule, this always occurs when a queen has to battle against several pieces. Factors which acquire particular importance in such cases are the security of the kings, together with the presence and also the mobility of passed pawns.

1 d4	d5
2 c4	e6
3 Nc3	Be7
4 Nf3	Nf6
5 Bg5	h6
6 B×f6	

In this way White tries to gain time, and, if the opportunity should arise, to obtain after c×d5 e×d5 a position from the Exchange Variation with an extra tempo. Of course, Black also acquires some plusses:

two bishops, which after a possible ... c5 can become highly formidable.

6 ...	B×f6
7 e3	0–0
8 Rc1	

An important link in Black's subsequent plan is the undermining ... c5, against which this move is directed. 8 Qc2, which occurred in earlier games (for example, Opocensky–Alekhine, Munich, 1941), allows Black an equal game by 8 ... c5, both after 9 0–0–0 c×d4 10 e×d4 Nc6 11 h4 Qc7 (Udovcic–Ivkov, Yugoslavia, 1956), and after K-side castling: 9 d×c5 Qa5 10 Be2 d×c4 11 0–0 B×c3 (Winter–Bondarevsky, Match Great Britain–USSR, 1947).

The immediate ... c5 can also be prevented by 8 Qb3, which, nevertheless, also allows Black equality: 8 ... d×c4 9 B×c4 c5 10 d×c5 Qa5 11 0–0 Nd7 12 Ne4 Be7 13 Rc1 N×c5 (Szabó–Gligoric, Helsinki, 1952).

| 8 ... | b6 |

In the given situation this system of development is hardly justified, since it leads to weaknesses on Black's Q-side. 8 ... Re8 also causes him considerable trouble after 9 Be2 d×c4 10 B×c4 Nd7 11 0–0 c5 12 Ne4! Correct is 8 ... c6 9 Bd3 Nd7 10 0–0 d×c4 11 B×c4 e5, with a reasonable game.

| 9 c×d5 | e×d5 |
| 10 Bd3 | Bb7 |

10 ... Be6 looks sounder, but even then 11 0–0 Bd7 12 e4 c6 13 e×d5 c×d5 15 Nb5 gives White significantly the better chances.

| 11 0–0 | Qe7 |

Black is already in difficulties. Thus White has an appreciable advantage after 11 ... c5 12 d×c5 b×c5 13 Qb3 Qd7 14 Bb5 Qd8 15 Rfd1, or 11 ... Nd7 12 Qb3 c6 13 e4. Comparatively best was 11 ... Re8.

12 Re1

Immediately exploiting the positioning of the queen on a file which may be opened.

| 12 ... | c5 |
| 13 e4 | d×e4 |

A pawn is lost after 13 ... c×d4 14 N×d5 B×d5 15 e×d5 Qd6 (*15 ... Qb4* is well met by *16 b3*, as well as the more active *16 Rc7!*) 16 Be4.

| 14 N×e4 | c×d4 |

The best chance. Totally bad is 14 ... Qd8 15 d×c5 B×b2 16 Rc2 Ba3 17 Nd6 Bc6 18 N×f7!, and wins.

| 15 Nc5 | Q×c5 |
| 16 R×c5 | b×c5 |

For the queen Black has obtained rook, bishop, and a strong pawn in the centre. White is required to play very precisely and actively.

| 17 Ne5! | B×e5 |

Otherwise the knight cannot be developed. 17 ... Re8 allows White by 18 Ng4 Nd7 19 R×e8+ R×e8 20 Bb5 Bc8 (*20 ... Rd8 21 B×d7 R×d7 22 N×f6+* and *23 Qg4+*) 21 N×f6+ to spoil Black's K-side pawn formation, and to retain an obvious advantage after 21 ... g×f6 22 h3 (with the threat of *23 Qa4*).

| 18 R×e5 | Nd7 |
| 19 Re7 | Bc6 |

20 h3	Rfe8
21 Qe1	Nb6
22 b3	

The two sides' chances have become clarified. The c5 pawn is securely blockaded, and Black must make every effort to remove the blockading bishop at d3. White, on the other hand, tries with his queen and bishop to worry the black king, while keeping control over a possible advance of the black d-pawn, and intending, should the opportunity arise, to penetrate with his queen onto the Q-side.

22 ...	Nd5
23 R×e8+	R×e8
24 Qc1	

The need for accuracy by White is excellently illustrated by the variation 24 Qa5 Nf4!

24 ...	Nc3
25 Kh2	

By removing his king from a possible check on the back rank, White restricts the opponent's tactical chances, prompts him to part with the open e-file, and begins the implementation of his basic plan.

25 ...	Rd8
26 Qf4	Nd5
27 Qf5	

27 Qe5 was slightly better, so as to meet 27 ... Nb4 with 28 Qc7. But I wanted to provoke 27 ... g6, so as to obtain possible access to f6. For example, 28 Qe5 Nb4 29 Bc4 d3 (29 ... Bd5 30 Qe7) 30 Qf6.

27 ...	Nb4
28 Qh7+	

"Pawn-grabbing" by 28 Q×c5 would have allowed Black to face the future with confidence after 28 ... N×d3 29 Q×c6 Nf4 followed by ... Ne6.

28 ...	Kf8
29 Bc4	Bd5

The attempt to advance the d-pawn leads to its loss: 29 ... d3 30 Qf5 Bd5 31 B×d3.

30 Bf1!

The only move. Now the threat of 31 Qh8+ forces Black to weaken all the white squares on the K-side.

30 ...	f6
31 a3	

The immediate "exploitation" of the weakening by 31 Qh8+ Bg8 32 Bc4 would have given winning chances to ... Black: 32 ... Nd5. Therefore the knight must be driven away from where it controls d5, and the coordination of the black pieces destroyed.

31 ...	Na2
32 Qh8+	Ke7
33 Q×g7+	Bf7
34 Bc4	Rf8
35 Qh7!	

The h6 pawn is of no significance. White's task is to neutralize the pawn pair c5–d4.

35 ...	Nc3
36 Qf5	B×c4

There is nothing else.

37 Q×c5+	Ke6
38 Q×c4+	Ke5
39 Qc5+	

Ivkov was in time trouble, and from inertia he makes a further couple of moves.

39 ...	Ke4
40 Q×f8	Kd3
41 Q×f6	Resigns

No. 44 Queen's Gambit

Romanishin–Geller

*46th USSR Championship
Tbilisi, 1978*

A rule is a rule!

Modern-day chess differs greatly from that which was played forty to fifty years ago. Much has changed regarding ideas about weaknesses, about methods of defence and counter-attack, and about the value of entire opening systems. But in this game my opponent broke an old rule, which even today holds true. The essence of it is: do not open up the position when the opponent has two bishops...

1 d4	d5
2 c4	e6
3 Nf3	Nf6
4 Nc3	Be7
5 Bg5	h6
6 B×f6	B×f6
7 e4	

This does not yet give Black an advantage, but it is the first step along an erroneous path. While the exchange on the previous move can be explained and understood—White did not wish to lose a tempo—the opening of the centre is obviously imprudent. However, the entire plan was prepared by White beforehand, in his home laboratory.

Better and more natural is 7 e3.

| 7 ... | d×e4 |
| 8 N×e4 | Nc6 |

It was tempting, of course, to retain the two bishops, but Black rightly considers it more promising to play to "outstrip" his opponent: he is the first to create pressure on the centre, by attacking the d4 pawn.

9 d5?

Now Black's position is preferable. In the following round Belyavsky repeated my opponent's opening experiment, against Georgadze, and hastened at least to deprive Black of the advantage of the two bishops by playing 9 N×f6+ Q×f6 10 Qd3, in the end managing to maintain equality. (A game Tatai–Geller, Las Palmas, 1979, continued *10 ... b6 11 Qe4 Bb7 12 Ne5 0-0-0 13 N×c6 Rd6 14 N×a7+ Kb8 15 Qe5 K×a7*, with an equal game.) But here the game is opened up even more, which is to Black's advantage.

| 9 ... | Ne5 |
| 10 Be2 | 0-0 |

It was possible to win a pawn, but the threat is stronger than its execution. White would have been very happy with 10 ... N×f3+ 11 B×f3 B×b2 12 Rb1 Be5 13 Qa4+ Bd7 (*13 ... Qd7 14 Q×d7+ K×d7 15 d×e6+ and 16 Nc5+*) 14 Qa3.

| 11 Qb3 | e×d5 |
| 12 c×d5 | |

| 12 ... | c6! |
| 13 Rd1 | |

After 13 d×c6 N×f3+ 14 B×f3 Qa5+ 15 Kf1 Qa6+ 16 Kg1 Q×c6 the white king is on "its" square, but as for its neighbour the rook.... It cannot easily come into play!

13 ...	N×f3+
14 B×f3	Qa5+
15 Rd2	Re8!

Also good is 15 ... Bg5, but the move played prevents the opponent from castling.

16 Kd1

If 16 0–0?, then 16 ... R×e4.

| 16 ... | Be5 |

Here we can take stock: Black's two bishops and the prospect of an attack on the king allow his position to be considered strategically won. But, as will be seen, for victory some 40(!) more moves were required. ...

| 17 Re1 | Bf5 |
| 18 g4 | |

After 18 Ng3 Bf4! 19 Rde2 R×e2 20 R×e2 Qc5 the white king ends up in a critical position.

| 18 ... | Bg6 |
| 19 Nc3 | |

| 19 ... | B×c3! |

A concrete approach to the demands of the position. Black parts with one of his fine bishops, but creates additional pawn islands in the opponent's position and removes one of the white king's defenders.

20 b×c3	c×d5
21 B×d5	Qc7
22 f3	

Bad is 22 Q×b7 Q×c3, when the white king is in a mating net.

| 22 ... | R×e1+ |

22 ... Qc5, with the threat of 23 ... R×e1+ and 24 ... Qg1+, was tempting, but White has 23 Rf1! Now, however, the exchange of a pair of rooks merely strengthens Black's pressure.

23 K×e1	Re8+
24 Kf1	b6
25 c4	Qf4
26 Rf2	

White's last hope was 26 Qc3!?, and if Black had been tempted by an ending with an extra pawn — 26 ... Re3 27 Qd4 Q×d4 28 R×d4 Ra3 29 Rd2 Bb1, then after 30 c5! Bd3+ 31 Kf2 b×c5 32 Rb2 White would have gained real chances of saving the game. But here too Black could have continued his pursuit of the king — 26 ... h5! 27 Qd4 Qg5.

26 ...	h5!
27 Qd1	Re3
28 Kg2	Qe5

With the threat of 29 ... Re1, 30 ... h×g4 and 31 ... Be4+.

29 f4	Be4+
30 Kf1	Bd3+
31 Kg2	

On 31 Q×d3 Black can interpose 31 ... Qa1+.

| 31 ... | Qd4 |
| 32 Rf3 | Qb2+ |

In time trouble, Black gains time on the clock.

33 Rf2	Qd4
34 Rf3	h×g4
35 R×e3	Be4+
36 R×e4	Q×d1
37 Re7	Kh7
38 R×f7	Qd3

Even in time trouble it was not at all necessary to give up a pawn. Black would have won more quickly after 38 ... a5.

39 R×a7	Kh6
40 Ra8	g6
41 Rh8+	Kg7
42 Rg8+	Kh7

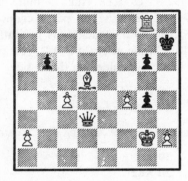

Here the game was adjourned.

43 Re8	b5!

Now the white bishop loses its support in the centre, and the queen acquires more scope.

44 Bg8+	Kg7
45 c×b5	Q×b5
46 Re5	

An attempt to create a so-called fortress, since on 46 Rd8 there follows 46 ... Qb6, when the rook no longer has a safe square on the 8th rank.

46 ...	Qb2+
47 Kg3	K×g8
48 Rg5	Kf7
49 R×g4	Qa3+
50 Kg2	Q×a2+
51 Kg3	Qb3+

Having laid waste the Q-side, the queen begins a zig-zag approach towards the white king. White's misfortune is that he can be attacked from the rear.

52 Kg2	Qc2+
53 Kg3	Qd3+
54 Kf2	Qd2+
55 Kf3	Qd1+
56 Kg3	Qe2
57 Rg5	Qe3+
58 Kg4	Qf2
59 Re5	Qg2+

White resigns: 60 Kh4 Q×h2+ 61 Kg4 Qg2+ 62 Kh4 Qf3 63 Kg5 Qg3+.

No. 45 Queen's Gambit

Timman–Geller

AVRO-Tournament
Hilversum, 1973

Mines always explode

The note to White's 14th move describes the mine which was "laid" under the variation which occurred in the game. Unfortunately, it did not explode in the World Championship Match, but it was not wasted. Sooner or later mines explode, and the more of them that a player has in his arsenal, the better.

1 d4	d5
2 c4	e6
3 Nc3	Be7
4 Nf3	Nf6
5 Bg5	0–0
6 e3	h6
7 Bh4	b6

This branch of the Queen's Gambit, which is associated with the names of Tartakover, Makogonov and Bondarevsky, has been tested at the very highest level—in matches for the World Championship.

103

8 c×d5	N×d5
9 B×e7	Q×e7
10 N×d5	e×d5
11 Rc1	Be6
12 Qa4	c5
13 Qa3	Rc8
14 Bb5	

Earlier White usually used to continue 14 Be2, but in a tournament in honour of the 25th anniversary of Victory Day (Moscow, 1970), in a game against me Furman employed the new move 14 Bb5. The idea of it is to provoke the advance of the a-pawn, which weakens both this pawn, and Black's entire Q-side. Our game continued: 14 ... a6 15 d×c5 b×c5 16 0–0 Ra7 17 Be2 a5 18 Rc3 Nd7 19 Rfc1, and White gained the advantage.

Soon after this game I found the correct plan for Black (*14 ... Qb7*), which Spassky and I examined together during his preparations for the 1972 World Championship Match. But in the 6th game of the match Spassky for some reason preferred the old method, and up to the 17th move followed the aforementioned Furman–Geller game, when he played 17 ... Nd7 18 Nd4 Qf8, but after 19 N×e6 f×e6 20 e4 had the inferior game.

14 ...   **Qb7**

It would seem that this continuation may shake the evaluation of 14 Bb5. With the white bishop at e2 the aim of this queen manoeuvre is easy to understand—in the event of 15 d×c5 b×c5 16 R×c5 R×c5 17 Q×c5 there follows 17 ... Q×b2. But here Black sacrifices a pawn, with completely different ideas in mind. In particular he threatens 15 . . c4 with the rapid advance of his Q-side pawns. Jan Timman chooses the most critical reply.

15 d×c5	b×c5
16 R×c5	R×c5
17 Q×c5	Na6!

This is the whole point. Black prevents his opponent from castling, since after 18 Qc6 Q×c6 19 B×c6 Rb8 (this is more exact than *19 ... Rc8*) the b2 pawn cannot be defended: on 20 b3 Black wins instantly by 20 ... Rc8, while after 20 0–0 R×b2 White has too many difficulties on the Q-side.

18 B×a6	Q×a6
19 Qa3	

Necessary, since 19 ... Rc8 was threatened.

19 ...	Qc4
20 Kd2	

Better is 20 Qc3, although here too Black has a marked advantage, for example, after the simple 20 ... Rb8. White assumes that his king will not be badly placed in the centre (he controls the black squares), but it transpires that his K-side is also weak.

20 ...	Qg4
21 Rg1	

21 ...   d4!

A breakthrough at the strongest (for White) point. Now on 22 e×d4 I was intending to play simply 22 ... Rb8, when one of the threats is 23 ... Bd5.

22 N×d4   Qh4
23 Re1

All the same White cannot defend his f2, and he attempts to consolidate his forces.

23 ...   Q×f2+
24 Re2   Qf1
25 N×e6   f×e6

White's extra pawn does not play any part. Much more important is the fact that his king, caught in the cross-fire of Black's heavy pieces, is unable to find peace either on the Q-side, or on the K-side. Such positions are very difficult to defend.

26 Qd6

In order to prevent a deadly rook check on the d-file.

26 ...   Kh8
27 e4   Rc8

Suggesting, once and for all, that the white king should forget about trying to shelter on the Q-side.

28 Ke3   Rf8

There is also no way over to the K-side.... Meanwhile, on the agenda is an unpleasant queen check at c1 and the invasion of the back rank by the rook.

29 Rd2

The attempt to maintain the status quo — 29 Kd2 — would have been met by the same move as in the game.

29 ...   e5!
30 Q×e5

The decisive mistake, but it is difficult by now to offer White any good advice. He is close to *zugzwang*, whereas Black was preparing to continue his attack, for example, by 30 ... Qf4+ 31 Kd3 Rf6.

Now comes the final attack.

30 ...   Qe1+
31 Re2   Qg1+
32 Kd2   Rd8+
33 Kc3   Qd1

The game could have been concluded at this point: White cannot defend all the squares on the d-file.

34 Qb5   Qd4+
35 Kc2   a6

The most energetic.

36 Q×a6   Qc5+

In view of mate in a few moves, **White resigned.**

No. 46 Queen's Gambit

Belyavsky–Geller

47th USSR Championship
Minsk, 1979

Victory brings the gold medal

Success in this game would practically assure me of the Championship gold medal several rounds before the finish, and I played it with considerable enthusiasm. My opponent, on the other hand, was battling both against me, and to some extent against himself. The point is that the opening which occurred in the game was borrowed by Aleksandr Belyavsky from me, and he frequently plays it himself. So that the task of my opponent was at the same time both difficult and not altogether pleasant....

1 d4	d5
2 c4	e6
3 Nc3	Be7
4 Nf3	Nf6
5 Bg5	h6
6 Bh4	0–0
7 e3	b6
8 Be2	Nbd7

By playing ... b6 before developing his queen's knight, Black has maintained control over the weakened squares a6 and c6. But now that White's king's bishop has made a move, the development of the knight is perfectly justified, since Bb5 will involve a loss of tempo. And, what is even more significant, in reply to the possible 9 B×f6 Black wants to recapture with the knight.

9 c×d5   e×d5

Also possible is 9 ... N×d5, but after 10 B×e7 Q×e7 11 Rc1 this leads to a totally different game.

| 10 0–0 | Bb7 |
| 11 Qb3 | |

The usual 11 Rc1 c5 12 d×c5 b×c5 would have led to one of the basic positions of the variation.

By the move in the game White attempts to prevent the creation by Black of a hanging pawn centre, by taking "X-ray" aim at the bishop at b7. But now a series of new nuances arise in the position, which Black promptly exploits.

11 ...   c5!
12 B×f6

White aims to give his opppnent an isolated pawn in the centre, and for the sake of this he parts with one of his bishops. Black was ready for this, and he had also taken account of the fact that after 12 d×c5, although 12 ... b×c5? was not possible due to the bishop at b7 being undefended, 12 ... N×c5! would have deprived the white queen of a3, a typical post when the opponent has a hanging pawn centre, while on the retreat to c2 the opposition of the queen and the black rook after 13 ... Rc8 would have been highly unpleasant.

12 ...   N×f6

Otherwise the d5 pawn is insufficiently defended.

13 d×c5   B×c5
14 Rfd1

White rather straightforwardly begins putting pressure on the opponent's isolated pawn. Nevertheless, the pressure of the bishop along the g1-a7 diagonal is appreciable, and he should not have weakened his f2. To be considered was Nb5-d4, so as to include the queen in the defence of e3, retain the f3 knight on the K-side, and then attempt to drive away the bishop from c5.

14 ...   Qe7
15 Nd4

White continues his plan of pressure on the d5 pawn, which includes transferring his bishop to f3 and retaining his knight at c3. In parrying the threat of 15 ... B×e3 16 f×e3 Q×e3+ and 17 ... Ng4, it was not yet too late to deviate from his original plan in favour of 15 Nb5 followed by Nbd4.

15 ...	Rad8
16 Rac1	Ne4
17 Bf3	Rfe8

Both sides have completed their planned set-ups, and the resulting position is undoubtedly more favourable to Black. Although for the moment this is not especially noticeable, his pieces are already eyeing White's insufficiently defended K-side.

18 Na4?

A loss of time, which transforms Black's attacking aspirations into something very real. White should have gone on to the defensive by 18 Nce2 or 18 Qc2.

| 18 ... | Ng5! |
| 19 Bg4 | |

Bad is 19 N×c5 b×c5, when, after the withdrawal of the knight from f3, Black takes on f3, completely destroying the white king's defences.

| 19 ... | g6! |

The very structure of the position suggested to Black an interesting plan — that of including in the attack...his h-pawn. It is now ready to rush forward.

| **20 Nc3** | **Ne4** |

All the same this move is necessary: in the event of 20 ... h5 21 Bf3 B×d4 (*21 ... h4?! — 22 B×d5*) 22 R×d4 N×f3+ 23 g×f3, White's rook along the 4th rank defends the approaches to his king, and also, because of the blockade at d4, Black is left with a bad bishop.

21 Qc2	h5
22 Bf3	h4
23 Qd3	Qe5

The threat of 24 ... Bd6 is now highly unpleasant, since on 25 g3 h×g3 26 h×g3 there follows 26 ... N×g3, with a strong attack.

24 Nce2

At the moment only the white-squared bishop is not participating in the attack, and by an original manoeuvre Black brings it into play.

| 24 ... | a5! |
| 25 Rc2 | |

White had not yet guessed the point behind the opponent's previous move, otherwise he would have reconciled himself to the painful necessity of 25 B×e4, when Black has two splendid bishops.

25 ...   Ra8!
26 a4

Here 26 B×e4 was essential: only in this way could White have continued to resist. True, he would have felt uncomfortable both in the middlegame (with an attack threatened!), and in the endgame (with two knights against two enemy bishops!).

26 ...   Ba6
27 Qb3

Only now did White see that the intended 27 Nb5 is refuted by 27 ... N×f2 28 K×f2 B×e3+ 29 Kf1(e1) Q×h2. But even the exchange down he is unable to hold out for long, since Black's attack continues.

27 ...   Bc4
28 R×c4   d×c4
29 Q×c4   Rad8

Renewing the threat of 30 ... N×f2.

30 Qb3   Rd6
31 h3   Rf6
32 Qc2   Ng5

For the second time the knight moves to this square, and this time it is decisive.

33 Bb7   Bd6
34 Nf4   R×f4
35 Nc6

After 35 e×f4 Q×f4 mate is inevitable.

35 ...   N×h3+
36 g×h3   Qg5+
37 Kf1   Rf6
38 Qd2   Bg3

White resigns

No. 47 Queen's Gambit

Psakhis–Geller

USSR Zonal Tournament
Yerevan, 1982

1 d4	d5
2 c4	e6
3 Nc3	Be7
4 Nf3	Nf6
5 Bg5	h6
6 Bh4	0–0
7 e3	b6
8 B×f6	B×f6
9 c×d5	e×d5
10 Qd2	Be6
11 Rd1	

This rare line of the Tartakover–Makogonov–Bondarevsky Variation was first played by Petrosian in his Candidates Match with Hübner (Seville, 1971). White's idea is to do everything possible to prevent the freeing advance ... c5.

Interestingly enough, a similar idea was carried out by Petrosian in one of the games of his 1969 World Championship Match with Spassky, where a position from the present game was even reached with an extra tempo for White: 6 B×f6 B×f6 7 e3 0–0 8 Qd2 b6 9 c×d5 e×d5 10 Rd1 Be6 11 g3 Nd7 12 Bg2 Be7 13 0–0 c6.

In both cases White failed to gain any advantage, and the line did not become popular. Then several years later it again occurred in this Zonal Tournament, in the game Georgadze–Geller...

11 ...   **Qe7**
12 g3

The Georgadze–Geller game quickly ended in a draw after 12 ... Nd7 13 Bg2 Rfd8 14 0–0 Rac8 15 Rc1 c5.

Lyev Psakhis obviously wanted to improve on White's play. It is difficult to say exactly what he had in mind, but one can make a suggestion. Thus instead of 14 0–0 there is the unexpected 14 Ng1!? with the idea of 15 Nge2 and Nf4, intensifying the pressure on d5 and thereby preventing ... c5. But despite the fact that White's entire preceding play has been directed against this advance, it proves possible to carry it out immediately.

12 ...   **c5!**

The plan with 11 ... Qe7 and 12 ... c5 had never been seen before, and it solves all Black's opening problems.

13 d×c5

More cautious was 13 Bg2 Nc6 14 0–0, but then Black has an easy game.

13 ...   **Rd8!**
14 c×b6?

After more than an hour's thought the USSR Champion chooses an over-optimistic move. However, the strongest continuation, 14 Bg2 b×c5 15 0–0, would have given Black the better chances after 15 ... Nc6.

14 ...   **d4!**
15 Bg2

15 N×d4 B×d4 16 e×d4 is of course bad because of 16 ... Bd5+, while the tempting 15 Ne4 meets with a brilliant refutation: 15 ... Bd5! 16 N×f6+ Q×f6 17 Q×d4 Q×f3 18 b7 Rd7!! 19 Qa4 (*19 b×a8=Q B×a8, or 19 Bb5 Q×h1+ 20 Kd2 Q×d1+! 21 K×d1 Bf3+*) 19 ... Q×d1+! 20 Q×d1 B×h1 21 f3!? R×d1+ 22 Ke2 Rd2+!, and Black wins.

15 ...   **Nc6**
16 N×d4   **N×d4**
17 e×d4

Possibly the best chance was 17 B×a8 R×a8 (*17 ...Nf3+ 18 B×f3 R×d2 19 R×d2* is insufficient) 18 e×d4 Bd5+ 19 Qe2 B×h1 20 Q×e7 B×e7 21 b×a7 (nothing is achieved by *21 d5 a×b6 22 Ke2 Bg2*) with three pawns for a piece, although with an inferior position.

17 ...   **Bh3+**
18 Kf1   **R×d4**
19 Qe3

Now White loses by force, but the proposed queen sacrifice 19 Q×d4 B×d4 20 R×d4 would also have failed to save him after 20 ... Qf6! 21 Rd3 (the other defence against the threat of *21 ... Qf3, 21 Rf4*, allows Black the advantage after *21 ... Qc6! 22 Rg1 B×g2+ 23 R×g2 Q×b6*) 21 ... Qf5! 22 Re3 a×b6 23 B×h3 Q×h3+ 24 Ke2 b5 25 a3 b4, when White is unable to set up a "fortress".

19 ...	Qb7!
20 f3	

Equally hopeless was 20 Rg1 R×d1+ 21 N×d1 Rd8 22 Nc3 B×g2+ 23 R×g2 B×c3+ 24 b×c3 Qa6+ 25 Ke1 Q×a2.

20 ...	R×d1+
21 N×d1	Qa6+
22 Kg1	Rd8
23 Nf2	Bd4
24 Qe1	B×f2+

White resigns, since after 25 K×f2 there follows 25 ... Q×b6+ 26 Kf1 Bc8!

It only remains to add that the Psakhis–Georgadze game from one of the later rounds again confirmed how harmless the entire variation is for Black: 5 ... h6 6 B×f6 B×f6 7 e3 0–0 8 Qd2 b6 9 c×d5 e×d5 10 Rd1 Be6 11 g3 Nd7 12 Bg2 Be7 13 0–0 c6 14 Ne1 Re8 15 Nd3 Bf5 16 Rc1 Rc8 17 Qe2, and a draw was agreed.

King's Indian Defence

No. 48 King's Indian Defence

Geller–Westerinen

Göteborg, 1968

A new line in opening theory

The King's Indian Defence has always occupied a special place in my sphere of opening interests. With my trainer at the time, grandmaster Eduard Gufeld, I had a lengthy discussion regarding the variation beginning with Black's 7th move. I considered it favourable for White. Of course, I was familiar with the game Portisch–Tal (Moscow, 1967), where White chose the solid 8 Ne1, clearing the way for his e- and f-pawns to occupy the centre. But I felt that a different solution was also possible, and here I gained the opportunity to try to uphold in practice my understanding of position. Grandmaster Heikki Westerinen (at the time he was still only an international master) "allowed" me to put forward a new opening set-up, which since then has found its way into all books on the King's Indian Defence.

1 d4	Nf6
2 c4	g6

3 Nf3	Bg7
4 g3	0–0
5 Bg2	d6
6 0–0	Nc6
7 Nc3	Bf5

Black has another aim, apart from the natural one of developing: he attempts to seize control over e4. But with this move—in combination with the development of the knight at c6—Black undertakes too much.

8 Re1

A prelude to the idea which I have already remarked on. For the moment White threatens the straightforward e2–e4.

8 ...	Ne4

9 Nd5

110

The idea of this manoeuvre is to exploit the position of the knight at e4, which is insufficiently defended only by the bishop at f5, which itself can be attacked.

| 9 ... | Re8 |

Black guesses his opponent's intention: after 9 ... e5 10 d×e5 d×e5 11 Ne3 there is the unpleasant threat of 12 N×f5, spoiling Black's pawn formation and giving White the advantage of the two bishops.

It should also be mentioned that, in reply to 9 ... Qd7 10 Ne3 Bh3 as played in Doda–Schmidt, Varna, 1972, White should have continued 11 Bh1!, when the threat of 12 d5 is highly dangerous. In addition, the knight at e4 is "hanging".

| 10 Ne3 | Bd7 |
| 11 d5 | Nb8 |

The knight has to retreat, since on 11 ... Na5 there follows 12 Qc2, when Black is forced to weaken his position by 12 ... f5, since 12 ... Nf6 loses to 13 b4, and 12 ... Nc5 to 13 Bd2 b6 14 b4.

12 Qc2	Nc5
13 Bd2	e5
14 d×e6	

Although this slightly activates the black pieces, there was absolutely no reason to allow Black to create a pawn outpost at e4.

| 14 ... | B×e6 |
| 15 Rad1 | |

White's positional advantage is undisputed. He is better developed, and all his pieces are concentrated towards the centre. He has the prospect of creating pressure both on the Q-side, and—after the exchange of black-squared bishops—on Black's insufficiently defended K-side.

15 ...	a5
16 Bc3	Nc6
17 B×g7	K×g7

| 18 Nd5 | B×d5 |
| 19 c×d5 | Nb4 |

It would have been better to retreat the knight again to b8, since now White drives back both knights with gain of tempo.

| 20 Qb1 | Qd7 |

Of course, Black would have liked to place his queen on f6, but in that case the white knight would have reached b5 in two jumps, when he would have had serious difficulties over the defence of his Q-side.

21 a3	Na6
22 b4	a×b4
23 a×b4	Na4
24 Qa1+	Kg8
25 Qd4	

Here we can take stock.

White has acquired a clear advantage in force on the K-side and in the centre. Now, in particular, he threatens both Ng5–e4, as well as the advance of his e2 pawn to e5.

| 25 ... | Nb6 |
| 26 e4 | |

Strategically this is the sounder plan.

At this point the attempt to invade at f6 does not work: 26 Ng5 Qe7 27 Ne4 Nd7, and White himself is blocking the advance of his e-pawn.

| 26 ... | Qe7 |
| 27 Qd2 | Qf6 |

28 Nd4	Nd7
29 Rc1	Re7
30 Bf1	Nb6

Practically forced in view of the threat of 31 B×a6 and 32 R×c7. At the same time Black threatens to win a pawn.

31 Re3

Seemingly overlooking his opponent's intention, White continues to prepare e4–e5 and in passing sets a well-camouflaged trap.

| 31 ... | N×b4? |

Westerinen falls into it!

32 Rf3!

An important *zwischenzug*.

If immediately 32 Q×b4, then Black regains his knight by 32 ... Ra4. But now he unexpectedly has insoluble problems over where to move his queen.

| 32 ... | Qe5 |

It turns out that 32 ... Qg7 or 32 ... Qh8 loses immediately to 33 Q×b4 Ra4 34 Q×b6! c×b6 35 Rc8+. But Black's position also collapses after the move in the game.

33 Nf5!

A spectacular blow, which reveals in reality how poorly defended the black king is.

| 33 ... | g×f5 |

Forced, since on 33 ... Rd7 there would have followed 34 Nh6+ Kg7 35 Ng4, with major gain of material.

| **34 R×f5** | **Q×e4** |

Or 34 ... Qh8 35 Q×b4 Ra4 36 Qb1 Ra×e4 37 R×c7, to White's advantage. But now too he has a very strong attack for the piece.

35 Qg5+	Kf8
36 Qf6	Ke8
37 Rg5	c6

In the event of 37 ... N4×d5 White wins by 38 Bb5+ c6 39 Q×d6 Kf8 40 Qh6+ Ke8 41 B×c6+ b×c6 (*41 ... Kd8 42 Qd6+*) 42 Rg8+ Kd7 43 Q×c6 mate.

38 Bh3

Black resigned in view of mate in a few moves, for example: 38 ... Kd8 39 Q×d6+ Nd7 40 Rg8+ Re8 41 Q×d7 mate.

No. 49 King's Indian Defence

Geller–Ljubojevic

*Interzonal Tournament
Petropolis, 1973*

Nevertheless f2–f4!

Two rounds earlier during my game with Hug I had conceived the idea of carrying out the advance f2–f4, which had previously not been played in the given variation. I did not succeed in doing so, and the idea remained "in reserve". Ljubomir Ljubojevic obviously had no suspicion of this, and at the critical point on the 9th move he did nothing to hinder White. As a result White seized the initiative on the K-side, and the Yugoslav grandmaster, who very much likes attacking, had to engage in an unpleasant business — defending.

1 d4	Nf6
2 c4	c5
3 d5	g6
4 Nc3	Bg7
5 e4	d6
6 Nf3	0–0
7 Be2	e5

The Yugoslav grandmaster more often plays 7 ... e6, which was the continuation I expected. Perhaps his choice was influenced by the fact that in the game with Hug I had played the opening stage rather unsurely.

8 Bg5

It would seem that this move was introduced into serious tournament practice by Petrosian. With the given pawn formation in the centre, it is obvious that Black will aim for ... f5, and it is against this advance that the move is aimed.

8 ...	h6
9 Bh4	

It has also been attempted by 9 Bd2 to exploit the weakening of Black's K-side. For example, 9 ... Ne8 10 Qc1! Kh7 h4, when the thematic 11 ... f5 is unpleasantly met by 12 h5, and if 12 ... g5, then 13 e×f5 B×f5 14 g4!

9 ...	Na6

Aimed, on the one hand, at preparing ...b5 (for which the knight should stand at c7), and, on the other hand, against White's usual plan in this position, involving b2–b4.

But the knight move looks rather awkward, and is obviously very slow. Black must break the pin as soon as possible, and therefore the natural 9 ... Qc7 is better. Incidentally, now the queen has to give up its convenient post at c7, and concede this square to the knight.

In the aforementioned game Hug continued 9 ... Qc7 10 Nd2 Nh7 11 0–0 (more usual is the quiet *11 Nb5 Qd7 12 f3 a6 13 Nc3 Qc7 14 a3 Nd7 15 Rb1* with standard play on the Q-side, or the sharper *11 g4 a6* and now either *12 Qc2*, as was played against me by Ivkov at Bled, 1961, or *12 Nf1* followed by *Ne3*; the text move is "working" on the new idea of *f2–f4*) 11 ... Bf6, and after the poor reply 12 Bg3 Qe7 13 Qc2 Nd7 14 Rae1 h5 Black obtained good counter-play. White should have preferred 12 B×f6 N×f6 13 a3, and if 13 ... Na6, then 14 f4.

10 Nd2	Qe8
11 0–0	Nh7

First 11 ... Nc7 would seem to be more accurate, but, by removing his control from c5, Black would have allowed White a free hand to attack on the Q-side by a2–a3 and b2–b4.

12 Nb5	Qd7

Black has nothing else, unless, of course, one considers 12 ... g5, which leads to a catastrophic weakening of the white squares after 13 Bg3 Qe7 14 Bg4.

13 Bg3	Nc7
14 f4	

In principle this plan is not new—the attempt to undermine Black's centre by f2–f4 in Benoni positions was made long ago by Botvinnik, but it would appear to be the first time it has occurred in the given position. White begins a battle for the key square e5. In doing so he exploits the fact that the black knights are a long way from e5, and cannot easily reach there.

The activated black bishop at g7 will all the same be tied in the main to the defence of the weak h6 square. As for the accompanying sacrifice of the b2 pawn, and in some cases the exchange at a1, during the game, to be frank, I did not examine it in any detail. It was obvious that for the sacrificed material White would gain fine play with good attacking chances. Later analysis confirmed this, for example: 14 ... e×f4 15 B×f4 N×b5 16 c×b5 g5 17 Bg3 B×b2 18 Nc4 B×a1 19 Q×a1, with the threat of 20 B×d6 Re8 21 Bh5. Both on 19 ... f5, and on 19 ... Q×b5, there can follow 20 B×d6 Rd8 21 e5.

Besides, placing Ljubojevic, a player with a sharp attacking style, in the position of defender, means forcing him to operate under the most unpleasant conditions.

It is not surprising that Black declines the sacrifices.

14 ...	e×f4
15 B×f4	Ne8
16 Nf3	

16 Qc2 was also good, but White wanted to provoke a further weakening of the opponent's K-side.

16 ...	Qe7

On 16 ... g5 17 Bg3 B×b2 White was again intending to sacrifice the exchange by 18 e5.

17 Qd2

Forcing Black to "part" with the white squares in the vicinity of his king.

17 ...	g5
18 Bg3	Nhf6
19 Bd3	

For the last time in the game offering Black a pawn: 19 ... N×e4 20 B×e4 Q×e4 21 N×d6 N×d6 22 B×d6 Rd8 23 Bc7, and if 23 ... Rd7 24 d6 Q×c4, then 25 Rae1 with sufficient compensation.

19 ...	Nh5
20 Bf2	Nf4
21 Rae1	

The e4–e5 breakthrough becomes a very real possibility (for example, 22 e5 d×e5 23 d6 and 24 B×c5), so Black takes countermeasures.

21 ...	a6
22 Nc3	Ng6
23 h3	

The immediate 23 Bg3 is not possible due to 23 ... g4.

23 ...	Kh8

A waiting move, and a poor one. In certain variations the black king can be checked from h6. In anticipation of White continuing the struggle for e5, Black should have played 23 ... Ne5 or completed his development by 23 ... Bd7.

24 Bg3	Qc7

24 ... Ne5 was now essential, although, by exchanging twice on e5, White would have retained the advantage.

25 h4

Black's position has become untenable, although White's attack is only one move ahead of the defence.

25 ...	g4
26 h5	g×f3

There is nothing else: 26 ... Ne5 27 N×e5 d×e5 28 Nd1, and Black cannot defend his

numerous weaknesses on the K-side, in particular his g4 pawn.

27 h×g6   f×g6

28 e5

Opening all the lines for an attack on the
king.

28 ...	Bf5
29 R×f3	d×e5
30 B×f5	R×f5
31 R×f5	g×f5
32 B×e5	Qb6

After 32 ... B×e5 33 Q×h6+ Kg8
34 Qe6+ White regains his piece, and maintains his attack plus an extra pawn.

33 d6

Renewing the threat of 34 Q×h6+.

33 ...	Kh7
34 Nd5	Qd8
35 d7	Qh4

Offering White a choice between the prosaic
36 d×e8=Q R×e8 37 Qc3, and the continuation in the game.

36 Qf2	Q×f2+
37 K×f2	B×e5
38 R×e5	Nd6
39 Re8	R×e8

Or 39 ... N×e8 40 d×e8=Q R×e8
41 Nf6+.

| 40 Nf6+ | Resigns |

No. 50 King's Indian Defence

Geller–Velimirovic

*Capablanca Memorial Tournament
Havana, 1971*

When a pin is more valuable than a rook

There were essentially two factors which
gave the following game such a fighting
nature. Firstly, my young opponent was a
player with a sharp attacking style, and I wanted to force him only to defend. Secondly,
the game took place in the sixth round,
when Dragoljub Velimirovic was leading
with a 100% score. I was naturally thinking
only in terms of winning.

In principle, of course, it is correct to
assert that one should simply "play chess",
depending on the nature of the position
reached. But before the start of a game
every player nevertheless tunes himself up
for a certain type of struggle, and for a certain
result. I, for example, always find it easier to
mobilize myself if I need to win. If, from the
tournament position, a draw suits me, I find
it much more difficult to force myself to aim
for the half point. ...

| 1 Nf3 | Nf6 |
| 2 c4 | |

This move order is dictated by the desire
not to allow Velimirovic his favourite Benoni
Defence with 3 ... c5.

2 ...	g6
3 d4	Bg7
4 g3	0–0
5 Bg2	d6
6 0–0	c5
7 Nc3	Nc6
8 d5	Na5

A well-known position has been reached,
where I prefer to have White: the knight
at a5 is, after all, rather out of play.

115

9 Nd2	e5

In my opinion, positionally this plan is not altogether justified. Black restricts his own bishop at g7, and the prospects for his knight at a5 become even bleaker. More solid is the usual line with ... a6, ... Rb8 and ... b5.

10 e4	Ng4

All this had occurred before, although in a slightly different position. The knight move had been played in reply to 10 Qc2, and also in the 10th game of the Petrosian–Spassky World Championship Match, 1966, with the inclusion of ... a6 for Black and Qc2 for White, and with a slight transposition of moves. The game continued 12 b3 f5 13 e×f5 g×f5, when by 14 Nd1 White provoked the opponent into an attack.

In the tournament at Amsterdam, 1970, Langeweg played against me 10 ... Ne8, and after 11 b3 (in earlier games with this variation, White replied *11 a3* immediately, or else made this move after *11 Re1 f5*; in both cases Black successfully solved his opening problems) 11 ... f5 12 e×f5 g×f5 13 Bb2 Nf6 14 Qc2 Bd7 (*14 ... a6* is slightly more accurate, immediately carrying out the usual plan of ... *Rb8* and ... *b5*) 15 Rae1 a6 16 Nd1 b5 17 Ne3 Nh5 18 Bf3 Qg5 19 B×h5! Q×h5 20 f4 White again obtained the advantage.

11 b3

In this position certain players prefer play on the Q-side, involving the preparation of b2–b4, and such a recommendation can be found in many opening guides. It is more critical, however, to emphasize the isolated state of the black knight by the move in the game, and "with an extra piece" to conduct the battle in the centre and on the K-side.

11 ...	f5
12 e×f5	e4?

Velimirovic attempts prematurely to seize the initiative, and runs into a counter-blow. Correct, of course, was the quieter 12 ... g×f5.

13 f6!

Already at this point White had decided to sacrifice a rook. To calculate all the variations at the board was of course impossible, but I was loathe to give up such an interesting idea. As for its correctness, I was reassured by reasoning of the following type: the resulting pin on the h4–d8 diagonal was bound to give White good play.

13 ...	N×f6

14 Nd×e4!!

By 14 Bb2 Black could have been forced to part with his breakaway e-pawn, but it was the position after 14 ... e3! 15 f×e3 Ng4 that he was hoping for. A forcing variation now begins.

14 ...	N×e4
15 N×e4	B×a1
16 Bg5	Bf6

Black cannot avoid the resulting pin, since if he moves his queen the bishop at a1 is lost, and with material almost equal (a pawn for the exchange) White gains a very strong attack.

17 N×f6+	R×f6
18 Qa1	Kf7
19 Re1	

Despite being a rook down, in the main sector of the attack White has an advantage in force, and it is difficult for Black to bring his Q-side pieces into play. Simple developing moves do not work. For example, on 19 ... Bf5 or 19 ... Bd7 there follows 20 Qc3! (with the threat of *21 B×f6 Q×f6 22 Q×a5*) 20 ... b6 (the only defence) 21 Re6!, and White wins, since the enforced 21 ... B×e6 leads to the opening of the long white diagonal after 22 d×e6+, and to loss of material for Black.

19 ...   Rb8

The alternative defence was 19 ... h6, but it would not have saved the game after the simple reply 20 B×h6. Here are some sample variations:

(*a*) 20 ... Bf5 21 Bg5 Rc8 22 g4 B×g4 23 Re4 Bf5 24 Rh4.

(*b*) 20 ... Qh8 21 Bg5 Bd7 (if *21 ... Bf5*, then *22 Qc3 b6 23 Re6*, whereas now in this variation Black has *23 ... Rf5*) 22 Re4! Rf5 (otherwise *23 B×f6 Q×f6 24 Rf4*; on *22 ... Rf8* there would have followed *23 Rh4 Qg7 24 Bh6 Qg8 25 B×f8 Q×f8 26 Rh7+ Ke8 27 Qe1+ Kd8 28 Q×a5+*) 23 Re7+ Kg8 24 Q×h8+ K×h8 25 Bd2, with a decisive advantage for White.

20 Re3   b6

Defending the knight which, as has been seen, is "hanging" in certain variations.

No better was 20 ... Bf5 21 h3! h5 22 g4 h×g4 23 h×g4 B×g4 24 Re4 Bf5 (*24 ... Bh5 25 Re6*) 25 Rh4.

21 Rf3   Bf5
22 g4   Qh8
23 B×f6

The simplest solution: White transposes into a won ending. 23 Bh3 is not altogether clear after 23 ... Rg8.

23 ...   Q×f6
24 Q×f6+   K×f6
25 g×f5   g×f5
26 Re3

An important link in White's plan of realizing his advantage. The frontal attack on the f5 pawn by 26 Bh3 would have allowed Black to maintain the balance: 26 ... Rg8+ 27 Kf1 Rg5. But now the white rook penetrates into the enemy rear.

26 ...   Nb7
27 Re6+   Kf7
28 Bf3

The threat of a bishop check at h5 completely destroys the coordination of the black pieces.

28 ...   Rg8+
29 Kf1   Kf8

Black cannot maintain control of h5 — 29 ... Rg5 30 h4.

30 Bh5   Rg5
31 Re8+   Kg7
32 Re7+   Kh6
33 R×b7

White has no reason to fear the rook ending: along with 33 Be8, this move leads to a straightforward win.

33 ...   R×h5
34 R×a7   R×h2
35 Rd7

White intends to obtain something of the order of three connected passed pawns. Black cannot successfully oppose this.

35 ...	Kg5
36 R×d6	Kf4
37 Ke2	b5
38 c×b5	Ke5
39 Rd7	Rh4
40 a3	

The mass of complex variations which remained behind the scenes demanded time of White, and it is not surprising that he was now seriously short of time. By the last move before the control he makes his task slightly more difficult. He could have won by force by 40 b6 Rb4 41 b7 h5 42 a4 h4 43 a5 h3 44 a6 h2 45 Rh7.

40 ...	Rh3
41 f3	Kd4

When short of time it was this move that White had overlooked. However, the game is extended by only five moves.

42 b6	Rh2+
43 Kf1	Rh1+
44 Kf2	Rh2+
45 Kg3	Rb2
46 b7	R×b3
47 a4	c4
48 a5	c3
49 a6	c2
50 Rc7	Resigns

No. 51 King's Indian Defence

Kolterman–Geller

Odessa Championship, 1949

Is it always worth sacrificing the queen?

This game was played at a time when the dynamic evaluation of a position had not yet become the property of every player, as it has today. This is why such an experienced and strong opponent as S. Kolterman, who had to his credit numerous victories over masters, and later even grandmasters, was lured into giving Black a weak pawn, allowing him too much in return. About myself, I can say that my handling of an open combinational struggle was initially correct, but at some point I ceased to control my actions from the point of view of their rationality. What told was an urge not only to win, but to win brilliantly, which in the given instance made the win more difficult. The pursuit of brilliancy is rightful only when it is simultaneously the swiftest way to achieve the goal.

1 d4	Nf6
2 c4	g6
3 Nc3	Bg7
4 e4	0–0
5 Nf3	d6
6 h3	Nbd7
7 Be3	

In the 1940s this system of development was highly popular. But as Black demonstrated the harmlessness of White's set-up, so it became less and less fashionable, although even now it is occasionally encountered.

7 ...	e5
8 d5	Nh5

Played in the spirit of the present day, although, of course, the idea was encountered even then. In 1951 Simagin played this against Moiseyev (without the inclusion of ... *Nbd7*), and in similar positions ... Nh5 was played by Bronstein. The idea behind it is obvious: Black wishes to advance ... f5, with his knight in a more active position than in the rear (after ... *Ne8*), and also in some cases to play ... Nf4. It is against this that White's reply is directed, and he attempts in this way to refute Black's opening strategy.

118

9 Nd2

Now ... f5 is ruled out for a long time, and it appears that White is free to prepare Q-side pressure by b2–b4 and c4–c5.

9 ...   c5!

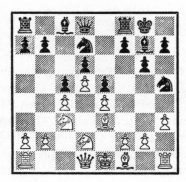

10 d×c6

White decides to open the centre, hoping to exploit the weakness of the d6 pawn, but this plan is erroneous. He should have seen through Black's plan and found the following manoeuvre: 10 g3 a6 11 Be2 Ndf6 12 a4 Bd7 13 Kf1!!, parrying the threat of 13 ... Qc8, carrying out artificial castling, and preventing the freeing advance ... b5.

Nowadays, perhaps, this may not seem especially complicated, but at that time, more than thirty years ago, it was not often that such plans were conceived.

10 ...   b×c6
11 Nb3   Ndf6
12 Qd2

On the one hand, the start of a premature attack on the d6 pawn, and, on the other hand, a timely controlling of the f4 square. The natural 12 Be2 would have allowed Black to carry out his plan of playing 12 ... Nf4. Therefore it is not possible to associate White's failure in the given position with any one move. The trouble is that, for the sake of a single weakness at d6, he has wasted a

mass of time, is behind in development, is deprived of the stable pawn triangle c4–d5–e4, and has allowed Black good piece play over the entire board.

12 ...   a5
13 Rd1   a4
14 Nc5

Both purposeful and ... forced, since on 14 Nc1 there would have followed 14 ... Qa5. But now, too, the undeveloped state of White's K-side is simply bound to tell!

14 ...   a3
15 b4   Ne8
16 Nb3

Had White's king been in a safe place, the struggle for the central d5 square by 16 b5 would have been perfectly justified. Black was intending to reply as in the game.

16 ...   f5
17 Bg5

On 17 Bc5 Black would have answered 17 ... Rf6, with the threat of 18 ... Qc7.

17 ...   Qb6

Much better than 17 ... Qc7, when 18 c5 gains in strength. Now White achieves nothing by 18 Be7 Rf7 19 B×d6 N×d6 20 Q×d6 Bf8, etc. The most interesting and correct continuation was 18 Nd5 Qb7 19 Ne7+ Kh8 20 N×c8 R×c8 21 c5 d5 22 e×d5, with a complicated game.

18 c5(?)   Q×b4
19 c×d6   Be6!

By opening the centre White has greatly sharpened the situation, and has gained the opportunity for tactical play. Thus, for example, 19 ... Nf4 loses to 20 Be7 Rf7 21 d7 Q×e7 22 d8=Q. But the fundamental evaluation of the position has not changed: the white king has still not castled. In some cases Black is threatening to exchange on b3 and to advance his a-pawn.

20 Be2   Nf4
21 Bf3

Castling was not possible due to 21 ... Q×c3.

21 ...   Bc4
22 Nc1

By defending d3, White intends by 23 g3 and 24 Nd3 to prepare, at last, to castle, but ...

22 ...   N×d6

The start of a combination involving a queen sacrifice.

23 Be7

Mate results from 23 Q×d6 Q×c3+ 24 Qd2 Q×f3! 25 g×f3 Ng2.

23 ...   Bh6
24 Qc2   f×e4!

Now after 25 B×e4 N×e4 or 25 B×d6 g×f3 the black queen is immune: 26 ... N×g2 mate is threatened.

25 R×d6   e×f3

The queen is again ready to die for the sake of victory: 26 R×g6+ h×g6 27 B×b4 N×g2+ 28 Kd1 Rfd8+, etc.

26 Rg1   N×g2+?

The explanation for this move is the author's false romanticism, which he had

not yet managed to overcome. In his pursuit of effect, Black again sacrifices his queen and allows the opponent to prolong the resistance. The prosaic 26 ... Qb2 would have immediately concluded the game.

27 R×g2   Q×d6
28 B×d6   f×g2
29 N3e2   Rf4!
30 f3

Of course, 30 B×e5 would also have lost to 30 ... Re8, but more tenacious was 30 Ng1, and if 30 ... Bd5, then 31 Nce2. However, White's position is nevertheless untenable, in view of the inevitable opening of the centre after ... e4 (in reply to the necessary *f2–f3*).

30 ...   Bd5
31 Ng1   Rc4
White resigns

No. 52 King's Indian Defence

Kotov–Geller

17th USSR Championship
Moscow, 1949

Energy encouraged

Even today this game is dear to my heart. Not only because, for the first time, it won me a creative award — the prize for the most brilliant game of the Championship. The point is that even today, more than thirty years later, I aim, as an ideal, for this kind of dynamic play. Each of Black's moves in this game is subordinate to one all-consuming idea: attack, attack, and again attack. Although, as was rightly stated by the chairman of the prize-awarding jury, the then World Champion Mikhail Botvinnik, the game cannot be called a complete one (both sides committed errors), Black's energy, in Botvinnik's words, deserved encourage-ment.

1 d4	Nf6
2 c4	g6
3 Nc3	Bg7
4 g3	0–0
5 Bg2	d6
6 Nf3	Nbd7
7 0–0	e5
8 e4	e×d4

This old (not to say ancient) variation of the King's Indian Defence had been enrich-ed by this time by the efforts in particular of Boleslavsky and Bronstein. Many theo-rists regard Black's last move as premature, but it also has its positive sides. The first of these is that it creates all the preconditions for lively piece play at an early stage of the game.

9 N×d4	Nc5
10 f3	

The plan associated with this move is rather passive. Since the attack on d6 does not in itself promise much, White cannot get by without the subsequent advance of his pawn to f4. Therefore it is usually prepared by 10 h3. In any case the e4 pawn is adequate-ly defended.

10 ...	Nfd7

Later, in a tournament at Szczawno Zdroj, 1950, I found a more effective plan: 10 ... a5 11 Be3 c6 12 Qd2 a4 13 Rad1 Qa5, with sufficient counter-chances.

11 Be3	c6
12 Qd2	a5
13 Rad1	Ne5

The prelude to a combinational storm. Botvinnik's recommendation of 13 ... Nb6 14 b3 Qe7 would have lost a pawn after 15 Nde2.

14 b3	a4

15 Nde2

A plausible but erroneous move, after which Black seizes the initiative. 15 f4, as suggested by Botvinnik, was essential. Then 15 ... Ng4 is bad because of 16 N×c6, while after 15 ... Ned3 16 N×a4 N×a4 17 b×a4 Nc5 18 N×c6 b×c6 19 B×c5 Bg4! 20 B×d6 B×d1 21 Q×d1 Re8 22 e5, with material approximately level, White retains a positional advantage; however, the position remains double-edged.

But Black has another interesting possibili-ty: 15 ... a×b3!? 16 f×e5 b×a2, and if 17 e×d6, then 17 ... Bg4 18 Ra1 Q×d6 19 R×a2 Rad8, when he is in no danger of losing. Black also has a satisfactory game after 17 N×c6 b×c6 18 B×c5 Bg4. Therefore 17 N×a2 looks more convincing, but then 17 ... Bg4 18 Ne2 (*18 e×d6 B×d1 19 R×d1 Q×d6 20 Nc3 Rfd8*) 18 ... B×e5 leads to the following highly interesting position.

For the sacrificed piece Black already has two pawns, and in addition the c4 pawn is weak. Even more important is the fact that the black pieces have taken up very strong positions, and that it is very difficult for White to find an active plan.

All this enables the position after Black's 14th move to be assessed as more promising for Black: even White's best continuation leaves him facing difficult problems.

15 ...	a×b3!
16 B×c5	N×c4
17 Qc1	b×a2

More resolute was Bronstein's suggestion of 17 ... b2! 18 Qc2 d×c5! 19 R×d8 R×d8. Although Black has only a rook against a queen, White cannot organize a serious defence. But during the game I was afraid of exceeding the bounds of permitted risk, especially since after the move played Black has an easy and, I would say, comfortable game.

18 N×a2	Qa5
19 Q×c4	Be6
20 Qc1	d×c5
21 Nac3	b5

This was the position Black was aiming for, when he embarked on the combination on the 14th move. For the piece he has three passed pawns on the Q-side, supported by two strong bishops.

22 Nb1

White loses his head. When making his 15th move he was hoping to win, but in fact because of it he has ended up by force in a difficult position. His one chance of saving the game was now to restrict one of the bishops, so as to attempt to neutralize the phalanx of black pawns by returning the piece. To this end he should have played 22 f4 Bb3 23 Rd6 b4 24 e5!

22 ...	b4
23 Nf4	Bb3
24 Rd6	c4
25 R×c6	c3
26 Nd5	B×d5
27 e×d5	Q×d5
28 f4	

Too late! The black pawns have advanced so far that White's main forces are unable to come to the help of their king, which now becomes the target for attack.

28 ...	Qd4+
29 Kh1	Ra2
30 Bf3	

The threat was 30 ... R×g2.

30 ...	Rb2
31 f5	Be5
32 Qe1	Rd8
33 Be4	Kg7!

Black's pieces are ideally placed. With his last move he provokes f5–f6, after which there is no longer an attack on g6, and he can throw forward his h-pawn.

34 f6+	Kg8
35 Ra6	h5
36 Ra5	h4
37 B×g6	

Now comes the concluding blow.

37 ...	R×h2+
38 K×h2	B×g3+
39 Q×g3	h×g3+
40 Kh3	f×g6

White resigns

No. 53 King's Indian Defence

Korchnoi–Geller

*USSR Team Championship
Moscow, 1963*

Whoever seizes the e4 square...

In this game attention should be paid to several crucial points:

1. One and the same move may be both correct, and erroneous, depending on the plan associated with it.

2. In many typical formations there is a square which dominates the entire position. In the King's Indian Defence this is usually e4. Here Black began the battle for it on the 12th move, and concluded it on the 37th.

3. In its very nature a queen sacrifice is so paradoxical, that at times it may be overlooked by even a tactically vigilant player.

1 d4	Nf6
2 c4	g6
3 Nc3	Bg7
4 e4	

Korchnoi had no doubt not forgotten our game from Curacao (No. 57), where a King's Indian, which transposed into a Grünfeld Defence, proved unfavourable for him. On this occasion he denies Black the possibility of changing the opening after 4 g3, and falls back on the Sämisch Variation.

4 ...	d6
5 f3	0–0

6 Be3	e5
7 d5	c6

The approved manoeuvre, which ensures Black counter-play on the c-file in the event of White aiming for a K-side pawn storm.

8 Qd2

Nowadays theory considers 8 Bd3 to be more accurate, if White is planning to castle K-side. But at the time when this game was played, such subtleties were not yet known, and had not even been thought about. In reply to 8 Bd3, after 8 ... c×d5 9 c×d5 I was intending to try not 9 ... Na6 10 Nge2 Bd7 11 Qd2 Nc5, which had already been played, but 9 ... Ne8, and if 10 Nge2, then 10 ... Bh6!, while on 10 Qd2 Black advances ... f5. Incidentally, even now this continuation is possibly the best for Black.

8 ...	c×d5
9 c×d5	Ndb7
10 Nge2	

In itself this move is not wrong, provided only that it is associated with the correct plan—that of castling Q-side. But White was intending to castle K-side, and therefore more logical was 10 Bd3 Nc5 11 Bc2.

10 ...	a6
11 Nc1	

This and the following move hand Black the initiative. White's diversion on the Q-side does not achieve anything tangible, and proves to be a loss of time. He should have continued either 11 g4, or 11 0–0–0 and 12 Kb1.

11 ...	Nh5
12 b4	

It goes without saying that on 12 g4 Black would be happy to offer a pawn sacrifice by 12 ... Nf4, obtaining in return more than adequate compensation in the form of superior development and the weakness of the black squares in White's position.

12 ...	f5
13 Nb3	Ndf6

The placing of the black knights is perfectly justified: one of them attacks e4, and the other keeps its sights on f4. It should be said that the entire game illustrates the importance of e4, the key square in positions of this type.

14 Bd3	Nf4

An even more favourable moment for this manoeuvre than on the 12th move. It is easy to see that White cannot accept the pawn sacrifice.

15 e×f5

Illogical, since the opening of the game favours Black, who has a lead in development. White was evidently afraid of castling, since after 15 0-0 N×d3 16 Q×d3 f4 17 Bf2 g5 Black's attack develops rather rapidly. Even so, that is what he should have played.

15 ...	N×d3+
16 Q×d3	B×f5!

White was counting on the strereotyped 16 ... g×f5, which would have given him a respite. But Black establishes piece control over e4, exploiting the fact that after 17 Ne4 B×e4 18 f×e4 Ng4 the white king is caught in the centre.

17 Qd2	Qc7
18 Rc1	Rac8!

The unpleasant opposition of white rook and black queen on the c-file demanded exact calculation, but I felt that any possible tactical complications would favour Black.

19 0-0

It is difficult to say whether Korchnoi's nerve failed him, or whether he underestimated Black's intended queen sacrifice, but, by wasting time on the completion of his development, White ends up by force in a very difficult position. He should have tried his luck in the variation 19 Ne4, although here too after 19 ... Qd7 20 N×f6+ B×f6 21 0-0 Qb5 Black has the advantage.

19 ...	Qc4!
20 g4	

On this tactical manoeuvre White was basing all his plans. If 20 ... Bd7, then 21 g5 Nh5 22 Ne4, and he has everything in order.

20 ...	N×g4!
21 Ne4	

Winning the queen, but losing the game. However, also unsatisfactory is 21 f×g4 Q×g4+ 22 Qg2 (*22 Kh1 R×c3 and 23 ... Be4+*) 22 ... Q×g2+ 23 K×g2 Bh3+! 24 K×h3 R×f1 25 Ne4 (*25 R×f1 R×c3,* and White loses his bishop) 25 ... Rf×c1! 26 B×c1 Bf8, and White cannot avoid the loss of a third pawn.

| 21 ... | N×e3 |
| 22 R×c4 | N×c4 |

Black has sufficient material for the queen, and his position can be regarded as won. White has no way of countering the pressure by the rooks on the f-file.

23 Qc1	b5
24 Rf2	Rf7
25 Qg5	Rcf8
26 Nbd2	Bf6

Of course, there was no point in Black exchanging for such a modest achievement as the win of a pawn, thereby losing his important white-squared bishop — 26 ... B×e4 27 N×e4 R×f3. He intends either to transfer his bishop from g7 to b6, or to capture the f3 pawn in a more favourable situation (*27 N×f6+ R×f6 28 Kg2 N×d2 29 R×d2 Bb1 30 Rf2 Be4*).

| 27 Qg3 | Be7 |

The bishop manoeuvre can be delayed. Black intends to remind White that the d5 pawn is also weak.

28 Re2	Nb6
29 Nc3	Bc8
30 Re3	Rf5

Of course, the point of this move does not lie in the one-move threats of 31 ... Rg5 and 31 ... Bg5. Black alternates his attacks on White's weaknesses. This is more effective than the straightforward 30 ... Bb7 31 Rd3. The white-squared bishop may still be required in the struggle for the dominant e4 square.

31 Nde4	Nc4
32 Rd3	Bd8
33 Nd1	

The threat was 33 ... Bb6+ and 34 ... Be3, winning the f3 pawn.

| 33 ... | Rf4 |
| 34 a4 | |

White has no counter-play, but he has to move something!

34 ...	Bb6+
35 Kg2	Bf5
36 Qe1	g5

Intending to weaken e4 by the flank attack ... g4.

37 Ndc3	g4
38 f×g4	B×g4
39 a×b5	a×b5
40 Kg3	Bf5
41 Kg2	Kh8

The subsequent play was preceded by adjournment analysis, which showed that White had no satisfactory defence.

42 Rg3	Bd4
43 h3	Bg6
44 Qe2	R8f7
45 Qe1	

White is obliged to await his fate.

| 45 ... | R7f5 |
| 46 Qc1 | |

Or 46 N×b5 R×e4 47 Q×e4 Rf2+. No better is 46 Qe2 B×c3 47 N×c3 (*47 R×c3*

R×e4 48 Q×e4 Rg5+) 47 ... Rd4 48 Kg1 Rd2, etc.

46 ...	B×c3
47 N×c3	Rf2+
48 Kg1	Nd2
49 Qa3	

On 49 Nd1 Black wins by 49 ... Rf1+ 50 Kh2 Nf3+ 51 Kg2 Ne1+.

49 ...	Rf1+
50 Kh2	Nf3+
51 R×f3	R5×f3
52 Qa8+	Kg7
53 Qc6	R1f2+
54 Kg1	Rc2
55 Qd7+	Kh6
56 Nd1	Rg3+

White resigns

No. 54 King's Indian Defence

Stein–Geller

*USSR Team Championship
Moscow, 1966*

Refutation of a refutation

My habit of returning again and again to positions which would appear to have been exhaustively analysed has often served me well, but in this game it could have let me down. Having refuted a theoretical recommendation in my analysis, I confidently went in for a double-edged continuation, intending to "catch" my opponent with it. But Leonid Stein made the correct first step on the way to refuting the refutation, and... stumbled on the second. Although not without its mistakes, the game was stirring and of a certain theoretical interest.

1 d4	Nf6
2 c4	g6

3 Nc3	Bg7
4 e4	d6
5 Bg5	

One of the sharpest continuations, with ideas of a K-side attack. Black must play very purposefully, so as to avoid ending up rather quickly in a difficult position.

5 ...	h6

Before undertaking any activity in the centre, it is useful for Black to determine the position of the white bishop, and to give himself additional chances involving the advance of his K-side pawns (unsatisfactory is *6 Be3 Ng4* or *6 Bf4 Nc6 7 d5 e5*).

6 Bh4	c5

At just the right time. An illustration of the dangers for Black of delaying is provided by the variation 6... 0–0(?) 7 f4 c5 8 e5.

7 d5	Qa5

This adds fuel to the fire, but it seems to me the most critical solution. The quiet 7 ... 0–0 would be more of a waiting move.

8 Bd3	

In the theoretical guides of that time, this move was accompanied by a question mark, and on the basis of the game Bisguier–Perez, Utrecht, 1961, 8 Qd2 was recommended instead. On studying the position after 7 ... Qa5, I came to the opposite conclusion. After 8 Qd2 the rook at a1 is undefended, and this gives Black good chances in the near future of playing ... b5. As for 8 Bd3, White could have made a significant improvement in comparison with the aforementioned game.

8 ...	g5
9 Bg3	N×e4!?

A rather risky continuation, by which Black wins a pawn, but affords White good attacking chances. 9 ... Nh5 looks sounder.

| 10 B×e4 | B×c3+ |

Black has to part with this bishop, since 10 ... f5 11 Qh5+ Kd8 12 Ne2 gives White a very strong attack.

| 11 b×c3 | Q×c3+ |
| 12 Kf1 | f5 |

13 Ne2?

By repeating the mistake made in the Bisguier–Perez game, White loses a highly important tempo. It soon transpires that the white queen, being tied to the defence of the rook at a1, cannot be transferred at the right moment to h5.

Correct was 13 Rc1 Qg7 (worse is *13 ... Qf6 14 h4 f×e4 15 Qh5+*, when White regains his pawn with a positional advantage) 14 h4 g×h4 15 Qh5+ Kd8 16 R×h4 (*16 B×h4 is unpleasantly met by 16 ... Qb2*) 16 ... f×e4 17 R×e4, and White has sufficient compensation for his slight material deficit.

13 ...	Qf6
14 Bc2	f4
15 h4	Rf8!

Emphasizing his advantage. It is clear that White cannot retreat his bishop, in view of 16 ... f3.

| 16 h×g5 | h×g5 |
| 17 N×f4? | |

In a difficult position White commits an oversight, which accelerates his defeat. The only defence was 17 Qe1, when, apart from 17 ... f×g3, Black also has 17 ... Nd7! 18 Bh2 Ne5 19 f3 Rh8, and again White's prospects are not very bright.

| 17 ... | g×f4 |
| 18 Bh2 | |

At the last moment Stein noticed that the planned 18 Bh4 would have lost to 18 ... Rh8.

18 ...	Nd7
19 g3	Ne5
20 Qh5+	Kd8
21 g×f4	Ng4

Winning the queen and the game.

| 22 Re1 | Rh8 |
| 23 Bh7 | Qg7 |

White resigned: if 24 Bg3, then 24 ... Nf6.

No. 55 King's Indian Defence

Uhlmann–Geller

Interzonal Tournament
Palma de Mallorca, 1970

Zugzwang as a result of carelessness

When a player considers that his offer of a draw is justified, but it is declined, he should endeavour to understand the reason for it being declined. Then he may be able to avoid the following typical psychological mistakes:

1. A subconscious desire to demonstrate quickly the justification for his offer. Hence he hastily makes the obvious move, which is by no means always the best.

2. A feeling of annoyance, provoking him into playing sharply "for a win", which is equivalent to playing "for a loss".

3. Finally, the conviction that he can achieve a draw "as he pleases". Here the

weakening of his sense of danger rarely goes unpunished.

The present game would appear to be an example of the third instance.

1 d4	Nf6
2 c4	g6
3 Nc3	Bg7
4 e4	d6
5 Be2	0–0
6 Bg5	

A continuation which became popular after the game Averbakh–Panno (USSR–Argentina, Buenos Aires, 1954). Thanks to the efforts of Polugayevsky and, in particular, Borisenko, the positions which result in the most common variations have been studied right down to the endgame. Therefore after

6 ...	c5
7 d5	

Black avoids the immediate opening of the centre (7 ... e6), and possible simplification of the type 8 Qd2 e×d5 9 e×d5 Re8 10 Nf3 Bg4 11 0–0 a6 12 a4 Nbd7 13 h3 B×f3 14 B×f3, with a slight advantage to White.

7 ...	h6
8 Bf4	

Along with 8 Be3, this occurs fairly often. 8 ... e6 is still possible, since 9 d×e6 B×e6 10 B×d6 Re8 11 B×c5 Qa5 12 b4 Qa6 gives Black a threatening initiative. But I did not care for 10 Qd2, and if 10 ... Qa5 — 11 B×h6 B×h6 12 Q×h6 N×e4 13 Rc1. Purely intuitively I sensed that Uhlmann was prepared for this variation, and I avoided it. Four rounds later it was "officially confirmed" that my intuition had not deceived me: in precisely this way Uhlmann crushed Uitumen (with the slight difference that on the 8th move the bishop retreated to e3).

Apart from 8 ... e6, other moves to be played in this position are 8 ... Nbd7 (Averbakh–Aronin, Moscow, 1954, Stahl-berg–Matanovic, Beverwijk, 1956, etc.), 8 ... Ne8 (Bronstein–Donner, Gotha, 1957), and 8 ... Qa5 (Gulko–Dzindzhikhashvili, Moscow, 1966). In the last of these White immediately committed an inaccuracy: 9 Qd2 instead of 9 Bd2!

8 ...	a6
9 Qd2	

Here too this gain of a tempo proves illusory. Necessary was 9 a4, as, incidentally, was played by Uhlmann in the first round against Gligoric (without the inclusion of 7 ... h6).

9 ...	Kh7
10 Nf3	

Now 10 a4 is less good in view of 10 ... Qa5, when White has to lose time on 11 Ra3 (otherwise Black plays ... b5, for example, *11 Nf3 b5 12 c×b5 a×b5 13 B×b5 N×e4 14 N×e4 Q×b5*). The move in the game allows Black to offer a sharp pawn sacrifice.

10 ...	b5
11 c×b5	a×b5
12 B×b5	Qb6!
13 Be2	

On 13 a4 Black would have replied as in the previous note: 13 ... N×e4, etc. The alternative was 13 Bd3, on which Uhlmann was evidently afraid of 13 ... Bg4, when Black gains indirect control over e5, and the e4–e5 advance is, after all, part of White's plans.

13 ...	Qb4!
14 e5	Nh5
15 Bg3	Ba6

Not so convincing is 15 ... N×g3 16 h×g3 d×e5 17 N×e5 Qd4, although in this variation, too, Black stands better.

16 B×a6

Perhaps slightly more accurate was first 16 e×d6, when Black has to decide what and when to capture. Is 16 ... B×e2 17 N×e2 Q×d2+ 18 N×d2 N×g3 19 h×g3 e×d6 20 Nc3 good for him? Should he sacrifice another pawn: 16 ... e×d6 17 B×d6 Re8 18 Kf1? Or should he agree to the opening of the h-file after 16 ... N×g3? However, things would probably have reduced to a simple repetition of moves, since accepting the sacrifice of the second pawn has its dangers for White.

16 ...	R×a6
17 e×d6	e×d6
18 0–0	Nd7
19 Rae1	

Sooner or later White has to remove his rook from its position opposite the bishop at g7. At the same time he takes measures against the threat of ... f5–f4. Especially, since he clearly cannot avoid losses on the Q-side....

19 ...	N×g3
20 h×g3	Nb6
21 Re2	Nc4
22 Qd3	Rfa8
23 b3	

In this way White saves one of his Q-side pawns, and forces the transition into an ending which is difficult, but not hopeless.

23 ...	Q×c3
24 Q×c3	B×c3
25 b×c4	R×a2
26 R×a2	R×a2
27 Rc1	

At this point White offered a draw. However, very exact play is required of him. The slightest mistake may prove to be that straw which broke the camel's back.

27 ...	Bf6
28 Kf1?	

Here it is! Essential was 28 g4!, since now the white pawns are blockaded, and the black king becomes very active.

28 ...	h5!
29 Ne1	g5
30 Rc2	Ra1
31 Ke2	Kg6
32 Nf3	Kf5
33 Nd2	g4!

It was not yet too late to... lose after 33 ... Rg1 34 Nf3 R×g2 35 Kf1. But now the threat of 34 ... Rg1 is extremely unpleasant.

34 Nf1	Bd4

Zugzwang, allowing the black rook to break through to the K-side. White cannot hold the position: 35 Ne3+ Ke5 36 Nf1 f5, and there is simply nothing that he can move, while after the advance of the black pawn to f4 the rook ending is easily won.

35 Nd2	Rg1
36 Nb3	Be5
37 Nd2	R×g2
38 Kf1	Rh2

39 Kg1	Rh3
40 Nf1	h4
41 Kg2	h×g3
42 f×g3	Ke4
43 Rf2	f6
44 Ra2	Rh8

Here the slight time scramble came to an end. The game was adjourned, but **White resigned** without resuming.

No. 56 King's Indian Defence

Adamski–Geller

Lugano Olympiad, 1968

Just like Baron Munchausen

It is unlikely that you will find anyone in the world who would believe the fascinating but incredible stories of the famous Baron Munchausen. In particular, of how the Baron once simultaneously brought down seven partridges with a single shot. I too was no exception. That was until I "killed" three opponents simultaneously with one shot. Moreover, at the board I had to consider only the "finishing off" moves: the fate of the games was decided by the study of a single interesting variation. But all this began back in 1967, at the Interzonal Tournament in Sousse, during my game with Reshevsky.

1 d4	Nf6
2 c4	g6
3 Nc3	Bg7
4 e4	d6
5 Be2	0–0
6 Bg5	Nbd7

A rather rare continuation in the Averbakh Variation. Theory considers it passive, since White is insured against the appearance of the knight at c6 with pressure on d4, and recommends 7 f4. But the move in the game

is more common, and leads to a familiar position, which is often reached after 6 ... c6 (by transposition).

7 Qd2	e5
8 Nf3	c6!

More exact than the immediate 8 ... e×d4 9 N×d4 Nc5, in view of 10 f3, when White gains some advantage, since 10 ... Re8 can be answered by 11 0–0–0.

9 0–0

Also to be considered is 9 d×e5 or 9 0–0–0 Qa5 10 Kb1 Re8, with approximate equality.

9 ...	e×d4
10 N×d4	

After 10 Q×d4 Black seizes the initiative: 10 ... h6 (but not *10 ... Nc5 11 e5*) 11 Bh4 g5 12 Bg3 Nd5! 13 Qd2 N×c3 14 b×c3 Nc5.

10 ...	Nc5
11 f3	

This allows Black to explode the bomb which failed to operate in the aforementioned game with Reshevsky. There I obtained the position which occurred here after White's 10th move. But since Reshevsky had moved his bishop to g5 in two goes (*Be3–g5*), Black had managed to make an extra move (...

Qe7), which proved indeed to be superfluous. Because, with the queen at e7, the combination carried out in the present game does not work. For example: 11 ... Nc5 (the numeration of the moves is of course increased by one) 12 f3 Nf×e4? 13 N×e4! (*13 f×e4 B×d4+ 14 Kh1 B×c3*) 13 ... N×e4 14 f×e4 B×d4+ 15 Kh1, and after 15 ... Q×e4 16 Rf4 Black loses a piece, while 15 ... f6 16 Bh6 leaves White the exchange up. I recall how, on calculating all this, I was very much put out, and even spent some time considering whether or not I could somehow "lose" a tempo, by returning the queen to d8 and maintaining the combinational motif.

Later, at home, it was established exactly when the combination would work, and when it would not. ...

Instead of the move in the game, White should play (as was demonstrated in a game with me by Polugayevsky, IBM Tournament, 1970) 11 Qf4 (*11 Bf3 is very passive*) 11 ... Qe7 (now this thematic move is appropriate) 12 Rad1 Nc×e4 13 N×e4 Q×e4 14 Q×d6, with slightly the more pleasant position.

11 ...	Nf×e4!
12 N×e4	N×e4
13 f×e4	B×d4+
14 Q×d4	

Now on 14 Kh1 Black has the simple reply 14 ... Qb6. This is why the queen must be on its original square!

14 ...	Q×g5
15 Q×d6	

White has maintained material equality, but his position is lost, since the e4 pawn is doomed.

15 ...	Qe3+
16 Rf2	Be6

The pin on the white rook enables Black not to hurry over capturing on e4, but first to complete his development. The exchange of queens merely delays the loss of the pawn.

17 Qf4	Q×f4
18 R×f4	Rad8
19 Bf1	Rd4
20 Rc1	Rfd8
21 Rf2	

All the same Black would have played 21 ... Bf5 or 21 ... f5.

21 ...	R×e4
22 b4	Red4
23 a4	Rd1

The exchange of one pair of rooks exposes the weakness of White's Q-side pawns.

24 Rfc2	R8d2
25 a5	Kf8
26 b5	c5
27 R×d2	R×c1
28 Kf2	Ke7
White resigns	

This occurred in the 9th round of the Olympiad Final, and in the 11th round we played the Danish team. My opponent Holm made his first 11 moves confidently enough, but sank into thought over his 12th move, then evidently remembered something, shook his head and ... stopped the clocks. The point was that the position on the board was the one from the Adamski–Geller game!

The "profits" from my thinking during the game with Reshevsky did not end at that. Immediately after the Olympiad I set off to Gori to the Karseladz Memorial Tournament. Obviously the games from the Olympiad had not yet become the property of all chess players, and in the game with Cikovani history repeated itself for the third time!

Grünfeld Defence

No. 57 Grünfeld Defence

Korchnoi–Geller

*Candidates Tournament
Curacao, 1962*

The idea came in transit

The opening in this game was dictated by considerations that were by no means idle.

The point was that once against the same opponent, in reply to 4 g3 I switched from the King's Indian to the Grünfeld, and played 5 c×d5 N×d5 6 Bg2 N×c3 7 b×c3 c5 8 e3 Nc6 9 Ne2 Bd7, etc., as Bronstein had played against me in the Amsterdam Candidates Tournament, 1956. White improved the variation, sacrificed the exchange, and won. And here, shortly before play was due to start, there came into my mind the rather unusual move 6 ... Be6. On the way to the tournament hall, without a board I briefly considered it, and decided...

1 d4	Nf6
2 c4	g6
3 Nc3	Bg7
4 g3	d5

For the moment, all according to plan!

| 5 c×d5 | N×d5 |
| 6 Bg2 | Be6 |

I made this move quickly, and White sank into thought. It is clear that any attempt to refute Black's innovation must lie in the boundless complications resulting from 7 Qb3 N×c3 8 Q×b7 Q×d4 9 Bd2 Nd5 10 Q×a8 Q×b2 11 Rd1 (*11 Rc1 Bc3!*), etc. At the board White decided against such a committing continuation; he possibly thought that the entire variation had been analyzed in detail by me.

Such a decision is understandable. But in that case White should have given up the idea of casting doubts on Black's 6th move, and should have quietly played 7 Nf3, after which Black will choose between 7 ... N×c3 8 b×c3 c5 and 8 ... 0–0, when 9 Ng5 does not work — 9 ... Bd5 10 e4 Bc4. The attempt in the game to drive the black bishop from e6 is clearly unsuccessful.

| 7 Ne4? | 0–0 |

Black has no reason to fear 8 Nc5: the bishop retreats to c8, whereas the knight (after ... *b6*) has no convenient retreat square. It can no longer return to the natural and important square c3.

8 Nf3	Na6
9 0–0	c6
10 a3	

It is not easy for White to complete his development. In particular, there is no good square for his queen's bishop. The attempt to play b2–b4, with the idea of fianchettoing the bishop, leaves him even further behind in development.

| 10 ... | Bf5! |

A concrete approach to the position. Showing that he is ready to part with one of his bishops, Black commences an immediate attack on the enemy centre.

11 Nh4	B×e4
12 B×e4	Qb6
13 e3?	

The critical and turning point of the game. Since 13 Nf3 would have cut off the retreat of his bishop from e4, and after 13 ... Rfd8 his queen would have felt uncomfortable, White should have begun a stubborn battle for equality. This aim was met by 13 B×d5 c×d5 14 Nf3, when White's position has no obvious weaknesses. The delay allows Black to occupy the d-file, after which his advantage becomes clear.

| 13 ... | Rad8 |
| 14 Qf3 | |

White is unable to cope simultaneously with the two threats of 14 ... c5 and 14 ... e5. He chooses what he considers to be the lesser evil.

14 ...	e5!
15 d×e5	B×e5
16 Bc2	Nc5
17 Rb1	

Thus Black has brought all his pieces into play, and has a marked lead in development. But there are no vulnerable points in White's position. The question now is whether or not White can complete his development, without suffering some material or positional loss in doing so. Therefore Black's task can be formulated as follows: he must not allow White

to free himself, i.e. play e3–e4 and develop his black-squared bishop. This should have been prevented by 17 ... f5, since 18 b4 Ne6 19 Bb2 B×b2 20 R×b2 a5 retains for Black a clear advantage.

The move in the game allows White to conclude his mobilization, although he remains with certain difficulties, and his position is nevertheless inferior.

17 ...	Qb5
18 e4	Nc7
19 Bh6	Rfe8
20 b4	

White's position is not yet ready for a counter-attack, and by this Q-side activity he merely creates additional weaknesses. 20 Rfd1 looks sounder.

20 ...	N5e6
21 Bb3	Rd3
22 a4	

Korchnoi was pinning all his hopes on this tactical stroke. The exchange of queens does indeed ease White's position, but the initiative remains with Black.

22 ...	R×f3
23 a×b5	Rc3
24 b×c6?	

A routine decision. For the second time in the game White does not have the courage to part with one of his bishops, and ends up in a difficult position. The correct 24 B×e6! N×e6 24 b×c6 would have given him saving chances.

| 24 ... | Nd4! |
| 25 Bd1 | b×c6! |

This capture, breaking up Black's Q-side pawns, is the strongest. Black gains the possibility of a frontal attack on the b4 pawn, provides a spring-board for his knight at b5, and with his pieces seizes all the important squares in the centre of the board.

26 Be3	Ncb5
27 Nf3	Bf6!

The attack on the e4 pawn forces White into exchanging, which increases still more the difference in activity of the black and white pieces.

28 N×d4	B×d4

The opposite-coloured bishops after 28 ... N×d4 29 B×d4 would have eased White's defence somewhat.

29 B×d4	N×d4
30 f3	Rb8

The outcome of the game can be considered settled. The black knight is significantly stronger than the white bishop, and White is unable to hold his b-pawn. 31 ... a5 is threatened, and so he gives up the pawn immediately.

31 Ra1	R×b4
32 f4	

32 R×a7 would have allowed Black a decisive attack: 32 ... Rb2, etc.

32 ...	Rb7
33 e5	h5
34 Rf2	c5
35 Rfa2	c4
36 Kf2	a5!

Black would be very happy to give up his extra pawn for the second rank.

37 Rd2	Nb3
38 Rd8+	Kg7
39 Ra3	Rc1
40 Ke2	Rb1

Here the game was adjourned. Although it lasted another 17 moves, White's position is hopeless. It is obvious that the exchange on b3 is impossible—the black pawn queens. All that White can try for is a counter-attack on the black king.

41 Ke3	Rb2
42 h3	Rh2
43 h4	Rb2
44 Ke4	a4
45 Ke3	Ra7
46 f5	

Black has prepared the advance of his c-pawn, so White can wait no longer.

46 ...	g×f5
47 Rc8	Rd7

This same move would have followed on 46 Rc8.

48 R×a4

Mate follows after 48 B×h5 Rd3+ 49 Kf4 Rf2+ 50 Kg5 R×g3.

48 ...	Rd3+
49 Kf4	Nd4

The quickest way. White does not have a perpetual check.

50 Raa8	Ne6+
51 K×f5	Rf2+
52 Ke4	R×d1
53 Rg8+	Kh7
54 Rh8+	Kg6
55 Rag8+	Ng7
56 g4	Re1+
57 Kd5	c3
White resigns	

134

Nimzo-Indian Defence

No. 58 Nimzo-Indian Defence

Geller–Bobotsov

Moscow, 1968

Dynamics versus statics

Black created an isolated pawn in his opponent's position, securely blockaded it, and... was unable to find any follow-up plan. This shows that the black pieces only appeared to be ideally placed, and that their actions were not united by a single concrete aim. At the same time, the dynamism of White's position fairly quickly made itself felt. A position was reached in which Black clearly sensed the danger, but was unable to avoid an inevitable sacrifice of the exchange.

The game was awarded a prize for an energetically conducted attack.

1 c4	Nf6
2 d4	e6
3 Nc3	Bb4
4 e3	c5
5 Nf3	b6
6 Bd3	Bb7
7 0–0	0–0
8 Na4	

I was making this move for the first time in my life, although the resulting position was familiar to me. It occurred in the game Bronstein–Geller (26th USSR Championship, Tbilisi, 1959),which after the obligatory moves 8 ... c×d4 9 e×d4 continued 9 ... d5 10 c5 b×c5 11 a3 c4 12 a×b4 c×d3 13 Bg5 Nbd7 14 Ne5, with the more agreeable position for White.

In later games Black tried to play more cunningly, associating his subsequent plans with the exchange on f3, for example: 9 ... B×f3 10 Q×f3 Nc6 11 Be3 d5 12 Rfd1 (a new move) 12 ... d×c4?! 13 B×c4 Rc8 (*13 ...*

Nd5 is better) 14 a3, and White gained a slight advantage (Korchnoi–Ljubojevic, Amsterdam, 1972).

In the game Portisch–Fischer (Palma, 1972) it was Black who employed an innovation: 9 ... Re8, and after 10 Bg5 h6 11 Bh4 B×f3 12 Q×f3 Nc6 13 B×f6 (*13 Qe3* is preferable) 13 ... Q×f6 14 Q×f6 g×f6 15 Be4 f5 he seized the initiative.

Bobotsov chooses a less successful path.

8 ...	c×d4
9 e×d4	Be7
10 Bf4	d6

Within just three moves it transpires that this is a highly significant loss of time. While the manoeuvre ... Bb4–e7 is balanced by the journey of the white knight from c3 to a4 and back, there is no justification for advancing the pawn from d7 to d5 in two goes.

11 Re1	Nbd7
12 Rc1	Rc8
13 Nc3	d5

Black has no other plan. But now the formation reached is similar to certain positions from the Queen's Gambit Accepted, in which, thanks to his greater command of space and his total mobilization, White has a clear advantage.

14 Ne5	d×c4
15 N×c4	Nd5

As often happens in positions of this type, control of d5 does not give Black equality, since it is difficult for him to find a target for counter-play.

Therefore to be considered was 15 ... Nb8, planning to attack the d-pawn by ... Nc6, although after 16 Nb5, with the threats of 17 N×a7 and 17 Nbd6, White retains the advantage, e.g.:

(a) 17 ... Qd5 17 Ne3 Q×a2 18 Ra1, with a decisive invasion of the 7th rank by the rook.

(b) 16 ... Bb4 17 Re2 Qd5 18 Ne3 R×c1 19 Q×c1 Q×a2 20 B×b8 R×b8 21 Qc7, and Black loses material.

16 Bg3	N×c3

Hardly a happy exchange, since it reinforces White's centre, but it is difficult to offer Black any good advice. His pieces appear to occupy ideal positions, but the cramped nature of his position makes it unattractive. On the immediate 16 ... N7f6 White could have continued either 17 Ne5, when the black queen has no good square, or 17 Nb5.

17 b×c3	Nf6
18 Ne5	Qd5

An outwardly active move. Preferable, however, was the more modest 18 ... Nd7, since the white knight cannot be tolerated at e5 for long.

19 Bf1	Rfd8

19 ... Q×a2 does not achieve anything: 20 Ra1 Qd5 21 c4 Qd8 22 R×a7. Black's last move is directed against c3–c4, and so White transfers the centre of the struggle to the opposite wing.

20 Bh4	Rc7
21 Re3	Ne4?

21 ... Rdc8 is better. Black attempts to relieve his position by exchanges, but in doing so he allows the white queen across to the K-side, after which the prospect of an attack by White is very much a reality.

22 B×e7	R×e7
23 Qg4	Nf6
24 Qh4	Kf8

By the premature flight of his king, Black decisively weakens his h7 pawn. 24 ... Rc7 was essential, although even then White has a pleasant choice between 25 Rf3 and 25 Rce1.

25 Rf3

The exchange sacrifice at f6 cannot be prevented!

25 ...	Rc7
26 R×f6	g×f6
27 Q×f6	Re8

Preparing to evacuate the king after 28 Qh8+ Ke7 29 Q×h7 Kd8. Therefore White brings up his reserves.

28 Re1	Qd8
29 Qh8+	

Now this is possible!

29 ...	Ke7
30 Q×h7	Kf8
31 Qh8+	Ke7
32 Qg7	Rg8
33 Q×f7+	Kd6
34 Nc4+	Resigns

No. 59 Nimzo-Indian Defence

Geller–Keres

20th USSR Championship
Moscow, 1952

An opportunity grasped

One of the most important features of this game was the search for a decisive continuation in the critical position. White held a positional advantage, in the form of superior development. In such an instance it is sufficient to miss an opportunity—and all will be lost. Meanwhile, the active side should normally be able to find a means of converting one type of advantage into another, more permanent one. Often this means is of a combinational nature, and the difficulty is to foresee and to sense the moment of crisis.

Here White managed to maintain his advantage by an exchange sacrifice. An additional difficulty was provided by the fact that at the same time an endgame was reached, and it had to be evaluated precisely. Meanwhile, the transition from one phase of the game into another is always complicated in itself, and it is frequently at these points that the attacker loses all the advantage accumulated in the previous play.

1 d4	Nf6
2 c4	e6
3 Nc3	Bb4
4 e3	b6
5 Bd3	0–0
6 Nf3	d5
7 0–0	Bb7

The players have chosen the popular—especially at that time—Rubinstein Variation, which affords both sides a wide range of possibilities in their choice of plan.

8 Bd2

White aims to bring all his pieces into play, and only then to declare his intentions. This move is rather modest, but 30 years ago, along with 8 Qe2, it was considered one of the main continuations. Nowadays White fights more actively for the initiative with 8 c×d5.

8 ...   d×c4

This surrender of the centre looks slightly premature. More acceptable, possibly, is 8 ... Bd6 9 Rc1 a6 10 Qc2 Nc6 11 a3 d×c4 12 B×c4 e5 (Konstantinopolsky–Steinsapir, Moscow, 1949), or 8 ... c5 9 c×d5 e×d5 10 Rc1 Nc6 11 d×c5 B×c5 12 Ne2 Ne4 (Geller–Matanovic, Stockholm, 1952).

9 B×c4   c5

In a game with Taimanov (19th USSR Championship, 1951), Averbakh continued here 9 ... Nbd7 10 Qe2 c5 11 a3 B×c3 12 B×c3 Ne4 13 Rac1 Rc8, with a satisfactory position.

10 a3   c×d4

This shows the drawback to the two preceding moves. Black is forced to part with his black-squared bishop, since 10 ... Ba5 11 d×c5 b×c5 12 Qe2! gives White the better game. To be considered was 10 ... B×c3 11 B×c3 Ne4 12 Be1, although again White has an advantage in the form of the two bishops.

11 a×b4	d×c3
12 B×c3	Ne4?

Black should have continued 12 ... Nc6 with the possible sequel 13 b5 Ne7 14 Bb4 Bd5, although here too White stands better. The attempt to achieve immediate equality leads Black into difficulties.

13 Q×d8   R×d8

14 Rfd1!

This is the whole point! Simplification is favourable to White, and the threat of mate at d8 allows him to retain his bishop, by withdrawing it to e1. In the resulting open position the advantage of the two bishops is bound sooner or later to make itself felt.

Now 14 ... R×d1+ 15 R×d1 Nc6 is bad because of 16 b5 N×c3 17 b×c6 N×d1 18 c×b7 Rb8 19 Ba6, when the threat of Ne5–c6 is irresistible.

14 ...	**Rc8**
15 Be1	**Kf8**

Radically eliminating the mating threats which could have arisen, for example, after 15 ... Nc6 16 b5 Nb4 (*16 ... Ne7 17 Rd7*) 17 B×b4 R×c4 18 R×a7.

16 Rd4

Gaining an important tempo for doubling rooks (*16 ... Nc6 is not possible*).

16 ...	**Ke7**
17 Rad1	**Rc7**
18 Ne5!	

The tangle of black pieces on the Q-side presents a rather sorry spectacle, and it cannot be unravelled. By 19 f3 Nf6 20 Bh4 White wishes to strengthen his position still further. Moreover, he has in mind the exchange sacrifice which occurs in the game. Were it not for this, Black would have been free to complete his development, with hopes of a draw.

18 ...	**f6**

This natural move leads unexpectedly and by force to a hopeless ending. Better was 18 ... Nf6, although even then after 19 f3 Nbd7 the white bishop comes very effectively into play at g3.

19 Bd3	**Nd6**

The main variation was 19 ... f×e5 20 R×e4 B×e4 21 B×e4 Nc6 22 b5 Rd8 23 Rc1, when White acquires a material advantage sufficient for victory. The attempt to complicate matters by 19 ... N×f2 runs into a refutation: 20 B×f2 f×e5 21 Bh4+ g5 (otherwise *22 Rf1+* and mate in two moves) 22 B×g5+ Kf7 23 Rh4.

20 B×h7!

There was a certain difficulty, not, of course, in the calculation, but in the necessity to evaluate exactly the position after the coming exchange sacrifice. Black cannot avoid it (*20 ... Nb5*) in view of the intermediate check at g6.

20 ...	**f×e5**
21 R×d6	**Bd5**
22 R6×d5	**e×d5**
23 R×d5	**Rc1**
24 Kf1	**Nc6**
25 Ke2	

Premature would have been 25 b5 Ke6!

25 ...	**Rd8**

Playing for the win of a pawn — 25 ...

Rh8 — would have allowed the white pieces to become dangerously active: 26 Be4 R×h2 27 b5, and even in the endgame the black king is uncomfortable. It is therefore understandable that Black should aim to exchange rooks.

26 R×d8	N×d8
27 Bc3	Ke6

Now White's problem is to set up some passed pawns on the K-side. It is solved as follows:

28 Bg8+	Kd6
29 f4	e×f4
30 e×f4	

It transpires that the g7 pawn cannot be defended.

30 ...	Ne6
31 Be5+	Kd5

Or 31 ... Kd7 (e7) 32 f5.

32 B×g7	Rc8
33 B×e6+	

White cannot preserve both his bishops (*33 Bf7 Rc7*), but there is no need to.

33 ...	K×e6
34 Kf3	Rc4
35 Bc3	Kd5
36 h4	a5
37 b×a5	R×c3+

The last chance, since the white pawns are irresistible.

38 b×c3	b×a5
39 h5	

It was perfectly sufficient to step immediately into the square of the last black pawn by 39 Ke2, but White shows that there is another way to win: 39 ... a4 40 h6 a3 41 h7 a2 42 h8=Q a1=Q 43 c4+.

39 ...	Ke6
40 Ke3	**Resigns**

No. 60 Nimzo-Indian Defence

Geller–Keres

26th USSR Championship
Tbilisi, 1959

Premature activity

On the 18th move Paul Keres made an active advance in the centre. Meanwhile, there was no justification for Black doing this, and the unwarranted disturbance of the equilibrium had irreparable consequences.

This can be explained roughly as follows. At first Black kept a strict eye on the opponent's threats, but then, as the position gradually became level, his sense of danger obviously receded into the background. Finally, equality on the board provoked something of an inner sigh of relief, and possibly a lack of vigilance at some point. The result was a premature advance, and Black's striving for victory rebounded into a defeat.

1 d4	Nf6
2 c4	e6
3 Nc3	Bb4
4 e3	b6
5 Nge2	Ba6
6 Ng3	

At that time I liked playing the white side of the Nimzo–Indian position resulting after a2–a3 B×c3+. The move in the game is an attempt to transpose into the a2–a3 variation with an extra tempo. I first employed it a year earlier against Matanovic in the USSR–Yugoslavia match, where 6 ... c5 7 d5 e×d5 8 c×d5 B×f1 9 K×f1 d6 10 e4 gave White a positional advantage. In addition, the move hinders the thematic advance ... d5, which would justify the development of the bishop at a6. Meanwhile, White intends after the possible 6 ... 0–0 to continue 7 e4 Nc6 8 Bd3 e5 (*8 ... d5?* led to a marked advantage for White in Portisch–Spassky,

Moscow, 1967) 9 d5 B×c3+ 10 b×c3, with a sharp and complicated game.

6 ...   h5

An interesting idea. Keres approaches the position in a concrete fashion, and provokes the answering move of the white h-pawn, after which K-side castling may prove dangerous for White. The alternative, 6 ... B×c3+ 7 b×c3 d5 8 Qf3 Qd7 9 c×d5 e×d5 10 B×a6 N×a6 11 Qe2 leads to a slight but persistent advantage for White (Bronstein–Portisch, Budapest, 1961).

7 h4   Bb7

It is essential to delay the development of White's K-side and to prepare ... d5, but now White gains a slight lead in development. It would be very interesting to try 7 ... Bd6, with the possible sequel 8 Nge4 N×e4 9 N×e4 Be7 10 g3 d5.

8 Bd2   a6

Black takes control of b5, and completes his preparations for the planned advance in the centre. Now on 8 ... Bd6 I was intending to play 9 f4 Ng4 10 e4 Be7 11 N×h5. During the game Keres was afraid of 9 Nge2, but White does not achieve anything after 9 ... c5 10 d5 e×d5 11 c×d5 Qe7!

9 Qc2   d5
10 c×d5   N×d5

The alternative was 10 ... e×d5. Obviously Black was pinning his hopes on open piece play.

11 N×d5

This leads to a rapid evaporation of White's advantage. He should have continued 11 0–0–0, when it is not easy for Black to neutralize the opponent's lead in development.

11 ...   B×d2+
12 Q×d2   Q×d5
13 Rc1   Nc6
14 Be2   0–0–0

The only way! Had Black been tempted by the obviously "poisoned" pawn at g2 (on *14 ... Q×a2* White wins by *15 Bf3*), his game would have rapidly gone downhill. For example, 14 ... Q×g2 15 e4 Rd8 (*15 ... 0–0–0 16 Qc3*) 16 d5! Ne5 (*16 ... e×d5 17 R×c6 B×c6 18 Qc3*, with the threat of *19 Bf3*) 17 R×c7 Ba8 18 Qf4, and Black's position is undefendable.

15 Bf3   Qd7
16 0–0   Ne7
17 B×b7+   K×b7
18 Rc3   e5?

By his imaginative play Keres has eliminated his opening difficulties, and after the correct 18 ... Ng6 19 Rfc1 Rc8 he would have had a perfectly good position. But after this premature undermining of the centre Black comes under a strong attack. It seems to me that Keres overlooked that on 19 Rfc1 Black cannot reply 19 ... c5, because of 20 Qe2!

19 Rfc1   e×d4

This decision to give up the queen for two rooks could have been justified if Black had been able to consolidate his position without loss of material. He is unable to do this, for the main reason that his king has no safe shelter. The best defence, in my opinion, was 19 ... c6, when White would have switched his heavy pieces to the d-file and occupied it: 20 Rd3 followed by Rd1. He would have carried out the same plan after 19 ... Rc8.

20 R×c7+	Q×c7
21 R×c7+	K×c7
22 e×d4	Nd5
23 Qd3	g6

No better is 23 ... Kb7 24 Qf3, when again White increases his material advantage.

24 Q×a6	Rd7
25 Ne4	Re8
26 Nc3	

Black cannot avoid the exchange of knights, and his rooks, which in the given position are unwieldy, are unable to oppose the queen supported by the pawns.

| 26 ... | N×c3 |
| 27 b×c3 | Re6 |

(see diagram previous column)

White's plan is crystal-clear: to exchange his a-pawn for the b-pawn, which will clear the way for his connected passed pawns in the centre. Black succeeds in countering this plan, but at a high price—his rooks become disconnected and come under attack by the queen.

28 a4	Rc6
29 a5	b5
30 Q×b5	R×c3
31 Qb6+	Kc8
32 a6	Rcc7

The attempt to place the rook behind the a-pawn ends in complete *zugzwang*: 32 ... Rc1+ 33 Kh2 Ra1 34 d5 and 35 d6, after which there is no defence against Qc6+.

33 d5	Rd8
34 d6	Rc1+
35 Kh2	Kd7
36 Qb7+	

White could have won two moves quicker by 36 Qa7+ K×d6 37 Qd4+, when Black loses a rook.

36 ...	K×d6
37 Q×f7	Rc5
38 Qf6+	

The king has nowhere to go: 38 ... Kc7 39 Qe7+, or 38 ... Kd7 39 Qd4+. Therefore **Black resigned.**

English Opening

Lengyel–Geller

Beverwijk, 1965

At the junction of two openings

The name of the opening in this case is highly arbitrary, since the play developed more along "Indian" lines. In this connection the game shows how important it is to study not so much the initial moves, but rather the typical positions which occur in each opening. Moreover, of considerable importance is not only a knowledge of the plans of the two sides, but also the nuances in the placing of the pieces and the methods of play in different cases. The Hungarian grandmaster Levente Lengyel was not familiar with the situation after Black's 15th move, otherwise he would hardly have been tempted into winning material.

1 Nf3	c5
2 c4	g6
3 Nc3	Nf6
4 g3	Bg7
5 Bg2	Nc6
6 0–0	0–0
7 d4	c×d4
8 N×d4	N×d4
9 Q×d4	d6

Black has avoided the symmetry, and hopes to gain counter-play in particular at the expense of the white queen, which has prematurely advanced into the centre. This position has occurred on numerous occasions, and it can be regarded as a starting-point for this variation of the English Opening. At the same time it has retained its topicality—it is sufficient to recall the 8th game of the Spassky–Fischer match.

Both sides have a variety of possibilities. In the first instance White must decide where to move his queen. Larsen's continuation 10 Rd1, and then 10 ... Be6 11 B×b7 Ng4 12 Qf4 (as he played against Tal in their 1965 Candidates Match) did not achieve anything for White.

10 Qh4 was introduced by me in a game against Suetin in the 1964 USSR Zonal Tournament, and after the poor reply 10 ... Rb8 White gained the advantage by 11 Bh6, which reinforces the position of the knight at c3 and restricts Black's counter-play against the Q-side. But when, in a later tournament in Chile in 1965, Smyslov played 10 Qh4 against me, Black obtained an easy game: 10 ... Be6 11 B×b7 Rb8 12 Bg2 Qa5, when White was unable to maintain his extra pawn.

Against Spassky, Fischer tried to deploy his pieces harmoniously, by improvizing, I would say, at the board: 10 Bg5, but after 10 ... Be6 he was forced to move his queen to f4, and then to lose time on Qd2. Black successfully overcame his opening difficulties.

10 Qd2 followed by the fianchetto of the queen's bishop appears to be well-founded, but here too, by playing 10 ... Be6 and if 11 b3 d5, Black equalizes, while 11 B×b7 Rb8 12 Bd5 N×d5 13 N×d5 Qd7 14 e4 Rfc8 15 Qe2 B×d5 16 c×d5 (*16 e×d5 Rb4*) 16 ... Qb5 17 Q×b5 R×b5 18 Rb1

Rc2 gives him sufficient compensation for the sacrificed pawn.

Therefore, in my opinion, the soundest move is Smyslov's 10 Qd3. This, incidentally, is what is played by all the supporters of this variation for White—Furman, Portisch, and also myself, although I more often have the given position with Black. This is also what Lengyel played.

10 Qd3   a6
11 Bd2

In recent times 11 Be3 has also been played, but the text move is considered more exact. The idea of it is to prevent the important move ... Qa5 followed by the transference of the queen to h5.

11 ...   Rb8

An unnecessary manoeuvre, since the place for this rook is on its initial square. Interesting play resulted in my game with Portisch (White) at the tournament in Skopje, 1968, after 11 ... Bf5 12 e4 Be6 13 h3 (*13 Nd5 N×d5 14 c×d5 Bd7*) 13 ... Nd7 14 b3, when Black unexpectedly sacrificed a pawn by 14 ... b5 15 c×b5 Ne5 16 Qe2 a×b5 17 Q×b5 Bc8!, and seized the weakened d3 square.

12 Rac1   Bf5
13 e4   Bd7

In principle d7 should have been retained for the knight, since by preventing ... b5 by the simple 14 a4, White could have retained his opening advantage. Later, in the Candidates Quarter-Final Match, Smyslov also gained an advantage by continuing against me 14 h3 b5 15 c×b5 a×b5 16 b4! Lengyel, on the other hand, is diverted by the idea of attacking the rook at b8, which subsequently was to attract Fischer in the aforementioned game with Spassky.

14 Be3   b5
15 c×b5   a×b5

16 Ba7   b4!

Also possible is 16 ... Ra8 17 Bd4 b4 18 Nd5 N×d5 19 B×g7 K×g7 20 Q×d5 Be6 21 Qd4+ Kg8 with a comfortable game, but the continuation in the game promises Black even more.

17 B×b8   b×c3
18 Ba7   c×b2
19 Rc3

The plausible 19 Rb1 achieves nothing for White after 19 ... Qa5 20 Qe3 (*20 ... Bb5 was threatened*) 20 ... Ng4 21 Qb6 Q×a2, when the threat of ... Ra8 is highly unpleasant.

19 ...   d5!

The black bishops will now be in their element!

20 e×d5   Bf5
21 Qb5   N×d5
22 Rc5

Not 22 Rb3 Nc3, when White is forced to give up two exchanges.

22 ...   Nc7

It turns out that the white pieces are cramped in a totally pawn-free part of the board, since they are tied down by the necessity of guarding the queening square of the formidable pawn at b2. The win for Black is not far off.

23 Qb7	Ne6
24 Rb5	

If 24 Rd5, then simply 24 ... Qc7. The only way to delay defeat, but not avoid it, was by 24 R×f5. White prefers to threaten 25 R×b2, and sets a little trap in passing.

24 ...	Bd3

Black happily falls into it, having in mind the continuation in the game.

25 Rd5	B×f1!
26 R×d8	R×d8

White's extra queen cannot prevent the rebirth of a new black opponent. Therefore **White resigned.**

No. 62 English Opening

Nikolayevsky–Geller

24th USSR Championship
Tbilisi, 1966/1967

Queens offered as presents

This is the only game I know of, in which the opponents happily exchanged queen sacrifices. What's more, both White and Black would have been well advised not to allow the offers. Nevertheless the black queen, which was the first to lay down its life, proved in the end to be more "valuable".

1 c4	g6
2 Nc3	Bg7
3 g3	c5
4 Bg2	Nc6
5 e3	Nf6

I think that in such positions Black should avoid complete symmetry. Only in this way can he hope to eliminate the advantage of the first move. Apart from the move made, 5 ... e5 followed by ... Nge7 also seems sensible.

6 Nge2	0–0
7 0–0	d6
8 h3	Bd7
9 b3	a6

10 d4!

Up till now events have developed rather slowly, and the two sides' forces have not come into contact. Now White creates tension in the centre, and at the right time closes the a1–h8 diagonal. The routine 10 Bb2 would have handed Black the initiative: 10 ... Qc8 11 Kh2 b5, and White cannot capture twice on b5 because of 13 ... Ng4+ and 14 ... B×b2.

10 ...	Rb8
11 a4	Nb4

Renewing the threat of ... b5, Black's only possible plan of counter-play.

12 d5?

White should have exploited the weakening of the pressure on d4 to begin an offensive with 12 e4. By eliminating the tension in the centre, White frees the opponent's hands for operations on the Q-side.

12 ...	b5

There was no reason to be tempted by 12 ... Bf5 13 Ra3 Qc8 14 Kh2 Bd3, since then 15 a5! would have hindered Black's basic strategic plan.

| 13 e4 | b×c4 |
| 14 b×c4 | e5! |

Black utilizes the opportunity to switch from a set-up typical of the English Opening to a King's Indian formation. Summing up, we can say that the opening has favoured Black. He is well developed, and his knight occupies an excellent post at b4. This latter factor forces White to commence operations on the K-side, whereas normally in this type of position he would aim to make use of the open b-file.

15 f4

After 15 d×e6 B×e6 16 Bf4 Ne8 White loses a pawn.

| 15 ... | e×f4 |
| 16 B×f4 | |

The attempt to retain a pawn phalanx in the centre — 16 g×f4 would have left White in an awkward dilemma after 16 ... Nh5: whether to wait for ... f5, or to play 17 f5, leaving the e5 square in Black's hands.

| 16 ... | Qe7 |
| 17 Qd2 | |

Fighting for the initiative by 17 e5!? d×e5 18 Bg5 (*18 d6 Qe6 19 Bg5 h6 20 B×f6 B×f6 21 Ne4 Bd8!*) 18 ... h6 19 B×f6 B×f6 20 Ne4 Bg7 21 d6 Qd8 does not achieve anything: the c5 pawn is immune in view of the weakness of the a7–g1 diagonal.

17 ...	Nh5
18 Bg5	Qe5
19 Rf3	

Other ways of defending the g3 pawn are no better, for example: 19 Ra3 Nc2! (*19 ... N×g3? 20 N×g3 Q×g3 21 Nb5 Qe5 22 Bf4*) 20 Bf4 N×a3 21 B×e5 B×e5. Thus in the given position the queen sacrifice is a universal weapon for Black.

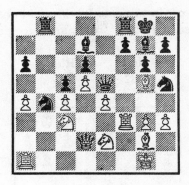

| 19 ... | Nc2 |
| 20 Bf4 | |

Capturing on c2 is equivalent to capitulation: the black bishops become enormously powerful.

20 ...	N×a1
21 B×e5	Nb3
22 Qd1	B×e5

For the queen Black has gained only rook and bishop, but his position can be considered won: his rooks will break into the white position along the open b-file.

| 23 Rd3 | Na5 |
| 24 g4 | Ng7 |

Unnecessarily cautious. Stronger was 24 ... Nf6, since the bishop at e5 is not liable to be attacked, and does not need to be able to retreat.

| 25 Kh1 | N×c4 |
| 26 Qc1 | Nb2 |

This too is not bad, but 26 ... Rb3 was better, carrying out the intended invasion plan.

27 Rf3	N×a4
28 Nd1	Rb4
29 Nf4	Rfb8

Black foresaw the possibility of a counter queen sacrifice on the 32nd move, but underestimated it. He should have prevented White from offering it by 29 ... Bb5 or

29 ... c4. In this case Black would not have required a further sixty moves to win the game!

| 30 Nd3 | Rb1 |
| 31 Qd2 | Nb2 |

32 N×e5!

An excellent idea. By returning the queen, White transposes into an ending where he is two pawns down, but where very exact play is required of Black.

32 ...	R×d1+
33 Q×d1	N×d1
34 N×d7	Rb1
35 e5!	d×e5
36 N×e5	Ne3+
37 Kh2	N×g2
38 K×g2	Rd1

Unpromising is 38 ... Ne8 39 N×f7 Rd1 40 Nh6+ Kg7 41 g5 Nd6 42 Ra3 R×d5 43 h4, when White gains a draw.

39 Rb3!

Nikolayevsky plays this part of the game splendidly. He would have had a difficult rook ending after 39 N×f7 Nf5 40 g×f5 K×f7 41 f×g6++ K×g6 42 Ra3 R×d5 43 R×a6+ Kg5.

| 39 ... | Ne8 |
| 40 Rb8 | Kf8 |

Here the game was adjourned. White's first moves after analysis are the strongest.

41 Nd7+	Ke7
42 N×c5	R×d5
43 N×a6	Nf6

Black intends to advance ... h5 and force his opponent to exchange on h5, rightly judging that he will have very real winning chances. White should have tried to prevent this plan, if only by 44 Nb4, but instead he makes a serious mistake in driving the black king off the 7th rank.

44 Rb7+	Kf8
45 Rb2	h5!
46 g×h5	

46 Rf2 loses in curious fashion after 46 ... Kg7 47 Kg3 h×g4 48 h×g4 Rg5 49 Rf4 Nh5+ 50 Kh4 N×f4 51 K×g5 Ng2, when White cannot avoid mate.

46 ...	N×h5
47 Rf2	Rb5
48 Nc7	Re5
49 Na6	Kg7
50 Nb4	f5
51 Nd3	Re4
52 Rf3	Kh6
53 Nf2	Ra4

While White has been bringing his knight into play, Black has strengthened his position and now intends to continue the offensive with his king, stealing up on the lone white pawn.

54 Rb3	Kg5
55 Nd3	Ra2+
56 Kf3	Ra5

Cutting off the white knight's road to e5 and to the rear of the black pawns.

| 57 Rc3 | Ra4 |
| 58 Nc5 | |

After 58 Ne5 one possibility is 58 ... Rf4+ 59 Kg2 Re4 60 Nf7+ Kh4, when the threat of ... Nf4+ is decisive.

146

| 58 ... | Rf4+ |
| 59 Kg2 | Kh4 |

60 Ne6

White tries for a counter-attack, since the attempt to create a fortress by 60 Nd3 Ra4 61 Nf2 does not succeed: 61 ... Nf4+ 62 Kh2 Ra2 63 Rf3 g5 64 Kg1 Ra1+ 65 Kh2 Rf1.

| 60 ... | Ra4 |
| 61 Rc6 | |

White loses immediately after 61 Nf8 Nf4+ 62 Kh2 g5.

61 ...	Ra2+
62 Kf3	Ra3+
63 Kf2	Ra2+

"Just in case" Black gains time on the clock by repeating the position.

| 64 Kf3 | Ra3+ |
| 65 Kf2 | Ng3 |

The natural capture of the pawn would have thrown away the win: 65 ... K×h3 66 Ng5+ and 67 R×g6, or 65 ... R×h3 66 Rc4+.

66 Nf4	Ne4+
67 Kg2	Ra2+
68 Kf3	Ra3+
69 Kg2	Ra2+
70 Kf3	Rf2+
71 Ke3	g5

72 Rh6+	Kg3
73 Ne2+	Kg2
74 Nd4	Nc5!

"Only" threatening mate by 75 ... f4.

75 Nc6	f4+
76 Kd4	Nb3+
77 Kc4	Rf3
78 h4	

White tries his last chance: suppose Black were to exchange?!

| 78 ... | Nd2+ |
| 79 Kd4 | Rg3 |

Here the game could have been terminated. The threat of ... f3–f2 forces White to give up his last pawn.

80 Nb4	Nf3+
81 Ke4	N×h4
82 Nd5	f3
83 Ne3+	Kh3
84 Kd3	Rg1
85 Kd2	Ra1
86 Rh5	Ra2+
87 Kd1	Re2
88 Nf1	Re5
89 Kd2	f2
90 Kd3	Kg2
White resigns	

No. 63 English Opening

Geller–Mikadze

Karseladze Memorial Tournament Gori, 1968

Take the pawn, please!

A crucial point of the game was the choice between a positional and a combinational procedure. I made it without hesitation. Of course, a part was played by my constant readiness to engage in open piece play.

Nevertheless, the main thing was the strict observance of a chess rule: the player with a lead in development can and should attack, disregarding, if necessary, loss of material. It was another matter that the position permitted a second solution, one that had been approved many years earlier.

So it was a matter of taste: to calmly follow the well-trodden path, or to seek complications.

1 Nf3	Nf6
2 c4	c5
3 Nc3	d5
4 c×d5	N×d5
5 g3	

Should White choose the text move, or should be play 5 e3 à 1a Keres with the possible development of his bishop at b5? I prefer the K-side fianchetto, which emphasizes the rather insecure position of the black knight at d5.

| 5 ... | Nc6 |
| 6 Bg2 | Nc7 |

This was introduced by Rubinstein and then analyzed in detail during the 1930s by Botvinnik, who used the pawn wedge b6–c5–e5–f6 to prepare an outpost at d4 for a knight. In the present game White does not prevent this, but intends to break up Black's centre.

| 7 0–0 | e5 |

Black has seized the d4 square, and yet accurate play is demanded of him, especially in the opening. Otherwise his lack of development may prove fatal.

| 8 b3 | Be6? |

This natural move is a mistake for the reason stated above. Black should have followed the well-known game Kirillov–Botvinnik (7th USSR Championship, 1931): 8 ... Be7 9 Bb2 0–0 10 Rc1 f6 11 Ne1 Bf5,

etc. The delay over the development of his K-side puts Black in a difficult position.

| 9 Bb2 | Rc8 |

Black cannot get by without supporting his c5 pawn.

| 10 Rc1 | f6 |

White's last few moves are the best in the given position, while Black's have been forced. Thus 10 ... Be7, for example, fails to 11 Na4. But now White has a choice between the sharp continuation in the game and the quieter 11 Ne1, with the idea of transferring the knight to d3 from where it attacks both of Black's central pawns. There is also the positional threat of B×c6. A game Flohr–Goldberg, 1955, continued 11 ... Qd7 12 Nd3 Bd6 13 Ne4 b6 14 f4 e×f4 15 N×d6+ Q×d6 16 N×f4, when White's advantage was obvious.

Even so, the opening up of the centre, in view of White's superior mobilization, seems to me more promising.

| 11 e3 | |

With the unequivocal intention of playing d2–d4.

| 11 ... | c4 |

Black's attempt to prevent this proves on closer examination to be a blank shot. His pieces become active for literally 2–3 moves, but are then forced to retreat, and in an inferior situation. But even 11 ... Be7 would have left Black in serious difficulties: 12 Na4 Na6 (or *12 ... b6 13 d4 e×d4 14 e×d4 N×d4 15 N×d4 c×d4 16 Re1*, etc.) 13 Qe2, and the threat of d2–d4 (with or without the preparatory *Rfd1*) is highly unpleasant.

12 Qe2!

This pawn sacrifice would seem to be the strongest continuation. On 12 ... c×b3 White carries out his plan: 13 d4, and if 13 ... Be7, then 14 Rfd1.

12 ...	Nb4

Black himself is prepared to part with a pawn for a moment, if only to avert the imminent explosion in the centre: 13 b×c4 Nd3.

13 Ne1

The exchange of offers continues! Now the capture on b3 is forced, since after 13 ... Nd3 14 N×d3 c×d3 15 Qh5+ Bf7 (or *15 ... g6*) 16 Qh4 Black cannot hold his Q-side.

13 ...	c×b3
14 a×b3	Nc6

Black's activity has expired, and now White's attack unfolds.

15 Nf3	Be7
16 d4	0–0
17 d×e5	f×e5
18 Ne4	

The position of his black-squared bishop draws White's attention to the g7 square. An endgame, where Black's Q-side pawns might have had something to say, is not destined to be reached.

18 ...	B×b3
19 N×e5	Bd5

There is nothing else. 20 N×c6 cannot be allowed, but also not possible is 19 ... N×e5 20 B×e5 Be6 (*21 Qb2, 21 Qg4* and *21 B×g7* were all threatened) 21 Rfd1.

20 Qg4

The storm factor has been brought to the necessary level. Black no longer has any defence.

20 ...	Be6
21 Q×g7+	K×g7
22 N×c6+	Bf6

A mistake, of course, but it merely accelerates the end. 22 ... Kf7 23 N×d8+ Rf×d8 24 Nc5 would have left White with an extra pawn and two long-range bishops.

23 N×d8	B×b2

And without waiting for the obvious 24 R×c7+, **Black resigned.**

No. 64 English Opening

Belyavsky–Geller

*Alekhine Memorial Tournament
Moscow, 1975*

Under fire from the bishops

In this game I was surprised by... the first move: I was mentally prepared for 1 e4. On the other hand, on the 6th move a surprise awaited my opponent, who, although still young, was already USSR Champion. In an unusual variation Aleksandr

Belyavsky, who works a lot and knows a lot, was forced at the board to work out something with which he was then obviously unfamiliar. White did not succeed in solving all the problems which arose, and the game concluded with a final position which rarely occurs in practice: a pure mate with two bishops.

1 c4	c5
2 Nf3	Nc6
3 Nc3	Nf6
4 d4	c×d4
5 N×d4	e6
6 g3	Qb6

In opening guides it is stated that this move was brought into practice by me. This is indeed so. But I should like to take the opportunity to say that Igor Bondarevsky, who was then my trainer, showed me the move more than twenty years before the present game. It was then that this move was first employed. It is true that, in playing this way, Black is taking something of a risk. On the other hand, it leads to a complicated strategic struggle — precisely that for which I was aiming. Besides, the move also contains a direct tactical threat, and for a certain time Black disturbs the coordination of the white pieces.

7 Nb3

In the game D. Byrne–Geller, match USA–USSR, 1955, White overlooked the threat, and, in analogy with certain outwardly similar variations of the Sicilian Defence, continued 7 Ndb5, but after 7 ... Ne5! the threat of 8 ... Qc6 cost him a pawn: 8 Bg2 a6 (8 ... N×c4 is also possible, since the line which used to be considered a refutation of this, 9 b3 Ne5 10 Bf4 — or 10 Be3 Qa5 11 Bf4 a6 12 B×e5 a×b5 — is unconvincing in view of 10 ... Nfg4 11 0–0 a6 12 Nd4 Ng6) 9 Be3 (slightly better is 9 Na3 B×a3 10 b×a3 N×c4 11 Qb3 Q×b3 12 a×b3, with some compensation) 9 ... Qa5 10 Bf4 a×b5 11 B×e5 b×c4.

Later White also tried 7 Nc2, depriving the black bishop of b4, which again leads to interesting play after 7 ... Bc5 8 e3 0–0 9 Bg2 Qa6.

7 ...	Ne5
8 e4	

Undoubtedly the strongest continuation (bad, for example, is 8 Be3 Qb4, when the c4 pawn is not easily defended). But White thought over this move for twenty minutes — an indication that he was not familiar with the 6 ... Qb6 variation.

8 ...	Bb4
9 Qe2	0–0

Against Taimanov in the 22nd USSR Championship, Moscow, 1955, I chose 9 ... a5, and after 10 Be3 Qc7 11 Bd2 0–0 12 a3 B×c3 13 B×c3 b6 14 f4 Ng6 15 Bg2 Ba6 16 Nd2 Rac8 the opening stage of the game had developed satisfactorily for Black. The text move is also perfectly good. After removing his king from the centre, Black is ready to open up the game.

10 f4

White cannot tolerate the knight at e5.

10 ...	Nc6
11 e5	Ne8
12 Bd2	

White does not want to allow the doubling of his pawns on the Q-side, but now the black queen remains at b6, from where it prevents K-side castling. More natural therefore is 12 Be3, which gives White the more pleasant game after:

(a) 12 ... Qc7 13 Bg2 f6 14 e×f6 B×c3+ 15 b×c3 N×f6 16 0–0 b6 17 f5 Ba6 18 f×e6 d×e6 19 Bf4 e5 20 Bg5 (Popov–Lutikov, USSR, 1977), or

(b) 12 ... Qd8 13 Bg2 f6 14 e×f6 N×f6 15 0–0 B×c3 16 b×c3 b6 17 Rfd1 Bb7 18 c5 Rb8 19 c4 (Schmidt–Ilic, Nis, 1977).

12 ...	f6

It is in this way that Black must open up the game. After 12 ... d6 13 e×d6 he cannot play 13 ... N×d6 in view of 14 c5 B×c5 15 Na4, while after 13 ... Nd4 14 N×d4 Q×d4 15 Rd1 it is not clear with what he should take on d6.

13 e×f6

13 c5 is interesting:

(a) 13 ... Qd8 14 a3 B×c3 f×e5 16 B×e5 b6 (an interesting try is *16 ... N×e5 17 Q×e5 b6 18 Bg2 Ba6 19 B×a8 Q×a8 20 0–0–0 Bc4 21 Nd2 Bd5*, with attacking chances for the sacrificed exchange) 17 Bg2, and now 17 ... Bb7! leads to a highly complex struggle.

(b) 13 ... Qc7 14 Nb5 B×d2+ 15 Q×d2 Qb8, and White cannot maintain his outpost at e5, while his c5 pawn will be attacked by ... b6.

13 ...	N×f6
14 Bg2	

On the intermediate 14 c5 Black should not play 14 ... Qc7, which after 15 Bg2 b6 16 Nb5 Qb8 17 B×b4 N×b4 18 B×a8 Q×a8 19 0–0 gave White a clear advantage in Magerramov–Chekhov, USSR, 1977, but 14 ... Qd8 followed by the undermining ... b6.

14 ...	d5!

In offering a pawn sacrifice, Black hopes to gain good piece play, since the position of the white king is now weakened.

15 0–0–0

Of course, on the Q-side White's king will come under attack, but he is not able to block the position. Thus 15 c5 Qc7 16 a3 fails to 16 ... B×c5! 17 N×c5 Nd4.

15 ...	a5!

Black is only interested in the initiative! The attempt to maintain material equality, 15 ... d×c4 16 Q×c4 Bd7, would have led to a marked advantage for White after 17 Na4! B×d2+ 18 R×d2 Qb4 19 Q×b4 N×b4 20 Nac5.

16 c×d5

White is unable to block the Q-side. For example, 16 c5 Qc7 17 Nb5 Qe7, when the c5 pawn requires defending and the threat of 18 ... a4 is highly unpleasant, while on 18 B×b4 a×b4 19 Kb1 Black continues 19 ... e5 with the threat of ... Bf5+.

16 ...	e×d5
17 B×d5+	

It might have been better to exchange a pair of knights by 17 N×d5 N×d5 18 B×d5+ Kh8, but what is White to do next?...

151

17 ...	Kh8
18 Qe3	

It was obviously on this that White was basing his defence, but the attack develops even without the queens! The alternative 18 Be3 Qc7 19 Nb5 would have allowed Black a choice between the quiet 19 ...Qe7 and the tactical 19 ... Nd4+ 20 N×c7 N×e2+ 21 Kb1 Bf5+ 22 Ka1 Rac8, when it is not easy for White to defend his hanging pieces.

18 ...	Q×e3
19 B×e3	Bg4
20 Rdf1	

On 20 Rd3 Black transfers his bishop to f5 with gain of tempo, cutting the white king's path into the corner.

20 ...	a4
21 Na1	

Alas, the knight has to move into the corner, since after 21 Nd2 B×c3 or 21 Nc5 N×d5 22 N×d5 B×c5 23 B×c5 Rf5 White loses material.

21 ...	a3
22 Bb3	Na5
23 Nc2	

This accelerates White's defeat. More tenacious was 23 Rf2 or 23 Bd4, although even then after 23 ... Rac8 his position can hardly be defended.

23 ...	N×b3+
24 a×b3	a2!
25 Na1	

In the variation 25 N×a2 R×a2 26 N×b4 Rc8+ White is either mated after 27 Kb1 Bf5+ 28 K×a2 Ra8+, or else he loses everything after 27 Kd2 R×b2+.

25 ...	Rac8
26 Bd4	Rfd8
27 B×f6	

27 Be5 is decisively met by 27 ... Ne4.

27 ...	g×f6
28 h3	

28 ...	R×c3+!

White resigned: 29 b×c3 Ba3+ 30 Kc2 Bf5 mate.

PART 2

Against World Champions

How does one defeat them? This question has always been of interest, both to experienced chess maestros, and to those who are merely taking their first steps along the wonderful and fascinating road of chess. After all, World Champions are distinguished by something special, otherwise they simply would not be champions.

It seems to me that World Champions can be defeated, provided that three essential conditions are satisfied.

The first is that you have to play against them. Perhaps not in a match for the World Championship, perhaps not in a major international tournament, but at least in a simultaneous display.

The second is that, when playing against them, you must always remember that they are Champions, and give every effort to the game, without thinking about the following day.

The third is that, when playing against them, you must completely forget that they are Champions. This will enable you to avoid being "hypnotized" by the opponent's personality, and will maintain your cheerfulness of spirit and clarity of mind.

The reader will realize, of course, that the content of these "rules" is not very serious. And I have permitted myself to hide behind their light-hearted tone, only because there is no scientifically based recipe for how to defeat Champions, there never has been, and there never will be.

But in every joke there is a dose of truth. If you play at full intensity, if you do not tremble before the formidable name of your opponent, and if, finally, you work seriously at chess, then you can hope for the most serious successes, and for the most joyous victories.

It is very difficult for me to give the exact number of games played against World Champions. The majority of them are Soviet players, and we have met even in not very important events, both individual and team. And there is no particular need to—it is sufficient to say that there have been about 200 such meetings. Of course, they were not all played with chess monarchs who were "ruling" at the time. Thus Max Euwe became Ex-World Champion at the time when I was only learning the moves of the pieces. Vasily Smyslov and Mikhail Tal each held the title for only one year, and Bobby Fischer, after becoming champion, did not play any more serious chess. But this is not so important. Champions—whether they be future or former—at any stage of their careers belong to the most interesting and distinctive of opponents.

Against the majority of them I have a successful record. If draws are discounted, my score against Botvinnik is 4–1, Smyslov — 10–7 (and altogether I have played about fifty games against him!), Petrosian — 4–2, and Fischer — 5–3. I have a 1–1 score against Euwe and Karpov, and only with two World

Champions do I have a minus score: against Tal 4–6, and against Spassky 6–9 (it is interesting that I have a plus score in tournaments, but in two matches I suffered six defeats without a single win).

I give here all the games I have won against World Champions, with the exception of one—against Tal from the 3rd cycle of the Candidates Tournament in Curacao, which was irreparably ruined by terrible mutual blunders in time trouble. It is "compensated" by two draws with the same opponent, which I hope will appeal to the reader.

Max Euwe

No. 65 King's Indian Defence

Euwe–Geller

Candidates Tournament
Zurich, 1953

The second and last...

During the game I realized that this was my second, and probably my last meeting with the highly-experienced Ex-World Champion: Max Euwe was beginning to cut down on his appearances. At any rate, he did not take part in the next World Championship cycle. And in this tournament Euwe avoided theoretical duels in complicated modern variations, and endeavoured to choose simpler continuations.

Black took all this into account when deciding on his tactics for the game. In addition, I was eager for revenge: in the first cycle of the event the Ex-World Champion, helped by the experience of three matches with the great master of combinations, Alexander Alekhine, had successfully parried my attack. ...

1 d4	Nf6
2 c4	g6
3 g3	Bg7
4 Bg2	0–0
5 Nf3	d6
6 0–0	Nbd7
7 Qc2	

In this way White vacates a square for his rook, simultaneously defends his c4 pawn, and prevents Black from initiating tactical complications in the centre after ... e5, ... e×d4 and ... Nb6. His plans clearly include an exchange of pawns in the centre.

7 ...	e5
8 Rd1	Re8
9 Nc3	c6
10 d×e5	

10 ... e4 and 11 ... d5 was threatened, so White carries out his plan and exchanges. A more complicated struggle results from 10 e4.

| 10 ... | d×e5 |
| 11 Ng5 | |

White's intention becomes clear: to occupy d6 directly by Ng5–e4–d6. But the time lost on this allows Black, by a series of manoeuvres, to create good preconditions for an attack.

11 ...	Qe7
12 Nge4	Nc5
13 Nd6	Rd8
14 N×c8	R×d1+
15 N×d1	

Capturing with the queen would have allowed Black to gain a further tempo by transferring his rook to the d-file.

154

15 ...	R×c8
16 Bd2	

Such a modest developing move indicates that at present White's advantage of the two bishops is of a purely theoretical nature. The obvious difference in the harmonious deployment of the minor pieces allows us to conclude that the opening battle has gone in favour of Black.

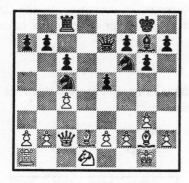

16 ...	Nfd7!
17 Bc3	f5
18 Ne3	Ne6
19 b4	

This outwardly active move is by no means an indication of White's aggression. He is simply vacating the b2 square for his queen, which was about to become rather restricted.

19 ...	Nd4
20 Qb2	Qf7
21 a4	Rf8

The concentration of Black's forces on the K-side becomes threatening. And if account is taken of the fact that White will be forced to take the knight at d4 with his bishop, and that his own knight is tied to the defence of his c-pawn, Black's positional advantage is bound to increase.

22 a5	f4
23 g×f4	Q×f4
24 Rf1	Nf6
25 c5	

The attempt to open up the game by 25 b5 would have merely suited Black: after 25 ... Ne4 White's Q-side pawns are also weak. Therefore the Ex-World Champion immediately begins erecting defensive barriers, blocking the position wherever it is possible.

25 ...	Ne4
26 B×e4	Q×e4
27 B×d4	e×d4
28 Ng2	a6

There is some point in Black blocking the Q-side, although 28 ... Re8 was also possible.

29 Qb3+	Kh8
30 Qd3	Qe5
31 f4	

This apparently hopeless weakening of the e-pawn and the e3 square is for the sake of the same idea: the creation of an impregnable fortress.

31 ...	Qe6
32 Rf3	Re8
33 Kf2	Rf8

On the threshold of time trouble Black limits himself to preventing the opponent from undertaking any freeing action. This is all the more justified, in that White is forced to await passively the development of events.

34 Kf1	Kg8
35 Kf2	Rf7
36 Kf1	Rf5

37 Kf2	Bf6
38 Kg1	Rd5
39 Kf2	Kg7
40 Kf1	Rh5
41 Kg1	Rd5
42 h3	

This advance does not spoil White's pawn formation. On the contrary, at h3 the pawn is more soundly defended.

42 ...	Kf7

After analyzing the adjourned position, Black intends to transfer his king to a safe shelter on the Q-side and then to launch a general storming of the K-side.

43 Kf2	Ke7
44 Kf1	Kd8
45 Ne1	

Sensing the futility of passive defence, White tries by the following knight manoeuvre to prepare counter-play against the black king.

45 ...	Kc7
46 Nc2	Kb8
47 Na3	Bd8
48 Nc4	Bc7
49 Nb6	Rd8
50 f5	

White consistently follows his overall plan of aiming for counter-play. Otherwise Black

himself would have put pressure on the f4 pawn by ... Qf6, etc.

50 ...	g×f5
51 Q×f5	Qh6
52 Qf7	

White intends, by invading the 7th rank with both heavy pieces, to give mate to the black king. The question to be settled is: who will be the first to create decisive threats? After a period of manoeuvring, the time has arrived when tempi have to be calculated.

52 ...	Qc1+
53 Kf2	Bh2!

With the rather unexpected threat of 54 ... Qg1 mate.

54 Qg7	Bf4
55 Kg2	Be3

56 Rf1?

Annotating this game in his book on the tournament, Bronstein recommends 56 Rf7, but then gives the variation 56 ... Qg1+ 57 Kf3 Qf1+ 58 Kg3 Bf4+! 59 Kh4 (*59 R×f4? Qg1+, or 59 Kg4 h5+*) 59 ... Qf2+ 60 Kg4 h5+ and wins. But this isn't so! After 61 Kf5? Black can indeed win, in rather cunning fashion: 61 ... Bc7+! 62 Kg6 Q×e2!! 63 R×c7 Qe4+ 64 Kg5 (*64 K×h5 Qf5+, 65 ... Qf4+ and 66 ... Q×c7*) 64 ... Qe3+! 65 Kf5 Q×h3+ 66 Ke5 Re8+ 67 Re7 R×e7+ 68 Q×e7 Qe3+

69 Kf6 Q×e7+, and one of the black pawns queens.

But White can continue 61 K×h5 Q×e2+ 62 Kh4! Qe1+ 63 Kh5!, and since 63 ... Qe5+ is bad in view of 64 Q×e5+ B×e5 65 Nd7+, Black is unable to drive the white king away from h4 and h5. In this case, as is easily verified, the above idea of retreating the bishop to c7 does not work: there is no threat of a check to the white king from f4 or g3. And this means that the venerable Ex-World Champion was not let down by his intuition, and that in pinning his hopes on counter-play he was in principle correct.

56 ...	Qd2
57 Rf7	

The tempo lost by White allows Black to win by force. But there was no longer any defence, since 57 Qg4 is decisively met by 57 ... d3, and 57 Kf3 by 57 ... Bh6.

57 ...	Q×e2+
58 Kg3	Qe1+
59 Kf3	

Moving on to the g-file would have led either to the variation in the game, or to the exchange of queens and the advance of the black pawn to the queening square.

59 ...	Qh1+
60 Kg3	

Similarly after 60 Ke2 d3+! 61 K×e3 Re8+ White cannot save his king.

60 ...	Qg1+
61 Kf3	Qf2+
62 Ke4	Re8+
63 Re7	Qh4+
White resigns	

Mikhail Botvinnik

No. 66 Queen Pawn Opening

Botvinnik–Geller

*19th USSR Championship
Moscow, 1951*

Disturbing the equilibrium

Whether or not to give perpetual check was what White had to decide on his 26th move. The position was level, but this was not the dynamic equilibrium of a middlegame, where one can hope to tip the scales in one's own favour, but equilibrium which demanded an accurate evaluation of the coming endgame. A mistake in this evaluation led to a defeat for White, since his trumps — a pawn mass in the centre and two strong bishops — nevertheless proved insufficient.

Every player has games which are especially memorable: the first game in a USSR Championship, the first appearance abroad in an international tournament. Among such games I include this one: my first ever meeting at the board with the leader of the Soviet Chess School, Mikhail Botvinnik.

1 d4	Nf6
2 g3	d5
3 c4	

Now Black can take the pawn. But the inaccuracy, strangely enough, was committed by the then World Champion back on the 2nd move, which allowed Black to transpose into a comfortable line of the Queen's Gambit. The point being that after 1 d4 d5 one doesn't play 2 g3.

3 ...	d×c4
4 Nf3	

If now 4 Qa4+ (as is usually played in the variation *1 d4 Nf6 2 c4 e6 3 g3 d5 4 Bg2 d×c4*), Black can play either to hold the pawn — 4 ... Nc6 5 Bg2 (*5 Nf3 Be6*) 5 ... Qd7 6 Nf3 e5, or can restrict himself to giving the opponent an isolated d-pawn — 4 ... Bd7 5 Q×c4 Bc6 6 Nf3 B×f3 7 e×f3 c6.

4 ...	Nc6

4 ... c5 is also possible, but then 5 Qa4+ followed by Q×c4 transposes into the Catalan Opening. But the position now reached is a strange conglomeration of the Queen's Gambit Accepted, the Catalan Opening, and, within another move, the Albin Counter-Gambit. It is not surprising that already at this point both sides began taking a long time over their moves.

5 Nc3	e5
6 N×e5	

It transpires that White has nothing better, since 6 d5 fails to 6 ... Nb4 7 e4 (*7 N×e5 Bf5*) 7 ... Bg4! 8 Qa4+ Qd7!

6 ...	N×e5
7 d×e5	Q×d1+
8 N×d1	Ne4
9 Bg2	Bb4+
10 Kf1	Nc5

The forcing operation begun by Black on his 5th move has enabled him to overcome completely his opening difficulties. Although, with the queens off, White's loss of castling is not especially terrible, even so Black's position would appear to be more promising.

11 Be3

It turns out that the apparently more energetic 11 Nc3, with the threat of Nd5, does not achieve anything: 11 ... Be6! 12 Nd5 0-0-0, and the bishop at b4 is immune in view of the mate on d1.

11 ...	Be6
12 Nc3	

It would have been rash to play 12 B×c5 (*12 a3? Nb3*) 12 ... B×c5 13 B×b7 Rb8 14 Bc6+ Ke7, when for the pawn Black gains strong pressure plus the two bishops.

12 ...	0-0-0
13 f4	

It might appear that White stands better. He has a pawn centre, he has prepared an exit for his king at f2, and Black's minor pieces on the Q-side have become entangled.

13 ...	B×c3!

Black's entire play is based on this. He does not cling on to the two bishops, but regains the important d5 square from White, and activates his pieces to the maximum. In addition, his Q-side pawns can begin to advance.

Incidentally, the text move would also have followed on 13 Rc1.

14 b×c3	Na4
15 Rc1	Bd5
16 Bh3+	

Were White to be deprived of the two bishops, he would stand markedly worse.

16 ...	Kb8
17 Rg1	Rhe8
18 Kf2	Be4

An inaccuracy, which allows White to equalize. Nowadays, without thinking, I would have played 18 ... b5 followed by

... Kb7, ... c5 and ... Kc6, which would have retained for Black the better position.

19 Rgd1!

By this pawn sacrifice, which cannot be declined (*20 Bd7* is threatened), White essentially ensures perpetual check.

19 ...	R×d1
20 R×d1	N×c3
21 Rc1	N×a2
22 Ra1	Nb4
23 B×a7+	Ka8
24 Bb6+	Kb8

The attempt to avoid the perpetual check — 24 ... Na6 — involved an unjustified risk, since after 25 B×c7 White would have halted Black's passed pawns, and would have been threatening to advance his pawn centre. Equally unjustified is White's decision to play for a win.

25 Ba7+	Ka8

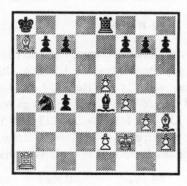

26 Be3+

White re-establishes material equality, but Black will now have the initiative.

26 ...	Na6
27 Ra4	Bd5
28 Bd7	Rd8
29 Bb5	Be6
30 B×a6	

After 30 B×c4 B×c4 31 R×c4 the black

pawns would have immediately begun advancing: 31 ... b5.

30 ...	b×a6
31 R×a6+	Kb7
32 Ra5	

In his first period of time trouble, Botvinnik finds the correct plan of defence: the white rook is placed behind the c4 pawn. The plausible 32 Ra1 would have merely delayed the invasion by the black rook into his position (*32 ... Kc6* followed by ... *Rb8–b2*).

32 ...	Rd1
33 Rc5	Rh1!

The king is lured onto a white square, since after 34 h4 h5 Black firmly blockades the entire K-side.

34 Kg2	Ra1
35 Rb5+	Kc6
36 Rc5+	Kd7
37 f5	

Evidently White did not like the fact that after the possible 37 ... c6 and ... Bd5 his rook would be shut in, since on 38 Bd2 Black gains a tempo by attacking the bishop, and the white rook does not manage to break out to a5. 37 Bd4, with the idea of e2–e4, is parried by 37 ... Ra2 38 Kf3 h5, when the white king is uncomfortably placed. Botvinnik's hopes associated with his compact pawn mass have not been justified, and he goes totally on to the defensive to exchange off the dangerous c4 pawn.

37 ...	B×f5
38 R×c4	Ra2
39 g4	

Otherwise there follows 39 ... h5.

39 ...	Be6
40 Rd4+	Kc8!

The way for the c-pawn has to be opened.

41 Kf3

In this position Black sealed his next move. White has a number of problems to solve.

41 ...	Ra5
42 g5	

42 Kf4 would have lost the g-pawn after 42 ... c5, 43 ... Ra4+ and 44 ... R(B)×g4. White had to choose between 42 h3 and the text move, which is more logical: after 42 ... R×e5 he has counter-play of the type 43 Rh4 Bf5 44 Bd4.

42 ...	c5
43 Rh4	c4

For the sake of the h-pawn it was not worth moving the bishop from its ideal post at e6, especially in view of Black's 46th move.

44 R×h7	g6
45 Rh8+	Kc7
46 Rd8	

Both the capture of the rook, and 46 ... R×e5 47 Bf4, lead to an obvious draw, but...

46 ...	Bd5+!

Now the white rook does not reach the first rank.

47 Kf2	c3
48 Rd6	c2
49 h4?	

Essential was 49 Bc1, which would subsequently have deprived Black of an important tempo. It would seem that, with his second period of time trouble approaching, White underestimated the strength of Black's reply.

49 ...	Bc4
50 Rd4	Ba6
51 Rf4	R×e5

Were the white bishop at c1, Black would not have had the threat of ... R×e3.

52 R×f7+	Kc6
53 Rf6+	Kd5

54 R×a6?	

The rook ending is completely hopeless for White. He should have tried 54 Bf4, although even then after 54 ... Re4! (54 ... R×e2+ 55 Kf3 Bd3 56 Rd6+ Kc4 57 R×g6 leads to a draw) 55 Bc1 R×e2+ 56 Kf3 Re1 57 Bd2 Bd3 it is not easy for White to draw, even with the small amount of material remaining.

54 ...	R×e3
55 Ra1	Rc3
56 Rc1	Kc4
57 Ke1	Kb3
58 Kd2	Kb2

White is in zugzwang: 59 e4 Rd3+.

59 R×c2+	R×c2+
60 Kd3	Kb3
61 e4	Rc4
62 e5	Kb4
White resigns	

160

No. 67 King's Indian Defence

Botvinnik–Geller

Budapest, 1952

The blockade of a flank

A game with Botvinnik is normally a battle against monumental strategy. And just as the visible part of an iceberg is only one sixth of it, so in this battle a large fraction of the ideas remains imperceptible. In play of this nature, particular significance is acquired by even the slightest inaccuracies. In the given case the only obvious slip was on White's 15th move, the fruits of which were exploited... 32 moves later. This happened partly for the added reason that the value of each move in the game, by both White and by Black, was fairly high, and behind every piece manoeuvre, without exception, there was a definite strategic problem.

1 d4	Nf6
2 c4	g6
3 g3	

When meeting Botvinnik, every King's Indian player had to be prepared to do battle against the fianchetto of the king's bishop. Such an adherence to a definite system of development allowed the opponent to avoid any possible surprises in the first few moves, but did not make his life any easier, since the resulting positions were handled splendidly by Botvinnik.

3 ...	Bg7
4 Bg2	0–0
5 Nc3	d6
6 Nf3	Nbd7
7 0–0	e5
8 e4	e×d4

Nowadays I more often play 8 ... c6. But at that time, firstly, I considered the continuation in the game to be better, and, second-ly, I used to aim more directly than I do now for dynamic piece play.

9 N×d4	Nc5
10 h3	Re8
11 Re1	a5

An unusual battle of nerves has begun. White is waiting for ... c6 (without which Black all the same cannot get by), so as to develop his bishop at f4 with gain of tempo. Black, for his part, puts off this move until the last possible moment, and before completing his development carries out the flank diversion which is usual in this position.

12 Qc2

The battle of nerves continues. In passing Black is offered the chance to win a pawn: 12 ... Nf×e4 13 N×e4 B×d4, but what is he to do after 14 Bg5 Qd7 15 Nf6+ B×f6 16 B×f6?

12 ...	a4

Who will be the first to "falter"? This is objectively stronger than 12 ... Ng4 13 Nb3!, and now:

(a) 13 ... N×b3 14 a×b3 Ne5 15 Be3 Nc6 16 Rad1, and Black has not managed to equalize (Stahlberg–Reshevsky, Candidates Tournament, 1953).

(b) 13 ... Ne5 14 N×c5 d×c5 15 Rd1 Bd7 16 Nb5 Qc8 17 Kh2 a4 18 f4 Nc6 19 Be3 Nb4 (Lipnitsky–Boleslavsky, 20th USSR Championship), and White could have con-solidated his advantage by 20 Qe2 b6 21 a3 Nc6 22 e5.

12 ... Nfd7 could have transposed into the game, but would have afforded White a greater choice.

In fact, 12 ... c6 could have now been played, since after 13 Bf4 Nfd7 14 Rad1 Ne5 15 b3 Qb6! 16 Be3 a4! 17 f4 Ned7 18 Rb1 a×b3 19 a×b3 Black has managed to bring his queen out to b6, and has a satisfactory position (Borisenko–Geller, 18th USSR Championship).

13 Be3

White at last "gives in". 13 Rb1 was still possible.

| **13 ...** | **c6** |
| **14 Rad1** | |

The alternative plan — of driving the knight from c5 by b2–b4 — would have involved the move mentioned in the previous note.

| **14 ...** | **Qa5** |

14 ... Nfd7 would again in a number of cases have transposed, but would have restricted Black's possibilities, for example after 15 f4. After the text move Black has good play, and it is not easy for White to make use of his spatial advantage.

15 a3?

A "self-blocking" move, after which the knight at c5 feels very much at home.

A later try was 15 f4 Bd7 16 Bf2 Re7 17 g4 Rae8 18 f5 g×f5 19 N×f5 B×f5 20 e×f5, when Black obtained a won ending: 20 ... R×e1+ 21 R×e1 a3! 22 g5 a×b2! 23 g×f6 R×e1+ 24 B×e1 B×f6 25 Q×b2 Nd3 26 Qe2 N×e1 27 Q×e1 Bd4+ 28 Kh1 Kf8 29 Qd2 Q×c3 30 Q×c3 B×c3 (R. Byrne–Kotov, match USA–USSR, 1954).

The frontal attack on the d-pawn by 15 Nde2 Nfd7 16 R×d6 Ne5 17 Rdd1 N×c4 18 Bd4 (Smyslov–Ciocaltea, Bucharest, 1953)

leads to a slightly inferior position for White, since 17 b3 a×b3 18 a×b3 B×h3 19 B×h3 Nf3+ 20 Kf1 N×e1 21 K×e1 N×e4 gives Black an irresistible attack.

Therefore White should have chosen 15 Bf4, when Black should not passively defend as in the match game Reshevsky–Najdorf, 1952 — 15 ... Bf8 16 Nf3 Be6 (*16 ... Rd8* is better) 17 B×d6 B×c4 18 B×f8 K×f8 19 e5 Nd5 20 Rd4 b5 21 Qd2, which leads to a clear advantage for White, but should actively seek counter-play: 15 ... Ne6 16 N×e6 B×e6 17 B×d6 (*17 b3 a×b3 18 a×b3 Nd7*) 17 ... B×c4 18 e5 Nd7.

White can also choose 15 Re2 Nfd7 16 Red2 (Averbakh–Ditman, Dresden, 1956, by transposition) 16 ... Qb4 17 Nb1 Nb6 18 Na3 Bd7 19 Ne2, with the better game.

| **15 ...** | **Nfd7** |
| **16 Bf1** | **Re7** |

Inviting White to declare his intentions, since he has made all the useful moves with his pieces, and must now take some positive action. But it will inevitably give Black good counter-chances, because his position is full of dynamism, and White already has some weaknesses (at b3, in particular).

17 f4

The signal for White to begin a pawn offensive in the centre, and simultaneously indicating the necessity for Black to regroup.

| **17 ...** | **Nf6** |

The return of the knight enables Black to complete his development, since the attack on the e-pawn gains a tempo.

| **18 Bf2** | **Bd7** |

The threat of 19 ... Rae8 compels White to take specific action.

19 e5	**d×e5**
20 f×e5	**Ne8**
21 Nf3	

Otherwise the e5 pawn cannot be defended.

21 ...	Bf5
22 Qe2	h5
23 Bd4	Nc7
24 Qf2	

24 Nh4 would have left the e-pawn undefended, and the knight would have had to return to f3.

| 24 ... | N7e6 |
| 25 Be3 | Rae8 |

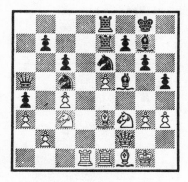

The most purposeful. Today I would possibly have considered the fate of the bishop at f5, and would have attempted to save it by 25 ... Rd8, gaining control of d3. This indicates not that the evaluation of the position has changed, but merely shows the inevitable metamorphosis of every chess player: that—alas!—prejudices have appeared.

26 Nh4

Botvinnik immediately gives up the pawn, at the same time breaking up the opponent's K-side pawns. But the centralization of the black pieces is so great that there is nothing terrible about this: White will not be able to get at the king.

| 26 ... | B×e5 |

The tempting 26 ... Ne4 27 N×e4 B×e4 would have lost a piece: 28 Bd2 Q×e5 29 Bc3.

27 N×f5	g×f5
28 Q×f5	Ng7
29 Qf2	B×c3
30 b×c3	Ne4
31 Qf4	N×c3
32 Rc1	

The position has clarified. The two good bishops do not compensate White for his pawn deficit, since his own king is exposed and his Q-side weak. Before the decisive regrouping, Black repeats moves to gain time on the clock.

32 ...	Na2
33 Rcd1	Nc3
34 Rc1	Ne4
35 Re2	Qf5
36 g4	

The exchange of queens at f5 would have lost White his g3 pawn. By the move played he restricts the black knight at g7, but he is unable to avoid simplification favourable to Black.

| 36 ... | h×g4 |
| 37 h×g4 | Qg6! |

The most accurate. Now White cannot get away with only exchanging the queens.

| 38 Rg2 | Ng5 |
| 39 Q×g5 | |

There is nothing else.

| 39 ... | R×e3 |

40 Q×g6	f×g6
41 c5	Ne6

Greed is always likely to be punished: 41 ... R×a3 42 Bc4+, and the black king has nowhere to go (*42 ... Kf8 43 Rf2+ and 44 Rf7+*).

42 Rb2	Re7
43 Bc4	Kg7
44 B×e6	R7×e6

For an instant White can restore the material balance, but then the black king breaks out at g5.

45 g5	Rb3
46 R×b3	a×b3
47 Rd1	Re2
White resigns	

The passed pawn will queen.

No. 68 Queen's Gambit

Botvinnik–Geller

*22nd USSR Championship
Moscow, 1955*

Whose weakness is weaker?

..Earlier in this opening variation Botvinnik had won against Keres. But I decided to repeat the opening. Firstly, because I had a definite liking for Black's position—the play could become highly interesting. And secondly, because I permitted myself a slight bluff (at that time I was liable to commit such a "sin"). The point was that the only way to refute Black's plan was via a mass of very sharp complications, and at that stage of his career Botvinnik did everything possible to avoid unclear, irrational positions. Moreover, Black had included the intermediate move ... h6 and ... in a word, his plan vindicated itself. ...

1 c4	Nf6
2 d4	e6
3 Nc3	d5
4 c×d5	

The favourite and deeply analyzed continuation of the then World Champion. If Black "simply" develops by ... Be7, ... 0–0, ... Ndb7, etc., he is "threatened" with the minority attack on the Q-side, of which Botvinnik had repeatedly shown himself to be a great master.

4 ...	e×d5
5 Bg5	c6
6 e3	h6
7 Bh4	Bf5

8 Bd3

It was only several years later, on the basis of a sufficient amount of practical material, that Igor Zaitsev, then a young master but now a grandmaster, published an analysis demonstrating that 8 Qf3 is favourable for White.

After 8 ... Bg6 9 B×f6 g×f6 (although in the game Geller–Portisch, Zagreb, 1955, Black somehow managed to survive in the variation *9 ... Q×f6 10 Q×f6 g×f6*, White has a clear advantage) 10 Qd1 Qb6 11 Qd2 Nd7 12 Nf3 Rg8 13 Be2 Bd6 14 0–0 White has markedly the better game (Krogius–Kovács, Budapest, 1965).

The critical and very sharp variation runs 8 ... Qb6 9 Q×f5 Q×b2 10 Qc8+ Ke7, and now:

(a) 11 N×d5+ c×d5 12 Qc1 Qb4+ 13 Ke2, Smyslov–Pachman, Munich Olympiad, 1958, when Black should have continued not 13 ... Qb5+? 14 Kf3 Qd7 15 B×f6+ K×f6 16 g3 with advantage to White, but 13 ... g5! 14 Bg3 Ne4 15 f3 Qb5+ 16 Ke1 Qb4+, with a draw.

(b) 11 Rb1! Q×c3+ 12 Kd1 g5 13 Bg3! (only a draw results from *13 R×b7+ Nbd7 14 Q×a8 Ne4!*, with perpetual check) 13 ... Ne4 14 Nf3 Bg7 (after *14 ... N×g3 15 h×g3* Black has a hopeless position, since *15 ... Kf6* is decisively met by *16 R×h6+!*) 15 R×b7+ Kf6 16 Be5+ Kg6 17 Nh4+ g×h4 18 Qe6+!, and, whether Black takes the queen or defends against the check, all the same he is mated.

At the board it was of course very difficult to evaluate such sharp and fantastic complications. Therefore White chose a quieter continuation, after which, however, Black has no opening difficulties.

8 ...	B×d3
9 Q×d3	Be7
10 Nge2	

After 10 Nf3 Black can establish himself at e4.

10 ...	Nbd7
11 0–0	0–0
12 f3	Re8
13 Bf2	

13 e4, which White would like to play, allows Black an advantage after 13 ... d×e4 14 f×e4 N×e4 15 N×e4 B×h4 16 Nd6 Rf8 17 N×b7 Qc7.

13 ...	c5

Beginning "the discussion of the question": which pawn is weaker—the black one at d5 or the white one at e3.

14 d×c5	B×c5
15 Rad1	Ne5

As compensation for his isolated pawn, Black's pieces have become very active, and it has to be said that this compensation is more than sufficient.

16 Qb5	Qb6
17 Q×b6	

17 ...	a×b6!

Black continues to pin his hopes on active play! For the sake of this he allows a further worsening of his pawn formation, since now his queen's rook, without making a single move, is aggressively placed.

18 b3

Preventing the invasion of the knight at c4. 18 N×d5 N×d5 19 R×d5 R×a2 was unsatisfactory, but to be considered was 18 Nf4, and if 18 ... Nc4, then 19 Nf×d5 N×d5 20 R×d5, simplifying the position.

18 ...	Nc6
19 Nf4	Nb4
20 Nd3?	

A mistake, provoked by the fact that White is still trying for an advantage. He should have given up this idea, and looked for simplification in the variation 20 Nf×d5 Nf×d5 21 N×d5 N×d5 22 R×d5 R×a2 23 e4 R×f2 24 R×f2 Ra8 25 R×c5 b×c5 26 Rc2, with drawing chances.

20 ...	N×a2
21 N×a2	R×a2

22 Rfe1	Bd6
23 h3	Rc2

Black's advantage stems not so much from his extra doubled pawn on the b-file, as from the ideal coordination and activity of his pieces.

24 Kf1

Slightly better is 24 Rc1 Rec8 25 R×c2 R×c2 26 Rc1 Rd2 27 Ne1, although even then after 27 ... Nh5 Black has every chance of success.

24 ...	Rc3
25 b4	b5

Fixing the weak white pawn on a black square, which with black-squared bishops on the board is of considerable importance.

26 Re2	Rb3
27 Be1	Nh5

After the exchange of Black's knight for the white bishop, the b4 pawn will be doomed.

28 g4	Ng3+
29 B×g3	B×g3
30 Kg2	

30 f4 is no better in view of ... Bh4–e7.

30 ...	Bd6
31 Kf2	Rc8

Black intends to win the pawn "at his leisure", after first improving to the maximum the positioning of all his pieces.

32 Red2	Rc4

The threat of 33 ... d4 forces White to do something. But this allows Black to retain his strong bishop.

33 Nc1	Rb×b4
34 R×d5	Rb2+
35 Ne2	

The exchange of one pair of rooks would merely favour Black, although the outcome of the game is already decided.

35 ...	Bb4
36 Kf1	Bc5
37 Nd4	b4
38 Rd8+	Kh7
39 Rc8	Rc3
40 Ne2	R×e3

White resigns

No. 69 King's Indian Defence

Botvinnik–Geller

Belgrade, 1969

With respect and gratitude

This was my last meeting at the chess board with Mikhail Botvinnik: a year later the long-time leader of world chess gave up practical play.

Here I should like to express my word of gratitude to Professor Botvinnik. Because he was not simply the World Champion, i.e. the strongest practical player. He showed the road which is now followed by all the leading grandmasters. This road is the study of chess, the maximum correlation of the game with science, and the entire chess world is deeply grateful to Botvinnik for this.

Of course, since 1970, when the five-times World Champion stopped appearing in events, theory has made great advances. Nevertheless, many of Botvinnik's ideas are topical even to this day.

I can also add that I personally gain the most satisfaction from chess when, like Botvinnik, I am engaged in studying the secrets of this ancient and eternally youthful game.

As for the present game, it is simultaneously both uncharacteristic of Botvinnik, and characteristic. The first, because he forgot the best move and lost his head (perhaps it was from him that I also copied this?!). The second, because, just as seventeen years earlier, we played my favourite King's Indian Defence, which Mikhail Botvinnik, who always stuck to his principles, did not want to avoid. And—the verysam e variation...

1 c4	g6
2 d4	Bg7
3 Nc3	d6
4 Nf3	Nf6
5 g3	0–0
6 Bg2	Nbd7
7 0–0	e5
8 e4	c6

Only here did we deviate from our 1952 game. My attitude to Black's 8th move is expressed in the notes to that game.

9 h3

White prepares to develop his bishop at e3 by depriving the black knight of g4.

9 ...   Qb6

One of the must popular and strongest continuations. Black begins an immediate attack on d4, by threatening the combination 10 ... e×d4 11 N×d4 N×e4! He also has ideas of attacking the unprotected c4 pawn (by ... *Qb4*).

10 Re1

Parrying both threats (the c4 pawn can now be defended by the bishop from f1).

| 10 ... | e×d4 |
| 11 N×d4 | Re8 |

It is curious to note that, in this heavily analyzed position, Black very recently (in the Malta Olympiad at the end of 1980) began employing the completely new continuation 11 ... Ne8, with the idea of defending d6 and beginning immediate counter-play against the active white knight in the centre. The drawback to this idea is that it hinders Black's development.

12 Re2

White defends in advance his f2 square, thus weakening the effect of the tactical ... Ng4. Botvinnik himself considers the strongest move to be 12 Na4, driving the black queen off the a7–g1 diagonal. The curious thing is that afterwards Botvinnik told me that during the game he had... forgotten this move! And so he employed a continuation recommended to him by Furman.

12 ...   Ng4

The alternative, which I have also played on a number of occasions, is 12 ... Qb4 13 Rc2 (indirectly defending the c4 pawn) 13 ... Nc5 14 Bd2 Qb6 15 Be3 a5!, as, for example, in the game Lengyel–Geller, Budapest, 1969.

13 Nc2

It is a matter of taste whether to play this or 13 Rd2. It should be said that in either case modern theory considers White's chances to be preferable, although the complex and sharp position is rich in mutual possibilities, and demands definite accuracy on the part of both sides.

13 ...	Nge5
14 Ne3	Nc5
15 b3?	

An oversight which leaves White a pawn down. Of course, 15 Q×d6? does not work, if only because of 15 ... B×h3 with the threat of 16 ... Rad8, but stronger is 15 Rd2 Be6!? with counter-play for Black.

| 15 ... | B×h3! |
| 16 Bd2 | |

On 16 B×h3 there would have followed 16 ... Nf3+ and 17 ... B×c3.

| 16 ... | B×g2 |
| 17 K×g2 | h5! |

The tragedy for White is not only that he has lost a pawn, but also that his K-side has been seriously weakened. It is here that Black begins an attack.

| 18 Rb1 | Qd8 |

With the threat of 19 ...-h4.

| 19 b4 | Ne6 |
| 20 f4 | |

Rather than passively await his fate, White provokes complications, but this exposes his king even more.

20 ...	Nd3
21 Nf1	B×c3!
22 B×c3	Nd×f4+

White resigned in view of the variation 23 g×f4 N×f4+ 24 Kf3 N×e2 25 Q×e2 Qh4, when for his two pieces Black already has a rook and three pawns, with the prospect of a fourth. In such a situation White did not wish to continue resisting, which would have merely prolonged the struggle.

Vasily Smyslov

No. 70 King's Indian Defence

Smyslov–Geller

Match for the Title of USSR Champion Moscow, 1955

All decided by tactics

In this case what I have in mind is not a tactical blow, but match tactics. This was the first match in my life, and what made it more difficult was the fact that prior to it I had a very bad record against Vasily Smyslov. On several occasions I had managed to obtain good or even winning positions against him, but by subtle and clever defence Smyslov had prevented their conversion into a win.

Before the match grandmaster Igor Bondarevsky, who was then my second, and I outlined the following tactics. Usually Smyslov had allowed me to be enterprising, and had very accurately exploited every slip, every weakening of the position. We decided that I should play extremely quietly and await the reaction of Smyslov to this unexpected turn of events. As part of our plan, when in the second and fourth games Smyslov chose the Slav Defence, I avoided the gambit continuation, although in an earlier game against him I had gained a big opening advantage with it. In the 5th game, in reply to 3 g3 (at the time Smyslov liked to fianchetto his king's bishop against the King's Indian Defence) I transposed into the Grünfeld Defence, and easily equalized.

It was obvious that in the 7th game, when the first player to win a game would now win the match, White would want more from the opening, and might play the Sämisch Variation against the King's Indian. Although in itself it is not bad, we regarded this as an achievement, since formerly Smyslov had not employed it.

That is in fact what happened. White handled the opening badly, came under an attack, and after six draws the match concluded in the first additional "round".

1 d4	Nf6
2 c4	g6
3 Nc3	Bg7
4 e4	d6
5 f3	

Thus Black is assured of the sharp struggle that he is aiming for.

5 ...	0-0
6 Be3	e5
7 Nge2	c6

This position had occurred frequently in the Semi-Finals of the 22nd USSR Championship. Especially interesting was the game at Gorky between Borisenko and Boleslavsky, in which Black carried out the idea prepared by his previous move: 8 Qd2 e×d4 9 N×d4 d5 10 c×d5 c×d5 11 e5 Ne8 12 f4 f6 13 e6 f5 14 e7 Q×e7 15 N×d5 Qd8 16 Bc4 Kh8 17 Bb3 Nf6 18 N×f6, and a draw was soon agreed.

However, it is by no means obligatory for Black to advance ... d5, since by 7 ... c6 he also prepared ... b5. Therefore on 8 Qd2,

which is undoubtedly best, I was intending to reply 8 ... a6 9 0-0-0 Nbd7 10 Kb1 b5 11 Nc1 Re8, with a complicated game.

8 d5

In the given position this is not especially promising, since ... c6 has already been played.

8 ...	c×d5
9 c×d5	Ne8
10 Qd2	

On 10 Nc1 there would have followed 10 ... Bh6!, which, in the event of the exchange (*11 B×h6 Qh4+*), weakens a complex of black squares in White's position.

| 10 ... | f5 |
| 11 h3? | |

It is difficult to understand how such a logically-thinking player as Smyslov could make such an illogical, passive and obviously bad move. Even his lack of familiarity with the position can hardly explain it. 11 Nc1 was of course necessary.

| 11 ... | Nd7 |
| 12 g3 | |

White is thinking of castling K-side, whereas his only chance was 12 0-0-0, with the possibility of subsequent play on the c-file.

| 12 ... | Nb6 |
| 13 b3 | |

13 Nc1 would not have protected the c4 square against invasion by the knight, since the white-squared bishop would have to go to g2.

| 13 ... | f4! |

The signal for the attack. Black is essentially developed, whereas White's pieces are scattered, his king is in the centre, and he has a mass of weaknesses on the K-side.

14 g×f4   e×f4
15 Bd4

15 B×f4 fails to 15 ... B×c3 16 Q×c3 R×f4 17 N×f4 Qh4+, but 15 Bf2 was better, leaving d4 free for the knight.

15 ...   Nd7

The black knight aims for e5.

16 h4   Ne5

A King's Indian player's dream! Nowadays, when all the typical positions have been studied, one cannot even hope to obtain such a comfortable game at an early stage.

17 Bg2   Bd7
18 Bf2   Rc8
19 Nd4   Qa5
20 Rc1   Nc7

The second black knight aims for c5, from where it can invade at d3.

21 Rc2   Na6
22 0–0   Nc5

The black pieces are ideally placed, and White tries to relieve the situation by exchanges.

23 Nce2   Q×d2
24 R×d2

There was no point in Black avoiding the exchange of queens, since he had worked out a fairly long combination.

24 ...   N×e4!

White's position explodes at the apparently most invulnerable point.

25 f×e4   f3
26 N×f3

White wrongly tries to hang on to his material. 26 Ne6 was better, although even then Black has a marked advantage: 26 ... f×e2 27 Re1 (*27 R×e2 Bb5*) 27 ... Bh6! 28 Rd×e2 R×f2! 29 R×f2 Nd3 30 Rfe2 N×e1 31 R×e1 Bd2 32 Re2 (*32 Rd1 Be3+ 33 Kh2 Rc2*) 32 ... Rc1+ 33 Kh2 Be1 34 Kh3 h5! 35 Re3 Rc3 36 R×c3 B×c3, and after the return of the black bishop to e1 nothing can prevent the black king's triumphant march into the centre of the board.

26 ...   N×f3+
27 B×f3   R×f3
28 B×a7   Rh3

For the pawn Black has obtained a very strong attack.

29 Bf2   Be5
30 Nd4   Bg4
31 Be1

On 31 Kg2 Black was intending to play 31 ... Rcc3.

31 ...   Re3
32 Bf2   R×e4
33 Re1   R×e1+
34 B×e1   Rc1

White resigned, since 35 Kf2 loses to 35 ... Bf6, and 35 Kf1 to 35 ... Bg3.

170

No. 71 Nimzo-Indian Defence

Geller–Smyslov

28th USSR Championship
Moscow, 1961

One move further

This game was judged to be one of the two best played in the tournament. Indeed, White achieved success thanks to his more accurate evaluation of the position arising before his 21st move. On this occasion violent measures were not required for the mounting of an attack on the black king.

It should also be added that prior to the game both players had $8\frac{1}{2}$ points out of 13, and were sharing 2nd–6th places. To the end of the Championship there remained six rounds, and only four players were to go through to the Interzonal Tournament. This rivalry intensified the battle, although Vasily Vasilievich and I very rarely had peaceful draws.

1 d4	Nf6
2 c4	e6
3 Nc3	Bb4

It was in this opening that Smyslov twice defeated me in the 1953 and 1956 Candidates Tournaments. Memories of these games may have played a part in his choice of the Nimzo-Indian Defence.

4 e3	0–0
5 Bd3	d5
6 Nf3	c5
7 0–0	d×c4
8 B×c4	Qe7

One of Smyslov's clever inventions, which he first employed in the 1959 Candidates Tournament against Gligoric. The drawback to the move is the possible pin on the knight along the h4–d8 diagonal.

9 a3	Ba5
10 Qc2	Bd7
11 Bd2	

In the aforementioned game Gligoric played 11 d×c5 Q×c5 12 Ne4 N×e4, and Smyslov equalized without difficulty. The text move does not relieve the tension in the centre, and would appear to be stronger. Especially since Black will soon be forced to exchange on d4, and after e×d4 there will be the unpleasant threat of Bg5, emphasizing the basic defect of his 8th move.

11 ...	Nc6
12 Rad1	c×d4
13 e×d4	Rac8
14 Qd3	

To be considered was 14 b4 Bb6 15 Qd3.

14 ...	B×c3!

Showing a subtle understanding of the position. After 14 ... Rfd8 15 b4 Bb6 16 Bg5 Black would have been faced with the threat of Ne4.

15 B×c3	Nd5
16 Bd2	Qf6

White's positional advantage has taken shape, in the form of his greater command of space. He has in prospect the manoeuvre Ba2–b1, which will force a significant weakening of the black king's position. With his last move Smyslov plans to transfer his knight from c6 via e7 to the K-side, but in so doing he allows the opponent immediate attacking possibilities. More accurate, therefore, was 16 ... Qd6 with the same idea.

17 Ng5

This knight move proves possible thanks to the black bishop at d7 being undefended, and once again shows how important is the coordination of all the pieces, without exception.

17 ...	Qg6
18 Qh3	h6

A mistake, after which White gains a serious, perhaps even decisive advantage. Essential was 18 ... Rfd8, and on 19 Bd3 — 19 ... f5, after which Black's position is quite tenable.

19 B×d5	h×g5

Forced, since after 19 ... e×d5 20 Q×d7 h×g5 21 Q×d5 Black loses a pawn.

20 Ba2	N×d4

When making his 18th move, Black had foreseen this position and considered it favourable: in winning the pawn, it would seem that he has in no way worsened his position, since 21 Bb4 is bad in view of 21 ... Ne2+ 22 Kh1 Nf4 followed by 23 ... Bc6. Satisfied with such an assessment, Smyslov cut short his calculation of the variation arising by force after 18 ... h6. But I had calculated a little further ...

21 Qg4!

This was overlooked by Black. Now White regains his pawn, and takes firm control of the d-file, after which he easily prepares a decisive offensive against the black king.

21 ...	Nf5
22 B×g5	Bb5
23 Rfe1	Nh6

Black's K-side is irreparably weakened by the absence of his h-pawn. It is practically impossible for him to play ... f6, and he is unable to parry White's attack involving the advance of his rook's pawn and Bb1.

24 Qf4	Rc5
25 h4	Bc6
26 b4	

The black rook will soon find things restricted on the 5th rank.

26 ...	Rf5
27 Qg3	Qh5
28 Rd4	

Preparing to double rooks on the d-file, and simultaneously preventing the black queen from going to g4.

28 ...	Rb5
29 Qf4	

Threatening 30 g4 and 31 Bb1. Black's position is dismal, and in search of counterplay he sacrifices a pawn, which, however, does not delay the end.

29 ...	e5
30 R×e5	R×e5
31 Q×e5	Re8
32 Qf4	Qe2
33 Bc4	

It was not yet too late to ... blunder away a rook by 33 B×h6 Q×a2 34 Qg5 Qa1+.

33 ...	Qe1+
34 Kh2	Re4
35 Rd8+	Kh7

On 35 ... Be8 there follows 36 R×e8+ R×e8 37 B×h6, winning.

36 Bd3	Resigns

No. 72 King's Indian Defence

Smyslov–Geller

USSR Team Championship Moscow, 1961

An extra tempo—is it harmful?

In this game a position typical of Réti's Opening with colours reversed was reached. It would seem that the extra tempo—the right of the first move—should give White a marked advantage. But in chess there is a paradox: what is good for Black may be inadequate for White. Thus a Sicilian formation with White is not especially promising, although in such a sharp opening the fate of the entire game can often depend on one tempo, and in other analogous cases the situation is the same. The present game once again confirms this paradox.

1 d4	Nf6
2 Nf3	g6
3 Bf4	Bg7
4 c3	

White chooses a set-up aimed at neutralizing the opponent's "King's Indian" bishop. But in doing so he avoids a battle for the centre, and cannot really hope for an opening advantage. Black has several ways of achieving a comfortable game. Thus he can prepare ... e5, gaining a tempo by attacking the white bishop, or he can first fianchetto his second bishop.

4 ...	b6
5 e3	Bb7
6 Nbd2	c5
7 h3	0–0

8 Be2	d6
9 0–0	Nc6
10 Bh2	Re8
11 Qb3	

White's intended piece attack on f7 is doomed to failure, since he has no superiority in the centre, or even equal control of it. To be considered therefore was 11 Re1 with the idea of Bf1 and e3–e4. It is interesting that this is what Black plays in analogous positions of the Réti Opening.

But after the move in the game, Black, who has ideally and freely developed his pieces, has no need to engage in prophylaxis such as ... h6: he can go his own way.

11 ...	Qc7
12 Ng5	e5
13 d×e5	N×e5!

13 ... d×e5? would obviously be a blunder: 14 Bc4 Nd8 15 Ndf3, and White gains a menacing initiative.

14 f4

A committing, although in many respects forced decision. Even at the cost of creating weaknesses in his own position, White is obliged to play actively, since otherwise, after driving back the knight from g5, Black will create pressure on the diagonal leading to g2 and will advance his pawn centre. Now the game enters a phase of sharp tactics.

14 ...	Nc6
15 Nc4	d5

Black does not have time for 15 ... h6, since by 16 f5 White begins a dangerous attack. In closing the a2–g8 diagonal, Black simultaneously forces the opponent to weaken the effect of the opposition of white bishop and black queen, since after 16 f5 Qd7 White loses material.

16 Ne5	Re7
17 Rad1	Rae8
18 h4	

By advancing his pawn to h5 and exchanging on g6, White tries to provide his knight with an eternal post at g5. But in doing so he weakens his control of g4, and Black immediately exploits this.

18 ...	Qc8

With the threat of 19 ... N×e5 20 f×e5 Ng4.

19 Bf3

By the counter-attack on d5 White parries the above threat, on which there would now follow 21 B×d5 with an attack on f7. But in principle White's strategy has already reached an impasse.

19 ...	h6

This move presents White with an unpleasant choice: whether to go in for the continuation in the game, or to "sound the retreat" —20 Nh3. But then he would have to reckon

with 20 ... N×e5 21 f×e5 Ne4 22 Nf4 B×e5 23 N×d5 B×h2+ 24 K×h2 B×d5 25 Q×d5 Qc7+ 26 Kg1 Ng3, when 27 Rfe1 is met by the extremely unpleasant 27 ... Nf5, and if 28 h5 then 28 ... R×e3! 29 Rf1 R3e5.

20 Ng×f7

White prefers to accept the challenge, especially since after 20 ... R×f7 21 N×f7 K×f7 22 B×d5+ N×d5 23 R×d5! Qe6 24 f5! Q×e3+ 25 Kh1 he would obtain a dangerous attack. But Black had in mind an important *zwischenzug*.

20 ...	c4!
21 Qc2	R×f7
22 N×f7	

The piece sacrifice 22 Q×g6 Rff8 23 Ng4 was tempting, with a strong attack after 23 ... N×g4 24 B×g4 Qd8 25 Be6+. But at the board I had prepared a variation which, I must confess, very much appealed to me: 23 ... Ne7!! 24 N×h6+ Kh8 25 Nf7+ R×f7 26 Q×f7 Qc5!, when the white queen is trapped. Threatened is 27 ... Q×e3+ or 27 ... Bc8 and 28 ... Rf8, while after 27 Qe6 Black wins immediately by 27 ... Bc8 28 Qe5 Nf5.

22 ...	K×f7
23 h5	g×h5
24 B×d5+	N×d5
25 R×d5	Ne7
26 R×h5	Qg4
27 Rh3	Nf5

The complications have ended to Black's obvious advantage. With material formally equal, the positional weaknesses in White's position are incurable, and his pieces — in particular his bishop and his rook at h3 — occupy truly tragic positions. All this means that the game is decided.

| 28 Re1 | Bf8 |
| 29 Qe2 | |

Without this it is impossible to bring the bishop out from h2 (if *29 Kh1*, with the idea of *Bg1*, then *29 ... Q×h3*).

29 ...	Q×e2
30 R×e2	Rd8
31 Bg3	

Both 31 e4 Rd1+ 32 Kf2 Bc5+ 33 Kf3 Rd3+ 34 Kg4 Ne3+, and 31 g4 Rd1+ 32 Kf2 Nd6 would have allowed Black a direct attack on the king. But now he carries out a plan of "suffocation".

31 ...	Rd1+
32 Kh2	Be4
33 b3	Kg6
34 b×c4	Be7

Depriving the white bishop of h4.

| 35 Bf2 | h5 |

Now g2–g4 becomes impossible.

36 Rb2	Bc5
37 Re2	a5
38 a4	Ra1

Now the d-file can be conceded ...

39 Rd2	R×a4
40 Rd8	Ra2
41 Kg1	Ra1+
White resigns	

After 42 Kh2 Rf1 44 Re8 a4 the advance of the pawn is decisive.

No. 73 Caro–Kann Defence

Geller–Smyslov

USSR Team Championship
Moscow, 1964

Even in the endgame combinations occur!

In many of Vasily Smyslov's games one notices his readiness to go into the endgame: this phase of the struggle is liked and known by the Ex-World Champion. But in this case White had no objections to going into an ending. He as though fell in with his opponent's wishes, relying on his two bishops and ... an unusual tactical blow planned beforehand. It led to the outcome already being clear in the region of the 20th move...

1 e4	c6
2 d4	d5
3 Nc3	d×e4
4 N×e4	Nd7
5 Bc4	Ngf6
6 Ng5	e6
7 Ne2	

A rare and rather quiet move, which is very appropriate for a team event (we were playing in the USSR Team Championship). The idea of it is to retain f3 for the retreat of the other knight, and to obtain a "French" type of position with a slight but persistent advantage.

| 7 ... | h6 |
| 8 Nf3 | Bd6 |

Otherwise White will himself occupy the h2–b8 diagonal with his bishop.

| 9 0–0 | Qc7 |
| 10 Re1 | |

It is important to take control of e4. A year earlier Simagin played the immediate 10 Nc3 against Smyslov, but after 10 ... b5 11 Bd3 b4 12 Ne4 N×e4 13 B×e4 Nf6 14 Bd3 0–0 15 Qe2 Bb7 followed by ... c5 Black obtained a satisfactory position.

10 ...	0–0
11 Nc3	a6

Black has to decide the problem of developing his Q-side, but he is not able to do this by 11 ... Nd5. White continues 12 Ne4 Bf4 13 B×f4 Q×f4 14 Ng3! (after *14 Bf1 b6 15 g3 Qc7 16 Bg2 Bb7 17 c4 N5f6 18 N×f6+ N×f6* the game is level, Stein–Pfleger, Tel Aviv Olympiad, 1964) 14 ... b6 15 Ne4 N×e5 16 R×e5, and since 16 ... Bb7 allows 17 Ne2 trapping the queen, he gains a clear advantage after 16 ... Qh4 17 Qd2 Bb7 18 Rae1.

However, the text move is also a loss of time. Approximate equality can be gained by the immediate 11 ... b5 12 Bd3 Bb7 (here, in contrast to the aforementioned Simagin–Smyslov game, *12 ... b4* is weaker in view of *13 Ne4 N×e4 14 R×e4! Nf6 15 Rh4*, with excellent attacking prospects), and now 13 Qe2 b4 14 Ne4 c5, or 13 a3 a6 14 b4 e5, or 13 Ne4 N×e4 14 B×e4 (*14 R×e4 c5 15 Rh4 c4*) 14 ... c5.

12 Ne4	b5

Conceding White the advantage of the two bishops, but the alternative 12 ... Bf4 13 B×f4 Q×f4 14 N×f6+ N×f6 15 Ne5 would also have given Black an unpleasant

position, since his queen is cut off from the rest of his forces. Perhaps the least evil was 12 ... N×e4 13 R×e4 c5, obtaining a French type position with the better game for White.

13 N×d6	Q×d6
14 Bf1!	

Sensing his opponent's desire to simplify and go into an ending, White does not impede him, although by 14 Bd3 c5 15 c3 he could have retained the queens.

14 ...	c5
15 d×c5	Q×d1
16 R×d1	N×c5
17 Be3	Na4
18 Bd4!	

Having cut off the knight's retreat, White intends to catch it by 19 b3.

18 ...	Nd5
19 Rac1	b4?

White has mobilized all his forces, whereas Black has in play only his two knights, one of which is tangled up on the edge of the board. Therefore there is no time for this move, and Black should have played 19 ... Nab6, preventing c2–c4 if only for an instant, and then completed his development.

Some "justification" for Black is the fact that the following tactical operation by White is unusual and by no means obvious.

20 a3!	b×a3

After 20 ... a5 21 Bb5 Nab6 22 Bc5 Rd8 23 a×b4 a×b4 24 B×b4 Black loses a pawn.

21 Ra1!	N×b2
22 Rdb1	Na4
23 R×a3	Bd7
24 c4	Nf4
25 Rb4	f6
26 Rb×a4	B×a4
27 R×a4	

By the temporary sacrifice of two pawns White has gained a material advantage, the realization of which, with the help of two bishops and a passed pawn, does not present any particular difficulty.

27 ...	Rfd8
28 g3	Ng6
29 Kg2	Ne7
30 Be3	Nf5
31 Bb6	Rdb8

Intruding on to the 2nd rank is impossible, and on to the 1st rank pointless.

32 c5	Ne7
33 Bc4	

This is much simpler than 33 R×a6 R×a6 34 B×a6 Nd5 35 Bc4 N×b6, when the game may drag out for a further twenty moves.

33 ...	Nd5
34 B×d5	e×d5
35 Nd4	Kf7
36 Nc6	Re8
37 Rd4	

The a-pawn is securely blockaded, and White sets about winning the d-pawn.

37 ...	Rec8
38 Na5	

There is no reason to hurry with 38 Nb4 — 38 ... a5.

38 ...	Ke6
39 Rd2	Rab8

40 Nb3	g6
41 Nd4+	Kd7
42 Nc2	Kc6
43 Nb4+	Kb5

And under the "threat" of adjournment, **Black resigned**, since he loses a minimum of two pawns.

No. 74 Nimzo-Indian Defence

Geller–Smyslov

Candidates Quarter-Final Match
1st Game
Moscow, 1965

With a favourable wind

This match commenced with a favourable "microclimate" for me as regards my purely chess "relations" with Smyslov. Out of my first nineteen meetings with the future (up till 1957) and then former (after 1958) World Champion I had lost seven whole games with one single victory (see Game No. 70), but in the next four I had picked up $3^{1}/_{2}$ points. The wind was clearly favourable, and a healthy confidence — but not overconfidence! — always adds to one's strength.

1 d4	Nf6
2 c4	e6
3 Nc3	Bb4
4 e3	c5
5 Bd3	d5
6 Nf3	d×c4
7 B×c4	a6
8 a3	Ba5
9 0–0	b5

9 ... 0–0 would have led to the normal position of this variation, and it is difficult to say why Smyslov chose this particular move order: a flank attack without castling.

10 Be2

I thus did not find out what my opponent had planned in reply to 10 Ba2 with the idea of d4–d5, since the text move leads to a completely different game.

10 ...	c×d4
11 N×d4	Bb7
12 Bf3	B×f3
13 Q×f3	Ra7

The apparently natural 13 ... Nbd7 loses to 14 Nc6. But now too, in spite of the further simplification, White has the more pleasant game. He has firm control of the d-file, and the slight disharmony among the black pieces is nevertheless perceptible.

14 b4	Bb6
15 Nc6	N×c6
16 Q×c6+	Nd7
17 Bb2	0–0
18 Rfd1	Qc8
19 Q×c8	

Nothing is achieved by 19 Qd6 Bc7!, when the threat of 20 Q×d7 is illusory in view of 20 ... B×h2+, while 19 Qe4 deprives the knight of this square, and Black continues 19 ... Rc7.

19 ...	R×c8
20 Rd6	

The apparently energetic 20 a4, suggested by Lilienthal, in fact allows too much simplification: 20 ... b×a4 21 N×a4 Bd8 22

Bd4 Rb7 23 Nc5 N×c5 24 B×c5, and now possible is either 24 ... a5 25 b×a5 Rb5 26 a6 Rb×c5 27 a7 Ra8 28 R×d8+ R×d8 29 a8=Q Rc1+, or 24 ... Bb6 25 R×a6 B×c5 26 b×c5 Kf8 27 c6 Rbc7.

20 ...	Bd8
21 Rad1	Rcc7
22 Ne4	Be7
23 R6d2	f6
24 f4	Kf8
25 Bd4	

At first sight White not altogether logically blocks the d-file and thus allows the black rooks to regroup. But in fact this is not quite so. Although all White's plans are associated with play on the K-side (*g2–g4–g5*), he must avoid simplification on the opposite side of the board. Meanwhile, Black was ready to play 25 ... a5 26 b×a5 b4 27 a×b4 B×b4, with further exchanges.

25 ...	Rab7

Slightly better is 25 ... Ra8 26 Kf2 Rac8, or 26 ... a5 27 b×a5 R×a5 28 Bc3! Raa7 (Black has difficulties after *28 ... Ra4 29 R×d7 R×d7 30 R×d7 R×e4 31 Bd4*) 29 Bb4 B×b4 30 a×b4, but here too White retains a definite advantage.

26 Kf2	Rc4
27 Kf3	Rbc7
28 g4	Rc2
29 h4	R×d2

30 R×d2　　　Kf7
31 g5

Black's only achievement has been the exchange of one pair of rooks, but during the four moves needed for this White has developed his initiative on the K-side, and intends to continue his offensive with h4–h5. Therefore Black cannot passively await the course of events.

31 ...　　　e5

After 31 ... f5 32 Nf2 the weakness of e5 makes itself felt; the threats of e3–e4 and h4–h5 are also unpleasant.

32 Bb2　　　Ke6
33 g×f6　　　g×f6
34 Rg2　　　e×f4

The attempt to maintain a pawn at e5 by 34 ... Kf7 leaves White with the advantage after 35 f×e5 N×e5+ 36 B×e5 f×e5 37 h5. Black therefore chooses a different way, and prepares to defend his f6 pawn.

35 e×f4　　　Kf7
36 Bd4　　　Rc4

The attempt to transfer the knight to c4 also achieves nothing: 36 ... Rc6 37 h5 Nb6 38 B×b6 R×b6 39 Rc2!, with a serious advantage.

37 Rd2　　　Ke6
38 Rd3

Prophylaxis. White defends his a-pawn, which later proves useful. Besides, Black is simply unable to improve his position.

38 ...　　　Rc6
39 Bf2　　　Nf8?

A mistake just before the time control. It was better to parry the threat of 40 f5+ by 39 ... Nb6, although in this case too Black is cramped after 40 B×b6 R×b6 41 Rc3, since 41 ... a5 is unpleasantly met

by 42 Rc7. But at f8 the knight is shut out of the game after White's next move.

40 h5　　　Rc4?!

A further time trouble inaccuracy, although Black's position is terribly difficult. Thus 40 ... Rc7 is met by 41 Bc5!, and 40 ... Kf7, with the idea of bringing the knight out to e6, by 41 f5.

41 Bc5!　　　Rc1

In this position the game was adjourned. White has several ways to win. Strong, for example, is 42 Re3, winning a pawn. The move sealed is also good.

42 f5+　　　Kf7
43 Nd6+　　　Kg8

Black also loses after 43 ... B×d6 44 R×d6 Rc3+ 45 Ke4 R×a3 46 Rd8.

44 Re3!

Forcing Black to exchange his bishop, after which the difference in the strengths of the remaining minor pieces proves decisive.

44 ...　　　B×d6
45 B×d6　　　Rd1

For the moment the knight remains shut in, since 45 ... Nd7 46 Re8+ Kf7 47 Re7+ leads to its loss.

46 Bc5　　　Nd7

At last! In addition, the cherished e5 square is within reach, but... it is too late.

47 Re8+	Kf7
48 Re7+	Kg8
49 Re8+	

Repeating moves to gain time on the clock.

49 ...	Kf7
50 Re7+	Kg8
51 h6!	N×c5

It transpires that after 51 ... Ne5+ 52 Ke2! White threatens 53 Re8+ Kf7 54 Rf8 mate, while 52 ... Rd8 53 Rg7+ Kh8 54 Ra7 leads to the loss of several pawns...

| 52 b×c5 | Rf1+ |
| 53 Ke2 | Rc1 |

The f5 pawn is indirectly defended by the variation 53 ... R×f5 54 c6 Rc5 55 c7, when Black loses his rook.

54 Rc7	a5
55 Kd2	Rc4
56 Kd3	Rc1
57 Kd4	Rd1+
58 Ke4	

Black resigned, since White's king will "lead" his pawn up to the queening square.

No. 75 Nimzo-Indian Defence

Geller–Smyslov

Candidates Quarter-Final Match
3rd Game
Moscow, 1965

Stop-go tactics

It would seem that even the most composed player can be deprived of complete mental balance, if in a match with him "stop-go" tactics are adopted: playing first quietly, and then more sharply. This was confirmed by the experience of my previous match with Smyslov for the title of USSR Champion. In the present game I was also "helped" by Smyslov himself. On the 6th move he avoided the exchange in the centre which had occurred in our initial meeting (see No. 74). It can be assumed that, since he was behind in the match ($\frac{1}{2}$ out of 2), my opponent was aiming for a more complicated game, but he chose an unfortunate moment to go in for it.

1 d4	Nf6
2 c4	e6
3 Nc3	Bb4
4 e3	c5
5 Nf3	0–0
6 Bd3	b6

An inappropriate time for this, allowing White energetically to seize space. Usually ... b6 is played before castling, and when White first develops his bishop at d3 and only then his knight at f3: otherwise White advances d4–d5 "free of charge".

7 d5!

This indicates that White is ready to sacrifice a pawn in the variation 7 ... e×d5 8 c×d5 Bb7 9 e4 Re8 10 0–0! B×c3 11 b×c3 N×e4. In return he has a pleasant choice between 12 c4 with excellent attacking chances, and 12 B×e4 R×e4 13 Ng5 with the possible sequel 13 ... Rh4 (parrying *14 Qh5*) 14 g3! Rh6 15 N×f7 K×f7 16 B×h6 g×h6 17 Qh5+, when it is unlikely that the "bare" black king can be saved.

If Black declines the pawn sacrifice by 11 ... d6, then, as shown by the game Geller–D. Byrne, match USSR–USA, 1955, White gains an advantage by 12 Re1 Nbd7 13 c4 Ng4 14 Bb2 Nde5 15 N×e5 N×e5 16 Bf1.

Black chooses a third path, and tries to seize the initiative.

7 ...	e×d5
8 c×d5	N×d5
9 B×h7+	K×h7

10 Q×d5	B×c3+
11 b×c3	Qf6
12 0–0	

Of course, not 12 Q×a8? Q×c3+ 13 Kd1 Nc6! 14 Rb1 Qd3+ 15 Nd2 Qd6 followed by ... Ba6, after which the black queen is much stronger than the two white rooks.

In the resulting middlegame White has good attacking chances, assisted by the weakened position of the black king and the opposite-coloured bishops. If some of the pieces, including the queens, were suddenly to disappear from the board, Black's pawn armada would give him the advantage in the endgame.

Hence the natural plans of the two sides.

12 ...	Nc6
13 e4	Kg8
14 Qh5	Ba6
15 Re1	Bc4

It is too dangerous to go pawn-grabbing: 15 ... Q×c3 16 Be3! Qf6 (parrying the threat of *17 Ng5*) 17 Rad1, when White's attacking potential is markedly increased (*17 ... Rad8 18 Bg5*, or *17 ... Bc8 18 Ng5 Qg6 19 Qh4* with the threat of *20 Rd6*).

| 16 Bg5 | Qg6 |
| 17 Qh4 | |

After the exchange of queens Black would also have incurred some weak pawns, but the opposite-coloured bishops would have

become a strong drawing factor. And White is thinking of more...

17 ...	f6
18 Bf4	Rfe8
19 Nd2	

Not a retreat—the knight is making way for the rook.

| 19 ... | Bf7 |
| 20 Re3 | Qh7 |

After 20 ... Qh5 21 Q×h5 B×h5 22 Nc4 the white knight invades very strongly at d6. Therefore Black offers the exchange of queens, while simultaneously controlling c4 and keeping the e4 pawn under attack.

| 21 Qg4 | d5? |

Black overlooks a concealed blow by his opponent. Essential was 21 ... Be6 with a complicated game.

22 Rh3!

| 22 ... | Qg6 |

It turns out that 22 ... Be6, as intended by Black, does not work because of 23 Q×e6+! R×e6 24 R×h7 K×h7 25 e×d5.

23 Qh4

The prosaic 23 Q×g6 B×g6 24 e×d5 was also good enough to win, but the attack on the king is stronger.

23 ...	Be6
24 Rg3	Qf7
25 Bh6	g6

25 ... g5 is crushingly met by 26 B×g5!

26 f4	f5
27 e5	d4
28 Nf3	

After 28 Rh3 Qh7 all the same Nf3 has to be played.

| 28 ... | d×c3 |
| 29 Rh3 | |

With the threat of 30 Bg5 Qg7 31 Bf6.

29 ...	Qh7
30 Ng5	Qe7
31 Re1?	

This is unnecessary, as White has no need to strengthen his position any further. Simplest is 31 Bf8! K×f8 32 Qh8+ Bg8 33 e6!, when against the threat of 34 Nh7+ there is no satisfactory defence. Also good is 31 R×c3, followed by returning the rook to h3. But now the dangerous black pawn remains alive, and even makes a step forward.

| 31 ... | c2 |

32 Bf8!

After the slight delay this move still wins.

32 ...	K×f8
33 Qh8+	Bg8
34 Nh7+	

It is paradoxical that here after 34 e6 Qd8 35 Nh7+ Ke7 36 Qf6+ Kd6 37 e7+ Kc7 38 e×d8=Q+ Ra×d8 White with his extra queen (!) may not be able to win because of the black pawn at c2.

34 ...	Kf7
35 e6+	Q×e6
36 Ng5+	Ke7
37 N×e6	B×e6
38 Qg7+	Kd6
39 Rd3+	Nd4
40 Rc1	Bd5
41 R×d4!	

White eliminates the chief enemy—the c2 pawn—and sets about gradually realizing his material advantage.

| 41 ... | c×d4 |
| 42 R×c2 | Rac8 |

Black is mated after 42 ... d3 43 Qc7+ Ke6 44 Qe5+.

43 Rd2

In this position the game was adjourned. There followed:

43 ...	Rc1+
44 Kf2	Re4
45 Q×g6+	Be6
46 Qg5	Kc6
47 h3	Kb5
48 Qg7	a5

No better is 48 ... R×f4+ 49 Kg3, followed by either 50 R×d4 or 50 Q×a7.

182

49 R×d4	Rc2+
50 Kg1	Re1+
51 Kh2	Ree2
52 h4	R×a2
53 h5	R×g2+

Otherwise Black will not even be able to give up his bishop for the h-pawn...

54 Q×g2	R×g2+
55 K×g2	a4
56 h6	Bg8
57 Rd8	Bh7
58 Rd7	Bg6
59 Ra7!	

After White avoids the trap 59 Rg7 a3 60 R×g6 a2, the game is over.

59 ...	Kb4
60 Rg7	

Now this is possible: 60 ... a3 61 R×g6 a2 62 R×b6+ Ka5 63 Rb8. Therefore **Black resigned.**

No. 76 Grünfeld Defence

Geller–Smyslov

Candidates Quarter-Final Match
5th Game
Moscow, 1965

The untouchable queen

The variation chosen by Smyslov did not catch me unawares. When preparing for the match, my trainer Semion Furman and I had rightly assumed that, if the match were to go in my favour and the E-World Champion would have to play for complications with Black, he might choose this complicated continuation. And that is happened. Although earlier the variation had occurred fairly often, I was able to exploit its defects.

1 d4	Nf6
2 c4	g6

3 Nc3	d5
4 c×d5	N×d5
5 e4	N×c3
6 b×c3	Bg7
7 Bc4	c5
8 Ne2	0–0
9 0–0	Nc6
10 Be3	Qc7
11 Rc1	Rd8

With his last two moves Black begins an original counter-attacking plan, the ultimate aim of which is to blockade White's pawn centre. At the same time Black intensifies the pressure on d4, prepares to complete his development, and is ready to meet f2–f4 with ... f5.

Thus in the game Gligoric–Smyslov (match USSR–Yugoslavia, 1959) after 12 h3 b6 13 f4 e6 14 Qe1 Na5 15 Bd3 f5 16 e5? Black was able to carry out his plan in the most favourable way. I happened to be watching this game, and it was immediately apparent to me that the Yugoslav grandmaster, on encountering an unfamiliar strategic plan, had acted insufficiently purposefully. Meanwhile, one is struck by the weakening of Black's K-side, and in particular of his f7. This gives White two possible ways of continuing:

(1) Manoeuvring with Qd2 and Bh6, or else 12 Bf4 Qd7 13 d5, as occurred in the games Balashov–Hort and Korchnoi–Stein from the Alekhine Memorial Tournament, Moscow, 1971. In the Gaprindashvili–Kushnir match, Riga, 1972, instead of 13 d5 Kushnir fives times employed the new continuation 13 d×c5?! This does not look very natural, and by the end of the theoretical debate Gaprindashvili had found a perfectly satisfactory way of deploying the black pieces.

(2) The more active one which occurs in the game.

12 f4	e6

The crucial reply to White's 12th move seems to me to be 12 ... Bg4, whereby Black continues the battle for d4.

The continuation chosen by Smyslov indicates Black's desire to blockade the white pawn centre. But the immediate attempt at a blockade — 12 ... Na5 13 Bd3 f5 (Vaganian–Rogoff, World Junior Championship, 1971) is inappropriate in view of the weakness of Black's K-side after 14 e×f5 g×f5 15 Ng3 e6 16 Nh5.

Incidentally, Smyslov played 12 ... e6 almost without thinking, and it became clear to me that he did not sense the danger. Therefore White allowed himself a prophylactic move, although it was already possible to launch an attack on the enemy king by the double-edged 13 f5.

13 Kh1   b6?

A loss of time and a weakening of the h1–a8 diagonal, after which White's offensive becomes menacing. It was essential, as in the game Tukmakov–Stein, Alekhine Memorial, Moscow, 1971, to play 13 ... Na5 14 Bd3 f5 15 e×f5 e×f5 (*15 ... g×f5 16 Ng3* leaves White with a strong attack) 16 d×c5 Be6, and now 17 Nd4 (in the game *17 Qc2* was played) with chances for both sides, although White still has a slight advantage.

14 f5   Na5

After 14 ... e×f5 the most effective continuation of the attack is 15 Bg5 Rf8 16 d5 Na5 17 d6 Qd7 Bd5 (this is where the weakening of the long white diagonal tells) 18 ... Bb7 19 e×f5.

15 Bd3	e×f5
16 e×f5	Bb7
17 Qd2	Re8
18 Ng3	Qc6
19 Rf2	

Simultaneously defending g2 and preparing a decisive offensive against f7. After the game the opinion was expressed that at this point Black should have curtailed White's attacking aspirations by 19 ... R×e3. But the exchange sacrifice would not have solved Black's problems, since after 20 Q×e3 c×d4 White has the following possibilities:

(*b*) 21 Qf4 d×c3 22 f6 Bf8 23 Nf5!, with a strong attack.

(*a*) 21 c×d4 B×d4 22 Qh6 Q×c1+ 23 Q×c1 B×f2 24 Qh6 Bd4 (*24 ... Bc5 25 Nh5!*) 25 f×g6 h×g6 26 B×g6 f×g6 27 Q×g6+ Kf8 28 Qd6+.

19 ...	Rad8
20 Bh6	Bh8
21 Qf4	Rd7
22 Ne4!	c4

This removes the tension from the centre and completely frees White's hands on the K-side. In addition, the black knight at a5 remains out of play, which gives White an advantage in force on the decisive part of the battlefield. During the game I was expecting the more tenacious 22 ... Qd7, although even then White has an undisputed advantage after 23 Re1! B×e4 (*23 ... Q×f4 24 Nf6+*) 24 R×e4 R×e4 25 Q×e4.

The game now enters a phase of forcing variations.

| 23 Bc2 | Rde7 |
| 24 Rcf1! | |

Threatening 25 f×g6 h×g6 26 Nd6, when Black does not have the earlier possibility of ... Re1+. I was less attracted by 24 f×g6 h×g6 25 Bg5, winning the exchange after 25 ... f5 or 25 ... Rd7 26 Nf6+ B×f6 27 B×f6 Re6 28 Qh4 R×f6, since the position promised more.

24 ...	R×e4

25 f×g6!	f6

The queen cannot be taken, of course, in view of 26 g×h7 mate. After 25 ... Q×g6 26 Q×f7+ Q×f7 27 R×f7 in order to avoid mate Black has to incur great loss of material, such as 27 ... Bg7 28 R×g7+ Kh8 29 R×b7 N×b7 30 B×e4.

26 Qg5!

This second queen sacrifice is dictated not by a pursuit of unnecessary brilliance, but by reasons of expediency. In view of the threat of 27 g7 Black's reply is forced.

26 ...	Qd7
27 Kg1!	

A finesse which is necessary for the rapid completion of the game, since the immediate 27 R×f6 B×f6 28 Q×f6 h×g6 29 Q×g6+ Kh8 30 Bg5 R4e6 31 Bf6+ R×f6 leads after 32 R×f6 to mate ... to the white king — 32 ... Re1. Moreover, Black has no useful moves, and the white queen is still untouchable.

27 ...	Bg7
28 R×f6	Rg4

28 ... B×f6 would have led to the continuation given in the note to White's 27th move.

29 g×h7+	Kh8
30 B×g7+	Q×g7
31 Q×g4	

The fourth and last queen sacrifice. **Black resigned.**

No. 77 Ruy Lopez

Geller–Smyslov

Interzonal Tournament
Palma de Mallorca, 1970

Both opening and endgame ...

This game is in the first place of theoretical interest, since with a new strategic plan White was able to cast doubts on the old Rubinstein system, which in its time was considered a reliable defence. In combination with Game No. 1 against Mecking, and the game with Hernandez mentioned in the notes, the present game can serve as a textbook example of how to play against the still popular Chigorin Variation of the Ruy Lopez.

The endgame which resulted here was also highly interesting and instructive.

1 e4	e5
2 Nf3	Nc6
3 Bb5	a6
4 Ba4	Nf6
5 0–0	Be7
6 Re1	b5
7 Bb3	0–0
8 c3	d6
9 h3	Na5
10 Bc2	c5
11 d4	Qc7
12 Nbd2	Nc6
13 d5	Nd8

The start of a plan which was mentioned in Game No. 1 against Mecking.

In Geller–Hernandez, Las Palmas, 1979, Black continued here 13 ... Na7, intending to transfer the knight via c8 to b6 and to set up pressure on White's Q-side. But after 14 Nf1 Bd7 15 a4! (less convincing is the 40-year-old theoretical recommendation of *15 Kh2 Kh8 16 g4 Ng8 17 Ng3 g6 18 Be3 Nc8*, when White has a comparatively slight advantage) it transpired that the immediate 15 ... Nc8 is not good in view of 16 a×b5. After the continuation in the game, 15 ... Rfb8 16 Ng3 Nc8 17 a5! the black knight was again prevented from coming into play, and White gained a clear advantage after 17 ... c4 18 Bd2 Bf8 19 Nh2 Ne7 20 Bg5! Ne8 21 Qd2.

14 a4   Rb8

The a-file has to be conceded, since after 14 ... Bb7 15 a×b5 a×b5 16 R×a8 B×a8 Black's white-squared bishop is out of play.

15 b4!

The exclamation mark belongs here not so much to this one move, as to White's fundamentally new plan. In the Spassky–Korchnoi Final Candidates Match in 1968, White played 15 a×b5 a×b5 and then b2–b4. But the opening of the a-file was premature, since Black adopted the formation of knight at b7, bishop at d7 and king's rook at c8, and then began exchanging rooks along the open a-file. This markedly weakened his opponent's attacking potential. But now Black is faced with difficult problems.

15 ...   c4

If Black had carried out the aforementioned set-up here, he would have obtained neither the Rubinstein plan, nor exchanges!

16 Nf1   Ne8
17 a×b5   a×b5

18 N3h2!

The way for the f-pawn is opened.

18 ...   f5

Black tries to find a target for counter-attack. And although this move makes the e4 square available to the white pieces, on the other hand the advanced pawn at d5 is slightly weakened, and in time it can be attacked by queen or knight. In addition, the advance of the white pawn to f5 is averted, and this would have led to an extremely cramped position for Black on both wings.

The capture on f4, on the other hand, would have given White the important d4 square, and would have allowed him to invade the 7th rank. For example, 18 ... f6 19 f4 e×f4 20 B×f4 Nf7 21 Qd4 Ne5 22 Ra7 Rb7 23 Rfa1, with a marked advantage.

19 e×f5   B×f5
20 B×f5   R×f5
21 Be3   Rf8

Otherwise the knight coming out to f6 would cut off the rook's retreat.

22 Nf3	Nf6
23 Ng3	Nf7
24 Ra7!	

This manoeuvre deprives the black queen of the b7 square, from where it would have attacked the d-pawn, and enables White to take complete control of the a-file.

| 24 ... | Rb7 |
| 25 Ra5 | Qd7 |

Necessary to prevent Nf5.

26 Qd2	Rfb8
27 Rea1	Bd8
28 Ra6	h6
29 Nh2	Bb6?

Apparently an active move, but in reality a loss of time. Better was the immediate 29 ... Bc7, although even then after f2–f3 followed by Ng4 White has an excellent game, since he gains the e4 square for a knight.

| 30 Nhf1! | Bc7 |

The passive bishop is nevertheless needed for the defence of the d6 pawn. 31 ... B×e3 32 N×e3 would have rid White of any worries over his d5 pawn, and would have allowed him to make an invasion along the open file.

31 Qd1

White begins an attack on the vulnerable d6 pawn, and Black is short of just one tempo to prevent the planned regrouping of the white forces.

31 ...	Nh8
32 Nh5	N×h5
33 Q×h5	Qf7
34 Q×f7+	K×f7

Or 34 ... N×f7 35 Ng3 Kf8 36 Ne4 Ke7 37 f4, and Black stands badly.

| 35 Ng3 | Ng6 |

Alas, ... Ne7 has not been played, and only with his knight at e7 could Black have hoped to halt the development of his opponent's initiative. Now he loses material.

| 36 Nf5 | Ne7 |

On 36 ... Rd8 White wins by 37 Ra7.

37 N×d6+	B×d6
38 R×d6	Nf5
39 Re6	Re7
40 Raa6	Rd8
41 Bc5	Red7
42 Kh2	Ne7

The sealed move. On 42 ... R×d5 there would have followed 43 g4 Nh4 44 Re7+ Kg8 45 Raa7, with the threat of mate in three moves.

43 R×e7+	R×e7
44 B×e7	K×e7
45 Re6+	Kd7

The resulting rook ending is interesting and extremely instructive. White is a pawn up, and he can increase his material advantage at the expense of one of the black pawns —e5, b5 or g7. But in each case Black gains counter-play, and the drawing tendencies of rook endings are well enough known. Hence the decision:

46 Kg3!!

A textbook illustration of a classical rule: the active deployment of the pieces is more important than a material advantage. It is confirmed by the following specific variations:

(*a*) After 46 Rb6 Ra8 47 R×b5 Ra3 Black picks up the c3 pawn, and his pieces are excellently placed.

(*b*) The tempting 46 Rg6 Ra8 47 R×g7+ Kd6 48 Rg6+ K×d5 49 R×h6 Ra3 allows the black c4 pawn to become highly dangerous, while in the event of 48 Rg3 Black does not reply 48 ... K×d5? 49 Re3 followed by Kg3–f3 and g2–g4, but 48 ... Ra2!, destroying the coordination of the white forces.

(*c*) Finally, 46 R×e5 Kd6 47 Re3 g5! is also not completely clear after either 48 Re6+ K×d5 49 R×h6 Ke4, or 48 g3 Rf8 49 Kg2 K×d5.

46 ...	Ra8
47 Kf3	Ra3
48 Ke4	R×c3

Now that material equality has been restored, the ending is hopeless for Black!

| 49 Rg6 | Rc2 |

Black has to give up the idea of creating two connected passed pawns, in view of 49 ... Rb3 50 K×e5 R×b4 51 R×g7+ Kd8, and now:

(*a*) Not 52 Ke6 c3 53 d6? Re4+ 54 Kd5 c2 55 Rc7 Rc4, when it is Black who wins, while after 53 Rg8+ Kc7 54 d6+ Kb7 55 d7 Rd4 56 Rc8 b4 57 Rc4 R×c4 58 d8=Q c2 White has to seek perpetual check.

(*b*) 52 Kd6! Ke8 53 Ke6 Kf8 54 Rf7+

Kg8 55 d6 Rb2 56 d7 Re2+ 57 Kf6 R×f2+ 58 Kg6 R×g2+ 59 K×h6 Rd2 60 Re7, when White wins the rook for his d-pawn and manages to stop the black pawns, e.g. 60 ... c3 61 Re8+ Kf7 62 d8=Q R×d8 63 R×d8 b4 64 Rc8 Ke6 65 Kg5 Ke5 66 h4 Kd4 67 h5 b3 68 h6 b2 69 h7 b1=Q 70 h8=Q+ .

50 R×g7+	Kd6
51 Rg6+	Kd7
52 Rg7+	Kd6
53 Rg6+	Kd7

Both here and later White repeats moves to gain time on the clock.

54 K×e5	Re2+
55 Kd4	R×f2
56 Rg7+	Kd6
57 Rg6+	Kd7
58 g4	Rd2+
59 Ke5	Re2+

Totally bad is 59 ... c3 60 R×h6 c2 61 Rc6, when White's king goes across to his passed pawns on the K-side.

60 Kd4	Rd2+
61 Kc5	c3
62 Rd6+!	Ke7

Black loses more quickly after 62 ... Kc7 63 R×h6 c2 64 Rc6+ Kd7 65 Kb6.

63 Re6+	Kd7
64 Re3!	c2
65 Rc3	Rh2

66 h4!

188

The number of extra pawns is again not so important. Of much greater significance is the fact that the black king should not reach d6 after 66 K×b5?!

66 ...	R×h4
67 R×c2	R×g4
68 Rh2	Rg6
69 K×b5	Kd6
70 Rh5	Kc7

On 70 ... Rf6 White wins by 71 Kb6 Kd7+ 72 Kb7 followed by the advance of the b-pawn, while after 70 ... Rg5 71 R×h6 K×d5 72 Kb6 a decisive role is played by the fact that the black king is cut off along the 6th rank.

71 Kc5	Rf6
72 Rh1	Kb7
73 b5	Rg6
74 Rh5	Kc7
75 Rf5	Rg1

No better is 75 ... Rg7 76 b6+ Kd7 77 d6 Rh7 78 Rf8 or 78 Re5 with the threat of 79 Re7+.

76 b6+	Kb7
77 Rf7+	Kb8
78 d6	Rc1+
79 Kd5	

Here the game was adjourned for the second time, but **Black resigned** without resuming. After 79 ... Rd1+ 80 Ke6 Re1+ 81 Kf6 Rf1+ 82 Kg6 Rg1+ 83 Kh7 (*83 K×h6 is also possible*) 83 ... Rd1 84 d7 he loses his rook.

No. 78 Ruy Lopez

Smyslov–Geller

41st USSR Championship
Moscow, 1973

Fashion is always individual!

As has already been mentioned, World Champions very often set the tone of chess fashion. And so at that time the Exchange Variation of the Ruy Lopez acquired great popularity, because it had been employed — and with success — by Bobby Fischer. The then World Champion had different ways of handling the resulting position: he would manoeuvre in the middlegame, go into an endgame... But apart from him, no one achieved any real successes with this old continuation.

In the present game, moreover, after spending almost an hour in total over his 8th and 10th moves, Black found a new and interesting plan, which later went into the theory books as the basic continuation of the variation.

1 e4	e5
2 Nf3	Nc6
3 Bb5	a6
4 B×c6	d×c6
5 0–0	f6
6 d4	Bg4
7 c3	Bd6
8 Be3	Qe7

Already at this point Black was considering a fundamentally new plan.

9 Nbd2	0–0–0
10 Qc2	

10 ...	e×d4!

Earlier here Black either endeavoured to hold the centre, or else launched into a counter-attack on the K-side, but in each case White gained an appreciable advantage:

(*a*) 10 ... Nh6 (with the idea of ... *Nf7*) 11 d×e5 B×e5 12 N×e5 f×e5 13 Nc4 (also possible is *13 c4* with the idea of *c4–c5* and an attack on b7) 13 ... Nf7 14 Na5 Be6 15 b4 (Berkovich–Pukshansky, USSR, 1969).

(*b*) 10 ... g5 11 d×e5 B×e5 12 N×e5 f×e5 13 Nc4 followed by f2–f3, Na5 and (in reply to ... *b6*) Qe2 (Makarichev–Pukshansky, Moscow, 1968).

By the move in the game Black concedes the centre, so as to immediately attack it!

| 11 c×d4 | Re8 |
| 12 e5 | |

The critical decision, but a debatable one. Now the central white squares come completely under Black's control. To be considered was 12 Rfe1, not fearing the exchange on f3.

| 12 ... | Bb4 |

Not, of course, 12 ... f×e5 13 Bg5 Nf6 14 d×e5 B×e5 15 Rfe1, and White wins a piece.

13 h3	Be6
14 Ne4	Qf7
15 a3	Bb3!

Black is markedly behind in development, a situation which is worsened after his next move. But this is more than compensated by his bishop dominating the white squares. Moreover, in driving it away White is bound to lose time, so that the position can be assessed as complicated, but more promising for Black. He has thus won the opening battle, although with only forty-five minutes left on his clock for the next twenty-five moves.

16 Qb1	Bf8
17 Ned2	Bd5
18 b4	Qg6
19 Qb2	

Here, in contrast to Game No. 73, Smyslov avoids going into an ending where the opponent has two splendid bishops.

19 ...	Ne7
20 a4	Nf5
21 Rfe1	

White achieves nothing by 21 b5 f×e5! 22 b×a6 b×a6 23 d×e5, when after 23 ... N×e3 24 f×e3 Bc5 the bishops dominate the board, and at d7 the black king will be completely safe.

21 ...	f×e5
22 d×e5	Be7
23 Re2	

By 23 b5 White concedes the c5 square, and after 23 ... N×e3 24 R×e3 Bc5 25 Re2 (not *25 Rc3 Bd4*) 25 ... Rhf8 Black has a strong attack. Therefore White entrusts the defence of f2 to his rook, and plans to exchange the black-squared bishops. On the immediate 23 Bc5 Black would have replied 23 ... Nh4.

23 ...	Rhf8
24 Bc5	B×c5
25 b×c5	

| 25 ... | Nd4! |

By exchanging one of the knights, Black goes on to the offensive, and in it the leading role continues to be played by his white-squared bishop.

| 26 Q×d4 | R×f3 |
| 27 Ne4 | |

The ending after 27 Qg4+ Q×g4 28 h×g4 Rc3 is completely hopeless for White.

27 ...	R×h3
28 Ng3	Rh5
29 Rae1	

The b1 square is attacked, and White defends his e-pawn so as to place the other rook on the b-file. But in any case his counter-attack is too late.

| 29 ... | Rg5 |
| 30 Rb2 | Rg4 |

Not allowing the white queen on to the b-file.

| 31 Qc3 | h5 |
| 32 Reb1 | h4 |

It is all over. The finish was:

33 R×b7	h×g3
34 f3	Qh6!
35 R×c7+	

Or 35 f×g4 Qh2+ 36 Kf1 Q×g2+ 37 Ke1 Qf2+ 38 Kd1 g2.

35 ...	K×c7
36 Qa5+	Kd7
37 e6+	K×e6
38 Qe1+	Kf6

White exceeded the time limit. But after 39 Q×e8 he is mated by force within a few moves.

No. 79 Sicilian Defence

Smyslov–Geller

*USSR Team Championship
Moscow, 1974*

Brute force of the dragon

By the time of this game between us, Vasily Smyslov no longer liked to engage in debates on sharp and topical opening schemes, but preferred quieter continuations. Taking account of this, after White's 3rd move I had no objection to a possible transposition into the Dragon Variation, since in this case the only danger facing Black is active, dynamic play by the opponent.

The reckoning proved correct. White played the opening passively, and the right of the first move did not bring him any advantage. And the "dragon" managed to win.

1 e4	c5
2 Nc3	Nc6
3 Nf3	

If White was seriously thinking of playing the Closed Variation, there was no point in him playing this move so early.

| 3 ... | g6 |

"The dragon raises its head" ...

4 d4	c×d4
5 N×d4	Bg7
6 Be3	d6
7 Be2	Nf6
8 0–0	0–0
9 h3	

Essentially a loss of time. In addition the e4 pawn can no longer be defended by f2–f3 — a whole complex of black squares on the K-side will be too weakened. White also had no need to prepare Qd2: in this case 9 ... Ng4 (after *9 Qd2*) is not considered the strongest, and all the same Black plays either for a draw by 9 ... d5, or else 9 ... Bd7.

Better therefore is the usual 9 f4.

| 9 ... | Bd7 |
| 10 Nb3 | |

It is not easy to explain this move: one senses that White has no unified plan of action. Evidence of this is provided by the fact that his last two moves do not harmonize in any way with each other.

10 ...	a5
11 a4	Nb4
12 Bf3	

Here too 12 f4 was more active, whereas now the c4 square is weakened, which Black immediately exploits.

12 ...	Be6
13 Nd4	Bc4
14 Re1	Rc8

Black's position is not perhaps yet superior, but it is more promising.

15 Be2

To be considered was 15 Ndb5, when, it is true, Black has the manoeuvre 15 ... Nd7. But now Black seizes the initiative.

| 15 ... | d5 |
| 16 e5 | |

Practically forced.

| 16 ... | Ne4 |
| 17 Bg4 | |

The threat was 17 ... N×c3 18 b×c3 B×e2 and 19 ... R×c3.

17 ...	e6
18 f4	N×c3
19 b×c3	Na6

As a result White's Q-side is broken up, and Black intends to set up very serious pressure against it by the most natural means — ... Nc5, ... Qd7, ... Ba6, etc. The occupation of d4 is only a slight consolation for White, since he is not able to mount an attack on the K-side.

Therefore White pins his hopes on disturbing the material balance.

20 N×e6	f×e6
21 B×e6+	Kh8
22 B×c8	Q×c8
23 Qd4	Nc7
24 Qc5	Qd7
25 Q×a5	Ne6

White has won a rook and three pawns for two minor pieces, so that formally he has a material advantage. But of much greater significance is the fact that the black pieces are ready to assail the white king.

26 Rab1	Qf7
27 Qa7	Ba6
28 Rbd1	g5!

Stronger than 28 ... N×f4 29 B×f4 Q×f4 30 R×d5, when for the moment White can still hold on. Moreover, Black had already found the theme of the concluding combination.

| 29 f×g5 | B×e5 |
| 30 Bf2 | |

30 R×d5 allows mate by 30 ... Qf1+.

192

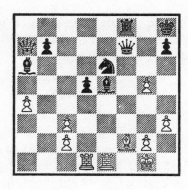

30 ...   d4!

The problem-like idea of interference: the white queen is shut out of play, and the bishop is attacked.

31 Bh4

The alternatives are no better:

(*a*) 31 R×e5 Q×f2+ 32 Kh1 Bf1! 33 Q×b7 Nf4 34 R×f1 (there is nothing else) 34 ... Q×f1+ 35 Kh2 Ne2.

(*b*) 31 B×d4 N×d4 32 c×d4 (*32 R×e5 Qf2+ 33 Kh1 Bf1 34 Q×b7 Nf3!*) and now possible is either the prosaic 32 ... Bb8 and 33 ... Qf4, or the more striking 32 ... Bg3! 33 Kh1 (if White moves his rook at e1 off the back rank, he is mated by *33 ... Qf1*, etc.) 33 ... Bf1! 34 d5 B×g2 35 K×g2 Qf3+ 36 Kg1 Bf2+.

32 ...	**Bb8**
33 Qb6	**Qf4**
34 g3	**Qf2+**
35 Kh1	**Be2**
White resigns	

Mikhail Tal

No. 80 Veresov Opening

Tal–Geller

Candidates Tournament Curacao, 1962

The second cycle

In order to understand the turning point in this game, one must remember certain surprises of the tournament (or, more correctly, match-tournament) at Curacao. Thus the very recent World Champion Mikhail Tal, who was considered one of the likely winners, after the first cycle had only 2 points out of 7, and was virtually propping up the tournament table. It was natural that in the second cycle he should play very riskily, in an attempt to catch up. I, on the other hand, was in the leading group, and could therefore play more quietly. This situation also gave Black a purely psychological advantage.

1 d4	**Nf6**
2 Nc3	**d5**
3 Bg5	

A rather unusual opening set-up. In the majority of cases White's strategic plan involves Q-side castling, the preparation of e2–e4, and (with luck) an attack on the K-side. The drawbacks to this scheme can be characterized by the words of grandmaster Savielly Tartakover, who wittily remarked: "Instead, after 1 d4, of tormenting himself for a long time over the preparation of e2–e4, wouldn't it be better for White to play 1 e4 immediately!"

3 ...   h6

One of the best replies to White's set-up is rightly considered 3 ... Nbd7 followed by ... c6 and the development of the queen at b6 or a5. But here Black preferred to clarify immediately the fate of the bishop at g5, especially since he does not lose a tempo in the exchange: an outlet for the bishop at f8 is opened.

4 B×f6	e×f6
5 e3	c6
6 Bd3	Bd6

Black aims for rapid development and avoids the creation of a "wall" by 6 ... f5, which would have restricted his opponent's attacking chances.

7 Qf3!

In any other case Black's previous move would have been justified. But now White establishes control over f5.

7 ...	0–0
8 Nge2	Re8

A slight loss of time. Although White has prepared castling on both wings, there could be no doubt—especially taking account of my opponent's style—that he was aiming to castle Q-side. To be considered therefore was 8 ... Nd7, not fearing 9 Qf5 g6 10 Qh3 Kg7, whereas after 9 0–0–0, in comparison with the game, Black would have gained an extra tempo for his counter-attack.

9 0–0–0	b5
10 g4	

Who will be the quicker?!—this is the essential point. Moreover, the combination 10 N×d5 c×d5 11 Q×d5 did not work because of 11 ... Qb6, when 12 Q×a8 fails

to 12 ... Bb7, while 12 Be4 can be simply met by 12 ... R×e4 13 Q×e4 Bb7 14 Qe8+ Bf8, with a good game for Black.

10 ...	b4
11 Na4	Nd7
12 h4	Nb6
13 N×b6	

The alternative was 13 Nc5 B×c5 14 d×c5 Na4 15 g5 f×g5 16 h×g5 N×c5 17 g×h6 N×d3+ 18 c×d3 g6 19 Rdg1, when, as in the game, White retains attacking chances.

13 ...	a×b6
14 g5	

White should not have been in a hurry to force events. After 14 Kb1 followed by Rdg1 and g4–g5 it would have been more difficult for Black to create counter-play, since his threats along the a-file can be parried by Nc1.

14 ...	f×g5
15 h×g5	R×a2

16 g×h6

Here 16 Kb1, retaining the rooks, was essential, since 16 ... Bg4 17 Q×g4 Qa8 would have failed to 18 Kc1 R×b2 (on 18 ... b3 there again follows 19 g×h6) 19 g×h6 Bf8 20 h×g7 B×g7 21 Rdg1, when White wins. Now, after the exchange of one pair of rooks, Black has nothing to fear.

16 ...	Ra1+
17 Kd2	R×d1+

18 K×d1	g6
19 Rg1	

The first consequence of White's inaccurate 16th move. In order to intensify the pressure on the g-file, he has to remove his rook from the h-file.

19 ...	Be6
20 Nf4	

The sacrifice on g6 does not work, either immediately — 20 B×g6 f×g6 21 R×g6+ Kh8, or after 20 Qh5 Kh8 21 B×g6 f×g6 22 Q×g6 Qe7. It has to be said that White appears to have no way to strengthen his attack.

20 ...	B×f4
21 Q×f4	Kh7

As often happens, the king feels safe under the cover of ... an enemy pawn.

22 Kd2	Qe7
23 Qe5	Rg8
24 f4	f6

24 ... Qh4 was also interesting, but ... time trouble was approaching, and from my tournament position I had no objection to a draw.

25 Qh5?

Here White should have admitted that his attack had been parried, and should have forced a draw by 25 R×g6 R×g6 (*25 ... f×e5?? 26 R×e6+*) 26 B×g6+ K×g6 27

f5+ K×h6 28 Qf4+ Kg7 29 f×e6 Q×e6 30 Qc7+ and 31 Q×b6. In continuing to play for a win, he oversteps the invisible boundary of the "safety zone".

25 ...	Bf7
26 Qh4	c5

The beginning of Black's counter-offensive.

27 c3	c4
28 Bc2	b5
29 Ke2	b3
30 Bb1	Qd6
31 Qh5	Qd7
32 Qh4	f5

Shutting the white bishop completely out of play.

33 Rg5	Be6

Black excludes any possible sacrifice on f5.

34 Qg3

White could have continued the struggle only by retaining his h-pawn. To do this he should have transferred his rook to the h-file, freeing g5 for his queen, although even in this case Black would have an undisputed positional advantage.

34 ...	K×h6
35 Qg2	Qf7
36 e4	

"Better an end without suffering, than suffering without end!" In the present position this aphorism is more than true, since against ... b4 (at the appropriate moment, of course) there is no satisfactory defence.

36 ...	f×e4
37 Qg3	Bf5
38 Ke3	Kg7
39 Rh5	Rh8
40 R×h8	K×h8
41 Qh4+	Kg7
42 Qd8	

Here the game was adjourned, but **White resigned** without resuming. After 42 ... Bd7 and 43 ... Qe6 the black queen breaks into the enemy position with decisive effect.

No. 81 Ruy Lopez

Tal–Geller

Kislovodsk, 1966

The loser is the one who makes the last mistake

The battle for first place in this traditional international tournament of the USSR Central Chess Club was mainly between three players—Mikhail Tal, Leonid Stein and myself. It was only by defeating both rivals (the game with Stein is also in this book—No. 3) that I managed to secure first prize. What's more, the game with the Ex-World Champion demanded particular composure on my part: at that time one had to play against Tal with a redoubled degree of caution, and to watch carefully for vol-cano-like erruptions of his chess fantasy.

1 e4	e5
2 Nf3	Nc6
3 Bb5	a6
4 Ba4	Nf6
5 0–0	Be7
6 Re1	b5
7 Bb3	0–0
8 h3	Bb7
9 d3	d6

The Closed Variation of the Ruy Lopez does not require h2–h3, and this gives Black equal chances. As the reader will already know from my notes to Game No. 4 with Zhukhovitsky, it was only later that I found the strongest plan for Black.

10 c3	Na5
11 Bc2	c5
12 Nbd2	Qc7

13 Nf1	Rad8
14 Qe2	Rfe8
15 Ng3	

15 ...	d5

Nowadays Black handles this position in analogy with the Smyslov Variation: he plays ... h6, ... Bf8, and is not too afraid of the white knight coming to f5. The move played, and especially the following one, are perhaps too audacious.

16 e×d5	R×d5

To be considered was 16 ... B×d5 with the possible sequel 17 Nf5 Bf8 18 Bg5 Re6, leading to great complications after 19 N×e5.

17 Bg5	g6

Essential, to prevent 18 Nf5.

18 b4?

A serious mistake. For the sake of return-ing his white-squared bishop to the a2–g8 diagonal (Tal has his sights on f7!), White irreparably weakens his d4 square, creates a weak pawn at b4, and drives the black knight to where it wants to go. The initiative passes completely to Black, whereas 18 d4! would have led to an interesting and double-edged position after 18 ... c×d4 19 c×d4 e4! 20 N×e4 N×e4 21 B×e7 N×f2 22 K×f2 Rd7 23 Bf6! R×e2+ 24 R×e2.

18 ...	c×b4

19 c×b4	Nc6
20 Bb3	Rdd8
21 Rac1	Nd5

Attacking the b4 pawn and—more important—threatening to invade at f4 after the exchange of black-squared bishops.

22 Ne4	B×g5
23 Nf×g5	Qe7

Releasing the pin on the knight, and threatening 24 ... Nd4.

24 Qg4	Nd4

In the first instance Black pursues a strategic aim: after the exchange of the white bishop or its eviction from b3, his K-side will be completely safe. Then the time will come to go after White's weak pawns.

25 Nc5	h5

Black takes the opportunity to exploit the insufficiently defended state of the knight at g5.

26 Qg3	Nf5
27 Qf3	Ba8

The bishop moves away from attack with gain of tempo, and White inevitably loses a pawn.

28 Nce4

Tal decides to maintain his second knight in its attacking position, so as to attempt to complicate matters. After 28 Nge4 Nd4 29 Qd1 N×b4 he is a pawn down, and without the least activity.

28 ...	Nd4
29 Qg3	N×b3
30 a×b3	Q×b4

30 ... N×b4 was also possible, but in the time scramble Black did not want to remove from the centre his well-placed knight.

31 d4

Resourceful, but now insufficient!

31 ...	e×d4

Simpler was 31 ... Q×d4, and if 32 Red1 Qb6, securely defending f6. Now a piece sacrifice allows White to complicate the game for a certain time.

32 N×f7	K×f7
33 Ng5+	Kf6!

After 33 ... Kg8(g7) Black has to reckon with the white knight going to e6.

34 Re4	Qd6?

In time trouble Black blunders away a whole rook! He could have won instantly by 34 ... Qd2, with a double attack on c1 and g5.

35 Q×d6+	R×d6
36 R×e8	K×g5
37 R×a8	d3

Although White is the exchange up, it is he who is fighting for a draw. Now 38 ... d2 39 Rd1 Nc3 is threatened.

38 Rac8	b4

Renewing the threat.

39 R8c5?

It is White's turn to blunder in time trouble. He could have drawn by 39 Rd1 Nc3 40 Rd2 Ne4 41 Rd1, when 41 ... d2 is bad because of 42 Rc2 with the threat of 43 f3.

| 39 ... | Kh6 |
| 40 R×d5 | |

It transpires that, by moving to c5, the white rook would have run into a fork in the variation 40 Rd1 Nc3 41 Rd2 Ne4.

40 ...	R×d5
41 Kf1	d2
42 Rd1	

With the time scramble over, **White resigned** because of 42 ... Rd3.

No. 82 Pirc Defence

Geller–Tal

Alekhine Memorial Tournament Moscow, 1975

March of the white king

A strategic struggle, tactics, a trap, an attack — it all happened in this game. And there was an original finish. Under fire from a sharp counter-attack in the middlegame, the white king literally forced its way through the ranks of its own and the enemy pieces deep into the opposing rearguard, until it was within a handshake of its black colleague.

Throughout my wide tournament experience, I do not recall a similar king march...

1 e4	d6
2 d4	Nf6
3 Nc3	g6
4 Nf3	Bg7
5 Be2	

This apparently modest continuation is not without bite, and is the one I most often employ. Harmoniously developing his pieces on central squares, for the moment White avoids disclosing his plans.

| 5 ... | 0–0 |

Black cannot engage in activity such as

5 ... c5, since 6 d×c5 Qa5 7 0–0! Q×c5 8 Be3 Qa5 9 Nc4 0–0 10 Nb3 Qd8 11 f4 leads to a position from the Sicilian Dragon, but with two extra tempi for White.

| 6 0–0 | Bg4 |
| 7 Be3 | Nc6 |

Theory considers this plan of piece pressure on the white centre to be the most reliable. Black prepares ... e5, so as to force White either to exchange, or to advance d4–d5.

| 8 Qd2 | e5 |
| 9 d5 | Ne7 |

As shown by the game Tal–Chikovani, USSR, 1978, the pawn sacrifice 9 ... B×f3 10 B×f3 Nd4 is incorrect, and does not give any compensation after 11 B×d4 e×d4 12 Q×d4 Nd7 13 Qd2 f5 14 e×f5 g×f5 15 Rae1 B×c3 16 Q×c3 Ne5 17 Re2.

10 Rad1

The basic position of the Pirc Defence has been reached. White has an advantage in space, and he must seek some way to attack. It is difficult to do this on the Q-side, since the knight at c3 hinders the advance c2–c4. Therefore he plans f2–f4. Black too must aim for ... f5, since he has no other plan. Especially since White's last move prevents ... c6, although also possible was 10 a4, cramping Black on the Q-side, as in Geller–Vasyukov, Kislovodsk, 1968.

| 10 ... ˙ | Bd7 |

Black wishes to preserve his bishop from exchange. A little earlier in the game Geller–Savon, USSR Spartakiad, Riga, 1975, he chose 10 ... Ne8 (10 ... Nd7 is also possible), which after 11 Ne1! B×e2 12 Q×e2 f5 13 f4! gave White a firm initiative, since in the given position the increased activity of the g7 bishop is less important than the specific weakness of the e6 square.

Here Black tries to improve the variation, by aiming to link the ... f5 advance with the more active sortie of his knight to g4.

11 Ne1

Introduced by the author of these lines. Since a black knight is not destined to reach e5, White aims to open up the game by f2–f4.

11 ...   Ng4

Possible, in analogy with the Karpov–Timman game, Amsterdam, 1976 (where *11 h3* was played), is the unexpected 11 ... b5, which after 12 f3 Qb8 13 Nd3 Rd8, with the idea of preparing ... c6, leads to a double-edged game.

12 B×g4   B×g4
13 f3   Bd7
14 f4   e×f4

After this game the best defence has been considered 14 ... Bg4, although even here 15 Rc1 (in Karpov–Timman, Tilburg, 1977, White chose the perfectly possible *15 Rb1*, but after *15 Nf3 f5 16 Rde1 B×f3 17 R×f3 Qd7 18 f×e5 d×e5 19 Bh6* the game is level, Geller–Timman, Wijk aan Zee, 1977) leaves White with the better game. Nevertheless, I think that the last word in this position has not yet been said.

15 B×f4   f5
16 Nf3!

Creating, in the first instance, the threat of 16 e5, after which Black will have no compensation for his numerous weaknesses. Therefore his reply is practically forced.

16 ...   f×e4
17 N×e4   Bg4

Without playing this Black has no convenient square for his queen.

Note also that 17 ... B×b2 18 c3 Ba3 would have been suicidal: without his black-squared bishop Black cannot ensure the safety of his king.

18 Rde1   Qd7

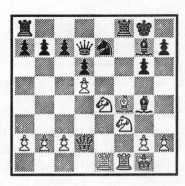

19 Neg5!

The result of the strategic battle is obvious. White has his sights set on e6, and Black is faced with a difficult defence.

19 ...   Rae8
20 c4

In the end it is not a rook which must be established at e6, but a knight! Therefore White defends his d5 pawn, preparing Nd4.

20 ...   Nc8
21 Nd4   R×e1
22 R×e1   Re8
23 R×e8+   Q×e8
24 h3

Opening, with gain of tempo, an escape square for the king.

24 ...   Bd7

After 24 ... B×d4+ 25 Q×d4 Bf5 26 Ne6! B×e6 27 Bh6 Qe7 28 d×e6 there is simply nothing that Black can move.

25 Nde6	B×e6
26 N×e6	Qf7
27 b3	

The exchange of rooks has to some extent insured Black against a possible direct attack, but strategically his position is still lost. In White's favour will be both the exchange of bishops, and the exchange of queens. Therefore, realizing the futility of "standing still", Black sacrifices a pawn in an attempt to gain counter-play.

27 ...	Qf6
28 N×c7	Qa1+
29 Kh2	Bd4
30 Qe2	

An inaccuracy, which makes the win more difficult. White could have won immediately by 30 Qc1! Q×a2 31 Qe1, when it is the black king which cannot escape the mating attack. But it's an ill wind — without this inaccuracy the marathon march of the white king from h2 to f8(!) would not have occurred.

30 ...	Ne7!

An excellent practical chance and an extraordinarily cunning trap!

31 Nb5

White saw that after 31 Q×e7 (first *31 Qe6+ Kh8* does not affect matters) 31 ... Qg1+

32 Kg3 Qf2+ 33 Kg4 Q×g2+ 34 Bg3 h5+ 35 Kh4 Qe4+!! 37 Q×e4 he would end up in a problem-like mate by the opponent's one remaining piece — 36 ... Bf6 mate!

31 ...	Bg1+

White would have had more trouble after 31 ... Qg1+ 32 Kg3 Nf5+ 33 Kf3 Bf6, with great complications. To be fair, however, it must be mentioned that both players were already short of time.

32 Kg3	Nf5+
33 Kf3	Nh4+

Slightly better is 33 ... a6, to which White would have replied 34 g4.

34 Kg4	Nf5
35 Qe8+	Kg7
36 Qd7+	Kh8

37 N×d6!

White calculated accurately that this would win by force, although he had literally seconds remaining on his clock.

37 ...	Qd1+
38 Kg5	Qh5+
39 Kf6	Bd4+
40 Ke6	Ng7+
41 Kf7	g5+

Here the time scramble ended and **Black resigned:** after 42 Kf8 there are no more checks.

Exceptions to the rule

It stands to reason that in their games collections players usually include only wins: after all, defeats do not number among one's achievements. But even so, there are no rules without exceptions. Instances are by no means rare when a victory is not at all pleasing in the creative sense (I have had this feeling even about some of my own games which have been awarded special prizes), while a defeat can be endured easily, because the game discovered something new, and provided aesthetic satisfaction.

In this book—and in this chapter—by way of an exception I have decided to include two drawn games. Both of them are well enough supplied with fantasy, with beautiful variations "behind the scenes", and cannot fail to please those who value in chess not only the competitive aspect, but also beauty. . . .

In the first of these games I have also made use of my opponent's notes.

No. 83 Sicilian Defence

Geller–Tal

44th USSR Championship
Moscow, 1976

1 e4	c5
2 Nf3	d6
3 d4	c×d4
4 N×d4	Nf6
5 Nc3	a6

"When preparing for the game against Geller, I constantly reminded myself that the Moscow grandmaster is an outstanding specialist in the field of opening theory. Even Karpov in his game with Geller attempted to avoid well-studied variations, and played the French Defence, which he had hardly ever employed before. I also wanted to play some unexpected variation, but in fact against such an opponent, and in the Sicilian, this is virtually impossible. . ." (M. T.).

6 Be2	e6
7 0–0	Nc6
8 Be3	Be7

The game has transposed into the old Scheveningen Variation, which is now enjoying its third or fourth youth.

9 Qe1

"A new continuation? Alas, it all leads merely to a transposition of moves. . ." (M. T.).

In certain cases in this set-up, Black can manage without developing his queen at c7. It is against this that White's selected move order is directed: as soon as the rook comes to d1, the black queen will have to move off the d-file.

9 . . .	0–0
10 Rd1	Qc7
11 f4	N×d4
12 B×d4	b5
13 e5	d×e5
14 f×e5	Nd7

"All this I played completely calmly, thinking that I was making moves that were well tried and tested by theory. But after 14 . . . Nd7 Geller glanced at me in surprise, and, as it seemed to me, sympathetically. After the game I learned that at home he usually tried to catch his son, a candidate master, in this variation, in lightning games. . ." (M. T.).

15 Ne4!

Black does not manage to exchange this knight—and this is an achievement for White: from the Q-side it transfers across to the K-side, which is where the main battle will develop.

15 . . .	Bb7

Black cannot take on e5, of course — 15 . . . N×e5 16 Qg3.

16 Nf6+

"Now I had no doubt that I had fallen into a prepared variation. I worked out (without the least pleasure!) a rather lengthy variation: 16 ... g×f6 17 e×f6 Bc5 18 Qh4 Kh8 (there is nothing better) 19 Bd3 B×d4+ 20 Kh1! B×g2+ 21 K×g2 Rg8+ 22 Kh3 N×f6 23 R×f6 Rg7 24 Q×d4. This sequence may also be terminated earlier—the end result has long been clear..." (M. T.).

The variations given by the Ex-World Champion are correct, but I once "caught" my son in a shorter and more beautiful variation: after 16... g×f6 White continued 17 Qg3+ Kh8 18 e×f6!! Q×g3 19 f×e7+, and White remains at least the exchange ahead.

16 ...   Kh8

The only move after which Black still has some hopes...

17 Qh4   h6
18 Qh5

Threatening 19 N×d7 Q×d7 20 Be3 Qc7 21 B×h6. In this situation there is no time to lose...

18 ...   Bc5!

"The bishop, which from d4 is intending in two leaps to carry out a raid on the h6 pawn, has to be exchanged. White can, of course, make things more difficult by 19

N×d7, but then after 19 ... Q×d7 20 B×c5 Black has 20 ... Qc6, when the bishop is nevertheless lost... I expected that after 19 N×d7 Q×d7 Geller would play 20 c3, when he would still have had the possibility of transferring his heavy pieces to the K-side and continuing his attack, which, it is true, would have lost some of its impetus.

"But after considerable thought Geller made another move, dictated, as soon becomes clear, by the soul of a chess artist." (M. T.).

19 Rf2?!!

"I must confess that this came as a surprise. At first I examined a continuation which seemed satisfactory — 19 ... B×d4 20 R×d4 N×e5 21 Rh4 Rfd8 (*21 ... Ng6 22 Q×h6+!*) and here, to my horror, I noticed that by 22 Qg5!! White would force immediate capitulation.

"But what if, instead of 21 ... Rfd8, Black plays 21 ... Qc5? Now 22 Qg5 is not possible because of 22 ... Nf3+. But it was after 21 ... Qc5 that my opponent had prepared a brilliant mating finish.

"Geller was intending to continue here 22 Q×h6+!! g×h6 23 R×h6+ Kg7 24 Rh7+ Kg6 25 Bh5+ Kg5 26 h4+! K×h4 27 B×f7+, and now, depending on Black's choice, his king is mated either at g3 — 28 Rh3, or at g5 — 28 Rh5.

"Of course, to be the co-author of such a work of art would have been honourable, but I nevertheless declined. It would have been a terribly crushing defeat..." (M. T.).

All the same, why did White play this? The point was that I was loathe to exchange my knight (*19 N×d7*), and I had to safeguard my king against pressure on the a7–g1 diagonal. Highly suitable for this was 19 Kh1!, when Black would appear to have no defence.

19 ...	Rad8
20 Ng4	Be4

Black is on his last line of defence...

21 N×h6	g×h6
22 Q×h6+	Kg8

"It transpires that for the completion of his attack White has insufficient force. However, Geller makes a last desperate attempt." (M. T.).

23 Rd3

"If Black takes the rook, nothing will save him. Also bad is 23 ... N×e5, since after 24 Rh3 White again gives mate. But the capture on d4 is sufficient for a draw..." (M. T.).

It is here that White's 19th move becomes important! Had he played his king to h1, after 23 Bd3!! his attack would have been irresistible.

23 ...	B×d4

It is clear that 24 R×d4 Bg6 25 Rh4 is parried by 25 ... Q×e5, while 24 Rg3+ Bg6 25 R×g6+ f×g6 26 Q×g6+ leads to perpetual check. And so we shook hands.

Drawn

No. 84 Queen's Gambit

Tal–Geller

46th USSR Championship
Tbilisi, 1978

1 c4	e6
2 Nc3	d5
3 d4	Nf6

4 Bg5	Be7
5 e3	0–0
6 Nf3	h6
7 B×f6	

This way of handling the opening is directed in the first instance against the possible Tartakover–Bondarevsky–Makogonov Variation.

At f6 the black bishop comes up against the securely defended d4 pawn, and sooner or later will have to return to e7. During this time White will prepare a minority attack, which is part of his plans.

7 ...	B×f6
8 Rc1	c6

A flexible continuation. Black does not persist with his aim of playing ... c5, as was the case in Game No. 43, Geller–Ivkov.

9 Bd3	Nd7
10 c×d5	

10 0–0 is analysed in the aforementioned Game No. 43.

10 ...	e×d5

This indicates Black's intention not to be restricted to defence, but to seek active counter-play.

11 b4!	Be7

To be considered was 11 ... a6.

12 b5	Ba3!

The white rook is diverted to c2, and some of Black's tactical ideas are later based on this nuance. Of course, it was impossible to foresee all the coming complications, but it was clear that the white knight was aiming for a4. With the rook at c2 it will be undefended, and later Black is able to exploit this factor.

13 Rc2

On 13 Rb1 Black had prepared 13 ... Qa5 14 Qb3 c5!, seizing the initiative. The same undermining of the white centre is also good after 13 b×c6 b×c6 14 Rc2 — 14 ... c5, and 15 N×d5 does not work in view of 15 ... c×d4 with the threat of 16 ... Qa5+.

| 13 ... | Bd6 |

Here 13 ... c5? would have favoured White, since after 14 N×d5 c×d4 15 N×d4 the queen check at a5 is harmless.

| 14 0–0 | Nf6 |
| 15 b×c6 | |

Eliminating ... c5, which was again on the agenda.

| 15 ... | b×c6 |
| 16 Na4 | |

White continues to battle for an opening advantage. After 16 e4 d×e4 17 N×e4 Be6 the game would have been level.

| 16 ... | Ne4! |

16 ... Bd7 17 Nc5 Qe7 18 Qc1! would have given White the better chances, and so Black offers a pawn sacrifice.

17 Ne5

Accepting the offer would have had its dangers: 17 R×c6 Bd7 18 Rc1 Ba3 19 Rb1 Qa5, with excellent counter-play.

| 17 ... | Qe8! |

With an "X-ray" attack on the undefended white knight. Now Black plans ... c5, after which the second white knight at e5 will also become uncomfortable. The routine 17 ... B×e5 18 d×e5 Qg5 19 f4 Qg6 20 Qc1 would have led to a position in which Black would have had no real counter to White's Q-side attack.

18 f3

Tal plays "in the spirit of Tal", and an exchange of combinational blows commences. 18 f4 suggests itself, reinforcing the knight at e5, after which it is by no means easy for Black to find a way to equalize. But there is one — 18 ... f6 19 B×e4 d×e4 20 Nc4 (20 N×c6?! Ba6 21 Rff2 Bb5) 20 ... Be7! 21 d5 Qf7 22 d6 (22 d×c6 Ba6) 22 ... Rd8, when both 23 Nc5 Be6 24 N×e6 Q×e6 and 23 Qd4 Be6 24 Rd1 B×c4 give Black roughly equal chances.

| 18 ... | c5!! |

Black also had other possibilities, for example: 18 ... f6 19 N×c6 Bd7 20 Qc1 Ng5, or 18 ... Ng5 19 f4 f6 20 Bg6 Qe7! (20 ... Qe6 21 R×c6!? f×e5 22 d×e5 Q×g6 23 R×d5 is also interesting) 21 f×g5 f×e5 22 R×f8+ Q×f8 23 Rf2 Qe7 24 g×h6 Be6. All would have led to very sharp and unclear positions. But the text continuation is more effective. Black continues to play for the initiative, and at the same time rids himself of his backward c-pawn.

19 f×e4   c×d4!

An unusually picturesque position: doubled white and black pawns, and both white knights "hanging".... It would have been a blunder to play 19 ... Q×a4? 20 e×d5, when 20 ... c×d4 fails to 21 N×f7!

20 Ng4!

In the event of 20 e×d4 Q×a4 it is White who has to fight for equality by 21 Nc6 (here *21 N×f7* does not work because of the *zwischenzug 21 ... Q×d4+*), while after 20 Nc6?! d×e4 21 Bb5 d3 the initiative passes to Black, although he has only two pawns for the piece.

20 ...   d×e4!

The knight at a4 was serving as a "bait": 20 ... Q×a4? 21 R×c8 Q×d1 22 R×f8+, while after 20 ... B×g4 21 Q×g4 Q×a4 White has an attack — 22 e5!

21 Bc4!

It appears that White should be able to decide the game by a direct attack on the king, but Black has in reserve a convincing counter. Thus after 21 R×c8 R×c8 22 Nf6+ g×f6 23 Qg4+ Kh8 24 R×f6 Rc1+ 25 Bf1 (*25 Kf2 d×e3+*) apart from 25 ... B×h2+ there is also 25 ... Qe6!, when it is White who has to concern himself over how to hold the draw.

21 ...   B×g4!

Black does not have time for 21 ... d3?, in view of 22 Rcf2 Be6 23 Rf6!! B×c4 24

N×h6+ g×h6 25 Qg4+ Kh7 26 R×h6+ K×h6 27 Rf6+, with mate in three moves.

22 Q×g4   Q×a4

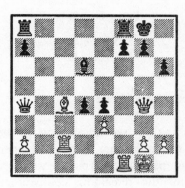

23 R×f7!

The tempo of the attack has to be maintained. After 23 Bb3? Qa5 24 Rcf2 Qe5 25 g3 d×e3 all the chances are with Black.

23 ...	**R×f7**
24 B×f7+	**K×f7**
25 Qf5+	**Ke7!**

25 ... Kg8? loses to 26 Qd5+ Kh7 27 Q×e4+ g6 28 Qb7+. But now, although the position of the black king appears dubious, White has nothing more than perpetual check.

26 Q×e4+	**Kd7**
27 Qb7+	**Ke6**
28 Qe4+	**Kd7**

The outcome would have been the same after 28 ... Be5 29 Rc6+ Kf7 30 Qd5+ Kf8 31 Qc5+ Kg8 32 Qd5+ Kh8! 33 R×h6+ g×h6 34 Q×e5+.

29 Qb7+

Drawn

Tigran Petrosian

No. 85 King's Indian Defence

Petrosian–Geller

*17th USSR Championship
Moscow, 1949*

Conversion of a bishop

This was our second meeting. In the first, in the Championship Semi-Final, there had been no particular struggle: we were well ahead of the remaining competitors, and neither had any objection to a draw. But here the situation was different. Participating for the first time in a very strong USSR Championship, and being still very young (formally I was still listed as a candidate master), we were pretty nervous and started extremely badly. A victory could provide a stimulus for either of the players. ...

1 d4	Nf6
2 Nf3	g6
3 c4	Bg7
4 Nc3	0–0
5 e4	d6
6 Be2	e5
7 d5	

Petrosian's favourite strategy—play with a blocked centre. By this White immediately predetermines the subsequent course of the game. The pawn formation favours his attack on the Q-side, while Black should seek counter-play on the other side of the board.

But for all that, Black can regard such an early stabilization of the centre as something of an achievement (which is why now *7 0–0* or *7 Be3* is more often played). Because, by controlling c5, he can delay White's attack on the Q-side.

7 ...	Nbd7

The most accurate continuation, 7 ... a5 followed by ... Na6, was developed by Leonid Stein and the author of these lines much later, roughly fifteen years after this game, as a reaction to the Petrosian System (in reply to *7 ... Nbd7 — 8 Bg5*).

8 0–0	Nc5
9 Qc2	a5
10 Nd2	

White intends to exchange off the knight at c5, but after the following reply by Black this move practically went out of use.

10 ...	Bh6!

Now White is unable to avoid the exchange of his very strong and important black-squared bishop for Black's passive bishop.

11 Nb3	B×c1
12 N×c5?	

White leaves his opponent with the renowned "bad King's Indian" bishop, overlooking that, deprived of its opponent, it has been converted into a "good" one! The lesser evil was 12 Ra×c1, although even here after 12 ... Nfd7 13 Nd2 (it is not possible to prevent ... f5, for example, *13 Bg4 N×b3 14 a×b3 f5! 15 e×f5 Nc5 16 Na4 Na6*, and Black has at least equal chances, Bobotsov–Petrosian, Kapfenberg, 1970) 13 ... f5 14 e×f5 g×f5 15 f4 e×f4 16 R×f4 Ne5 Black has active counter-play, Hort–Stein, Los Angeles, 1969.

12 ...	Bh6
13 Nd3	Nd7
14 a3	f5

Black is well ahead of the opponent in carrying out his plan, and the initiative is completely with him. In addition, White has no way of countering the King's Indian bishop.

| 15 b4 | Nf6 |

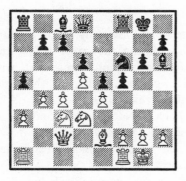

16 Nb2

The attempt by 16 f3 to hold on to e4, the key square in the King's Indian Defence, does not succeed: 16 ... Be3+ 17 Kh1 (*17 Nf2 a×b4 18 a×b4 R×a1 19 R×a1 f×e4 20 N×e4 N×e4 21 Q×e4 Bd4*, with the decisive threat of *22 ... Bf5*) 17 ... Bd4, and White cannot maintain material equality without making a decisive positional concession such as 18 e×f5.

The approved idea in such positions of 16 e×f5 g×f5 17 f4 is not good here because of 17 ... e4, when the black-squared bishop is terribly strong. Besides, also very tempting here is 16 ... B×f5, and White is in difficulties under the sweeping fire of the two bishops.

| 16 ... | f×e4 |
| 17 c5 | |

Since 17 N×e4 N×e4 18 Q×e4 is not possible in view of 18 ... Bf5 19 Qf3 Qg5 with a very strong attack, White hopes to transfer his knight via c4 to the defence. But he does not succeed in this: in turn the doubled black e-pawns perform the role of a battering-ram.

| 17 ... | a×b4 |
| 18 a×b4 | R×a1 |

Weakening the defence of f2.

19 R×a1	Bf5
20 Qb3	e3
21 f3	e4

An attack plus an extra pawn—the rest is not difficult.

22 Nc4	e×f3
23 B×f3	Ng4
24 g3	

Otherwise the queen would burst in at h4.

24 ...	Qf6
25 Bg2	Bd3
26 h3	Qf2+
27 Kh1	Q×g3

Mate is inevitable, and **White resigned.**

No. 86 Nimzo-Indian Defence

Geller–Petrosian

*Candidates Tournament
Amsterdam, 1956*

Blockade or breakthrough?

Such were the fundamentally different strategic plans carried out by the two opponents. Everything was decided by one question—which was stronger? At first Black's chances of blockading the centre were preferable, but a barely perceptible mistake equally imperceptibly changed the situation, and the energy of White's breakthrough brought him success.

1 d4	Nf6
2 c4	e6
3 Nc3	Bb4
4 e3	d5
5 Nf3	0–0
6 Bd3	c5
7 0–0	Nc6
8 a3	B×c3
9 b×c3	Qc7

After the usual 9 ... d×c4 10 B×c4 Qc7 a so-called "Tabiya" is reached—the basic position in this variation of the Nimzo-Indian Defence, in which both formerly, and now, 11 Bd3 is considered the strongest. Black wishes to avoid this, and employs a continuation which first occurred six months before this game, in the 23rd USSR Championship.

10 Qc2

An attempt to transpose after all into the "Tabiya". Later it was established that White does better to continue 10 c×d5 e×d5 11 Nh4 or 11 a4.

10 ...	Na5
11 c×d5	

In this way White can hardly hope for an opening advantage. But the attempt to maintain control of c4 by 11 Ne5 also does not achieve anthing: after 11 ... d×c4 12 N×c4 N×c4 13 B×c4 c×d4 14 c×d4 Bd7 15 Qe2 Rac8 16 Bd3 Ba4 the game is level, Borisenko–Khasin, 23rd USSR Championship, Leningrad, 1956.

11 ...	c4
12 Be2	e×d5
13 Nd2	

From here the knight defends the b3 square, and simultaneously participates in the preparation of e3–e, the typical break-

through in such positions. A new position has arisen with completely new problems.

13 ...	Bg4

White's plan obviously has to be opposed. Therefore during the game I first thought 13 ... Re8 to be more dangerous, with the idea of ... g6 and ... Bf5. But then I noticed 14 f3, after which both 14 ... R×e3 15 Ne4 R×e4 16 f×e4 N×e4 17 Bf4, and 14 ... Qe7 15 e4 d×e4 16 f×e4 N×e4 17 N×e4 17 N×c4 led to a complicated struggle with fair chances for White.

By the move played Black hopes by the exchange of bishops to weaken the white squares in the opposing position, to set up a blockage, and then to mount an attack on the K-side.

14 B×g4	N×g4
15 g3	f5
16 Rb1	

A useful move—in some cases the rook is ready to attack the d5 pawn from b5.

16 ...	Nc6?

A mistake. From its active position (it was constantly threatening to invade at b3, and forced the white knight to remain at d2) the knight transfers to a square where there is nothing for it to do. Better was Euwe's suggestion of 16...b6, parrying a possible

Rb5, freeing the queen from the necessity of guarding the knight, and aiming after the possible sequel 17 a4 Rae8 18 Ba3 Rf6 19 Rfe1 Qf7 20 Nf1 Rfe6 for pressure on the e-file and activity on the K-side. But Black, who was obviously very pleased with his position, played this part of the game quickly and carelessly, without attaching significance to certain important details.

17 a4	Qd7
18 Ba3	Rfe8

Black should have continued 18 ... Rf6. Now it transpires that his queen's rook is out of it, and with only one rook he is unable to prevent the e3–e4 break-through.

19 Rfe1	b6

20 Re2

Black's planless play has led to a sharp change in the picture.

20 ...	Qe6

Or 20...g6 21 Rbe1 Re6 22 f3 Nf6 and 23 e4.

21 Rbe1	Qh6
22 Nf1	Qh5
23 f3	Nf6
24 Nd2	Re6
25 e4	Rae8
26 e5	Nd7

27 Nf1!

A tactical way of realizing the advantage achieved. The immediate 27 f4 would have allowed Black after 27 ... Nf6! 28 Nf1 Ne4 29 Ne3 Rd8 to hold his weak d5 and f5 pawns, while acquiring an excellently-placed knight in the centre. But now the threat of 28 Ne3 forces Black to accept the opponent's "Greek gift".

27 ...	Q×f3
28 Rf2	Qd3

28 ... Qh5 29 Q×f5 would be equivalent to capitulation.

29 Qc1

The point of White's plan. The threat of 30 Re3 forces Black to part with a piece.

29 ...	N×d4
30 c×d4	Q×d4
31 Rd1	Qg4

Black wishes to leave the e5 pawn to the mercy of the knight, since 31 ... Q×e5 32 Bb2 Qd6 (*32 ... Qe4 33 Rd4*) 33 R×f5 is totally unpromising for him. But he does not manage to achieve this.

32 Ne3	Qe4
33 Rf4	

The most exact. The queen is "driven" to e5, where it deprives its knight of this square.

33 ...	Q×e5
34 N×d5	Qe2

35 Rf2	Q×d1+

Otherwise Black loses either the exchange (*36 Nc7*), or his c-pawn.

36 Q×d1	Re1+
37 Rf1	R×d1
38 R×d1	Ne5
39 Ne3	

In time trouble White overlooks 39 Ne7+ followed by the capture of the f5 pawn, but this is of no great importance.

39 ...	c3
40 Kf2	g5
41 h3	Rc8
42 Rd5	Nc4
43 Bc1	Nb2
44 N×f5	Rc4

Only 44 ... Rc5 would have prolonged the resistance.

45 Rd8+	Kf7
46 Nd6+	Resigns

No. 87 King's Indian Defence

Petrosian–Geller

USSR Team Championship
Moscow, 1961

A surprise ... to whom?

No one is insured against surprises in the opening, although, of course, any player will endeavour to reduce their possibility to a minimum. But at the board one is nevertheless forced to solve rather unexpected problems. In such situations everyone reacts in a different way. I am one of those who endeavours without fail to find the drawbacks to the new continuation, if, of course, my positional understanding and experience tell me that they may exist. I would agreee that, from the purely practical point of view, this is not always sensible, and that such a search demands a great deal of effort and practically "guarantees" time trouble, but there is nothing I can do about it!...

In the present game I was able to discover the weak aspects of White's 6th move, which, I must confess, was an absolute surprise, and had never been analysed by me.

1 c4	g6
2 d4	Bg7
3 Nc3	Nf6
4 e4	d6
5 Be2	0–0
6 d5!?	

At first sight a rather strange move. Instead of developing a piece, White advances a central pawn which was not attacked by anything, and affords the opponent a wide choice. Had such a move been made by a player of other than Petrosian's class, he would have been reproached for his lack of knowledge of the basic laws of opening play. ...

As for the considerations by which Petrosian was guided at this point, only he himself can answer.

There were probably several causes which gave rise to such an early pawn advance. Firstly, in itself this move is not so bad: White creates the pawn wedge which cramps Black in the usual King's Indian set-ups. Secondly, under its cover White intends to comfortably deploy his pieces, since a stereotyped attack on the pawn centre by ... c6 and ... e6 will also demand considerable time on Black's part. Thirdly, at the board Black is forced to solve new problems, and in this case the width of choice can often prove counter-productive: with time restricted it is not easy to establish precisely which continuation is in fact the strongest.

After some thought Black managed to find what is probably the most convincing plan, of avoiding ... e6 and of aiming for activity on the Q-side. In military language, the pressure on White's pawn centre is carried out by "a turning movement from the right".

6 ...	Na6!
7 Bg5	

It transpires that the natural 7 Nf3 creates opening difficulties not for Black, as should be the case, but for White. In the later game Uhlmann–Geller (Moscow, 1967) the following position was reached (here it could have occurred after *7 Nf3 Nc5 8 Qc2 c6 9 Bg5*).

There followed 9...c×d5 10 c×d5 (*10 e×d5* would have given Black a further tempo—*10 ... Bf5*) 10 ... Bd7 11 Rc1 Rc8, and White was forced to waste time on the retreat 12 Qb1, after which Black had an excellent game. In fact he made an inopportune piece sacrifice: 12 ... Nf×e4 13 N×e4 Bf5 14 Nfd2 Qb6 15 0–0 B×b2 16 Nc4 B×c1

17 N×b6 B×g5 18 N×c8 B×e4 19 N×e7+, which led to a rather unusual balance of forces. After inaccuracies by White in the endgame, the final result was a draw.

7 ...	Nc5
8 f3	c6
9 Qd2	

Additional weaknesses would appear in White's position after the "active" 9 b4 Na6 10 Rb1 (*10 a3 N×d5*) 10...c×d5 11 c×d5 Bd7, when the c-file is under Black's control.

9 ...	c×d5
10 c×d5	Bd7
11 h4	

Not for the sake of an attack, but merely to develop the king's knight. Isn't this the best indication of how unconvincing White's strategy has been?

11 ...	Rc8
12 Nh3	

12 ...	b5!
13 Nd1	

It transpires that White's centre is by no means so solid, and he is forced to defend passively. On 13 N×b5 B×b5 14 B×b5 there would have followed 14 ... Nf×e4! 15 f×e4 N×e4 16 Qb4 (the unpleasant *16... Qa5+* was threatened) 16 ... Ng3, and, in spite of his extra piece, White's scattered forces create a sad impression.

13 ...	Nh5
14 g4	

Castling is "forbidden" in view of the bishop capture at h3.

14 ...	Ng3
15 Rg1	N×e2

In such a situation the absence of the white-squared bishop is soon bound to tell.

16 K×e2	b4!

Immediately preparing an invasion along the weakened white squares. Accepting the pawn sacrifice would merely mean that the b-file would also be open for the attack. In the first instance White concerns himself over somehow safeguarding his king and maintaining material equality.

17 Kf2	Qa5
18 Ne3	

Parrying the threat of 18 ... Nb3, and defending against a possible invasion at c2, but there is no way of covering the d3 square...

18 ...	Qa6
19 Kg2	h6

An important *zwischenzug*. Had Black played not 18 ... Qa6, but 18 ... Bb5, White would now have been able to reply 20 B×e7, and on 20 ... Rfe8 — 21 B×d6. But now the d6 pawn is defended, and the threat of capturing on e7 is eliminated: from e7 the bishop would have nowhere to retreat to.

20 Bf4	Nd3
21 Rgb1	h5

Having drawn away White's heavy pieces to the defence of the Q-side, Black begins sounding out the weaknesses in the immediate vicinity of the white king.

22 Bg5	h×g4
23 f×g4	Rc7
24 Nf2	Bb5
25 Nh3	

White's position is strategically hopeless, and he should have tried to complicate the game somehow by 25 a4, with the probable sequel 25 ... N×f2 26 K×f2 (*26 a×b5 N×e4,* etc.) 26 ... Bd3 27 Rd1 B×e4 28 Q×b4. Evidently fearing a swift debacle, he prefers to defend passively.

25 ...	Rfc8

The "turning movement from the right" has been accomplished, and it remains to carry out the invasion.

26 h5	Qb6
27 h×g6	f×g6
28 Kh2	

Taking measures to defend the e4 pawn. It is surprising that for almost the entire game White stubbornly maintains material equality, and indeed the end comes with equal material on the board.

28 ...	Qd4
29 Qg2	Rf8
30 b3	

White is unable to achieve any coordination between his three piece-pawn "islands".

30 ...	Nc5
31 Rd1	Q×e4
32 Rac1	Bd3
33 Rd2	Bc3

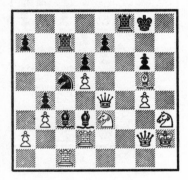

Strictly speaking, the game could have been terminated here.

| 34 Rf2 | Q×g2+ |
| 35 K×g2 | Be4+ |

The bishop takes the place of the queen, vacating its own for the second invasion by the knight.

36 Kg3	Nd3
37 R×f8+	K×f8
38 Rf1+	Kg7
39 Nf4	Be5

Luring the white bishop to f4, and preventing White from evicting the bishop from its excellent post at e4 (39 ... N×f4 40 K×f4).

40 Nc4	N×f4
41 B×f4	Bc3
42 Rd1	Rc5
43 Be3	

The attempt to hold the d-pawn (43 Ne3) would have led to the loss of the a-pawn (43 ... Ra5). Now an exchange occurs, but it is a clearly unequal one: the black passed pawns in the centre cannot be stopped.

43 ...	R×d5
44 R×d5	B×d5
45 B×a7	Be4
46 Bb6	d5
47 Na5	Kf6
48 Nc6	e5
49 Bc5	d4
50 N×b4	

The material balance has been restored, but after

| 50 ... | d3 |

White resigned.

No. 88 French Defence

Geller–Petrosian

USSR Spartakiad
Moscow, 1963

War of nerves

How can it be explained why the normally far-sighted and cautious Tigran Petrosian had a completely hopeless position by the 13th move—a very rare instance, if not the only one in his career? The point was probably that this game saw the meeting of two players, who were familiar not only with the chess style and habits, but also the way of thinking, and the slightest likes and dislikes of each other. In such games it is especially important to win the psychological battle, to triumph in the war of nerves. I fancy that what hindered Petrosian was precisely this thorough knowledge of his opponent.

1 e4	e6
2 d4	d5
3 Nc3	

The first move in the present game which has a psychological point to it. Usually in the French I prefer to develop my knight at d2, but here a part was played by my knowledge of the opponent's favourite positions. Petrosian feels very much at home in the positions with an isolated d-pawn arising after 3 Nd2 c5 4 e×d5 e×d5, and so White decided to choose a slightly sharper variation.

3 ...	Bb4
4 e5	b6
5 Nf3	

In the French Defence Black is always faced with the problem of his white-squared bishop, and therefore the idea of exchanging it (after ... *Ba6*) in itself merits approval. But in the given case it involves a loss of time on the move ... b6, and I decided to aggravate Black's lack of development. To do this White must not move his king's bishop, so that after ... Ba6 he can take on a6, and, having "lured" the knight there, force it to retrace its steps.

In addition, I took account of the fact that (both before and after this game) this variation had occurred frequently in Petrosian's games, and instead of the theoretical 5 Qg4 (or *5 a3 B×c3+ 6 b×c3 Qd7 7 Qg4 f5 8 Qg3* etc.) 5 ... Bf8 6 Bg5 Qd7 (*6 ... Ne7? 7 B×e7 Q×e7 8 N×d5*) 7 0-0-0 h6 8 Be3 Ba6 9 Nge2, I chose a different line.

5 ...	Qd7

The "natural" 5 ... Ba6 would have forced Black after 6 B×a6 N×a6 7 Qd3 either to take on c3 (when White would have managed without *a2–a3!*), or to make the awkward 7 ... Qc8, since 8 Qb5+ would have been threatened.

6 Bd2	Bf8

This further loss of time is to a certain extent forced. Black was perfectly well aware of his opponent's intentions, and 6 ... Ba6, apart from anything else, would have been psychological capitulation. 6 ... c5 is also not possible because of 7 Nb5. By the retreat of his bishop Black prepares this

thematic advance, but White's lead in development becomes threatening. Black should probably have reconciled himself to the exchange of his black-squared bishop after 6 ... Ne7 7 a3.

7 a4	

A move which is again dictated by a knowledge of the opponent. Petrosian is obviously aiming to castle Q-side, and White decides to "frighten" him with a possible attack on the king.

7 ...	Nc6

It would seem that Black was "frightened" ...

8 Be2	Nge7
9 0-0	f6?

With his development incomplete, Black begins undermining White's pawn centre, which inevitably leads to the opening up of the position. Perhaps he was afraid that after the normal (and correct) 9 ... Bb7 10 Re1 White would succeed in securely consolidating his e5 pawn? But at least he wouldn't have been threatened with an immediate debacle.

10 Re1	f×e5?

A second and decisive mistake. Now 10 ... Bb7 was absolutely essential. There was also 10 ... f5, it is true, but, firstly, this would have signified an admission that the previous move was incorrect (...*f5* could have been played immediately), and, secondly, Black is playing to undermine the centre, and not to set up a "wall".

After, say, 9 ... f5, Black has a fairly solid position, but White has a marked advantage in space, and he dominates the position. Whereas Black will be practically forced to wait, White can prepare b2–b4, with the additional possibility in some cases of play on the K-side.

The move played allows White to obtain a won position by force.

| 11 Bb5! | Ng6 |

Attempting somehow to "patch up" the position in the centre, since 11 ... e4 12 Ne5 Qd6 13 Bf4 leads to loss of material, as does 11 ... e×d4 12 N×d4 Qd6 (or *12 ... a6 13 B×c6 N×c6 14 N×e6*) 13 N×c6 N×c6 14 Bf4 Qd7 15 Q×d5.

| 12 N×e5 | Ng×e5 |
| 13 R×e5 | a6 |

It turns out to be rather difficult for Black to hold on to both of his central pawns. On 13 ... Be7 there can follow 14 Qf3 Bf6 (*14 ... Bb7 15 Rae1*) 15 N×d5 B×e5 16 Nf6+, and on 13 ... Bd6 — 14 R×e6+. Therefore Black immediately parts with his d-pawn, and at least gets rid of the unpleasant pin on his knight. But it is too late to save the game.

| 14 B×c6 | Q×c6 |
| 15 N×d5 | Bd7 |

15 ... Bd6 does not work, if only because of 16 Qf3.

| 16 Bg5 | Bd6 |
| 17 Qh5+ | Kf8 |

After 17 ... g6 there are three white pieces *en prise*, but after 18 Qe2 B×e5 19 Q×e5 how is Black to parry the threats of 19 Q×h8+ and 19 N×c7+?

| 18 Qf3+ | Kg8 |

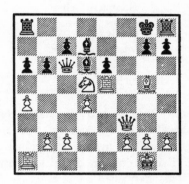

| 19 R×e6 |

Exploiting the fact that his rook is immune, White goes into an ending in which his advantage is increased to two pawns.

19 ...	Rf8
20 Ne7+	B×e7
21 Q×c6	B×c6
22 R×e7	Rf7
23 Rae1

The quickest way of realizing the advantage. White creates a powerful passed pawn in the centre.

23 ...	B×a4
24 b3	Bc6
25 R1e6	Bd5
26 Re8+	Rf8
27 R6e7	h6
28 R×f8+	K×f8

29 R×c7	Kg8
30 Bf4	g5
31 Be5	Rh7
32 Rc8+	Kf7
33 c4	Bb7
34 Rd8	Ke6
35 Rd6+	Kf5

36 f3	g4
37 Rf6+	Kg5
38 f4+	Kh5
39 R×b6	Be4
40 Kf2	Rb7
41 R×b7	B×b7
42 d5	Resigns

Boris Spassky

No. 89 Queen's Gambit

Spassky–Geller

*Candidates Tournament
Amsterdam, 1956*

The proverb loses its effect

An old Russian proverb states that the first pancake always comes out spoiled, and, as though to justify it, against young players I have rather often lost my first game. This happened in later years in my meetings with Belyavsky, Romanishin, and others. It also happened in the 1955 USSR Championship against the 18-year-old Boris Spassky. But the present game, with the player who was then the youngest grandmaster in the world and a candidate for the World Championship, was the third, and hence the "rule of the first pancake" did not extend to it. . . .

1 d4	d5
2 c4	e6
3 Nc3	c5
4 e3	Nf6
5 Nf3	Nc6
6 a3	c×d4
7 e×d4	Be7
8 Bd3	

The position with an isolated pawn, in which White has good piece play, was well in keeping with the style of the young Spassky. Otherwise it would not have been too late for him to transpose by 8 c5 into the Panov Attack against the Caro–Kann Defence. But now a position from the Queen's Gambit Accepted is reached with an extra tempo for Black.

8 ...	d×c4
9 B×c4	0–0
10 0–0	a6
11 Bg5	b5
12 Ba2	Bb7
13 Rc1	b4
14 a×b4	N×b4
15 Bb1	Qa5

This game was a basic one for the theory of the given variation. The two sides' plans are already clear. White has no other possibility other than an attack with pieces on the black king. Black has secure control over d5 and intends to mount pressure on the c- and d-files. The position is full of life, and success depends completely on the energy with which each side conducts the game.

16 Ne5　　　Rac8

Also in keeping with Black's main plan was 16 ... Rad8, tying White to the defence of his d-pawn. But the continuation in the game has a quite specific justification, and indirectly preserves from exchange an important defender—the knight at f6.

17 Re1

It turns out that 17 B×f6 B×f6 18 Nd7 does not achieve anything in view of 18 ... Qg5 19 Be4 B×e4 20 N×e4 R×c1 21 Q×c1 Q×c1 22 R×c1 Rd8 23 Nd×f6+ g×f6 24 N×f6+ Kg7, when Black regains his pawn.

17 ...　　　Nbd5

For the moment direct pressure on the d-pawn by the king's rook is premature: on 17 ... Rfd8 White has the combination 18 B×f6 B×f6 19 B×h7+. But 17 ... Rcd8, as suggested by certain commentators, is inconsistent: Black could have played this a move earlier. Therefore he continues his Q-side play. However, preferable with the same aim was 17 ... g6!?, immediately eliminating the pressure of the white-squared bishop on h7, followed by ... Rfd8.

18 Qd3　　　g6
19 Qh3　　　Qb4?

But this is an excessively optimistic assessment of the position. The concentration of white forces on the K-side is already considerable, and Black should have taken certain prophylactic measures.

Thus 19 ... Nh5!? promises him a satisfactory game, White having nothing better than to exchange the black-squared bishops by 20 B×e7 (in the event of *20 Bh6* Black

seizes the initiative — *20 ... Ndf4! 21 Qg4 f5 22 Qd1 Rfd8*) 20 ... N×e7, and if now 21 Nd7 Rfd8 22 Nc5, then 22 ... R×d4! 23 N×b7 Qb4, while 23 N×e6 is strongly met by 23 ... Rd2.

After the text move White could have begun a very strong attack.

20 Bh6　　　Rfd8

21 Ba2?

He misses the opportunity! 21 N×f7! K×f7 22 Q×e6+ Ke8 would have led to an interesting, very sharp position, where for his piece White has two pawns and an attack.

It is true that nothing is achieved by 23 Bc2 (with the terrible threat of *24 Ba4+*), due to 23 ... N×c3 24 Q×f6 (or *24 b×c3 Qd6*) 24 ... Ne4!, when 25 B×e4 does not help in view of 25 ... R×c1.

But a lengthy and painstaking analysis enabled a very dangerous continuation for White to be found: 23 Bg5!! (with the threat of *24 B×f6*) 23 ... Qd6 (*23 ... Rc6* fails to *24 N×d5*, and *23 ... Rd6* to *24 Qe5! Kd8* —24 ... Kf7 or 24 ... Kf8 is met by 25 Ba2!, winning material — *25 B×f6*) 24 Qh3! N×c3 (bad is *24 ... Qd7 25 N×d5 N×d5 26 B×g6+*, or *24 ... Rd7 25 N×d5 N×d5*— or 25 ... R×c1 26 N×f6+ Q×f6 27 B×c1 — *26 Q×h7!*) 25 b×c3 Bd5 26 B×f6 Q×f6 27 Q×h7 Bf7 28 Re3, and in view of the irresistible threat of 29 Rf3 (on *28 ... R×d4* there follows *29 Rce1 Rd7 30 Rf3*) White wins a fourth pawn for his piece.

Need it be said how difficult it would be to find such manoeuvres and to calculate such variations at the board, in the tense atmosphere of a game?

To be fair, it should also be mentioned that we have not yet completely exhausted Black's defensive resources. For example, 24 ... Nf4!?, and White has to choose between 25 R×e7+ Q×e7 (it is easy to see that *25 ... K×e7 26 Q×h7+* loses for Black) 26 B×f4 R×d4 27 Bg5, and 25 Qh6 N4h5!, when in view of the unpleasant threat of ... Ng4 it would seem that White has to force a draw by 26 B×g6+.

21 ...   Rd6!

A typical idea: the rook copes excellently with the task of defending the weak points along the 6th rank.

22 Bg5   Q×d4
23 Rcd1

It turns out that the tempting 23 N×d5 N×d5 24 N×f7 K×f7 25 Q×h7+ is parried by the "unexpected" 25 ... Qg7!

23 ...   Nf4
24 B×f4

Already White has to think in terms of maintaining the balance, since 24 Qh4, for example, loses to 24 ... Ne2+ 25 N×e2 Q×d1 (*25 ... Q×e5* is also good) 26 f3 h6! 27 R×d1 R×d1+ 28 Kf2 h×g5 29 Qa4 Bc5+ 30 Kg3 Rd2.

24 ...   Q×f4
25 R×d6

25 N×f7 is an attempt to maintain the balance by tactical means:

(a) 25 ... R×d1?! (this justifies White's idea) 26 R×d1 (*26 N×d1* favours Black after *26 ... Bb4!*, and if *27 Q×e6 Re8!*, or *27 R×e6 Qd2! 28 Nd6 Bd5*, or *27 Rf1 Kg7!* and

the white knight at f7 is doomed) 26 ... Bc5 27 B×e6 Q×f2+ 28 Kh1 Rb8 29 Nd8+ Kg7 30 N×b7 R×b7 31 b3.

(b) 25 ... R×c3! 26 b×c3 (or *26 Q×c3 R×d1 27 R×d1 K×f7*) 26 ... Ne4, leading to variations similar to those in the game.

25 ...   B×d6
26 N×f7

Desperation.

26 ...   R×c3!

Better than 26 ... K×f7:

(a) 27 Q×e6+ Kg7 28 Qf7+ Kh6 29 Q×b7 Q×h2+ 30 Kf1 Qh1+ 31 Ke2 Re8+ and Black wins.

(b) 27 B×e6+ Kg7 28 B×c8 B×c8 29 Q×c8 Q×h2+ 30 Kf1 Qh1+ 31 Ke2 Q×g2, with an unclear position.

27 Nh6+

No better is 27 b×c3, and now:

(a) 27 ... K×f7 28 Q×e6+ Kg7 29 Qf7+ Kh6 30 Q×b7.

(b) 27 ... Bc5 28 Rf1 Ne4 29 Q×e6, and it is Black who has to force a draw by 29 ... B×f2+ 30 Kh1 Ng3+ 31 h×g3 B×g2+ 32 K×g2 Q×g3+.

(c) 27 ... Ne4! 28 Nh6+ (or *28 Rf1 N×f2!*) 28 ... Kg7 29 Ng4 h5, and White loses material.

27 ...   Kg7
28 b×c3   Bc5

The white knight cannot escape.

29 Qg3	Q×g3
30 h×g3	K×b6
31 B×e6	Ne4

Black's pieces are so active that the realization of his advantage does not present any difficulty.

32 Re2	N×c3
33 Rb2	Bc6
34 Kh2	Bb5
35 f3	Kg7
36 Rb3	Bd4
37 Bc8	a5
38 Ra3	a4
39 g4	g5
40 g3	Kf6
41 f4	Bc6
42 Bf5	h6

White resigns

No. 90 Ruy Lopez

Geller–Spassky

*25th USSR Championship
Riga, 1958*

The price of one move

Black did not make any serious mistake. But one inaccuracy (on the 11th move) led to several others, and since White consistently and undeviatingly followed his plan, he was able to convert his positional advantage into a win. The game was awarded a prize as one of the best in the Championship.

1 e4	e5
2 Nf3	Nc6
3 Bb5	a6
4 Ba4	Nf6
5 0–0	Be7
6 Re1	b5

7 Bb3	0–0
8 c3	d6
9 h3	Nb8

The system with the transfer of the knight from b8 to d7 was first suggested by the Hungarian master Breyer, and was introduced into modern tournament practice by Borisenko and Furman. Black reinforces his e5, the key square in the Ruy Lopez, and obtains a sound but more cramped position than in the Chigorin Variation. At that time the Breyer Variation was highly fashionable.

| 10 d4 | Nbd7 |
| 11 c4 | |

At the time this was considered one of the strongest replies to the system chosen by Black. White vacates c3 for his knight.

11 ...　　　　　　**Bb7**

An inaccuracy, which has grave and lasting consequences. It is now known that Black does best to continue 11 ... c6, which in the present game became clear literally within two moves.

The attempt to disturb the harmonious development of the white pieces by 11 ... b4 suffered a fiasco in the game Geller–Filip (Amsterdam Candidates Tournament, 1956): 12 c5 Bb7 13 Qc2 e×d4 14 c6! d3 15 Qc4 Nb6 16 c×b7! N×c4 17 b×a8=Q Q×a8 18 B×c4 N×e4 19 B×d3 d5 20 a3!, with a clear advantage to White. Only, on 20 ... Nc5

219

he should retreat his bishop to f1, and not to c2, which is strongly met by 21 ... b3!

12 Nc3

Were his pawn already at c6, Black would have been able to play 12 ... b4. But now this move is bad in view of the possible piece sacrifice: 13 Nd5 c6 14 N×b4 d5 15 N×c6! Black is forced to give up the idea of an attack on the e4 pawn, and to go on to the defensive by blocking his queen's bishop.

12 ...   c6
13 a3

Radically eliminating Black's possible counter-play associated with ... b4, and retaining the white-squared bishop on the a2–g8 diagonal. It soon transpires that in the given position this second factor is of particular importance.

An alternative was 13 c5, when since 13 ... Qc7 (*13 ... d×c5 14 d×e5*) 14 c×d6 B×d6 15 d×e5 gives White an excellent game, Black has to reply 13 ... e×d4 14 c×d6 B×d6 15 N×d4, when White has an advantage in the centre and the convenient f5 square for his knight. But I did not want to force matters.

13 ...   Qc7

This passive move leads to serious difficulties for Black. He should have tried to relieve the tension in the centre by ... d5. It is true that the direct 13 ... b×c4 14 B×c4 d5 (or *14 ... N×e4 15 N×e4 d5 16 d×e5 d×c4 17 Qe2*) does not work in view of 15 d×e5!, when White has the advantage both after 15 ... d×c4 16 e×f6 N×f6 17 Qa4 Qd3 18 Bg5, and after 15 ... N×e4 16 N×e4 d×e4 17 e6!

As was later shown by Keres, Black should have played 13 ... e×d4 14 N×d4 b×c4 15 B×c4 d5!, and if 16 Bd3, then 16 ... c5 (or *16 ... d×e4 17 N×e4 c5*) 17 Nf5 d4.

14 Bg5   Rae8

The bishop at e7 has to be defended, since in certain variations it comes under attack. On 14 ... h6 there could have followed 15 Be3, when the knight is free to go from f3 via h4 to f5. After 14 ... Rfe8 15 Rc1 the black queen has no convenient retreat square.

15 Rc1   Qb8
16 Ba2

Having reinforced his e5 square, Black was ready to play 16 ... b×c4 17 B×c4 d5. The bishop retreat allows White to interpose 17 d×e5 with a clear positional advantage. At the same time White plans a Q-side offensive. It is obvious that Black has not managed to solve satisfactorily his opening problems.

16 ...   Kh8

17 b4!

Threatening by 18 d×e5 d×e5 19 c5 to cramp completely the opponent's position. In great difficulties, Spassky finds the only way of complicating the game, by resorting to tactics, but it, too, is insufficient to equalize.

17 ...   c5

According to Keres, it would have been useful to interpose 17 ... h6, and if 18 Be3, then 18 ... c5 gains in strength. On 18 Bh4 Black could have continued 18 ... Nh7 19 Bg3 Ng5.

18 b×c5   e×d4

18 ... d×c5 19 d5 b4 would have afforded White a pleasant choice:

(*a*) 20 a×b4 c×b4 21 Na4 Nc5 22 N×c5 B×c5 23 B×f6 g×f6 24 Nh4 a5 25 Bb3, with an attack on the K-side.

(*b*) 20 Na4 a5 21 a×b4 a×b4 22 Bb3, with strong positional pressure.

Therefore Black was very hopeful of the intermediate exchange in the game, intending after 19 N×d4 d×c5 20 Nf5 to obtain counter-play by 20 ... b4!

19 c6!

Only in this way can White maintain his initiative. Black is unable to retain his white-squared bishop (*19 ... B×c6 20 N×d4,* with a big advantage), after which a whole complex of white squares in his position becomes vulnerable.

19 ...	**d×c3**
20 c×b7	**Q×b7**
21 c×b5	**Q×b5**

The e4 pawn is immune: 21 ... a×b5 22 R×c3 N×e4 23 R×e4 Q×e4 24 Re3.

22 R×c3   Nc5

It is again taboo: 22 ... N×e4 23 R×e4 B×g5 24 R×e8 R×e8 25 B×f7 Rf8 26 Q×d6, and White has the better position plus a material advantage. Also bad is 22 ... Qb2 23 Qc2 Q×c2 24 R×c2, or 22 ... Ne5 23 Nd4 followed by 24 Nf5.

23 Rce3   Ne6

24 e5!

Black has no way of countering this decisive breakthrough in the centre. Now 24 ... d×e5 25 R×e5 leads to the loss of a pawn, as does the tactical trick which occurs in the game.

24 ...	**Ng4**
25 h×g4	**N×g5**
26 e×d6	**N×f3+**
27 g×f3	**Bg5**
28 a4	

White could have realized his advantage more quickly by 28 Bc4! Qd7 29 R×e8 R×e8 30 R×e8+ Q×e8 31 d7, when he wins a second pawn by 32 B×a6. The queen sacrifice 28 ... R×e3 29 B×b5 R×e1+ 30 Q×e1 a×b5 31 d7 and 32 Qe8 would also not have saved Black.

28 ...	**Qd7**
29 R×e8	**R×e8**
30 R×e8+	**Q×e8**
31 d7	**Qf8**

With the opposite-coloured bishops it is not so much White's extra pawn which is important, as the insecure position of the black king—after all, the queens are still on the board!

31 ... Qe7 is decisively met by 32 f4.

32 Qe2

White quite correctly avoids going into a pawn ending, which would still have demanded exact calculation: 32 B×f7 Q×f7 33 d8=Q+ B×d8 34 Q×d8+ Qg8 35 Q×g8+ K×g8. Now he threatens the simple 33 Qe8.

| **32 ...** | **Qe7** |
| **33 Qd3** | **h6** |

White's white-squared strategy triumphs, since 33 ... g6 leads to immediate capitulation after 34 f4!

34 Bc4!

An essential finesse: after 34 B×f7 Q×f7 35 d8=Q+ B×d8 36 Q×d8+ Kh7 37 Qd3+ Qg6 White would again have had to work out a pawn ending at the board. Therefore the black a-pawn is lured on to a square where it can be attacked.

34 ...	a5
35 B×f7	Bh4

Now 35 ... Q×f7 36 d8=Q+ B×d8 37 Q×d8+ Kh7 38 Q×a5 is conclusive, since the f3 pawn cannot be taken in view of the exchange of queens.

36 Kg2	Bf6
37 Bc4	Qd8
38 Qd5	Bg5
39 Qf7	Resigns

Against the threat of 40 Qe8+ Kh7 41 Bd3+ there is no defence.

No. 91 Ruy Lopez

Spassky–Geller

*USSR Zonal Tournament
Moscow, 1964*

A harmless surprise

White chose the Exchange Variation of the Ruy Lopez not because he wanted to avoid a struggle: this was the start of the Zonal

Tournament, and it was here that the future World Champion began his storming of the chess Olympus. It was simply Boris Spassky resorting to his favourite opening tactic—a psychological surprise. But, as a rule, such a surprise is really dangerous only in sharp opening schemes, whereas here, relying on the enduring laws of strategy and on his general positional understanding, Black gradually assumed the initiative. There were few complicated variations here, it was very much a manoeuvring struggle.

1 e4	e5
2 Nf3	Nc6
3 Bb5	a6
4 Ba4	Nf6
5 0–0	Be7
6 B×c6	d×c6
7 d3	Nd7
8 Nbd2	

The most natural continuation, 8 d4, which has the aim of obtaining a pawn majority on the K-side (which is the idea of the Exchange Variation), has also been shown on many occasions to hold no danger for Black — 8 ... e×d4 9 N×d4 0–0 10 Nc3 Bf6, and if 11 f4, then 11 ... Nb6! The text move shows that White is by no means aiming for simplification.

8 ...	0–0
9 Nc4	Bf6

Nowadays this continuation is rightly considered inferior, and precisely why will soon be seen. 9 ... f6 leads to equality.

10 Bd2	Re8

By over-protecting e5 with his rook, Black wishes to relieve his knight of this duty and then develop his Q-side.

11 a4?

A mistake. White does nothing to hinder Black's plan, and meanwhile after 11 Bc3 it would have been very difficult to carry out, since 11 ... b5 is bad because of 12 Na5.

11 ...	Nf8
12 a5	

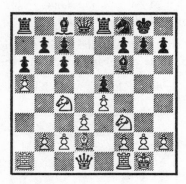

12 ...	b5!

Black takes the opportunity to force the opponent into choosing between straightening his pawns by 13 a×b6 c×b6, and conceding the c4 square. Black, with his two bishops, is perfectly happy in either case.

13 Ne3?

Nevertheless White should have chosen the alternative, since now the entire march of the white pawn from a2 to a5 proves pointless.

13 ...	c5
14 b3	Be6
15 Bc3	Ng6
16 Nd2	Qd7
17 g3	

White himself is hoping to obtain play on the K-side, and does not want to allow the knight in at f4. Even so, he should have reconciled himself to this as the lesser evil, and played 17 Re1 followed by Nf1–g3. The text move markedly weakens the white squares on the K-side (White has no white-squared bishop!), and he is unable to commence a pawn offensive.

17 ...	Bh3!
18 Ng2	Be7
19 Re1	

The intended 19 f4 has to be deferred, since after 19 ... e×f4 20 g×f4 Nh4 White loses the exchange.

19 ...	Rad8
20 Ne3	Bg5
21 Qf3	f6
22 Qe2	

Both 22 Nf5 and 22 Nd5 are bad because of 22 ... b4, as is 22 g4 B×e3 23 Q×h3 Bd4 followed by ... Nf4 with domination of the black squares.

22 ...	Nf8

At the first opportunity the knight heads for d4!

23 f3	Ne6
24 Qf2	Nd4
25 Ndf1	Qf7
26 f4	

In an inferior position and also short of time on the clock, White tries to ease his defence by exchanges.

| 26 ... | Bh6! |
| 27 B×d4 | |

Practically forced, since 27 ... Qh5 and 28 ... Nf3+ was threatened, while after 27 f×e5 f×e5 28 Q×f7+ K×f7 White has no way of opposing the powerful black bishops.

27 ...	c×d4
28 Nf5	Qg6
29 N×h6+	Q×h6
30 Nd2	c5

Black has the initiative on both wings, but especially dangerous is the threat of ... c4, against which White begins taking measures.

31 Rac1	Rd7
32 Qf3	Qg6
33 f5	Qg5
34 Qf2	Rc8

Both sides are ready to undermine the opposing pawn chain, the only, highly important, difference being that the black king is completely safe, whereas things may become unpleasant for White's.

| 35 Kh1 | Rdc7 |
| 36 c3 | |

Before carrying out the intended exchanging manoeuvre with his knight, White wishes to open the c-file for counter-play, since on the immediate 36 Nf3 Qg4 37 Ng1 there would follow 37 ... c4. White is unable to avert this breakthrough by waiting tactics:

Black is ready to play ... g6, and after the exchange of pawns to transfer his bishop to e6.

| 36 ... | d×c3 |
| 37 R×c3 | Rd8! |

A new target—the d3 pawn.

| 38 Nf3 | Qg4 |
| 39 Ng1 | h5 |

Not only to undermine White's K-side, but also to create an escape square for the king.

| 40 N×h3 | Q×h3 |

Here the game was adjourned for the first time, and was resumed within an hour and a half. Strategically the outcome is decided. Black has the superior pawn formation and a spatial advantage, and the opposing king cannot feel safe. But the exchange of queens does not ease White's defence, since then the weakness of his pawns becomes more appreciable.

41 Qe2

41 R×c5 is most strongly met by 41 ... Rcd7.

41 ...	Rd4
42 Kg1	Kh7
43 Rec1	Rcd7
44 Rd1	Qg4!

Here the exchange of queens is especially favourable, since the pawn at g4 blockades White's K-side.

45 Q×g4

45 Kf2 is decisively met by 45 ... R×e4!

45 ...	h×g4
46 R×c5	R×e4
47 Kf2	

Or 47 d×e4 R×d1+ 48 Kf2 Rh1!

47 ...	Rb4
48 Rc3	Kh6
49 Ke3	Kg5
50 Rc6	

It is impossible to defend all the weak pawns at b3, d3 and f5. If 50 Rf1, then 50 ... Rbd4 with the threat of 51 ... b4.

50 ...	R×b3
51 R×a6	K×f5
52 Rb6	Ra7

Stronger was the immediate 52 ... Rd4 followed by ... Ra4.

53 Rf1+	Kg6
54 Ra1	Rd7
55 Rd1	

If 55 a6, then 55 ... Rd×d3+ 56 Ke2 Ra3.

55 ...	Rd4
56 a6	Ra4
57 Rd2	Rba3
58 R×b5	R×a6

Here the game was adjourned for the second time. Black's extra pawn plus the weaknesses at d3 and h2 leave White with no chance of saving the game.

59 Rb4	R6a4
60 Rbb2	Kg5
61 Ke2	g6
62 Ke3	Ra1
63 d4	

White cannot maintain the status quo for long.

63 ...	R4a3+
64 Ke4	Re1+
65 Kd5	e4

The black pawn is quicker!

66 Re2	R×e2
67 R×e2	Kf5
68 Rf2+	Rf3
69 Re2	e3
70 Re1	g5
71 Re2	

Or else he has to concede e4 to the black king.

71 ...	Kg6
72 Ke6	f5
73 Ra2	

On 73 d5 Black wins by 73 ... f4 74 d6 Rf1 75 d7 Rd1 with the threat of 76 ... Rd3.

73 ...	f4
74 d5	e2!

This is simpler than 74 ... Rf2.

White resigned, since after 75 R×e2 Re3+ 76 R×e3 f×e3 the black pawn queens with check.

No. 92 Queen's Gambit

Geller–Spassky

Moscow, 1967

Rook in a trap

The opening variation which occurs in this game has a long life and an interesting biography. It was introduced by Botvinnik, and then was taken up by Spassky, Portisch, and other leading grandmasters. It has also occurred in a number of my games, both with White and with Black, and it was employed in the World Championship Match in Merano. Each side has a number of interesting possibilities, and everything depends on how they are handled.

The outcome of the game was decided by a trap which suddenly snapped shut around a black rook.

1 d4	d5
2 c4	e6
3 Nc3	Be7
4 c×d5	

It is with this move that the aforementioned variation begins.

4 ...	e×d5
5 Bf4	c6
6 e3	

Less good is the plan involving Q-side castling — 6 Qc2 g6 7 0-0-0 (yet to be tried in practice is Tal's idea of *7 e4 d×e4 8 d5*) 7 ... Nf6 8 f3 Na6 9 e4 Nb4, and now:

(*a*) 10 Qb3?! Be6 11 e5 Nd7 12 a3, and now the piece sacrifice 12 ... a5! 13 a×b4 a×b4 14 Nb1 c5 gave Black a winning attack, Korchnoi–Spassky, Final Candidates Match, Kiev, 1968.

(*b*) 10 Qd2!? d×e4 11 N×e4 N×e4 12 f×e4 Be6 13 d5 c×d5 14 Bb5+ Bd7 15 B×d7+ Q×d7 16 Ne2 0-0!, and here too Black has an excellent game.

6 ...	Bf5
7 g4	

Only in this way can White fight for an opening advantage. Neither the quiet 7 Bd3 (Botvinnik–Portisch, Palma-de-Mallorca, 1967, and other games), nor 7 Nge2 Nd7 8 Ng3 Bg6 9 Be2 Ngf6 10 h4 h5! (weaker is *10 ... h6?! 11 h5 Bh7 12 Bd3*, when White gains a spatial advantage) 11 Bg5 Bd6 12 Rh3

Qb6 13 Qd2 0-0 (Portisch–Geller, Portoroz, 1973), is particularly promising for him.

| 7 ... | Be6 |

8 h3

An even sharper and more complicated game results from 8 h4!?, which was also first played by Botvinnik. Since it is risky for Black to accept the pawn sacrifice (*8 ... B×h4?! 9 Qb3 b6 10 Nf3* followed by *Ne5* with a powerful initiative), Black must defend on the K-side and seek counter-play on the opposite wing. For example, 8 ... Nd7 9 h5 Qb6! 10 Rb1 Ngf6 11 f3 h6 12 Bd3 0-0 13 Nge2 (the position is very sharp after *13 g5 h×g5 14 B×g5*) 13 ... c5 14 Kf1 Rfe8 15 Kg2 Rac8 16 Qe1 Nh7 17 Qf2 c×d4 18 e×d4 Bd6 (Furman–Geller, 43rd USSR Championship, Leningrad, 1975).

8 ...	Nf6
9 Nf3	0-0
10 Bd3	c5

Here too this is the best way of creating counter-chances.

11 Kf1

On 11 0-0 Black has the extremely unpleasant 11 ... h5 12 g5 Ne4.

11 ...	Nc6
12 Kg2	c×d4

This relieving of the central tension is premature, and does not promise Black full equality. In the 13th game of the Korchnoi–Karpov World Championship Match, Merano, 1981, Black preferred 12 ... Rc8, and after 13 Rc1 Re8 14 d×c5 B×c5 15 Nb5 Bf8 16 Nfd4 he could have continued 16 ... Qb6 or 16 ... Qd7!? Also to be considered is Romanovsky's idea of 12 ... Re8 followed by ... Nd7–f8.

13 N×d4

I wanted to carry out Botvinnik's idea in full, by placing my pawn at f3 in the event of the exchange on d4. In the 14th game of the Botvinnik–Petrosian World Championship Match, Moscow, 1963, White also gained the better game by 13 e×d4.

13 ...	Bd6
14 B×d6	Q×d6
15 Nce2	Rfe8
16 Rc1	Bd7

Parrying the positional threat of 17 N×c6 b×c6 18 Qc2 Bd7 19 Nd4.

| 17 Bb1 | Rad8 |
| 18 Qb3 | |

Instead of 18 Qd3, which he would seem to have been preparing (and to which Black would have replied *18 ... g6*), the white queen changes course.

| 18 ... | Rb8 |

Practically forced, since 18 ... b6 19 N×c6 B×c6 20 Nd4 is unsatisfactory for Black.

| 19 Rhd1 | h5 |

Sensing that he may have a lot of trouble with his d5 pawn, Black begins a counter-attack against the white king's advanced pawn screen. He has in mind a combinational solution to his defensive problems.

| 20 g5 | Ne4 |
| 21 Nf3 | |

The d5 pawn is hanging, and 21 ... Be6 is unpleasantly met by 22 Nf4. Therefore Black follows his intended path.

21 ...	B×h3+!
22 K×h3	N×f2+
23 Kg2	N×d1
24 R×d1	Qc5

White would have parried 24 ... Qe6 by 25 Kf2 followed by Nf4.

| 25 R×d5 | |

But here 25 Kf2 is less convincing in view of 25 ... Ne5 26 N×e5 R×e5 and then ... Rbe8.

25 ...	Q×e3
26 Q×e3	R×e3
27 Nc3	Rd8?

Black's combination was correct, and after 27 ... Re7 he would have retained roughly equal chances.

| 28 R×d8+ | N×d8 |

29 Be4!

This was overlooked by Black. His rook is trapped, and loss of material is inevitable.

29 ...	Kf8
30 Kf2	R×e4
31 N×e4	

Now Black's only hopes are associated with the fact that two lone knights cannot give mate, and so for the three white pawns he merely has to give up his knight and all five of his pawns. But he cannot achieve this.

31 ...	Ke7
32 Ke3	Ke6
33 Kf4	Kd5
34 Nc3+	Kc4
35 Ke4	

Threatening 36 Ne5+, and in the event of 35 ... f6 — 36 g6.

35 ...	Nc6
36 Nd5	f5+
37 g×f6	g×f6
38 N×f6	

Black has exchanged one white pawn, but what can he do now?

| 38 ... | h4 |
| 39 Ng4 | Nb4 |

The threat of 40 Nge5+ did not leave Black time for the diverting 39 ... h3.

| 40 Ne3+ | Kc5 |
| 41 N×h4! | |

This move was sealed by White (the routine *41 a3* would have allowed Black to continue fighting with *41 ... h3*), and **Black resigned** without resuming. Indeed, after 41 ... N×a2 42 Kd3 a5, even if Black should succeed in giving up his knight and a pawn for White's last pawn, he will still have one of his own pawns left. But in this case, according to a well-known analysis by the chess composer Troitsky, the two knights can weave a mating net without particular difficulty.

No. 93 Sicilian Defence

Geller–Spassky

*USSR Spartakiad
Moscow, 1964*

The idea remains "behind the scenes"

Ex-World Champion Boris Spassky first played 9 ... e5 in the first game of his Candidates Semi-Final Match with Karpov, Leningrad, 1974, and then in the same year he employed it against Mecking at the Nice Olympiad. Even at the cost of a tempo, Black is ready to go into the Boleslavsky Variation, in which the black pawn reaches e5 in one move. I made an analysis of this continuation, and, it would seem, managed to grasp certain nuances of the position. In the present game I was able to confirm in practice an idea for White, based on an interesting piece sacrifice. It is described in the note to Black's 12th move, since the sacrifice in fact remained "behind the scenes".

1 e4	c5
2 Nf3	d6
3 d4	c×d4
4 N×d4	Nf6
5 Nc3	e6
6 Be2	

In the present game I did not aim to force matters, but preferred to develop my pieces quietly.

6 ...	Be7
7 f4	0–0
8 0–0	Nc6
9 Be3	e5

A rather unusual continuation. As already mentioned, with the loss of a tempo Black transposes into the Boleslavsky Variation.

10 Nb3

In the aforementioned game Mecking played 10 Nf5, which allowed Black a good game after 10 ... B×f5 11 e×f5 d5.

| 10 ... | a5 |

The present game shows that it is incorrect to weaken the b5 square. To be considered therefore was the more modern treatment of 10 ... e×f4 11 B×f4 Be6, as in Geller–Kasparov, Moscow, 1981.

| 11 a4 | Nb4 |
| 12 Kh1 | |

Here Karpov played 12 Bf3. It cannot be said that the king move is stronger, but for the moment I decided to leave the bishop at e2 to control the c4 square.

| 12 ... | Qc7 |

Black prepares ... Be6–c4. The immediate 12 ... Be6 was interesting, so as on 13 f5 Bd7 14 Bf3 to reply 14 ... Bc6 with the idea of ... d5. Against this White intended 15 Qe2 d5 16 Rad1, and if 16 ... d4 then 17 N×d4 e×d4 18 B×d4, with a strong attack.

| 13 Rc1 | |

At first sight played rather straightfor-wardly, but in fact the position of the rook at c1 contains a threat: White defends his c-pawn and prepares Nb5 and c2–c3.

| 13 ... | Be6 |
| 14 Nd2 | |

It will be apparent that the main struggle now revolves around the c4 square, on to which White tries not to allow the enemy bishop.

| 14 ... | e×f4 |
| 15 Nb5! | |

15 R×f4 can be met by 15 ... d5, while if White takes on f4 with the bishop, after a subsequent Nb5 the black queen would be able to go to b6.

| 15 ... | Qd8 |
| 16 B×f4 | |

Here we can take stock. The opening phase has ended in favour of White, who has achieved an active position. His knight at b5 is very well placed, whereas the position of its opponent at b4 is insecure in view of the threat of c2–c3.

| 16 ... | Nc6 |

Even so, this retreat seems premature to me. Better was 16 ... Rc8, retaining for the moment the outpost at b4. Subsequently the knight could have gone via a6 to c5.

| 17 Qe1 | |

The rook at c1 has played its part, and it is time to vacate another square for it.

| 17 ... | d5 |

This decision of Black to open up the game merely favours White, whose pieces are much more active. To be considered was 17 ... Ne5 followed by ... Nfd7.

| 18 Rd1 | Qb6 |

In search of a comfortable post for his queen, Black moves it for the third time...

| 19 e×d5 | |

19 e5 is also good.

| 19 ... | N×d5 |

After 19 ... B×d5 20 Nc4 Black has nothing better than to exchange on c4 and concede the advantage of the two bishops.

20 Nc4   Qc5
21 Bc1

21 Bg3 appears stronger, but I did not want to move off the c1–h6 diagonal. The point is that, after the retreat of the black knight from d5, White may acquire the very dangerous threat of Be3. At the same time he prepares c2–c3, b2–b3 and Ba3, against which Black has to take immediate measures.

It should also be mentioned that, in the unusually deployed quartet of knights, the white ones are operating to much greater effect.

21 ...   Nf6

It was probably worth giving up the exchange by 21 ... Qb4 22 Qg3 Q×a4 23 Bh6 g6, but retaining certain counter-chances.

22 b3

Beginning a pursuit of the enemy queen, which, encircled by the white knights, feels highly uncomfortable.

22 ...   Rfd8

22 ... Bg4 was perhaps preferable, since now Black loses a pawn by force.

23 Ba3   R×d1
24 B×d1   Qg5
25 B×e7   Bd5

Black tries to complicate matters by the sacrifice of a piece. It is clear that after 25 ... N×e7 26 Nc7 White has both an extra pawn, and the better position (*25 ... B×c4 is bad because of the simple 27 b×c4*).

26 Bf3   Re8

Black loses quickly after 26 ... B×f3 27 g×f3 Re8 28 B×f6! R×e1 29 R×e1, when 29 ... Q×f6 allows mate by the rook at e8, while on 29 ... g×f6 there follows 30 Rg1.

27 h4

27 B×d5 R×e7 (*27 ... Q×d5 28 Nc7*) 28 B×f7+ is also sufficient, but the text move is more energetic.

27 ...   Qg6

27 ... Qh6 was slightly more tenacious, although after 28 B×d5 R×e7 (*if 28 ... N×d5, then 29 Bg5! R×e1 30 R×e1*) 29 B×f7+ it transpires that 29 ... R×f7 is bad because of 30 Ncd6 Rf8 (*30 ... Re7 31 Nf5*) 31 Qe6+ Kh8 32 Nf7+, while on 29 ... K×f7 there follows 30 Nbd6+ Kf8 (*30 ... Kg8 31 Nf5*) 31 Qg3 Qg6 32 Qh3, with decisive threats.

28 Ne5   N×e5
29 Q×e5   B×f3
30 g×f3

Having failed to regain his piece, **Black resigned.**

No. 94 Sicilian Defence

Geller–Spassky

Alekhine Memorial Tournament
Moscow, 1975

Improvization on a familiar theme

In our era of profound knowledge, improvization in the opening succeeds more and more rarely. A careful analytical check is required on any impromptu arising opening idea. But there is no rule without its exceptions. After Black's 2nd move in this game I decided, contrary to my preparations, to transpose into the Closed Variation. This is explained by the fact that I had a sudden thought: with White Spassky does not like playing against the King's Indian Defence, and the Closed Variation of the Sicilian is virtually a King's Indian by the first player.

The improvization succeeded. Moreover, its theme was very familiar to me: I have been playing King's Indian set-ups throughout the whole of my chess career.

1 e4	c5
2 Nf3	e6
3 d3	Nc6
4 g3	d6

Black declines the tacit offer to play against King's Indian formations, otherwise he would have replied 4 ... d5.

5 Bg2	g6
6 0–0	Bg7
7 c3	e5

Otherwise White will immediately play 8 d4.

8 a3	Nf6

The development of the king's knight at e7 is more harmonious in such positions, avoiding the blocking of the f-pawn. But in anticipation of the advance of the white b-pawn, Spassky reserves e7 for his other knight.

9 b4	0–0
10 b5	Ne7
11 a4	a6

Black initiates counter-play on the Q-side. The attempt to prepare a counter-blow in the centre (... d5) by 11 ... Qc7 could have run into 12 c4, when the white knight can advance to d5 at the appropriate moment, whereas there is practically no way of a black knight reaching d4.

12 Na3	a×b5
13 N×b5	Nc6?

A mistake. Black should have guarded g5 by 13 ... h6.

14 Bg5!	h6
15 B×f6	B×f6
16 Nd2	

Threatening 17 Nc4, and simultaneously preparing for activity on the K-side with f2–f4.

16 ...	Na7

To be considered was 16 ... Be6, when although after 17 Nc4 B×c4 (*17 ... d5 18 e×d5 B×d5 19 B×d5 Q×d5 does not work— 20 Nb6*) 18 d×c4 Be7 White retains a certain positional advantage, opposite-coloured bishops remain on the board.

17 Na3	Nc6

On 18 Nb5 Black will reply 18 ... Na7, and on 18 Nc4 — 18 ... Na5, but...

18 Rb1	

Tying the bishop at c8 to the defence of the pawn.

18 ...	Bg7

The attempt at counter-play on the Q-side, 18 ... Qa5, achieves nothing after 19 Nac4:
(*a*) 19 ... Q×c3? 20 Rb3 Qd4 21 h3!, with the irresistible threat of 22 Nf3.

(b) 19 ... Q×a4 20 N×d6, and Black is unable to defend his weaknesses at b7 and c5.

19 Ndc4	Ra6

The threat of 20 Nb5 is parried (20 ... Na5), but the white knights continue their dance.

20 Ne3!

The other knight heads for c4, and the pressure on the b-file is maintained.

20 ...	Ne7
21 Nac4	Bd7
22 a5	Bc6
23 Qb3	h5

Black hopes to activate his g7 bishop, since he cannot free himself by 23 ... d5: 24 e×d5 N×d5 25 N×d5 B×d5 26 B×d5 Q×d5 27 Q×b7 Q×b7 28 R×b7 Rd8 29 Rfb1!, followed by the rapid advance of the a-pawn.

24 Nd5	Bh6

25 f4

Having regrouped his forces, White begins a K-side offensive, with the aim of provoking new weaknesses in the opponent's position.

25 ...	e×f4
26 g×f4	B×d5
27 e×d5	Nf5
28 Be4?	

White should have simply played 28 Q×b7, retaining all the advantages of his position. But by this point both players were already seriously short of time, and this affected the normal course of events.

28 ...	B×f4
29 B×f5	

Alas, the bishop is immune in view of the queen check...

29 ...	Qg5+
30 Kh1	Q×f5
31 Q×b7	Re8?

The exposed position of the white king attracts Black, and he commits a decisive mistake. Meanwhile, White's position was still superior, and therefore Black should have aimed in the first instance for equality. To this end, best was 31 ... Ra7! diverting the white queen from the defence of d5, and forcing perpetual check after 32 Q×a7 (if *32 Qc6?*, then *32 ... Re7, 32 ... Rc7* or *32 ... Ra5*) 32 ... Q×d5+ 33 Kg1 Qg5+ 34 Kf2 Qh4+ 35 Ke2 Qg4+.

32 Rf2!

This quiet move is decisive. White simultaneously defends the 2nd rank, opens a loophole for his king at f1, and creates the decisive threat of 33 Q×a6, or — after the withdrawal of the rook from a6 — 33 N×d6. Of course, after the hasty 32 Q×a6? Re2 Black's idea would have been justified.

32 ...	g5

32 ... Ra7 is now insufficient: 33 Q×a7 Q×d3 (*33 ... Q×d5+ 34 Kg1 Qg5+ 35 Kf1*) 34 Rbf1.

33 Rg1

33 Q×a6 Q×d5+ 34 Kg1 Q×d3 35 Qb5 would have won immediately, but with his flag nearly horizontal White makes a "solid" move, parrying the threat of 33 ... Q×d3 by 34 R×f4.

Black could have exploited this chance opportunity, but for him, too, the last few seconds were ticking away...

33 ...	Rea8

Now it is all over. After 33 ... h4! the position would have remained sharp, at any rate in a time trouble situation. Thus 34 Q×a6 is then bad in view of 34 ... Q×d5+ 35 Rfg2 h3.

34 N×d6	R×d6

34 ... Qf6 is most simply met by 35 Ne4.

35 Q×a8+	Kh7
36 c4	Rf6

Mate follows after 36 ... Q×d3 37 R×f4 g×f4 38 Qg8+.

37 Qb7	Qh3

Or 37 ... Q×d3 38 Qb1, exchanging queens.

38 Qb2	Be5
39 Qe2	

Black exceeded the time limit.

Bobby Fischer

No. 95 Sicilian Defence

Geller–Fischer

Candidates Tournament
Curacao, 1962

Breaking the blockade

The variation which occurred in this game was fashionable at the time, and was therefore intensively analyzed by the theorists. These included Bobby Fischer, who was well known for his predilection for certain opening schemes, one of which was this variation for Black. A little earlier, at the Stockholm Interzonal Tournament, Fischer had tried the flank development of his queen's bishop against me, but had failed to equalize. It was clear to me that the American grandmaster would not simply abandon his favourite variation, but would try to find an improvement for Black. And, of course, counter-measures were taken on my part, so that Black's 10th move did not catch me unawares.

1 e4	c5
2 Nf3	d6
3 d4	c×d4
4 N×d4	Nf6
5 Nc3	a6
6 Be2	e5
7 Nb3	Be7

This game was played in the second round, but a month later in our game from the 16th round Fischer deviated here and followed Najdorf's handling of the opening (see Game No. 14): 7 ... Be6 8 0–0 Nbd7 9 a4 Be7 10 f4 Qc7 11 f5 Bc4 12 a5 0–0 13 Be3 b5 14 a×b6 N×b6, and after 15 Kh1 Rfc8 16 B×b6! Q×b6 17 B×c4 R×c4 18 Qe2 he again ended up in an inferior position.

But here he was keen to employ his planned 10th move.

8 0–0   0–0
9 Be3   Qc7

Nowadays this is considered inaccurate, since the queen prematurely determines its position and comes under attack after Nd5. Therefore a more accurate move order has been found: 9 ... Be6 followed by ... Nbd7. But at that time 9 ... Qc7 was universally played.

10 a4   Be6

Deviating from our Stockholm game, where Fischer played 10 ... b6 against me. However, I had succeeded in finding a plan for occupying d5, after which the entire variation with 10...b6 ceased to appeal to its supporters. For example, the game with Fischer continued 11 Qd2 Bb7 12 f3 Bc6 13 Rfd1 Nbd7 14 Qe1 h6 15 Qf1 Qb7 16 Bc4 Rfc8 17 Rd2 Nf8, and now the knight manoeuvre 18 Nc1! Ng6 19 N1a2, with d5 as the final goal, placed Black in a difficult position.

In my game against Bolbochan from the same tournament, I carried out the same manoeuvre after 11 ... Be6 12 Rfd1 Ndb7 13 f3 Qb7 14 Nc1! Rfd8 15 N1a2 Nc5 16 Nb4 a5 17 Nbd5 N×d5 18 N×d5 B×d5 19 Q×d5 Q×d5 20 R×d5, and in spite of the enforced transition into an ending White retained a clear advantage.

In the same tournament Stein tried against me 10 ... Nbd7 11 a5 b5 12 a×b6 N×b6, but after 13 Na5 Be6 14 B×b6! Q×b6 15 Nd5 N×d5 16 e×d5 Bd7 White gained the advantage in view of the weakness of the a6 pawn and the c6 square.

The text move looks stronger, but White still gains the better position. It is clear that, after developing his queen at c7, it is no longer easy for Black to equalize.

11 a5   Nbd7
12 Nd5   N×d5

Also possible is 12 ... B×d5, as in the later game Bradvarevic–Nemet (Bled, 1963): 13 e×d5 b5 14 a×b6 N×b6, although here too White retained the advantage: 15 c4! a5! (the threat was *16 Na5;* White also stands better after *15...N×c4 16 Qc2 Rfc8 17 Rfc1 N×e3 18 Q×c7 R×c7 19 R×c7 Ne×d5 20 Rb7*) 16 R×a5 R×a5 17 N×a5 Nb×d5 18 Bd2 Nf4 19 b4, and the passed b-pawn is rather unpleasant for Black.

But in general Fischer likes the two bishops, and without extreme necessity he rather rarely parts with them. Here too he sticks to his convictions, and the scales tip markedly in White's favour.

13 e×d5   Bf5
14 c4   Bg6
15 Rc1

The manoeuvres with the black bishop have cost time, and White has built up a serious attack on the Q-side. He now intends to pierce Black's defences with 16 c5.

15 ...   Nc5

Fischer was obviously afraid of sharpening the position — 15...f5 16 c5 f4 (or *16...d×c5 17 N×c5 N×c5 18 b4 f4 19 B×c5 Bd6*) 17 c×d6 Q×d6 18 Bc5 N×c5 19 N×c5. Meanwhile, that is what he should have played, although White's position would have remained attractive. On the other hand, the attempt to blockade the critical c5 square proves illusory, and Black's game can no longer be saved.

16 N×c5		d×c5
17 b4!		

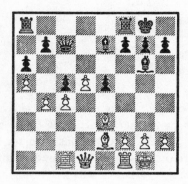

The blockade is nevertheless broken. Now 17...c×b4 allows 18 Bb6 and 19 c5 with a complete positional bind, while 17 ... f5, aiming for counter-play on the K-side, would merely create additional weaknesses.

17 ...	Rac8
18 Qb3	Bd6
19 Rfd1	

Threatening to win a pawn, which would not have worked a move earlier—19 b×c5 B×c5 20 B×c5 Q×c5 21 Q×b7 Q×a5 22 Ra1 Qd2. In defending it Black is forced to waste a further tempo.

19 ...	Qe7
20 b×c5	B×c5
21 B×c5	R×c5
22 Ra1!	

Without the transfer of his rook to b6 it is difficult for White to combine the threat of winning the b-pawn with the advance of his d-pawn.

22 ...	Rd8
23 Ra4	Bf5
24 Rb4	Bc8
25 Rb6	Rd6

Fischer defends tenaciously. The capture of the a-pawn would merely have aggravated Black's position: 25...R×a5 26 d6 Qd7 27 Bf3, and the b-pawn cannot be defended.

26 Qb4	Qc7
27 R×d6	Q×d6
28 Rb1	Qc7

Slightly better was 28 ... g6, creating an escape square for the king, when for the moment 29 Qa3 does not work due to 29 ... R×d5.

29 Qa4!

A further link in the same strategic plan. White's other rook heads for b6, and this will force Black into the unfavourable exchange of his b-pawn for the white a-pawn.

29 ...	Bd7
30 Qa3	R×a5
31 R×b7	Q×b7
32 Q×a5	

The idea conceived in the opening has been carried out, so to speak, in its purest form: the two connected passed pawns in the centre are irresistible. All that is required of White now is accuracy.

32 ...	g6
33 h3	Qb1+
34 Kh2	Bf5

The alternative was a hopeless queen ending after 34 ... Qc2 35 Qd8+ Kg7 36 Q×d7

Q×e2 37 Qc7! a5 38 f4 a4 39 f×e5 a3 40 e6 a2 41 Q×f7+ Kh6 42 Qf6.

35 Qc3	Qe4
36 Bf3	Qd4
37 Q×d4	

White has calculated that his pawns will be quicker.

37 ...	e×d4
38 g4	

The bishop is driven into the path of the white pawns, which will give them some important additional tempi. It is easy to check that Black does not achieve anything either by the bishop sacrifice — 38 ... a5 39 g×f5 a4 40 d6 Kf8 41 c5, or by 38 ... Bc2 39 c5 d3 40 c6 Ba4 41 d6.

38 ...	Bc8
39 c5	a5
40 c6	Kf8
41 d6	

This move was sealed, and **Black resigned** without resuming. The alternatives are equally bad:

(a) 41 ... Ke8 42 Bd1 Ba6 43 g5 Bb5 (43 ... Kd8 44 Bg4) 44 c7 Bd7 45 Ba4.

(b) 41 ... a4 42 c7 a3 43 Bc6 a2 44 d7 B×d7 45 B×d7 a1=Q 46 c8=Q+.

No. 96 Sicilian Defence

Fischer–Geller

*Candidates Tournament
Curacao, 1962*

Passion is not always an ally...

It seems to me that Fischer's conduct of this game was prompted by two simultaneous feelings. Firstly, he aimed irrepressibly for a struggle, seeking for this all possible and impossible resources. And, secondly, he was passionately dreaming of ... revenge for his defeat in the first cycle of the tournament. All this led to the future World Champion overreaching himself in a position where he was obliged to think only of a draw ...

1 e4	c5
2 Nf3	d6
3 d4	c×d4
4 N×d4	Nf6
5 Nc3	Nc6
6 Bc4	

Of course, I, like everyone else, was well aware of Fischer's particular liking for the Sozin Attack, which begins with this move. And before this game I prepared an improvement in a variation which I thought might occur.

However, for the moment everything proceeds "according to theory".

6 ...	e6
7 Bb3	

The notes to Game No. 99 give Fischer's evaluation of this move and my opinion regarding it ...

7 ...	Be7
8 f4	

8 0–0 is usually played, but here White chooses a sharper continuation. An understandable decision, especially since a little earlier, at the Stockholm Interzonal Tournament, Fischer had defeated Olafsson in this way. But it was for this move that Black was prepared ...

Digressing slightly, I should like to mention that my duel with the American grandmaster in this variation of the Sozin Attack was continued in the 4th game of the 1972 World Championship Match in Reykjavik. There after 8 Be3 0–0 9 0–0 a6 10 f4 N×d4 11 B×d4 b5 12 a3 Bb7 13 Qd3 Spassky, whom I was seconding, answered 13 ... a5! and obtained good counter-play, which developed into a strong attack. And although the game finally ended in a draw, after this the Sozin Attack disappeared from Fischer's repertoire.

8 ...	0–0
9 Be3	N×d4
10 B×d4	b5

The natural counter to White's aggressive 8th move. Black simply forces his opponent, in spite of his lack of development, to open the centre, since 11 a3 Bb7 is clearly in Black's favour.

11 e5	d×e5
12 f×e5	Nd7
13 0–0	

Black has the better position after 13 N×b5 Qa5+ (or even *13 ... N×e5* immediately) 14 Nc3 N×e5.

13 ...	Bc5!

The prepared improvement! In the afore-mentioned Fischer–Olafsson game White gained the advantage after 13 ... b4 14 Ne4 Bb7 15 Nd6. But now he has to worry over his own weakness—his e5 pawn.

14 B×c5	

If 14 N×b5, then 14 ... Qb6, and Black regains his pawn, maintaining a strong initiative.

14 ...	N×c5
15 Q×d8	R×d8

16 N×b5	Ba6
17 Bc4	

Forced, since after 17 Nc7 B×f1 18 N×a8 Bb5 (*18 ... B×g2* is also good) the white knight would be extremely awkwardly placed, while the rook ending after 17 a4 N×b3 18 c×b3 Rab8 is unpromising for White.

17 ...	Rab8
18 a4	

18 ...	N×a4!

This equalizes completely. The logic of the position should now have dictated to White the forced drawing variation 19 R×a4 B×b5 20 B×b5 R×b5 21 R×a7 R×b2 22 Rf×f7 Rd1+ 23 Rf1 R×f1+ 24 K×f1 R×c2. But my opponent was definitely after revenge...

19 Nd6?	B×c4
20 N×c4	N×b2
21 Nd6	

The exchange on b2 would have led to the aforementioned rook ending, but with the significant difference that White would have lost an important tempo, and, as a consequence, his e-pawn.

21 ...	Rd7
22 Rfb1	Rc7

22 ... Rb6 23 c4 Na4 fails to 24 c5!, when the weakness of the back rank rules out both

24 ... N×c5 25 R×b6, and 24 ... R×b1+ 25 R×b1 N×c5.

23 h3

This move is not essential. Better drawing chances were offered by the immediate 23 c4 with the idea of 24 Nb5, although Black has the strong reply 24 ... Rb4!, retaining his extra pawn.

| 23 ... | Rb6 |
| 24 c4 | h6 |

An escape square has been opened, and White is forced to part with his strong knight and go into a rook ending a pawn down.

| 25 Nb5 | Rc5 |

Not 25 ... R×c4?? 26 R×b2 a6 27 Nd6.

| 26 R×b2 | a6 |
| 27 Rf2 | |

Or 27 Rab1 a×b5 28 R×b5 Rbc6.

27 ...	a×b5
28 Ra7	R×e5
29 Rf×f7	Rg5

30 Rfb7

Practice shows that in a double-rook ending the realization of an extra pawn involves greater difficulties, and to be considered therefore was 30 c×b5 Rb×b5 31 Rf2. It would seem that the American grandmaster had no doubt that the single-rook ending was drawn, since all the pawns are on one side of the board. In principle this is so, but nevertheless White's defence is not now so simple. It is sufficient to recall the well-known ending Botvinnik–Najdorf, Moscow, 1956, in which the World Champion converted a similar position into a win. So that for a draw very exact play is demanded of White.

30 ...	R×b7
31 R×b7	b×c4
32 Rc7	Rf5
33 R×c4	Kf7
34 g4	

An inaccuracy. Of course, the white king has to come into play, but for this 34 g3 was more appropriate, retaining the possibility in certain cases of continuing h3–h4 and Kg2–h3–g4. But now the white king is cut off along the third rank, and the white pawns are insufficiently defended.

34 ...	Rf3
35 Kg2	Rd3
36 Rc7+	Kf6
37 h4	Ra3
38 Rb7	Rc3

Both sides have been making waiting moves before the time control, but White suddenly changes the character of the position.

39 g5+	h×g5
40 h×g5+	Kg6
41 Re7	Re3

42 Kf2?

This last move before the adjournment loses by force. White could still have drawn by 42 Kh2!!, so as to answer 42 ... Re5 with 43 Kh3, not allowing the black rook to take the g5 pawn with check or to leave the e-file with check. And in the event of 42 ... K×g5 43 R×g7+ Kf6 44 Rg1 Rf3 45 Kg2 Rf5 46 Re1 a theoretically drawn position would have been reached.

42 ...	Re5

By this sealed move Black wins a second pawn, and with it the game.

43 Kf3	Rf5+
44 Ke3	

In the event of 44 Ke4 Black of course would not have continued 44 ... e5?? 45 R×g7+, but 44 ... Rf7! 45 R×e6+ K×g5, and since here White's king is cut off on the so-called "long" side of the board, he is lost. Something similar also occurs in the game.

44 ...	e5
45 Ke4	R×g5
46 Re8	Rg1!
47 Kf3	

The e-pawn is immune, since the pawn ending after 47 Re6+ Kf7 48 R×e5 Re1+ 49 Kf5 R×e5+ 50 K×e5 Kg6! 51 Kf4 Kh5 is lost.

47 ...	Rf1+
48 Kg3	Rf5
49 Rb8	

Or 49 Kg4 Rf4+ 50 Kg3 Kf5 51 Rf8+ Ke4 52 Rg8 Rf3+ 53 Kg2 (53 Kg4 Rf1) 53 ... Rf7, and Black completes his regrouping.

49 ...	Kg5
50 Re8	Kf6
51 Rf8+	Ke6
52 Re8+	Kf6
53 Rf8+	Ke6
54 Re8+	Kd5

Before the second control Black gains time on the clock by repeating moves.

55 Ra8	Rf7
56 Kg4	Re7

The control is passed, the rook is ideally placed, and Black has merely to escape from the checks and advance his pawns.

57 Ra5+	Ke6
58 Ra6+	Kf7
59 Kf3	Re6
60 Ra8	e4+
61 Ke3	g5

All the conditions have been fulfilled, and the win is not far off.

62 Ra1	Kg6
63 Rb1	Re5
64 Kd4	Kf6
65 Re1	

Or 65 Rf1+ Ke6 66 Ke3 (66 *Re1 g4 67 Rg1 e3*) 66 ... Rf5 67 Ra1 Rf4 68 Ra5 Kf6 and the king breaks through at h4.

65 ...	Ra5!

A typical plan. Black gives up one of his pawns to break through with his king and obtain a theoretically won position.

66 R×e4	Kf5!

Here the pawn ending would have been drawn.

67 Re8	Kg4
68 Ke3	Kg3

White resigned in view of the following plan, which is again typical: 69 Ke2 g4 70 Rg8 Rf5 71 Rg7 Kh3 72 Rg8 g3 73 Rg7 Kh2 74 Rh7+ Kg1 75 Rg7 g2 76 Ra7 (*76 Rh7 Re5+ 77 Kd3 Kf2 78 Rf7+ Kg3 79 Rg7+ Kf3 80 Rf7+ Kg4 81 Rg7+ Rg5*) 76 ... Rh5 77 Kf3 Kh1.

No. 97 King's Indian Defence

Geller–Fischer

*Capablanca Memorial Tournament
Havana, 1965*

Pleasing to... ICCF

This is the only "correspondence" game in my long chess career, and it was played under highly unusual circumstances. The point was that the American State Department refused to allow Fischer to travel to Cuba to take part in a very interesting tournament. But Fischer found a way out. He played his games sitting in the Marshall Chess Club in New York, using a long-distance telephone link. This caused the games to last some two to three hours longer, but none of the participants in Havana objected to such an unusual "innovation", which would undoubtedly have pleased the International Correspondence Chess Federation. Although the games with the then permanent USA Champion were a considerable physical strain.

As for the chess content of the game, Edmar Mednis called it "another positional masterpiece by Geller against Fischer". This is perhaps over-stating it, but indeed it cannot be denied that White's play is logical and consistent. ...

1 c4	g6
2 Nc3	Bg7
3 d4	Nf6
4 e4	d6
5 f3	c6

Against the Sämisch Variation Fischer used to employ various continuations, and all without particular success. On this occasion he chooses a line which is directed in the first instance against the possibility of Q-side castling by White (... *a6* and ... *b5*).

6 Be3	a6
7 Bd3	

"The sharpest line for White is 7 Qd2, 8 0–0–0, followed by an attack on the K-side by h2–h4, Bh6, etc. It is understandable that, in a game with Fischer, Geller does not aim for early tactical complications. He wishes to obtain a sound, solid position." This is written by Mednis in his book *How to Beat Bobby Fischer*.

I cannot agree with this. I never avoided complications in meetings with the future World Champion, since it was his play in irrational positions that I regarded as Fischer's less strong side. The point was quite different, and lay in an objective, purely chess evaluation of the opening variation. After White's Q-side castling, Black acquires a clear plan of an attack on the king, and it is easier for him to achieve a satisfactory position.

The following moves by both sides must be criticized, but only from the position of our present-day knowledge.

7 ...	b5
8 c×b5	

After this game it was established that Black should first play 7 ... 0–0, since after 7 ... b5 White could have gained a serious advantage by 8 e5. This was confirmed in:

(a) 8 ... d×e5 9 d×e5 Ng8 10 f4 Nh6 11 Nf3 Bf5 12 Be2! Q×d1+ 13 R×d1 f6 14 Nd4! f×e5 15 f×e5 0–0 16 0–0 Nf7 17 N×f5 g×f5 18 e6 Ne5 19 g4! (Spassky–Kavalek, San Juan, 1969).

(b) 8 ... Nfd7 9 f4 0–0 10 Nf3 Nb6 11 b3 (Portisch–Kavalek, Beverwijk, 1975). But perhaps in this last variation Black, without wasting time on castling, should immediately attack the c4 pawn with 9 ... Nb6!?

8 ...	a×b5
9 Nge2	0–0
10 b4	

In this way White prevents ... b4 and prepares a2–a4 with subsequent pressure on the Q-side.

10 ...	Nbd7
11 0–0	Bb7

Slightly better is 11 ... Nb6 12 a4 b×a4 13 N×a4 Ba6, and now:

(a) 14 Nb2 B×d3 15 Q×d3 Qc7 16 Qb3 Qb7 17 Ra5, and White has only a minimal advantage (Filip–Bolbochan, Havana, 1966).

(b) 14 B×a6 R×a6 15 Qb3 Qb8, with a satisfactory game for Black (Pachman–Geller, Moscow, 1967).

12 Qd2	e5
13 Rfd1	e×d4
14 N×d4	Ne5
15 Bf1	Nfd7
16 a4!	Nb6!

By tactical means (17 a×b5 R×a1 18 R×a1 Nbc4 19 Qc1 N×e3 20 Q×e3 Qb6, with the threats of 21 ... N×f3+ and 21 ... Nc4) Black forces the exchange of one pair of knights.

17 Qc2	b×a4
18 N×a4	N×a4
19 R×a4	R×a4
20 Q×a4	

The clash of opening plans has led to a position favourable for White. The whole question reduces to whether or not he can exploit the persistent weakness of Black's hanging pawns.

20 ...	Qe7
21 Qb3	Ra8
22 Nc2	Bc8
23 Nd4	

White had only one minute per move left to the time control, and he naturally wanted to gain even a little time on the clock.

23 ...	Bd7

Understandably, Black does not wish to fall in with his opponent's intentions. But nevertheless this move must be criticized, since the black knight unexpectedly finds itself in danger.

24 h3!	

With the threat of 25 f4.

24 ...	Rb8
25 Qa3	

On 25 f4 there would have followed 25 ... c5.

25 ...	d5

Saving the knight by 25 ... f6 would have been quite suicidal, whereas now the play becomes sharper in White's time trouble.

26 e×d5	c×d5
27 Nc2!	

27 ...   B×h3

It is difficult to give a definite assessment to Black's idea, but it would nevertheless seem to be his best practical chance. 27 ... Be6 is strongly met by 28 Bc5, when White's passed pawn, supported by his bishops, is ready to advance. On 27 ... Bf5 the same reply 28 Bc5 followed by Ne3 is unpleasant, while after 27 ... Nc4 28 Qa7! Rd8 29 R×d5 N×e3 30 Q×e3, as Mednis rightly points out, Black loses a pawn without any compensation.

28 Bc5!

There was absolutely no point in allowing Black to confuse matters after 28 g×h3 N×f3+ 29 Kf2 (*29 Kg2? Nh4+*, or *29 Kh1? Qe5!*) 29 ... Qf6 30 Kg3.

28 ...	**Qg5**
29 f4	**Qh5**
30 R×d5	

This is simpler than 30 Rd2 Bf5 31 f×e5 B×e5, when, in spite of being a piece down, Black may be able to create some threats in the opponent's time trouble. But now exchanges are inevitable, leading to a won ending for White.

30 ...	**Bf5**
31 Ne3	**Ng4**

31 ... Nc6 is well met by either 32 N×f5 or 32 g4.

32 N×g4	**Q×g4**
33 Qa7	**Re8**

Bad is 33 ... Q×f4 34 Bd6.

34 Qc7	**h5**
35 Rd8	**R×d8**
36 Q×d8+	**Kh7**
37 Be3	

Strategically the game is decided, since sooner or later the b-pawn will cost Black a piece.

37 ...   Bh6

This meets with a refutation and leads to the loss of a pawn. But White's task would have been even easier after Mednis's recommendation of 37 ... h4 with the idea of exposing the white king by ... h3. By continuing 38 Qg5, White would win immediately. Other moves by Black, 37 ... Be6 for example, would have allowed the b-pawn to advance.

38 Qf6

With the threat of 39 Bd4.

38 ...	**Bg7**
39 Q×f7	**Qd1**
40 Qc4	**h4**

Black would have done better to refrain from this, although the outcome of the game is all the same decided.

41 Qe2

The sealed move.

41 ...	Qa1
42 Kh2	Bd4

Otherwise how else can the pawn be prevented from advancing by force to b6?

43 Bf2!	B×f2
44 Q×f2	Kg7

The weakness of his h-pawn forces Black to lose a tempo, and the white pawn begins its march.

45 b5	Be4
46 b6	Bb7
47 Qe2	Kf6
48 Qd3	

With the threat of 49 Qd6+, 50 Qd7+, 51 Q×b7, 52 Qf3 and 53 b7 with an easy win.

48 ...	Ke7
49 Qc4	Kf6
60 Qd3	

Gaining time on the clock by repeating moves.

50 ...	Ke7
51 Qe3+	Kd6

White would have answered 51 ... Kf6 in the same way...

52 Be2!

Transposing into an accurately calculated pawn ending.

52 ...	Qb2
53 Bf3	B×f3
54 Qe5+	Q×e5
55 f×e5+	K×e5
56 g×f3	Kd6
57 f4	

"Chess is a tragedy of one tempo. One is always short of it, either for a win, or a draw", said grandmaster Savielly Tartakover. As if to confirm this aphorism, **Black resigned,** since in the forced variation 57 ... Kc6 58 Kh3 K×b6 59 K×h4 Kc6 60 Kg5 Kd7 61 K×g6 he is indeed short of just one tempo: 61 ... Ke7 62 f5 Kf8 63 Kf6 Kg8(e8) 64 Ke7(g7).

No. 98 Sicilian Defence

Fischer–Geller

Monte Carlo, 1967

On the edge of the abyss

The commencement of battle in this game was preceded by the following considerations. At that time the "Fischer problem" was undoubtedly not so acute as it was later, but even then it was clear to me that the vulnerable point of the American grandmaster was in double-edged, "hanging", irrational positions. When the play was of this nature, Fischer often failed to find a win even in a won position. It was this that led to the decision to challenge Fischer to a very sharp game, and, what's more, in his favourite variation. Players who are devoted to certain opening systems know how unpleasant it can be to "play against oneself" in the purely psychological sense.

To be objective, it must be pointed out that with such a decision there is always another side to the coin, as was indeed the case here. The opening subtleties of the variation were well known to Fischer, whereas I had to search very hard for good continuations in an unfamiliar situation. Unexpectedly this introduced an additional nuance into the course of the game. The point was that Fischer had started with 5 points out of 5, and his only rival was Vasily Smyslov. At the start I had lost one game, and in view of the short distance of nine rounds (or essentially even eight, since one player had dropped out, and all the others were given a win against him), I was no longer a real contender for first place.

In the event of Fischer losing the present game from the last round, Smyslov by winning would catch the leader. It is natural that Fischer could not avoid being worried by this. But while I was thinking, Smyslov quickly agreed a draw. Fischer got up from the board, made sure of this personally, calmed down, and accepted the challenge. Had the tournament situation been different, he might have been more cautious. But when both players aim for complications, the storm on the chess board can achieve immense proportions. It is sufficient to say that analyses of our game continued to be published for a further four to five years. ...

1 e4	c5
2 Nf3	d6
3 d4	c×d4
4 N×d4	Nf6
5 Nc3	a6

It was this line that Fischer used to systematically and readily employ with Black. It is sufficient to recall that he even chose the variation which occurs in the game on two occasions in his World Championship Match. Normally Fischer used to play 6 Bc4 here —not, in my opinion, the continuation that Black has to fear most.

| 6 Bg5 | e6 |
| 7 f4 | Qb6 |

Exploiting the fact that White's last move has temporarily cut off his black-squared bishop from its defensive duties, Black declares his readiness to accept the sacrifice of the b-pawn, and to be subjected to a strong attack on his king stuck in the centre. The less committing 8 Nb3 would have looked like moral capitulation on White's part.

| 8 Qd2 | Q×b2 |
| 9 Rb1 | |

The 9 Nb3 employed by Spassky against Fischer (Reykjavik, 1972), is less common. The mass of complicated variations resulting after this would require a special and rather extensive analysis.

| 9 ... | Qa3 |
| 10 f5 | |

Fischer had several times refuted the attack begun with the usual 10 e5, and probably for this reason he follows the game Gipslis–Korchnoi (31st USSR Championship, Leningrad, 1963). The continuation selected leads to a game in which Black's chances are perhaps not inferior, although he has to withstand a sharp attack. Later this was confirmed in, among others, the game Kavalek–Fischer (Sousse Interzonal, 1967), which ended in a draw.

| 10 ... | Nc6 |

The most natural reaction to White's last move. It is tempting, of course, to bring the queen home, but 10 ... Qc5 loses almost by force: 11 f×e6 f×e6 12 B×f6 g×f6 13 Na4 Bh6 14 Q×h6 Q×d4 15 Nb6 Qc3+ 16 Qd2. There is no time to prepare ... Qc5 by 10 ... b5, while 10 ... Be7 allows White to set up decisive pressure on e6: 11 f×e6 f×e6 12 Bc4.

11 f×e6	f×e6
12 N×c6	b×c6
13 e5	

White's universal idea in this variation — he opens all the lines in the centre. If he limits himself to the sacrifice of only one pawn, 13 B×f6 g×f6 14 Be2, as in Hennings–Kavalek, Sinaia, 1965, this can lead to the exchange of queens: 14 ... Rg8 15 0–0 (*15 Bh5+ Ke7, and 16 0–0 fails to 16 ... Qc5+*) 15 ... Qc5+ 16 Kh1 Qg5.

13 ...   **Nd5**

The most dangerous continuation for Black, after which White retains his attacking black-squared bishop.

The alternatives were 13 ... Nd7, aiming for equality, and the usual 13 ... d×e5 14 B×f6 g×f6 15 Ne4 Be7 16 Be2, and now, as played by Fischer, 16 ... h5. But I was playing this variation for the first time in my life. It was inconceivable to try and work out all the possible complications at the board, and I decided that Black's pawn centre should enable his king to "sit it out".

14 N×d5

14 Ne4 is unpleasantly met by 14 ... d×e5 with the threat of 15 ... Bb4, but possible was 14 Rb3 Qa5 15 Be2 N×c3 16 R×c3 d5 17 0–0, when for the pawn White has good prospects.

14 ...   **c×d5**

14 ... e×d5 would have cost Black a piece: 15 e6! B×e6 16 Qe2.

15 Be2

A new move. Earlier 15 c4 was usually played, and then either 15 ... d×e5 16 c×d5 Be7, or 15 ... d×c4 16 B×c4 d5 17 Be2 (*17 B×d5 e×d5 18 Q×d5 Bb4+*) 17 ... Bc5 (Vogt–Espig, East German Championship, 1967).

15 ...   **d×e5**
16 0–0

The position would have been still sharper after 16 Rf1, not allowing Black to develop his king's bishop with gain of tempo. For example, 16 ... Be7 17 Bb3 B×g5 (*17 ... Qd6 18 Rbf3*) 18 Q×g5 Qe7 19 Qh5+ g6 20 Q×e5 Rf8 21 R×f8+ Q×f8 22 Qc7, retaining the initiative for the pawn. However, Black too could have attempted to improve the defence — 16 ... Ra7!?

16 ...   **Bc5+**

The later efforts of analysts established that here too 16 ... Ra7 was a better defence. Thus in Bednarsky–Sakharov, Varna, 1968, after 17 c4 Qc5+ 18 Kh1 d4 19 Qc2 Be7 20 Qa4+ Rd7 21 Bd2 Rf8 22 Bh5+ g6 23 Bf3 R×f3 24 R×f3 e4 25 R3f1 e3 Black completely equalized.

17 Kh1   **Rf8!**

Necessary, since White's threats had become very real. In general, any exchanges are in Black's favour.

Up to this point Fischer had played very quickly, obviously following his prepared analysis. Here for the first time he sank into thought and ... made the usual move in this sort of position.

18 c4   **R×f1+**
19 R×f1   **Bb7**

Later it was asserted by Khasin that by interposing 19 ... h6 Black could have parried the attack: 20 Bh5+ Kd7 21 c×d5 h×g5 22 d×e6+ Kc7 23 Qd5 Ra7 24 Bf3 Rb7.

But what is Black to do if White is not so generous: 20 Bh4 g5 21 Bg3 Bd4 22 c×d5 e×d5 (*22 ... Qc3 23 Qd1 e×d5 24 B×e5 B×e5 25 Q×d5*) 23 B×e5, or 23 Qc2 Qd6 24 Qh7? It must be wrong to weaken the g6 square!

20 Bg4?

Fischer's only mistake in the game, made after more than twenty minutes' thought. It is easy to condemn him for it, but avoiding it was much more difficult. Objectively, the black king should hardly be able to survive under the fire of the four remaining white pieces, but finding a way to win at the board was not so simple: there are too many continuations of the attack to be analysed. It was here that the correctly evaluated aspect of Fischer's character came into effect: in unfamiliar sharp positions he was apt to lose his way.

He had to make a choice between:

(*a*) 20 Rf3.

(*b*) 20 Bd1.

(*c*) 20 Qc2.

(*d*) The continuation in the game.

Let us examine them all, if only briefly.

(*a*) 20 Rf3 Qa4 21 Qb2! Qd7 22 Rb3! (*22 Q×e5 Bd6*) 22 ... Rb8 (*22 ... Bd4 23*

Qb1!, or 22 ... Bc6 23 Rb8+ R×b8 24 Q×b8+ Kf7 25 Bh5+! g6 26 Qh8 g×h5 27 Q×h7+ Kf8 28 Bh6+ Ke8 29 Qg8+ Ke7 30 Qf8 mate*) 23 Q×e5 Bd6 24 Qe3, with advantage to White.

But after the correct 20 ... Qb4! 21 Q×b4 B×b4 22 Rb3 a5 23 a3 h6 24 Be3 d×c4 25 B×c4 Bd5! 26 B×d5 e×d5 27 a×b4 d4 28 Bg1 a×b4 29 R×b4 Kf7 Black can · successfully defend.

(*b*) 20 Bd1.

This was suggested by Lilienthal, and threatens the spectacular 21 Qd3! or 21 Qb2! and mate after Ba4+. Black fails to save the game after 20 ... Kd7 21 Rf7+ Kc8 (*21 ... Kc6 also loses*) 22 Bg4, or 20 ... Bc6 21 Qe2!, or 20 ... d×c4 21 Qc2! (*21 Qc3 Q×a2*).

Black would have had to play 20 ... Be7, and now:

Not 21 Rf3 B×g5 22 Q×g5 Qb4 23 Q×e5 0–0–0!! (*23 ... Qe7 24 Ba4+ Kd8 25 Rg3 g6 26 Rb3 Rc8 27 Rb6*).

21 B×e7! K×e7 (*21 ... Q×e7 22 Ba4+ Kd8 23 Qa5+ Kc8 24 c5!*) 22 Qg5+ Kd6 23 Rf7 Re8(!) 24 c5+ (*after 24 R×b7 Qd3 25 h3 Q×d1+ 26 Kh2 Qd4 27 Q×g7 Black gives perpetual check*) 24 ... Q×c5 (*24 ... K×c5 25 R×b7 Qd3 26 Qc1+!*) 25 R×b7 Qf2 26 h3 Qf1+ 27 Kh2 Qf4+ 28 Q×f4 e×f4 29 R×g7 e5 30 R×h7 (in the event of *30 g3 f3! 31 B×f3 e4* White's chances of success are problematic), and White should win in this rather sharp ending.

(*c*) 20 Qc2.

After the game I pointed out this attacking possibility to Fischer. It is difficult to parry the threat against h7.

20 ... Be7 loses quickly to 21 Bh5+! (but not the natural *21 Q×h7 B×g5 22 Qh5+ Kd7*, and the king hides behind the pawns) 21 ... g6 (*21 ... Kd8 22 Rf8+ Kd7 23 Rf7 Re8 24 R×g7*) 22 B×g6+ h×g6 23 Q×g6+ Kd7 24 B×e7!

Also inadequate is 20 ... g6 21 Bg4 Be7

22 Qf2! 0–0–0 23 B×e6+ Kb8 24 B×e7 Q×e7 25 B×d5 B×d5 26 c×d5.

Three months later in the USSR–Yugoslavia match (Budva, 1967) Bogdanovic chose 20 ... e4 against Tal, but had to resign after 21 Bg4 Be7 22 Qf2! 0–0–0 23 Bf4 Bd6 24 B×e6+ Kb8 25 Qb6 B×f4 26 Q×d8+ Ka7 27 Rb1 Qd6 28 B×d5! B×d5 29 Q×d6 B×d6 30 c×d5.

Now it will be understandable how difficult it was for Fischer to choose one of the two correct continuations of the attack, where in addition the win lay at the end of long and complicated variations. After all, apart from those given, he had to work out a mass of other possibilities. The position is so sharp that just one mistake will lead to White's defeat: his boats have already been burned.

And that is precisely what happened in the game.

20 ...	d×c4
21 B×e6	Qd3
22 Qe1	Be4!

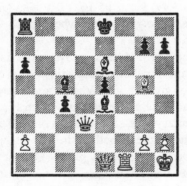

The outcome of the game is decided. The idea of this last move is to paralyze White's heavy pieces. The bishop in the centre is simultaneously both a shield and a sword, and Black threatens to bring into play his "reserve" rook via the route ... Rb8-b2. True, the following variation had to be checked: 23 Bf5 B×f5 24 Q×e5+ Kd7 25 Q×g7+ Kc6 26 Qf6+ Bd6, and White is forced into an inferior ending, in which the recently helpless c4 pawn becomes Black's main trump. Fischer at this point looked very dismayed.

| 23 Bg4 | Rb8 |

Now 24 Be2 is not possible due to 24 ... Rb2!, while 24 Bf3 would have led to the hopeless ending which we have already seen: 24 ... B×f3 25 Q×e5+ Kd7.

24 Bd1

Renewing the threat of Ba4+, which was so terrible four moves earlier.

| 24 ... | Kd7 |
| 25 Rf7+ | Ke6 |

Contrary to the normal state of affairs, Black's king in the centre is now safe, whereas its white colleague, which is in its customary place, is in a trap. On 26 R×g7 there follows 26 ... B×g2+ 27 K×g2 Rb2+ 28 Kh1 Qd5+. Therefore **White resigned.**

No. 99 Sicilian Defence

Fischer–Geller

"Solidarity Tournament"
Skopje, 1967

Under the microscope of analysis

Like the previous game with Fischer, this encounter provoked a great deal of competitive and analytical interest among chess players. Competitive, because this was my third successive victory over the American grandmaster, and in terms of number of moves the game was barely beyond the bounds of a miniature. It was of a certain significance for theory, and the incredible tension in a position, where everything was decided by one tempo, provoked numerous analytical works. It was only several years later that the analysts, having refuted and corrected one another, came to a unanimous conclusion. And although immediately after the game it seemed to me to be complete and consistent, it later had to be included among those played according to the principle of "two on the swing". Personally this gives me less satisfaction, but the wealth of possibilities in the positions arising was so great, and the oscillation amplitude from win to loss so small and imperceptible, that this game is undoubtedly one of my most memorable.

As a point of information, I should also like to point out that Black, in spite of his "love" for time trouble, spent on the twenty-two moves of this highly complex encounter less than an hour and a half. The time spent by White was greater....

1 e4	c5
2 Nf3	d6
3 d4	c×d4
4 N×d4	Nf6
5 Nc3	Nc6

Black naturally wishes to vary his opening schemes—see Game No. 98.

6 Bc4

It is possible that the Rauzer Attack—6 Bg5—is more dangerous for Black, but the Sozin Attack, which commences with this move, is Fischer's childhood love. I have several times managed to find means of active counter-play against it. In general, when playing the American grandmaster, it was best to aim for positions with chances for both sides.

It should be mentioned that, after his failure in the present game and against Larsen (Interzonal Tournament, Palma de Mallorca, 1970) where Fischer also chose 0–0–0, he reverted to his former set-up with K-side castling in his match with Spassky. I have already mentioned this in my notes to Game No. 96. But after the fourth game of the match Fischer did not play the Sozin Attack again.

| 6 ... | e6 |
| 7 Be3 | |

In his notes to this move in his book *My 60 Memorable Games*, Fischer writes that "Bb3 cuts down Black's options", and cites mainly the Fischer–Dely game from the same tournament in Skopje. I think that 7 Bb3 is a double-edged weapon, since it also cuts down White's options. For example, in the variation with Q-side castling Black has constantly to reckon with the fact that White has not wasted a tempo on the retreat of his bishop. Thus in a game with me at Budapest, 1973, Velimirovic after 7 Be3 Be7 8 Qe2 N×d4 9 B×d4 0–0 10 0–0–0 Qa5 continued 11 e5 d×e5 12 B×e5, with interesting play. So that, if he is planning 0–0–0, White is not obliged to hurry over moving his bishop to b3.

| 7 ... | Be7 |

"Too routine", writes Fischer. "Black should start quicker action on the Q-side. More reasonable is 7 ... a6 8 Bb3 Qc7 9 Qe2 (or *9 f4*) 9 ... b5 10 0–0–0 Na5 (*10 ... Bb7* is also possible, whereupon White might reply *11 f3*)."

In the Sozin Attack, move order is very important for both sides, since any transposition gives both White, and Black, a wide choice of continuations. From Fischer's commentary it is seen that he himself is not altogether sure whether in the proposed variation White should play 9 Qe2 or 9 f4, since in the latter case the recommended 11 f3 is no longer possible. Moreover, after 7 ... a6 8 Bb3 Qc7 9 f4 b5 Black has to reckon with the immediate 10 f5 b4 11 f×e6. So that at present it is hardly possible to give any categorical directions in the given position.

| 8 Bb3 | 0–0 |
| 9 Qe2 | |

White retains the choice on the following move of the side on which to castle.

9 ...   Qa5

Here too Black is not obliged to play an early ... a6. In the game Tal–Bolbochan (Havana Olympiad, 1966) after 9 ... a6? 10 0–0–0 Qa5 White could have set his opponent a number of difficult problems by 11 Rhg1! with the idea of g2–g4–g5.

10 0–0–0

The critical decision. On 10 0–0 it would be interesting to try 10 ... N×d4 11 B×d4 b6 with the threat of ... Ba6.

10 ...   N×d4

Of course, Black would have liked to play 10 ... Bd7 immediately, without revealing his cards, but then White can gain the advantage by 11 Ndb5 Ne8 12 Bf4 a6 13 N×d6 N×d6 14 B×d6 B×d6 15 R×d6 Qg5+ 16 Qd2 Q×g2 17 Rhd1 Be8 18 Qf4. This variation is also cited by Fischer.

11 B×d4

The first debatable point in the game. To be considered was 11 R×d4, retaining the possibility of 12 g4. With the bishop at d4, g2–g4 can be parried by ... e5, whereas now White would have in reserve the tempo-gaining Ra4, or even an exchange sacrifice, for example in the variation 11 R×d4 Bd7 12 g4 e5 13 Nd5.

11 ...   Bd7

It stands to reason that at the board I did not even consider variations resulting from 11 ... Qg5+ and ... Q×g2. As it is the game is about to become open, and Black's chances lie in a counter-attack on the Q-side. For this ... b5 must be prepared as soon as possible, which is what the move played is aimed at.

12 Kb1

A useful prophylactic move, intensifying the threat of 13 B×f6.

Immediate activity with 12 Rhg1 would have been highly dubious:

(a) 12 ... Bc6 (recommended by Kholmov, who gives the move an exclamation mark) 13 g4 e5 14 Be3 N×e4 15 B×e4 (Kholmov suggests 15 Nd5) 15 ... B×e4 16 Bd2, and Black loses a piece.

(b) 12 ... Rfc8(!) 13 g4 e5 (or 13 ... b5 with chances for both sides) 14 Be3 R×c3 15 Bd2 Bb5! 16 Qe1 R×c2+ 17 K×c2 Qa6, with the threats of ... Bd3+ or ... Be2, when Black has fine counterplay for the sacrificed exchange.

12 ...   Bc6?

This frees White's hands. The bishop stood very well at d7, hindering the advance of White's K-side pawns (*f2–f4* or *g2–g4*), which would have been countered by ... e5. Black should have chosen between 12 ... Rfd8, 12 ... Rfc8, or, as was played in one of the later rounds against Fischer by Sofrevsky, 12 ... Rad8. This game continued 13 Qe3! (Fischer's exclamation mark) 13 ... b6 14 B×f6! g×f6 15 Nd5!! and White won. But by continuing 13 ... Bc6 (instead of *13 ... b6?*) Black would have maintained the balance, since 14 B×a7 is not convincing due to 14 ... Nd7, when it is not clear how the bishop at a7 can be freed.

However, 12 ... Rfc8 nevertheless looks the most thematic.

13 f4   Rad8
14 Rhf1

There were also some reasonable alternatives:

(*a*) 14 g4 (Kholmov) 14 ... e5 (White also has the better game after *14 ... d5 15 e×d5! N×d5 16 N×d5 B×d5 17 Bc3 Qc5 18 B×d5 R×d5 19 R×d5 Q×d5 20 Qd1 Qc5 21 f5 e×f5 22 g×f5*) 15 f×e5 d×e5 16 Bf2 R×d1+ 17 R×d1 Rd8 18 Rf1.

(*b*) 14 f5 e×f5 (*14 ... e5 15 Bf2 d5? 16 e×d5 N×d5 17 N×d5 B×d5 18 Q×e5*) 15 e×f5 Rfe8 16 Qf2.

Commenting on the move in the game, Fischer writes: "I already had in mind the ensuing sacrifice". It should be mentioned that this idea is not an original one, and that a similar sacrifice had been seen earlier (for example, Stein–Osnos, 29th USSR Championship, 1961).

14 ...   b5

15 f5!

The start of a long and forcing variation with numerous complicated branches, which ends in White's defeat. Meanwhile, thanks to Black's mistake on the 12th move, White's position is won, but to show this requires very energetic and exact play in a highly complex position. As in the previous game, this proves to be beyond Fischer's powers, although he begins the attack correctly and strongly.

15 ...   b4
16 f×e6

This piece sacrifice is simultaneously both correct and forced, since after 16 Nd5 e×d5 17 e×d5 Black seizes the initiative, for example by 17 ... N×d5 18 B×d5 B×d5 19 Q×e7 Q×a2+ 20 Kc1 Rc8! 21 Q×a7 (or *21 B×g7 Bb3!*, etc.) 21 ... Qc4! 22 Rf2 Be4 23 Rdd2 b3.

16 ...   b×c3
17 e×f7+

Both in the game, and in his notes, Fischer overlooks the suggestion by Murey and Boleslavsky of 17 R×f6!:

(*a*) 17 ... g×f6 18 e×f7+ (*18 Qg4+ Qg5! 19 e×f7+ R×f7 20 Qe6 Rf8 21 Q×e7 Qd2!!*) 18 ... Kh8 (or *18 ... R×f7 19 B×f7+ K×f7 20 Qc4+* and *21 Q×c6*, and White gains the advantage) 19 Qg4! Rb8 (against the threat of *20 Qe6*, Black is not saved by *19 ... Bd7* in view of *20 Qh4 Kg7 21 Rd3 R×f7 22 Rg3+ Kf8 23 Q×h7!*) 20 Qe6 Qd8 21 Rf1 Rb4 (trying to defend against *R×f6*) 22 B×c3 R×e4 23 R×f6! (nevertheless!) 23 ... Re1+ 24 B×e1! B×f6 25 Ba5!!, with a spectacular win.

(*b*) 17 ... B×f6 (more tenacious) 18 B×f6 g×f6 19 e7, and White has an undisputed positional advantage, for example, 19 ... Qe5 20 e×d8=Q R×d8 21 Qc4 Be8 22 Q×c3.

Fischer chooses another path, which is objectively no less strong, but is more complicated.

17 ...   Kh8
18 Rf5   Qb4!

Reminding White that he too has a vulnerable point—b2. In some cases Black has in mind ... R×f7.

19 Qf1

"A hard move to find—it took around forty-five minutes. The threat of R×f6 must be attended to", writes Fischer. Indeed, Black's task would have been very simple after 19 b×c3 Qb7 (with the threats of ... B×e4 and ... R×f7), or 19 B×c3 Q×e4, while White also achieves nothing by 19 R×f6 B×f6 20 B×f6 g×f6 21 Qf2 R×f7.

It can be asserted that at this point Fischer had already planned 20 a3, in order to mount his attack "in comfort". But if 19 Qf1 is regarded merely as a prelude to the subsequent 20 Qf4, then 19 Rf1 does not deserve an exclamation mark, since 19 Qf2 is equally good...

19 ...   N×e4

"Objectively best is 19 ... Ng4", suggests Fischer, although in this case White wins: 20 B×c3 Qb7 (*20 ... Q×e4 21 Rd4*) 21 Rh5 B×e4 (*21 ... Ne5 22 Qf5 h6 23 Qg6!*) 22 Bd5 B×d5 (*22 ... B×c2+ 23 K×c2 Ne3+ 24 Kd3 Q×d5+ 25 R×d5 N×f1 26 R×f1, and 26 ... Bf6 fails to 27 R×f6*) 23 Qf5 h6 24 R×d5 Nf6 25 B×f6 B×f6 26 R×h6+ g×h6 27 Q×f6+ Kh7 28 Rh5 (Murey).

The text continuation sets Fischer the most difficult problems.

20 a3?

This loses in paradoxical fashion. As Fischer writes, a couple of hours after the game he found the problem-like win 20 Qf4!!, with the threat of 21 Rh5. Black has no way of equalizing, for example, 20 ... c×b2 21 Rh5!, and now:

(a) 21 ... Bf6 22 Qf5 h6 R×h6+!! g×h6 24 Qg6, with inevitable mate.

(b) 21 ... Nf6 22 Rh6!, when Black can avoid the thematic R×f6 only by going into a hopeless ending: 22 ... d5 23 R×f6 Rd6 24 R×d6 Q×d6 25 Q×d6 B×d6 26 Rf1, and 26 ... B×h2 fails to 27 Bc5, while the threat of 27 Rf6! is maintained (Murey).

(c) 21 ... Nc3+ 22 K×b2 N×d1+ (*22 ... R×f7 23 Q×f7 N×d1+ 24 Kb1!! Q×d4 25 R×h7+! K×h7 26 Qh5 mate*) 23 Kc1 R×f7 24 B×f7!, with the decisive threat of 25 R×h7+ K×h7 26 Qf5+.

White also wins after 20 ... Nd2+ (his task is very simple after *20 ... d5 21 Qe5 Nf6 22 R×f6 B×f6 23 Q×f6!*) 21 R×d2 c×d2 22 c3!!, and:

(a) 22 ... Qb7 (or *22 ... Q×b3*), and Black succumbs to the mating combination 23 B×g7+! K×g7 24 Qg4+ Kh8 25 Qd4+.

(b) 22 ... Qc5 (best, although it does not get Black out of his difficulties) 23 Kc2! Bd7 (*23 ... Qe5!? 24 R×e5 d×e5 25 Q×e5 Bf6, with the hope of 26 Q×f6? d1=Q+!, leads to a hopeless position after the correct 26 Qc5 B×d4 27 c×d4 Rc8 28 K×d2 Ba4 29 Qe7 B×b3 30 a×b3 Rcd8 31 Ke3*) 24 B×c5 B×f5+ 25 Q×f5 d×c5 26 Kd1 Rd6 27 Qe5 Rd7 28 Qe6 Rb7 29 Bc2, and against 30 Qf5 there is no satisfactory defence.

This is the truth, established after many years of painstaking analysis. The number of moves with two exclamation marks demanded of White shows how difficult it was to find all this during the restricted time of one game. A calculation of all the variations was impossible, and intuition in sharp situations was not Fischer's strongest weapon.

20 ...   Qb7
21 Qf4

(see diagram next page)

21 ...   Ba4!!

A counter-attacking manoeuvre, based on an imperceptible nuance: by driving away the queen and avoiding the variations associated

with 20 ... Qc5, White has fatally weakened his b3 square.

22 Qg4

The point of Black's last move would have been shown in the variation 22 Qh6 Bf6 23 R×f6 B×b3 24 R×d6 Ba2+!, or 24 c×b3 Q×b3 25 Rf2 Q×d1+ and 26 ... Q×d4. The game continuation also loses.

22 ...	Bf6!
23 R×f6	B×b3!

White resigned, since he cannot simultaneously parry 24 ... Ba2+ and 24 ... N×f6.

Anatoly Karpov

No. 100 French Defence

Geller–Karpov

44th USSR Championship
Moscow, 1976

Knights on the attack

This game began, before we sat down at the board, with an interesting psychological duel. The point was that, not long before this, I was Anatoly Karpov's second in the Final Candidates Match, and participated in his preparations for the World Championship match with Fischer, which did not in fact take place. I was therefore familiar with the World Champion's opening repertoire, and it was evidently for this reason that in the present game he decided to avoid his usual lines, expecting me to play 3 Nd2, which I most often choose. I realized what his idea was.... Moreover, in the variation which occurred he had had no experience at that time, whereas, as the reader will see, the position was familiar to me.

1 e4	e6
2 d4	d5
3 Nc3	Bb4
4 e5	Qd7

The idea of this move, and the essence of the entire variation chosen by Black, are described in the notes to Game No. 88 with Petrosian.

5 Nf3

The alternatives are 5 Nh3 or 5 Ne2 followed by the transfer of the knight to f4, as well as the approved 5 a3, which immediately clarifies the position and gives White, in the opinion of theory, the better game after 5 ... B×c3+ 6 b×c3 b6 7 Qg4 f5 8 Qg3 Ba6 9 B×a6 N×a6 10 Ne2. But I wanted to follow a less familiar path, but one in which I nevertheless had some experience (again Game No. 88). Moreover, White continues his development without loss of time.

5 ...	b6
6 Bd2!	

6 Bd3 is more often played, but, firstly, all the same the white-squared bishop will be exchanged, and, secondly, White continues his tactics of developing as quickly as possible, and, thirdly, he plans an attack on Black's centre and frees c1 for his rook.

6 ...	Ba6

After this the game deviates from the aforementioned game with Petrosian, where 6 ... Bf8 was played.

7 B×a6	N×a6
8 0–0	

8 Qe2 is also possible, but White saves e2 for carrying out his plan.

8 ...	Nb8

A loss of time, which, however, could have gone unpunished, had White not succeeded in opening up the game. To be considered was 8 ... B×c3 9 B×c3 Ne7, when Black is assured of castling K-side.

9 Ne2	Be7?

After this the black king fails to find a safe shelter. 9 ... B×d2 10 Q×d2 Ne7 was now essential.

10 Rc1

Threatening to open up the game by c2–c4, when White's lead in development is bound to tell.

10 ...	b5
11 Nf4	h5

Otherwise the K-side cannot be developed, since 11 ... Nh6 loses to 12 Nh5, and if 12 ... Nf5, then 13 g4.

12 b3

Stronger was 13 a4?!, and if 12 ... b×a4 13 c4!, while after 12 ... a6 13 a×b5 a×b5 14 Ra1 White breaks through on the Q-side.

12 ...	Ba3
13 Rb1	a5?!

In this way Black prevents the trapping of his bishop by 14 b4, but 13 ... Be7 was more tenacious.

14 c4!	c6

After 14 ... b×c4 15 b×c4 d×c4 16 d5 e×d5 17 e6 f×e6 18 Ne5 the black king is assailed by all White's forces.

15 c5

The opening of lines will not escape White, since to save his bishop Black himself will be forced to do it.

15 ...	Bb4
16 Bc1	a4
17 Nd3	

Clearing the white bishop's path to the K-side, but more resolute was 17 a3! Ba5 18 b×a4 b×a4 19 Q×a4 Qa7, and now 20 Bd2 Bc7 21 R×b8+! Q×b8 22 Q×c6+ Kf8 23 Ng5.

However, a similar idea is carried out in the game, but a few moves later.

17 ...	Ba5
18 b×a4	b×a4
19 Q×a4	Qa7
20 Bg5	Bc7

After 20 ... Qa6 21 Rb3 Ne7 22 Rfb1 Nd7 23 Ra3 the threat of 24 Nb4 cannot be parried.

21 R×b8+!

Launching a direct attack on the enemy king stranded in the centre.

21 ...	Q×b8

21 ... B×b8 loses immediately to 22 Q×c6+.

22 Q×c6+	Kf8
23 Nf4	Ra7

Or 23 ... Ne7 24 B×e7+ K×e7 25 Ng5 Rh6 26 N×f7 K×f7 27 Qd7+ Kg8 28 N×e6 R×e6 29 Q×e6+ Kh8 30 Q×d5, and White already has five pawns for the piece, plus a continuing attack.

By the text move Black frees his queen from having to defend his bishop, and thus prepares his next move.

24 Nh4!

With the threats of 25 Nhg6+ f×g6 26 N×e6+ Kf7 27 Qd7+ and mate in two moves, or 25 N×e6+ f×e6 26 Ng6+ Kf7 27 N×h8+ and 28 Q×e6, again with a quick mate. So Black transfers his queen to the defence of the vulnerable points g6 and e6, at the same time, apparently, forcing the exchange of queens.

24 ...	Qe8

25 Q×e6!!

It turns out that the defence of the queen is nevertheless insufficient!

25 ...	f×e6
26 Nfg6+	Q×g6

Or this will become forced after 26 ... Kf7 27 N×h8+ Kf8 29 N4g6+.

27 N×g6+	Ke8
28 N×h8	

White's big material advantage assures him of a win.

28 ...	Ra4
29 Rd1	Ne7
30 B×e7	K×e7
31 Ng6+	Kf7
32 Nf4	

White would perhaps have won more quickly by 32 Nh4!? B×e5 33 Nf3 Bf6 34 h4 R×a2 35 Kf1, when although his material advantage is reduced to one pawn, Black has no way of opposing the impending advance of the c-pawn.

32 ...	B×e5
33 d×e5	

After 33 N×e6? K×e6 34 d×e5 K×e5 it may not be possible to win ...

33 ...	R×f4
34 Rc1!	Ke8
35 c6	Kd8
36 c7+	Kc8

Now White is playing not only with two extra pawns, but also an "extra" king.

37 g3	Ra4

Or 37 ... Rf5 38 g4 g5 39 a4! g×f4 40 a5 f×g3 41 a6 g×h2+ 42 Kh1 Rf2 43 Ra1, and the a-pawn will cost Black his rook.

38 Rc6	R×a2
39 R×e6	g5
40 Rd6	Rd2
41 e6	K×c7
42 e7	

Black resigned—if 42 ... Re2, then 43 R×d5 R×e7 44 R×g5.

Main Tournament and Match Results

Year	Event	Score	Place
1946	Ukrainian Championship, Kiev	$11^1/_2/17$	4–6
1947	Ukrainian Championship, Kiev	$9^1/_2/16$	6
	USSR Championship Semi-Final, Sverdlovsk	7/12	5–6
1948	Ukrainian Championship, Kiev	11/18	5–8
	Candidate Master Tournament, Baku	9/15	3–5
1949	Ukrainian Championship, Odessa	$13^1/_2/19$	2–3
	USSR Championship Semi-Final, Tbilisi	$11^1/_2/16$	1
	17th USSR Championship, Moscow	$12^1/_2/19$	3–4
1950	Ukrainian Championship, Kiev	$12^1/_2/17$	1
	Szczawno Zdroj	$12^1/_2/19$	5–6
	USSR Championship Semi-Final, Kiev	9/15	3
	18th USSR Championship, Moscow	9/17	7–10
1951	USSR Championship Semi-Final, Sverdlovsk	13/19	2
	19th USSR Championship, Moscow	$11^1/_2/17$	2–3
1952	Budapest	12/17	2
	Olympiad, Helsinki	$10^1/_2/14$	–
	Interzonal Tournament, Stockholm	13/20	4
	20th USSR Championship, Moscow	12/19	3
1953	Candidates Tournament, Zurich	$14^1/_2/28$	6–7
1954	21st USSR Championship, Kiev	$9^1/_2/19$	10–11
	Olympiad, Amsterdam	5/7	–
	USSR Championship Semi-Final, Gorky	15/20	1
1955	22nd USSR Championship, Moscow	12/19	1–2
	Interzonal Tournament, Göteborg	12/20	5–6
	Zagreb	12/19	4–5
1956	Candidates Tournament, Amsterdam	$9^1/_2/18$	3–4
	Olympiad, Moscow	$7^1/_2/10$	–
1957	Ukrainian Championship, Kiev	$12^1/_2/17$	1–2
	Szczawno Zdroj	$12^1/_2/15$	1
	USSR Championship Semi-Final, Kiev	12/19	2
1958	25th USSR Championship	10/17	7–8

Year	Event	Score	Place
	Ukrainian Championship, Kiev	12$\frac{1}{2}$/16	1
	USSR Championship Semi-Final	11/15	2–3
1959	26th USSR Championship, Tbilisi	9$\frac{1}{2}$/19	10–11
	Ukrainian Championship, Kiev	18/21	1
	Dresden	11/15	1–2
	USSR Championship Semi-Final, Yerevan	12/15	1
1960	27th USSR Championship, Leningrad	13$\frac{1}{2}$/19	2–3
	Copenhagen	10$\frac{1}{2}$/13	2
1961	28th USSR Championship, Moscow	12/19	3–4
	European Team Championship, Oberhausen	6$\frac{1}{2}$/9	–
	Bled	10$\frac{1}{2}$/19	6–7
1962	Interzonal Tournament, Stockholm	15/22	2–3
	Candidates Tournament, Curacao	17/27	2–3
	Olympiad, Varna	10$\frac{1}{2}$/12	–
1963	Havana	16/21	2–4
	31st USSR Championship, Leningrad	11$\frac{1}{2}$/19	4–6
1964	Zonal Tournament, Moscow	5/12	7
1965	Beverwijk	10$\frac{1}{2}$/15	1–2
	Havana	15/21	2–4
	Santiago	10$\frac{1}{2}$/13	2
1966	Kislovodsk	8$\frac{1}{2}$/11	1
	Prague	10$\frac{1}{2}$/13	3
	34th USSR Championship, Tbilisi	12$\frac{1}{2}$/21	2
1967	Monte Carlo	6/9	3–4
	Moscow	8$\frac{1}{2}$/17	9–12
	Skopje	13/17	2–3
	Interzonal Tournament, Sousse	14/21	2–4
1968	Göteborg	7$\frac{1}{2}$/9	1
	Skopje	13$\frac{1}{2}$/19	2
	Kislovodsk	10/14	1
	Olympiad, Lugano	9$\frac{1}{2}$/12	–
	Gori	7/10	2–3
1969	Wijk-aan-Zee	10$\frac{1}{2}$/15	1–2
	37th USSR Championship, Moscow	13$\frac{1}{2}$/22	3–4
	Belgrade	9$\frac{1}{2}$/13	5–6
1970	Moscow	9/13	2–4
	'Match of the Century', Belgrade (v. Gligoric)	2$\frac{1}{2}$/4	–
	European Team Championship, Kapfenberg	4/6	–

Year	Event	Score	Place
	Amsterdam	10/15	4
	Olympiad, Siegen	8/12	–
	Interzonal Tournament, Palma de Mallorca	15/23	2–4
1971	Havana	$10^1/_2$/15	2
	39th USSR Championship, Leningrad	$9^1/_2$/21	14
1972	Kislovodsk	9/14	3
1973	Budapest	$10^1/_2$/15	1
	Hilversum	$9^1/_2$/14	1–2
	European Team Championship, Bath	$4^1/_2$/5	–
	Interzonal Tournament, Petropolis	$11^1/_2$/17	2–4
	Match-Tournament, Portoroz (v. Portisch and Polugayevsky)	3/8	3
	41st USSR Championship, Moscow	$8^1/_2$/17	7–8
1974	Amsterdam	8/15	6–7
1975	Wijk-aan-Zee	8/15	8–10
	Teesside	$9^1/_2$/14	1
	Moscow	12/17	1
	43rd USSR Championship, Yerevan	$8^1/_2$/15	6–8
1976	Las Palmas	$10^1/_2$/15	1
	Interzonal Tournament, Biel	10/19	9–11
	Sochi	$7^1/_2$/15	8–9
	44th USSR Championship, Moscow	$8^1/_2$/17	8–10
1977	Wijk-aan-Zee	8/11	1
	European Team Championship, Moscow	$2^1/_2$/5	–
	Sochi	10/15	2–3
	45th USSR Championship, Leningrad	8/15	5–7
1978	Bogota	12/15	1
	Zonal Tournament, Lvov	$3^1/_2$/14	15
	Odessa	9/13	1
	Novi Sad	$11^1/_2$/15	1
	46th USSR Championship, Tbilisi	9/17	5–8
1979	Las Palmas	$10^1/_2$/15	4
	Novi Sad	9/13	2–3
	47th USSR Championship, Minsk	$11^1/_2$/17	1
1980	European Team Championship, Skara	4/6	–
	Lone Pine	6/9	3–4
	Las Palmas	$8^1/_2$/11	1–3
	Olympiad, Malta	$6^1/_2$/9	–
	48th USSR Championship, Vilnius	$6^1/_2$/17	14–15

Year	Event	Score	Place
1981	Match-Tournament of 4 USSR Teams, Moscow	4/6	–
	Moscow	4/13	14
	Manila	8/11	3
1982	Zonal Tournament, Yerevan	8/13	4
	London	6/13	10
	Moscow	8/13	3–4
	Interzonal Tournament, Moscow	$7^1/_2$/13	5–6
	Sochi	$7^1/_2$/15	8–10
1983	Linares	5/10	7–9
	50th USSR Championship, Moscow	$6^1/_2$/15	14–15
	European Team Championship, Plovdiv	3/4	–

Matches

1955	Smyslov: USSR Championship Play-Off	4–3
1962	Keres: Candidates Play-Off for 2nd Place	$3^1/_2$–$4^1/_2$
1965	Smyslov: Candidates Quarter-Final	$5^1/_2$–$2^1/_2$
1965	Spassky: Candidates Semi-Final	$2^1/_2$–$5^1/_2$
1966	Larsen: Candidates Match for 3rd Place	4–5
1968	Spassky: Candidates Quarter-Final	$2^1/_2$–$5^1/_2$
1971	Korchnoi: Candidates Quarter-Final	$2^1/_2$–$5^1/_2$

Index of Openings

(Numbers refer to games)

Index of Opponents

(Numbers refer to games)